"*Business Competitiveness and Sustainability: Theory, Practice, and Future Challenges* brilliantly navigates the complexities of organizational success in a dynamic environment. Through contemporary research and illustrative case studies, this insightful book by Marco Arraya and João Ferreira offers invaluable tools for scholars, students, and practitioners to analyze and enhance organizational performance. A must-read for those seeking to master strategic management and innovation in today's VUCA world."

Hussain Rammal, *The University of Adelaide, Australia*

"The authors outline a multi-dimensional and multi-stakeholder set of perspectives on the key determinants and drivers of competitiveness and sustainability. In so doing, they aim to unlock the 'black box' of sustainable competitive advantage and highlight the key enablers of it – their figure on organization competitiveness dimensions showcases and amplifies those."

Elias G. Carayannis, *Professor of Science, Technology, Innovation and Entrepreneurship; Director, European Union Research Center, School of Business, George Washington University, USA*

"The two editors have assembled an excellent group of scholars who bring diverse expertise and perspectives to understand the complex and multifaceted topic of organizational competitiveness as well as sustainability. This volume is a valuable resource for researchers, practitioners, and students seeking a deeper understanding of this critical subject."

Wendy D. Chen, *Senior Associate Editor, Management Decision and Assistant Professor of Texas Tech University, USA*

BUSINESS COMPETITIVENESS AND SUSTAINABILITY

This book presents seven internal dimensions that have a direct impact on an organization's global competitiveness and sustainability: purpose, leadership, passion, people-centered, customer-centric, infrastructure, and viability.

An organization operates as a complex adaptive system that is impacted by external factors that make up its environment. These external factors, in turn, compel managers to make decisions and take deliberate actions that stimulate the organization's internal dimensions to enhance its competitiveness. Therefore, a competitive organization achieves a sustained level of productivity that leads to growth and the attainment of its objectives, resulting in increased income and well-being. Chapters in this book provide readers with a framework that demonstrates how these dimensions can be studied and analyzed individually, as well as how cultivating a coherent, mutually reinforcing system can enhance an organization's competitive advantage. This book also includes illustrative case studies and proposes an instrument to measure an organization's competitiveness.

Providing a strategic framework for enhancing competitiveness in VUCA environments, this book will interest scholars and students in strategic management, competitiveness, innovation, and international business.

Marco Arraya is an Assistant Professor at Universidade Europeia (Lisboa), Portugal. He holds a PhD in Strategic Management from Universidade Aberta, Portugal. Marco has co-edited several books and published in international journals, and his research interests include competitiveness, dynamic capabilities, strategic management, and organizational change. He has much experience in competitive industries as CEO.

João J. Ferreira is a Full Professor of Management at the University of Beira Interior (UBI), Portugal, and an affiliated member of the UBI Research Unit in Business Sciences (NECE). He has edited and co-edited several books on strategy and entrepreneurship and published over 200 papers in premier international journals. His main research interests include strategy, competitiveness, and entrepreneurship.

Innovation and Technology Horizons

Series Editor: Vanessa Ratten, La Trobe University, Australia

As business landscape constantly shifts in today's digital age, this timely series looks at how business and society can harness technological innovation to succeed and drive progress. The books in this series identify new innovation capabilities and emerging technologies and investigate the managerial implications of such technologies. As business processes become increasingly complex, the series also explores how businesses can transform themselves with new digital technologies while aligning themselves with today's societal goals. This series provides direction through research on innovation and technology management and will be of benefit to anyone who is keen to thrive in an evolving business environment.

The Business of Data
Commercial Opportunities and Social Challenges in a World Fuelled by Data
Martin De Saulles

Economics of the Fourth Industrial Revolution
Internet, Artificial Intelligence and Blockchain
Nicholas Johnson and Brendan Markey-Towler

Business Competitiveness and Sustainability
Theory, Practice, and Future Challenges
Edited by Marco Arraya and João J. Ferreira

For more information about this series, please visit www.routledge.com/Innovation-and-Technology-Horizons/book-series/ITH

BUSINESS COMPETITIVENESS AND SUSTAINABILITY

Theory, Practice, and Future Challenges

Edited by
Marco Arraya and João J. Ferreira

Routledge
Taylor & Francis Group
LONDON AND NEW YORK

First published 2025
by Routledge
4 Park Square, Milton Park, Abingdon, Oxon OX14 4RN

and by Routledge
605 Third Avenue, New York, NY 10158

Routledge is an imprint of the Taylor & Francis Group, an informa business

British Library Cataloguing-in-Publication Data
A catalogue record for this book is available from the British Library

Library of Congress Cataloging-in-Publication Data
Names: Arraya, Marco, author.
Title: Business competitiveness and sustainability : theory, practice, and future challenges / edited by Marco Arraya and João J. Ferreira.
Description: Abingdon, Oxon ; New York, NY : Routledge, 2025. |
Series: Ith innovation and technology horizons | Includes bibliographical references and index. |
Identifiers: LCCN 2024036630 (print) | LCCN 2024036631 (ebook) | ISBN 9781032695907 (hbk) | ISBN 9781032696003 (pbk) | ISBN 9781032695969 (ebk)
Subjects: LCSH: Organizational effectiveness. | Competition.
Classification: LCC HD58.9 .B873 2025 (print) | LCC HD58.9 (ebook) |
DDC 658.4/012—dc23/eng/20240819
LC record available at https://lccn.loc.gov/2024036630
LC ebook record available at https://lccn.loc.gov/2024036631

ISBN: 9781032695907 (hbk)
ISBN: 9781032696003 (pbk)
ISBN: 9781032695969 (ebk)

DOI: 10.4324/9781032695969

CONTENTS

MORE ABOUT THE EDITORS

Marco Arraya is an Assistant Professor at Universidade Europeia (Lisboa), Portugal; an affiliated member of the Graduate School of Business Leadership, University of South Africa, Pretoria, South Africa; and an affiliated member of the NECE Research Unit in Business Sciences, Covilhã, Portugal. He holds a PhD in Strategic Management at Universidade Aberta, Portugal. His main research interests include dynamic capabilities, strategic management, and organizational change. He has published his work in multiple international academic journals, including the *European Journal of Training and Development*, *International Journal of Management Concepts and Philosophy*, *European Journal of Management Studies*, and *Sport, Business, and Management: An International Journal*. Marco has extensive experience in competitive industries, in C-suite positions.

João J. Ferreira is a Full Professor of Management at the University of Beira Interior (UBI), Portugal. His research interests include strategy, competitiveness, and entrepreneurship. He is the editor of the Studies in Knowledge Management and Entrepreneurial Ecosystems book series by De Gruyter. He has edited or co-edited several books on strategy, innovation, knowledge transfer, and entrepreneurship and has published over 400 papers in premier international journals, including *Technological Forecasting & Social Change*, *IEEE Transactions in Engineering Management*, *Journal of Business Research*, *R&D Management*, *Journal of Technology Transfer*, *Management Decision*, *Service Business*, *Regional Studies*, *International Journal of Information Management*, *Journal of Intellectual Capital*, *Business Strategy and the Environment*, and many others. João is currently serving on the editorial boards of several journals, and he is a co-editor of the *Journal of Small Business and Enterprise Development* and an associate editor of the *Management Decision*, *Journal of Management and Organization*, *Journal of Global Information Management*, *Journal of the Knowledge Economy*, and others.

MORE ABOUT THE CONTRIBUTORS

Federico Cosenz, Ph.D., is a Professor of Business Management at the University of Palermo (Italy), Department of Political Sciences and International Relations. Therein, he serves as the Rector's delegate for performance management & governance. He teaches master-level courses, such as Business Strategy and Planning & Control Systems. His main research interests concern business model design and innovation also from a sustainability perspective, SME growth management, simulation for business planning and strategic learning, and system dynamics modelling. He has published in several academic and professional journals, such as Long Range Planning, Journal of Business Research, Business Strategy and the Environment, Journal of Small Business Management, Management Decision, European Management Review.

Rodolfo Damiano received his PhD in Economics and Statistics from the University of Palermo, Italy, in 2022. He is RTDa (Research Fellow) at the University of Palermo. His research interests include accounting narratives and sustainability reporting. He has published articles on sustainability reporting in journals such as *Meditari Accountancy Research* and *Utilities Policy.*

André de Waal, MSc, MBA, PhD, is an Academic Director of the HPO Center, an organization which conducts research into high-performance organizations. He is also a partner at the Finance Function Research & Development Center, a company that aims to help finance functions transform into a high-performance department. André has been a consultant and partner with Arthur Andersen for 16 years. André was also an Associate Professor of Organizational Effectiveness at the Maastricht School of Management for 13 years. He was selected by managementboek.nl as one of the Dutch Masters in Management, ten people who have influenced management thinking in The Netherlands the most over the past decade. André has published more than 500 articles (including more than 140 academic publications) and 36 books. His articles can be read on www.hpocenter.com and www.andredewaal.eu.

Elisabeth Figueiredo is a PhD candidate in Psychology at the University of Salamanca Salamanca, has a Master's degree in Management, with a specialization in Human Resources Management from the Institute of Management and Health Organizations of the Catholic University of Portugal – Regional Center of Viseu, Degree in Mathematics and Natural Sciences, from the Polytechnic Institute of Viseu. Elisabeth taught Mathematics and Natural Sciences. His research interests include relationship marketing, reward systems, work passion, and telework.

Marco Figueiredo is a candidate for PhD in Management from the University of Beira Interior (UBI), Portugal. He holds a Master's degree in Management from UBI. He is a Researcher at the NECE-UBI Research Centre for Business Sciences and recently published his first paper in *the Journal of International Management.* His research interests are strategic management, international business, advanced technologies, and corporate governance.

Daniel Roque Gomes is a Coordinator Professor at the School of Education of the Polytechnic University of Coimbra. He holds a Postdoc by SOCIUS – ISEG Lisbon School of Economics and Management, and a PhD in Psychology with specialization in Work and Organizational Psychology by ISCTE-IUL. He was the Administrator of the Polytechnic University of Coimbra from 2017 to 2021 and is currently the Vice President of the Polytechnic University of Coimbra in charge of the Quality Management, Human Resources Management, and Academic Affairs of the institution. His research focuses on human resource management, organizational behavior, and internal communication.

Harri Hokkanen is a Visiting Lecturer at Tampere University in Finland and Senior Manager at Accenture. His research focuses on industry transformations, new business forms, the changing roles of companies, and adaptive business models, specifically in the retail sector. His work has appeared in a variety of journals, including the *Journal of Marketing Management*, *Journal of Business Models*, and *The International Review of Retail, Distribution, and Consumer Research.*

Julie Linthorst, MSc, is an entrepreneur, researcher, and management consultant who specializes in the areas of futureproofing, strategic management, and sustainable HRM. She holds an MSc in Work and Organizational Psychology from the University of Amsterdam, where she is currently pursuing a PhD in the future. After having worked at globally recognized consultancy firms and with Arthur Andersen as Senior Manager Human Capital, Julie started Yoconfio.nl and Futurebels to create a positive future of work. She has worked for large international firms, SMEs, and government agencies. Julie volunteers to support poverty alleviation, decent work, and social inclusion. Her research has been published in multiple peer-reviewed journals, and she has spoken at several scientific conferences such as the European Academy of Management (EURAM), British Academy of Management (BAM), and Work and Organization Psychology (WAOP).

Clara Margaça has a doctorate in Psychology from the University of Salamanca, where she is currently a Margarita Salas Researcher. She conducts transdisciplinary research on entrepreneurial intentions, entrepreneurship, sustainability, and its relationship with psychological variables. Her research interests include emotional and ecological intelligence, positive psychological capital, social enterprises, and sustainable development education. She has been the author of several articles in high-impact journals and book chapters in the fields of psychology and entrepreneurship. Clara was a visiting researcher at the Nova Southeastern University (USA), and participated in different Erasmus+ missions, namely at Trinity College Dublin. She has received the Extraordinary Doctorate Award (2022) from Salamanca University.

José António Porfírio is an Associate Professor with habilitation at Universidade Aberta in Portugal, holding a PhD in Management (specialization in Strategy). He works mostly in the fields of Corporate Strategy, Entrepreneurship, and Family Business, with several studies published in reference journals. He is the Dean of the Social Sciences and Management Department at Universidade Aberta and the Coordinator of the Master in Management. Professionally, José also has a long experience as coordinator of several European projects in the domains of Entrepreneurship, Family Business, and Social Inclusion, and an experience of more than 20 years as manager and consultant for several companies in Portugal, and for the UNCTAD TrainForTrade Program of the United Nations in Geneva, where he works since 1999 as a consultant on distance-learning and foreign trade.

Carlos Rey is a Professor of Strategic Management and Director of the Chair Management by Missions and Corporate Governance at Universitat Internacional de Catalunya (UIC Barcelona). He is also the Founder of DPMC, a provider of strategy and change management services for companies such as Coca-Cola, Sony, Camper, Repsol, or Bristol Myers Squib. Formerly, he was Executive Vice President of HUF International. He received the extraordinary doctorate award for the research on corporate purpose and missions. He is co-author of *Management by Missions*, published in six languages, *Purpose-Driven Organizations: Management Ideas for a Better World* and other books and articles in leading journals like *Long Range Planning* and *Journal of Business Ethics*.

Neuza Ribeiro is a Coordinator Professor at the School of Technology and Management, Polytechnic University of Leiria, Portugal and a Researcher of CARME – Center of Applied Research in Management and Economics. She holds a Postdoc in Management and a PhD in Industrial Management with a specialization in Organizational Behavior at Aveiro University. She was a guest professor at the Faculty of Economics, University of Coimbra and at ISCAC, Polytechnic Institute of Coimbra. She was Head of the Department of Management and Economics at the School of Technology and Management during 2015–2017, and the coordinator of CARME during 2019–2022. Her research focuses on human resource management and organizational behavior.

Tawfiq Rkibi has a PhD in Management from Grenoble University, France. He is a Full Professor at the Universidade Europeia of Lisbon, Portugal, where he coordinates the doctoral program in management. Previously, he was a rector at the same university and president of the International University of Casablanca, Morocco. His areas of teaching and research relate to business and corporate strategies, as well as international business and global marketing.

Ricardo M. Rodrigues has a PhD in Management and, since 2020, has been an Assistant Professor in the Management Department at ISEG, teaching several courses in the scientific area of Strategic Management and Marketing at ISEG's undergraduate and master's degrees. Within the scope of ADVANCE, CSG, he develops research in the areas of Management, covering topics such as Strategy, Internationalization and Corporate Governance. At the same time, within the scope of CEGE/ISEG, of which he is Director, he participates in the promotion of applied projects, with the involvement of Professors from the ISEG's Management Department to national and foreign organizations. He has also participated in the organization of scientific events at ISEG. Outside of ISEG, he has participated in the governing bodies of non-profit organizations that aim, among other objectives, to support young people and the elderly.

Marcantonio Ruisi is a Full Professor of Business Management at the University of Palermo, Italy. He teaches master-level courses such as business strategies and entrepreneurship. He is the Coordinator of Executive Master in Cultural Heritage Management, Rector's Delegate for Spin-off and Innovative Start-ups and Coordinator Start-Cup (Business Plan Competition), Vice President of SISTUR (Italian Society of Tourism Science), and Coordinator of the Summer School "Methodology in Business Administration Studies" SIDREA (Italian Society of Accounting and Business Administration Scholars). He is the author of many scientific articles and books in the field of entrepreneurship, destination management, strategic alliances and virtue ethics.

Helen E. Salavou is currently an Associate Professor of Business Administration at the Athens University of Economics and Business and Director of the Athens MBA. Her main research interests involve entrepreneurship (traditional and social), innovation, and the strategy of small firms. She is the founding member of the research unit of social entrepreneurship and the Scientific Director of the education programs titled "Social and Green Entrepreneurship" and "Youth and Adolescent for the Future" at the University. She has published her work in international journals and participated in several national and international research projects since 1997. Parallel to her academic career, she has contributed as a consultant and mentor to numerous entrepreneurial initiatives.

José Carlos Sánchez-García is a Full Professor and Director of the Doctorate Program in Psychology at the University of Salamanca, Director of the Chair of Entrepreneurship at the University of Salamanca, and also President of the Association for Training, Research and Development of Entrepreneurship. He received the OPA Award for his research and promotion of entrepreneurship at the university and Juan Huarte de San Juan Award for his career as a psychologist and promotion of Psychology. He is also a Visiting Professor at different European and Latin American universities and presidents of various International Congresses on Entrepreneurship and Innovation.

Carlos A. P. F. Silva has a PhD in Management in the field of Strategy from Universidade Aberta, a Master's in International Economics from ISEG (Technical University of Lisbon), and a degree in International Relations from Universidade Lusíada. He is an Associate Professor at the Faculty of Social Sciences and Technology at the European University, where he has been teaching since 2015. He has taught several curricular units in the areas of management, international business, and strategy in undergraduate and master's degrees, and in PhD in Management. He is a consultant in international business, internationalization, international marketing, and brand management. He developed internationalization programs and projects, as well as consultancy on market entry and business opportunities for national and international companies.

Mika Yrjölä is a University Lecturer of Marketing at Tampere University, Finland. His research background includes executive decision-making, business models, value propositions, and omni-channel retailing. He has published his work in multiple international academic journals, including the *Journal of Retailing and Consumer Services*, *Journal of Marketing Management*, and *Journal of Business and Industrial Marketing*.

INTRODUCTION

Marco Arraya and João J. Ferreira

Since the advent of for-profit organizational structures, there has been lingering uncertainty regarding how to build an organization that consistently achieves excellence, adapts swiftly to unforeseen changes in its internal environment, effectively addresses the competitive challenges of its external environment while delivering outstanding value to stakeholders, particularly customers, and generates exceptional financial outcomes for investors. Despite the passage of time, a clear and definitive answer to this question remains elusive in the ever-evolving business world, where mediocrity in strategy and operations is met with harsh consequences and success is born from relentless economic dynamism and the pursuit of improved competitiveness through innovation and adaptation.

Competitiveness has gained considerable attention from think-tankers, policymakers, C-level executives, and managers when discussing organizational performance. The concept of an organization's competitiveness is complex and multifaceted, making it challenging to define. It refers to an organization's ability to thrive and grow under the influence of both internal and external factors. This entails combining an organization's diverse resources and capabilities in a cohesive manner (Ferreira et al., 2022). By doing so, a competitive organization can leverage its resources and capabilities to create and deliver high-quality products that customers are willing to pay in a more attractive package than competitors, thereby securing a significant market share and profit (Joshi & Singh, 2010; McLaughlin, 2017; Usubamatov et al., 2013).

Essentially, the objective is to surpass the competitor performance. However, this definition is comprehensive and studying it can be challenging. To effectively examine competitiveness, it is essential to analyze the core dimensions of the system. This process requires an interdisciplinary approach that considers multiple factors and sources of competitiveness as well as their interconnections and relationships.

DOI: 10.4324/9781032695969-1

Nevertheless, maintaining high competitiveness requires adaptability, innovation, collaboration, and coherence. Adaptation to the market, creativity, knowledge creation and dissemination, competencies, and infrastructure (resources and capabilities, processes, and routines), such as peer collaboration, are key factors for competitiveness (Siudek & Zawojska, 2014), but they will only be important factors if they act as a coherent system (Arraya, 2022). Thus, an organization's competitive level is a predictor of its survival, growth, and sustainability. However, formally, most organizations do not measure or manage their competitive levels. Determining and measuring its main endogenous dimensions involves evaluating a system that provides coherence and allows the organization to have the right to play and win the game (Leinwand & Mainardi, 2010). In other words, it recognizes the most important and fragile dimensions for the organizational competitive level, statistically linking the scores resulting from the perception of employees and comparing the variations over time. If so, they discover the state-of-the-art of each assessed dimension and the differences between them. The organization is better managed by identifying and addressing problems before they become dramatic for organizational sustainability.

The main focus of this book is the competitiveness of organizations. To this end, we propose and examine seven critical strategic dimensions that possess significant characteristics that affect businesses: purpose, leadership, passion, people-centric, customer-centric, infrastructure, and viability. We introduce two dimensions – customer-centric and viability – that capture the organization's capacity to surpass rivals and swiftly adapt to fluctuations and demands (Chikán et al., 2022; Yang et al., 2015). Additionally, we highlight five dimensions – purpose, leadership, passion, people-centric, and infrastructure – that contribute to making the organization more competitive (Alonso & Leiva, 2019; Carew et al., 2009; De Waal, 2021; Do & Mai, 2020). Collectively, these dimensions explain why some organizations outperform others (see Figure 0.1).

Drafting organizations that possess a well-defined, unambiguous purpose focused on customers, inclusive and people-oriented leadership, robust infrastructure

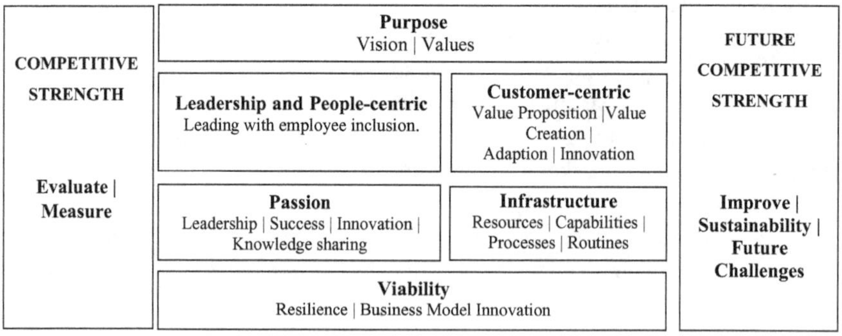

FIGURE 0.1 Organizational competitiveness dimensions.

serving as the backbone of the organization, and passionate employees call for coherence and continuous vigilance. This book offers a comprehensive examination of the seven strategic critical dimensions that contribute to the competitiveness and exceptional performance of any organization, with a focus on academic rigor and practical expertise. The aim of this book is to provide readers with a multifaceted understanding of the significance of these seven dimensions in enhancing organizational competitiveness as well as how measuring them facilitates the implementation of improvements that drive competitiveness. The insights and framework outlined in *Business Competitiveness and Sustainability* serve as indispensable resources for policymakers, C-suite executives, managers, and observers of organizational trends.

Business Competitiveness and Sustainability are ideal textbooks for studying organizational competitiveness because of several key characteristics. First, the textbook examines all seven strategic dimensions independently and as a cohesive multidimensional system, making it scalable for any organization. Second, the framework enables readers to comprehend the functioning of dimensions and their influence on an organization's performance as well as how they can be used as a system to achieve better outcomes and superior organizational performance. Third, by considering the dynamic consequences of the dimensions on competitiveness, the framework provides new managerial insights and guidance for more effective strategies, ultimately changing the way organizations operate in markets and creating new opportunities.

Ultimately, although the ideas presented in this book are coherent, succinct, and applicable, their continuous evolution is often disregarded. Changes are rarely straightforward, because they are frequently characterized by complexity, uncertainty, and stress. Therefore, accurately gauging the competitive standing of an organization entails familiarity with the current state-of-the-art, thereby facilitating forthright and innovative responses to the challenges of change. This book provides academic rigor, empirical research, the fundamental aspects of competitiveness, and a framework for evaluating an organization's competitive level. Using this, readers can develop strategies to adapt, reflect, evolve, and flourish in an ever-changing world.

The book is structured according to a funnel approach, with the aim of progressing from a broader context to an epicenter focused on the evaluation of company competitiveness, culminating in an analysis of future peer competitiveness challenges. Chapter 1 delves into the central concepts of productivity and competitiveness, which are essential to economic and business literature. Chapter 2 examines critical issues in the field of competitive advantage from 1985 to 2023, highlighting valuable work on theorizing the concept of competitive advantage as the ultimate manifestation of performance superiority. Chapters 3–8 explore the significance of the seven core dimensions of this book – purpose, leadership, passion, people-centric, customer-centric, infrastructure, and viability – in the context of competitiveness. Chapter 9 analyzes the relationship between internationalization strategies and digital transformation, examining whether internationalization arises with the creation of companies and whether they are originally digital. Chapter 10 presents the "firm competitiveness fit stress-test" tool, which evaluates the seven dimensions discussed in detail in this book, revealing which factors drive a company's competitiveness and which require special attention to achieve its goals. Finally, Chapter 11 provides a descriptive review of the literature to identify and analyze the main challenges affecting organizations, focusing on their present and future implications.

References

Alonso, S., and Leiva, J. C. (2019). Business competitiveness in Costa Rica: A multidimensional approach. *Tec Empresarial, 13*(3), 28–41.

Arraya, M. (2022). The relationship between distinctive capabilities system, learning orientation, leadership and performance. *European Journal of Management Studies, 27*(2), 205–227.

Carew, D., Kandarian, F., Parisi-Carew, E., and Stoner, J. (2009). Is your organization high performing? In Ken Blanchard (Eds). *Leading at a higher level, revised and expanded edition: Blanchard on leadership and creating high performing organizations*, 2nd Edition (pp. 3–16). Pearson.

Chikán, A., Czakó, E., Kiss-Dobronyi, B., and Losonci, D. (2022). Firm competitiveness: A general model and a manufacturing application. *International Journal of Production Economics, 243*(C), 1–13, 108316.

De Waal, A. d. (2021). The high performance organization: Proposed definition and measurement of its performance. *Measuring Business Excellence, 25*(3), 300–314.

Do, T. T., and Mai, N. K. (2020). High-performance organization: A literature review. *Journal of Strategy and Management, 13*, 297–309.

Ferreira, J. J. M., Fernandes, C. I., and Ferreira, F. A. F. (2022). What makes organizations unique? Looking inside the box. *Journal of Business Research, 139*(C), 664–674.

Joshi, R. N., and Singh, S. P. (2010). Estimation of total factor productivity in the indian garment industry. *Journal of Fashion Marketing and Management, 14*(1), 145–160.

Leinwand, P., and Mainardi, C. (2010). The coherence premium. *Harvard Business Review*, June, 86–92.

McLaughlin, S. A. (2017). Dynamic capabilities: taking an emerging technology perspective. *International Journal of Manufacturing Technology and Management, 31*(1/2/3), 62–81.

Siudek, T. and Zawojska, A. (2014). Competitiveness in economic concepts, theories, and empirical research. *Acta Scientiarum Polonorum Oeconomia, 13*, 91–108.

Usubamatov, R., Ismail, K. A. and Sah, J. M. (2013). Mathematical models for productivity and availability of automated lines. *The International Journal of Advanced Manufacturing Technology, 66*, 59–69.

Yang, J., Zhang, F., Jiang, X., and Sun, W. (2015). Strategic flexibility, green management, and firm competitiveness in an emerging economy. *Technological Forecasting and Social Change*, 101, 347–356.

1

PRODUCTIVITY AND COMPETITIVENESS IN THE DIGITAL ERA

More inseparable and interdependent

Carlos A. P. F. Silva and Tawfiq Rkibi

1.1 Introduction

Literature reviews are an essential component of academic research, providing a comprehensive examination of existing literature related to a specific research question or area (Boote & Beile, 2005). They capture current knowledge and facilitate the identification of advancements in the field (Randolph, 2009).

Literature reviews lay the foundation for scientific advancement, enabling researchers to build upon the theories and findings of previous studies. By synthesizing available literature, researchers can identify gaps in knowledge and areas needing further investigation (Jesson et al., 2011). This is our intention when preparing this chapter. Additionally, literature reviews help contextualize new research findings within the broader scholarly conversation (Hart, 1998).

Approaches to conducting literature reviews vary, including systematic reviews, which aim to minimize bias through structured methods, and narrative reviews, offering a broader overview of a field (Higgins & Green, 2011). The latest one is more our approach in the present chapter. Criteria for selecting sources include publication date, relevance, and academic rigour, ensuring the review's currency and credibility (Petticrew & Roberts, 2006).

The literature provides us with benefits and disadvantages or challenges to this methodology. Conducting a literature review enhances the academic knowledge base, guides the formulation of research questions and hypotheses, and informs research design and methodology (Tranfield et al., 2003). These reviews ensure research questions are grounded in relevant academic discourse, increasing the research's relevance and impact (Fink, 2019).

Despite their benefits, literature reviews face criticism for potential bias in source selection and the risk of emphasizing published studies over unpublished or

DOI: 10.4324/9781032695969-2

negative findings (MacLure, 2005). The rapid pace of knowledge generation also poses a challenge, requiring continuous updates to remain current (Greenhalgh & Peacock, 2005).

We may consider that literature reviews are fundamental to the integrity and advancement of academic research. Despite challenges, the methodology of literature reviews continues to evolve, addressing these issues and maintaining their role as a cornerstone of scholarly research (Grant & Booth, 2009).

After this first methodological approach it is important to refer how the chapter is organized. First, a conceptualization of productivity and competitiveness and then a interrelation between them and productivity. The idea is to have a broaden visualization of this constructs. In today's highly competitive business landscape, productivity and competitiveness are crucial factors that can determine the success or failure of a company (Duginets & Olena, 2021). Today, businesses face severe tests in both national and international markets due to intense competition from foreign companies. Consequently, widespread attention is being given to the problem of increasing the productivity and long-term profitability of businesses. The productivity and competitiveness of a company play a vital role in its growth and survival (Zakaria et al., 2020). Any business has to show a considerable set of efforts and possess a clear strategic vision in order to stay afloat and keep or expand the market share (Duginets & Olena, 2021). The strengthening of competition is accompanied by the emergence of numerous competing enterprises both in domestic and foreign markets, forcing companies to constantly develop their potential and search for new ways to increase their competitiveness and attract clients. The importance of productivity and competitiveness cannot be overstated in today's highly competitive business landscape. In order to thrive in today's competitive business environment, companies must prioritize productivity and competitiveness (Zakaria et al., 2020). This importance lies in that it enables a business firm to exhibit superior performance in one aspect or more in a manner that is considered superior to that of other competitors. The productivity and competitiveness of a company are crucial factors that determine its success or failure in today's highly competitive business landscape. Productivity and competitiveness are key drivers for a company's success and survival in today's highly competitive business landscape.

Afterwards, the relation to the digitalization of businesses is also commented. In today's rapidly changing and interconnected world, the concepts of productivity and competitiveness have taken on new dimensions with the advent of digital transformation (Магомедов et al., 2020). Digital transformation refers to the integration of digital technologies into all aspects of a business, fundamentally changing how it operates and delivers value to customers (Horal et al., 2020). The digital transformation is driven by the recognition that technology can significantly enhance productivity and competitiveness in various industries (Vaska et al., 2021). Digital transformation has impacted value creation, delivery, and capture in almost every industry, allowing firms to co-create value with customers through customized manufacturing, adoption of servitization strategies, expansion of product and service portfolios, creation of digital platforms and ecosystems, and addressing sustainability issues (Gebayew et al., 2018).

1.2 Productivity: concept and the digitalization agenda

The concept of productivity refers to the efficiency and effectiveness with which inputs are transformed into outputs in each process or system. This concept is crucial in understanding the production and consumption dynamics within management (Morgan et al., 2002). By analysing the relationship between inputs and outputs, productivity analysis provides insights into the efficiency of the transformation process. This analysis can help identify areas where improvements can be made to optimize resource utilization and enhance overall performance (Adagba et al., 2021). Additionally, productivity analysis enables organizations to measure the impact of various management, human resources, operational, marketing strategies, and initiatives on their overall performance. By integrating insights from manufacturing, accounting, customer service, and R&D management, organizations can adapt successful practices and mindsets to improve its efficiency and effectiveness. However, productivity is not just about generating more output with the same number of inputs, but also about optimizing resource utilization and enhancing overall performance. In today's management landscape, the concept of productivity is crucial in understanding how efficiently and effectively inputs are transformed into outputs (Sheth & Sisodia, 2002).

In recent years, the impact of digital transformation on productivity is significant (Pousttchi et al., 2019). By implementing digital technologies and optimizing operational processes, organizations can streamline tasks, automate manual processes, and eliminate inefficiencies. This leads to an increase in productivity as employees can work more efficiently and focus on higher-value tasks, rather than spending time on repetitive or manual tasks. Digital transformation also enables organizations to access and analyse vast amounts of data, which can provide valuable insights for decision-making and process improvement (Pousttchi et al., 2019). Furthermore, digital technologies, such as artificial intelligence and machine learning, can automate routine tasks, allowing organizations to allocate resources effectively and optimize their workforce's productivity. Measurement of productivity in the context of digital transformation can be complex. Traditional productivity measures, such as output per hour or output per worker, may not fully capture the impact of digital transformation. Instead, organizations may need to consider new metrics that consider the efficiency gains, cost savings, and value creation enabled by digital technologies.

So, the concept of productivity plays a pivotal role in determining the success and efficiency of businesses, organizations, and individuals (Priya & Aroulmoji, 2020). As we have seen, productivity is commonly defined as the ratio between output and input, where output refers to the goods or services produced, and input refers to the resources or factors used in the production process. Several factors contribute to the need for increased productivity in today's business landscape:

- First, the intense competition from foreign companies in both national and international markets pushes businesses to constantly improve their productivity levels. This increased competition can lead to a decline in market share, profitability, and overall business performance if productivity levels are not effectively managed;
- Second, the advancements in technology and digitalization have led to increased expectations of efficiency and effectiveness (Dedrick et al., 2003). Organizations are now expected to deliver products and services at a faster pace, with higher quality, and at competitive prices. To meet these demands and stay ahead of the competition, businesses must continuously strive to improve their productivity (Priya & Aroulmoji, 2020).

One widely used measure of productivity is Total Factor Productivity, which is the ratio of aggregated inputs to aggregated outputs. Total Factor Productivity (TFP) represents the efficiency and effectiveness with which inputs (labour, capital, etc.) are transformed into outputs in the production process. It is a crucial indicator of an economy's health and potential for growth, as it encompasses improvements not accounted for by increases in input quantities. Historically, the concept of TFP emerged as economists sought to understand the sources of economic growth beyond simple capital accumulation (Solow, 1957). Measuring TFP involves estimating the output not explained by the quantity of inputs used in production. This typically requires a production function approach, where the output is related to inputs such as labour and capital, with TFP acting as a residual factor (Hulten, 2001). However, measuring TFP accurately is challenging due to issues like data availability, the choice of methodology, and the need to account for the quality of inputs.

Several factors can influence TFP, including technological advancements, which enhance the ways in which inputs are used; human capital, particularly education and skills, which improve labour productivity; and the policy and institutional framework, which can either foster or hinder efficiency and innovation (Acemoglu & Autor, 2011). In this sense, TFP is considered a key driver of economic growth. Studies have shown that differences in TFP levels are significant determinants of the variations in economic performance across countries (Hall & Jones, 1999). Enhancements in TFP can lead to sustained economic growth without the need for additional capital or labour.

Despite its importance, enhancing TFP poses significant challenges, including the need for investment in research and development, education, and infrastructure. Future research could focus on understanding the specific mechanisms through which policy and innovation influence TFP in different economic and institutional contexts (Comin & Mestieri, 2018).

It is when we consider changes in the economy that we should readdress the productivity issue. The fourth industrial revolution brought a big effort in digitalization. Digital transformation is a comprehensive and company-wide process that involves the adoption of digital technologies to revolutionize and optimize business operations, enhance customer experiences, and create new business models (Verhoef et al., 2021). This process goes beyond simply digitizing existing processes and involves significant changes to an organization's properties and ways of doing business (Kraus et al., 2021). It involves rethinking and redesigning processes, products, and business models to leverage the full potential of digital technologies (Vial, 2019).

This evolution has also had a significant impact on competitiveness. Organizations that embrace digital transformation and effectively leverage digital technologies gain a competitive edge in the market (Pousttchi et al., 2019). They are able to respond more quickly to changing market demands, deliver personalized and seamless customer experiences, and create innovative products and services (Vial, 2019). This way, the notion of scale has also changed. Additionally, digital transformation allows organizations to expand their reach and enter new markets through online platforms and digital channels (Pousttchi et al., 2019). It's becoming more and more difficult to separate productivity and competitiveness and if, in the past, productivity and competitiveness were often measured using traditional metrics such as revenue, market share, and cost reduction, organizations are now able to track metrics such as website traffic, social media engagement, and online sales to assess their productivity and competitiveness. These new metrics provide valuable insights into customer engagement, the effectiveness of digital tools, and the overall effectiveness of a company's online presence.

With the advent of digital transformation, new metrics have emerged to better capture the impact of digital technologies on productivity and competitiveness (Pousttchi et al., 2019). The measurement of productivity in the context of digital transformation can be complex and may require new metrics that consider the efficiency gains, cost savings, and value creation enabled by digital technologies. Digital transformation and productivity are closely intertwined concepts (Vial, 2019). Digital transformation is a catalyst for improved productivity and competitiveness in organizations. By adopting digital technologies and embracing the opportunities they offer, organizations can streamline processes, automate tasks, and enhance collaboration. These new metrics may include factors, such as digital adoption rates, digital maturity of processes, customer engagement through online platforms, and speed of response to market changes (Verhoef et al., 2021). This data-driven approach allows organizations to analyse and optimize processes in real time, enabling them to identify bottlenecks, inefficiencies, and areas for improvement. Additionally, the evolution of digital transformation has led to a shift in how competitiveness is perceived (Pousttchi et al., 2019) and we may consider that digital transformation has intensified the interrelation between productivity and competitiveness. Productivity gains from digital transformation enable organizations to streamline their operations, optimize their processes, and automate manual tasks, and organizations may offer competitive pricing and deliver products and services in a timelier manner. Digital transformation also enhances competitiveness by enabling organizations to adapt quickly to market changes and customer demands. By leveraging technologies, such as Big Data, artificial intelligence, and machine learning, organizations can anticipate trends, identify patterns, and make data-driven decisions. Additionally, digital transformation enables organizations to innovate and create new business models that differentiate them from their competitors delivering unique value propositions, personalized customer experiences, and innovative products and services. Under this context, organizations also consider the impact of digital technologies on their overall competitive position and market share (Miklošík & Evans, 2020).

1.3 Competitiveness: conceptualization

Competitiveness is a fundamental concept in the field of industry (Dangayach & Deshmukh, 2003). It refers to the ability of a company or industry to effectively compete and thrive in the marketplace. This ability is determined by a variety of factors, including the structure of the industry, the strategic position of the company within that industry, and its ability to differentiate itself from competitors. There are several key sources that emphasize the importance of competitiveness in industry. Becoming competitive in the market is not an easy endeavour; it requires paying attention to the importance of innovation in all organizational processes and activities (Alghanmi, 2020). Innovation also plays a crucial role in enhancing competitiveness as it allows businesses to exhibit superior performance and gain a competitive advantage over their rivals. To understand the concept of competitiveness in industry, it is crucial to analyse the inherent structure and competitive forces that exist within an industry. One of the key sources that explores this topic is Michael Porter's framework, which provides a comprehensive approach to analyse industry structure and understand the forces of competition that shape it (Porter, 1980). By analysing the structure of an industry and understanding the underlying forces, companies can identify opportunities and threats, as well as determine their own position within the industry (Porter, 2008). Porter's five forces framework is a widely recognized tool that helps companies analyse the competitiveness of their industry. According to Porter's framework, every industry has an inherent structure driven by five competitive forces:

- The threat of new entrants;
- The bargaining power of buyers;
- The bargaining power of suppliers;
- The threat of substitute products or services; and
- The intensity of competitive rivalry.

These competitive forces determine the profit structure of an industry and can either drain away economic value or create opportunities for companies to gain a competitive advantage. To effectively compete in the marketplace and improve relative performance, companies need to understand and navigate these competitive forces. Without competitiveness, companies risk losing market share to their competitors and ultimately failing. Furthermore, understanding competitor analysis allows companies to uncover their competitors' strategies, strengths, and weaknesses. This knowledge can inform a company's own strategic decisions and help identify areas where they can gain a competitive advantage. Companies that can effectively navigate and respond to the competitive forces in their industry are more likely to achieve higher profitability. They can capture a larger share of the market, command higher prices for their products or services, and achieve cost efficiencies (Shehabat, 2020).

As we have seen, in today's global market, competition among companies has become increasingly fierce. Companies are constantly striving to gain an edge over their competitors to succeed and thrive, and this is where the importance of competitiveness comes into play. Competitiveness is essential for companies as it enables them to stand out from their competitors and achieve superior performance (Bahorka et al., 2023). Competitiveness is crucial for companies for several reasons:

- First, competitiveness drives innovation. To stay ahead of the competition, companies need to constantly innovate and improve their products, services, and processes. This not only allows them to meet the evolving needs and demands of customers but also helps them to differentiate themselves in the market;
- Second, competitiveness leads to increased efficiency and productivity. When companies strive to be competitive, they are motivated to streamline their operations, eliminate waste, and optimize their resources. Any process or function that enables organizations to gain a competitive advantage on a global scale is considered valuable (Stroh & Caligiuri, 1998);
- Third, competitiveness drives customer satisfaction (Bahorka et al., 2023). In a competitive market, companies are constantly vying for the attention and loyalty of customers. They invest in understanding customer needs and preferences, delivering high-quality products and services, and providing exceptional customer experiences;
- Lastly, competitiveness drives economic growth and success. When companies are competitive, they are more likely to attract investment, create jobs, and contribute to the overall prosperity of an economy.

Competitive companies are more likely to attract investment, create jobs, and contribute to the prosperity of an economy (Qin & Gu, 2008). Competitiveness is also crucial for places and destinations (countries, regions, cities, etc.) (Adamo et al., 2019;

Bahorka et al., 2023), and competitiveness in the tourism sector drives innovation, encourages the development of new attractions and experiences, and improves the quality of services provided to tourists (Ricafort, 2021).

Additionally, competitiveness also fosters collaboration and cooperation within industries. By being competitive, companies are motivated to collaborate with other stakeholders, such as suppliers, partners, and industry associations, to leverage their strengths and create new opportunities. Competitiveness also leads to a constant drive for improvement and innovation. Competitive companies are constantly seeking ways to improve their processes, products, and services to stay ahead of their competition.

Competitiveness in today's markets is heavily influenced by an organization's ability to harness digital transformation. Organizations that effectively implement digital transformation strategies are better positioned to compete in the digital era. They can adapt to changing customer demands, offer personalized experiences, and deliver products and services more efficiently (Williams et al., 2022). As we've seen when exploring productivity, digital transformation enables organizations to explore new markets and opportunities, expand their product offerings, and establish partnerships with other digital platforms or service providers. These factors contribute to increased market share, customer satisfaction, and overall competitiveness.

To maintain competitiveness in a digital world, organizations need to adopt strategies (Vial, 2019) that embrace the implications of digital transformation and drive better operational performance (Williams et al., 2022). This includes:

- Embracing a culture of innovation and continuous improvement: organizations need to foster a culture that encourages experimentation, learning, and adaptability.
- Creating a customer-centric approach: in the digital era, organizations need to prioritize customer experience and satisfaction.
- Developing strategic partnerships and collaborations: in a digital world, organizations cannot operate in isolation. They must collaborate and form strategic partnerships with other organizations to leverage their combined capabilities and resources.
- Investing in digital capabilities and infrastructure: to remain competitive, organizations need to continuously invest in the latest digital technologies and infrastructure. This includes implementing robust IT systems, cloud computing, data analytics, artificial intelligence, and automation tools.
- Adopting agile methodologies: agile methodologies, such as scrum or kanban, enable organizations to respond quickly to changing market dynamics and customer needs. These methodologies emphasize flexibility, iterative development, and frequent feedback, allowing organizations to adapt their strategies and offerings based on evolving market trends and customer preferences.
- Fostering a culture of continuous learning and skill development: in the digital age, organizations need to prioritize upskilling and reskilling their workforce to ensure they have the necessary digital competencies and expertise.

- Embracing data-driven decision-making: in the digital era, organizations have access to vast amounts of data. They should use this data to drive decision-making and strategy development.

Digital transformation provides organizations with the tools and capabilities to enhance their productivity and competitiveness and this leads to better coordination and efficiency, enabling teams to work together seamlessly and make faster, more informed decisions (Soule et al., 2015). Additionally, digital transformation facilitates data-driven decision-making, as organizations can gather and analyse large amounts of data to gain insights into customer preferences, market trends, and operational performance (Vial, 2019).

1.4 Measuring productivity and competitiveness in the digital transformation world

Let's start with an example of analysis in the Portuguese case. One of the greatest national scholars on competitiveness and productivity has been former minister Augusto Mateus. In a very general way, he considers productivity in Portugal, when compared to most of the European space where Portugal competes, to be much lower.

He considers that to increase competitiveness and productivity, greater collaboration between companies is crucial, but also a constructive and ambitious economic policy designed by the State. On the other hand, it bases the competitiveness model on unregulated tradable goods and a workforce that has been qualified, but whose salaries are competitive compared to other competing geographic realities and in the same sectors (Mateus, 1995).

When we think about the measurement of productivity and competitiveness, we should consider that it can be challenging due to their intangible nature. However, there are various indicators and metrics that can be used to evaluate and compare productivity and competitiveness levels (Kurilova & Antipov, 2020). Let's revise productivity measurement. Productivity can be measured by metrics, such as output per employee, revenue per employee, or cost savings achieved through process optimization. Competitiveness, on the other hand, can be assessed through market share, customer satisfaction ratings, brand recognition, and financial performance.

Quantitative measures of productivity can include metrics such as revenue growth, cost reduction, and efficiency improvements (Vial, 2019). These metrics provide tangible evidence of the impact of digital transformation on an organization's bottom line. On the other hand, measuring competitiveness in the digital era involves assessing factors, such as market share, customer satisfaction, brand reputation, and the ability to adapt to changing market conditions. Qualitative measures, such as innovation and agility, also play a crucial role in assessing competitiveness in the digital age. Overall, the measurement of productivity and competitiveness in the context of digital transformation is a complex task that requires consideration of various quantitative and qualitative factors.

As we've seen, digital transformation plays a significant role in shaping productivity and competitiveness in today's business landscape (Vial, 2019), and measuring productivity and competitiveness in the context of digital transformation requires a comprehensive approach that considers both quantitative and qualitative factors (Kuang et al., 2023). By leveraging digital technologies, organizations can improve their productivity by automating tasks, streamlining processes, and enabling efficient collaboration. These advancements lead to increased output, cost savings, and faster decision-making, enhancing competitiveness by enabling organizations to differentiate themselves through innovative products, personalized customer experiences, and seamless integration across different channels and platforms.

The measurement of productivity and competitiveness requires a shift in traditional metrics to account for the impact of digital technologies (Kuang et al., 2023). Traditional productivity metrics may no longer be sufficient to capture the full impact of digital transformation (Verhoef et al., 2021). Instead, organizations need to consider new metrics that account for the efficiency and effectiveness of digital technologies in enabling value creation and delivery (Kuang et al., 2023).

One approach to measuring productivity in the context of digital transformation is through the concept of "digital intensity" (Vial, 2019). Digital intensity measures the extent to which digital technologies are integrated into an organization's processes, operations, and business models. It considers the level of investment in digital technologies, the extent of digital skills and capabilities within the organization, and the degree of integration between digital technologies and core business functions. Another approach to measuring productivity and competitiveness in the context of digital transformation is through the use of key performance indicators that specifically address digital transformation goals and objectives (Pousttchi et al., 2019). These may include metrics, such as digital revenue growth, customer acquisition and retention rates in digital channels, time to market for new digital products or services, and customer satisfaction with digital experiences (Verhoef et al., 2021).

Additionally, the measurement of productivity has also evolved in the era of digital transformation. Unlike traditional methods of measuring productivity, which focused mainly on output and efficiency, digital transformation has introduced new metrics for assessing productivity in the digital age (Miklošík & Evans, 2020). However, with digital transformation, productivity is measured not only in terms of output but also in terms of customer engagement, digital tools utilization, and the ability to deliver value through innovative products and services (Pousttchi et al., 2019).

The evolution of digital transformation has brought about a shift in the understanding of productivity and competitiveness. Productivity and competitiveness are no longer solely focused on internal efficiency and cost reduction, but rather on the ability to leverage digital technologies to create value for customers and stay ahead in a rapidly changing digital landscape. So, digital transformation has intensified the interrelation between productivity and competitiveness. Organizations that are more productive due to their effective use of digital technologies are also more competitive in the marketplace. They can deliver products and services more efficiently and effectively, meet customer demands in a timely manner, and stay ahead of their competition.

The complexity of productivity metrics arises from the need to accurately capture the efficiency of resource utilization and the value added by labour and capital in the production process. The Office for National Statistics' Productivity Handbook cited by Crowhurst et al. (2015) emphasizes that productivity measures are essential for understanding economic dynamics and formulating policies aimed at enhancing efficiency and growth. These measures serve as critical indicators for assessing how economies and individual businesses convert resources into tangible outputs.

In the realm of organizational performance, the Productivity Measurement and Enhancement System (ProMES) exemplifies a targeted approach to improving productivity measurement. It highlights the importance of feedback mechanisms in fostering an environment of continuous improvement and efficiency enhancement. Furthermore, Pritchard et al. (2008) contribute to the understanding of productivity by analysing the ProMES through a meta-analysis, showcasing its impact on organizational outcomes.

Here are some of the most prominent ways of measuring productivity:

- Output per Hour (or Unit of Time) – One of the most direct measures of productivity is the output per unit of time, which quantifies the amount of work produced within a specific period. Drucker (1999) emphasizes the importance of output measurement in enhancing organizational performance, suggesting that what gets measured gets managed. This method is particularly effective in manufacturing settings, where output is easily quantifiable (Goldstein, 2002).
- Efficiency Ratios – Efficiency ratios, which compare the input and output to assess resource utilization, provide insights into organizational waste and efficiency improvement areas. Kaplan and Norton (1996) introduced the Balanced Scorecard, a strategic management tool that includes efficiency ratios to evaluate performance from multiple perspectives.
- Profitability Metrics – Profitability metrics, such as Return on Investment (ROI) or profit margins, offer indirect productivity measures by assessing the effective use of resources to generate profit. Schmenner and Swink (1998) argue that profitability is often a reflection of productivity improvements, underscoring the relationship between efficient resource use and financial performance.
- Goal Completion Rates – Tracking the rate of goal completion is essential in measuring productivity, especially when quality is as important as quantity. Locke and Latham (2002) have demonstrated the positive impact of setting specific and challenging goals on performance, highlighting the role of goal setting in productivity improvement.
- Quality Adjusted Output – Considering the quality of output alongside quantity offers a more nuanced understanding of productivity. Deming (1986)

emphasizes quality improvement as a key driver of productivity, suggesting that high-quality processes lead to reduced costs and improved output.
- Employee Satisfaction and Engagement Surveys – Employee satisfaction and engagement have been linked to productivity, with research by Harter et al. (2002) showing a strong correlation between engaged employees and business outcomes. This underscores the importance of considering employee perspectives in productivity assessments.
- Benchmarking against Industry Standards – Benchmarking performance against industry standards provides a relative measure of productivity. Camp (1989) discusses the benefits of benchmarking for identifying best practices and setting performance standards.

Accurate productivity measurement is thus foundational for strategic decision-making, enabling policymakers and business leaders to identify opportunities for innovation and competitive advantage. By leveraging comprehensive productivity metrics, entities can better navigate the complexities of the global economy, ensuring sustainable growth and development.

For those engaged in the study or management of productivity, the methodologies and insights provided by these sources offer valuable frameworks for understanding the multifaceted nature of productivity and its critical role in economic and organizational success. Although we are in this rush for digitalization, other methods and/or metrics being used are:

- Overall efficiency – measuring the organization's ability to produce more outputs with fewer inputs (Pousttchi et al., 2019).
- Process execution speed – measuring the time it takes to complete tasks or processes, from start to finish (Verhoef et al., 2021).
- Error rate reduction – measuring the percentage of errors or rework in processes, aiming to minimize them and improve efficiency (Pousttchi et al., 2019).
- Innovative output – measuring the organization's ability to generate new ideas and solutions that lead to improved products or services.

Competitiveness, as we've seen, is a critical indicator of an entity's ability to succeed in the global marketplace. This concept, while universally acknowledged, offers a challenge in its measurement due to the complexity and breadth of factors involved. Academic literature provides various methodologies to assess competitiveness, ranging from macroeconomic indicators to firm-level efficiency metrics. We'll explore some of these traditional methodologies to shed light on the multifaceted nature of competitiveness.

- Productivity as a Benchmark – Productivity, often measured by output per labour hour, is a primary indicator of competitiveness. Porter (1990) posits that the competitive advantage of nations is founded on their ability to innovate and upgrade, which is directly related to productivity levels. High productivity means that an economy can produce more goods and services with the same number of resources, a key driver of competitiveness.

- Innovation and Technological Advancement – The capacity for innovation and the adoption of new technologies are pivotal in maintaining competitiveness. Schumpeter (1942) highlights the role of technological innovation in economic growth and competitiveness, arguing that the creative destruction process is essential for continuous development. Innovation indicators include research and development (R&D) spending, patent applications, and the rate of new product introductions.
- International Trade Performance – Competitiveness is also measured by a country's or firm's performance in international markets. Krugman (1994) challenges traditional measures of competitiveness by arguing that trade performance, including export volumes and market shares, reflects an entity's ability to compete globally. Positive trade balances and increased market shares are indicative of high competitiveness.
- Price and Cost Competitiveness – Price levels and cost structures are critical for competitiveness, especially in industries where price competition is intense. According to Ricardo (1817), comparative advantage suggests that nations should specialize in producing goods for which they have a lower relative cost of production, thereby enhancing their competitiveness.
- Human Capital and Skill Levels – The quality of human capital, including education and skill levels, is a significant determinant of competitiveness. Becker (1964) emphasizes the importance of human capital in economic development, suggesting that investments in education and training directly contribute to competitiveness by enhancing productivity and innovation capacity.
- Economic Stability and Infrastructure – Economic stability, characterized by low inflation and sustainable public finances, alongside well-developed infrastructure, is essential for competitiveness. These factors ensure a stable environment for business operations and investments, facilitating efficient production and distribution of goods and services.

Considering this metrics, we may say that in the digital age, productivity and competitiveness have evolved significantly (Bai, 2021) and with the integration of new technologies, such as Big Data, Internet of Things, artificial intelligence, and cloud computing, manufacturing enterprises have become more agile, flexible, and adaptable to changes in the external environment (Xiao, 2022). They can leverage these technologies to streamline processes, automate tasks, and improve decision-making (Mergel et al., 2019).

In the past, competitiveness was often measured by comparing an organization's performance to its competitors in terms of market share, sales growth, and profitability (Ianenko et al., 2020). However, in the digital age, competitiveness goes beyond these traditional measures (Meraghni et al., 2021) including factors such as agility, adaptability, and the ability to leverage technology effectively and disrupting traditional notions of productivity and competitiveness by introducing new metrics and methods for measurement.

The digital transformation has reshaped the global economic landscape, introducing new criteria for measuring competitiveness. In this context, competitiveness reflects not only the ability to innovate and maintain market share but also the capacity to adapt to and leverage digital technologies. Let us look at some updated methodologies.

- Digital Innovation and Technological Adoption – In the digital age, innovation extends beyond traditional R&D, encompassing digital technologies, platforms, and ecosystems. Schwab (2016) describes this shift as the Fourth Industrial Revolution, characterized by the fusion of technologies blurring the lines between physical, digital, and biological spheres. Metrics for assessing digital innovation include digital R&D expenditure, the adoption rate of emerging technologies (e.g., AI, IoT, blockchain), and digital patent applications.
- Digital Infrastructure and Connectivity – Competitiveness now heavily relies on digital infrastructure, including broadband access, cloud computing capabilities, and mobile connectivity. Castells (1996) highlights the importance of the information society, where economic and social activities are increasingly mediated by digital networks. Indicators of digital infrastructure quality, such as internet penetration rates, broadband speed, and digital services availability, are crucial for competitiveness.
- Data Analytics and Decision-Making – The ability to collect, analyse, and utilize Big Data has become a competitive advantage. Davenport (2014) argues that data analytics transforms decision-making processes, enabling more informed and strategic business moves. Competitiveness metrics in this domain include data analytics investments, the sophistication of data analytics tools, and the integration of data-driven decision-making in strategic planning.
- Cybersecurity Measures – As digital operations expand, so does the risk of cyber threats, making cybersecurity capabilities a vital component of competitiveness. Kshetri (2013) suggests that robust cybersecurity measures are not only essential for protecting assets but also for maintaining consumer trust and operational integrity. Competitiveness indicators related to cybersecurity include investment in security technologies, the maturity of cybersecurity policies, and incident response capabilities.
- Digital Skills and Literacy – The digital transformation has elevated the importance of digital skills and literacy across the workforce. The OECD (2017) notes that digital skills are critical for individuals and organizations to navigate and thrive in the digital economy. Thus, measures of competitiveness increasingly consider the digital literacy levels of the population, the availability of digital education and training programs, and the integration of digital skills in the workforce.

It's no surprise that these advancements have also led to the emergence of other new metrics and methods for measuring productivity and competitiveness in the digital age (Joshi, 2011; Antipov et al., 2020).

Digital transformation has also allowed for the measurement of customer satisfaction and experience through online reviews, ratings, and social media engagement (Meraghni et al., 2021). These measurements provide valuable insights into the overall competitiveness of an organization and its ability to meet customer expectations in the digital age. With the increasing adoption of digital solutions, organizations can target specific key performance indicators that directly translate into financial benefits. Moreover, digital transformation has led to the evolution of competitiveness itself.

Likewise, digital transformation has also led to the emergence of digital platforms, which have revolutionized the way organizations operate and compete. These platforms enable organizations to reach a wider audience, engage with customers in real time, and gather valuable data for analysis (Shpak et al., 2020). By analysing this data, organizations can gain insights into customer preferences and behaviour, allowing them to tailor their products and services to meet specific needs. As well, digital platforms also facilitate collaboration and knowledge sharing among employees, leading to increased innovation and creativity.

The interrelation between productivity and competitiveness in the context of digital transformation is apparent (Verhoef et al., 2021), but digital transformation plays a crucial role in improving productivity and enhancing competitiveness. By embracing digital technologies and leveraging them effectively, organizations can streamline processes, eliminate inefficiencies, and automate repetitive tasks (Shpak et al., 2020). This improves productivity by allowing employees to focus on more value-added activities and enables organizations to deliver products and services faster and at a lower cost. Also, digital transformation allows organizations to adapt quickly to changing market conditions and customer needs (Verhoef et al., 2021). This agility and responsiveness enhance competitiveness by enabling organizations to stay ahead of the competition and deliver superior customer experiences (Gurbaxani & Dunkle, 2019). For example, the shift to digital platforms and online marketplaces has opened new opportunities for organizations to expand their reach and tap into new markets. Implementing e-commerce strategies and digital marketing techniques can help organizations increase their market share and attract new customers (Vaska et al., 2021). Besides, digital transformation also enables organizations to leverage data and analytics to gain a competitive edge. By harnessing the power of data, organizations can make more informed decisions, identify trends and patterns, and develop targeted strategies to drive growth and outperform the competition (Vial, 2019).

1.5 Productivity and competitiveness: the importance of a high correlation

The interrelation between productivity and competitiveness in the context of digital transformation is evident (Hirt & Willmott, 2014). Digital transformation has the potential to improve productivity by enabling more efficient processes and leveraging technology to automate tasks (Xiao, 2022). This, in turn, allows businesses to allocate resources more effectively and focus on strategic initiatives. Additionally, digital transformation enhances competitiveness by providing organizations with the tools and capabilities to better understand and meet customer needs (Hirt & Willmott, 2014). By leveraging data analytics and artificial intelligence, companies can gain valuable insights into customer preferences and behaviour, allowing them to tailor their products and services accordingly and digital transformation enables businesses to respond to market trends and changes more quickly and effectively.

By leveraging real-time data and analytics, companies can make informed decisions and adapt their strategies in a timely manner. With digital transformation, companies can also expand their reach and compete on a global scale (Gurbaxani & Dunkle, 2019). Through digital platforms, companies can reach a broader audience and enter new markets, increasing their competitive edge. The evolution of digital transformation has played a significant role in reshaping the concepts of productivity and competitiveness (Hirt & Willmott, 2014).

The interrelation between productivity and competitiveness lies in the fact that improving productivity can enhance an organization's competitiveness in the market. Improving productivity allows organizations to produce goods or services more efficiently and effectively, which can lead to lower costs, higher quality, faster delivery times, and ultimately, increased customer satisfaction (Priya & Aroulmoji, 2020).

In today's highly competitive business landscape, productivity and competitiveness are crucial factors that can determine the success or failure of a company (Duginets & Olena, 2021) and play a vital role in its growth and survival (Zakaria et al., 2020). Today, businesses face severe tests in both national and international markets due to intense competition from foreign companies. Consequently, widespread attention is being given to the problem of increasing the productivity and long-term profitability of businesses. Any business has to show a considerable set of efforts and possess a clear strategic vision in order to stay afloat and keep or expand the market share (Duginets & Olena, 2021). In order to thrive in today's competitive business environment, companies must prioritize productivity and competitiveness (Zakaria et al., 2020). This importance lies in that it enables a business firm to exhibit superior performance in one aspect or more in a manner that is considered superior to that of other competitors (Duginets & Olena, 2021).

Another way of putting things is that the relationship between productivity and competitiveness is a symbiotic one. Improving productivity directly impacts an organization's competitiveness in the market. The more productive an organization is, the better it can utilize its resources and produce goods or services efficiently (Pousttchi et al., 2019). When an organization is competing with other companies in the market, it needs to continuously innovate and improve its processes to stay ahead (Kurilova & Antipov, 2020). This drive for innovation and process improvement leads to increased productivity.

By implementing digital technologies and integrating them into various aspects of the organization, such as operational processes, resources, and internal operations, organizations can streamline their workflows, automate repetitive tasks, and improve overall efficiency. However, it is important to note that digital transformation alone is not enough to drive productivity and competitiveness. Organizations must also focus on developing a digital mindset and building digital capabilities across the organization. This involves fostering a culture of continuous learning and adaptation, encouraging employees to embrace digital tools and technologies, and providing the necessary training and support for their successful usage. The evolution of digital technologies and the competitive environment necessitate the development of new skills in data analysis (Kuang et al., 2023). This includes the ability to gather and interpret data, as well as the proficiency in using advanced analytics tools and techniques (Vial, 2019). These skills are crucial for organizations to extract valuable insights from data and make informed business decisions. Moreover, as digital transformation continues to evolve, organizations must also adapt their strategies and business models to remain competitive. They need to continually identify new opportunities for innovation and embrace emerging technologies to stay ahead of the curve. Organizations need to leverage digital technologies to create new value propositions, enhance customer experiences, and drive innovation (Schneider, 2019).

Modern organizations are not yet able to simultaneously use all the directions and possibilities of digitalization (Setiawan, 2020). They often only utilize individual technologies, which negatively affects their development and reduces their competitive advantages. Consumers increasingly value their time and expect instant feedback, well-designed information resources, online chats, and an individual approach (Vial, 2019). To meet these high demands, organizations need to accelerate the digitization of their business processes and embrace the implications of digital transformation. This transformation is driven by several factors. As information and communication technology (ICT) advances, so does the development of innovation and the software and digital content industry.

Strategy and organizational changes are also crucial for organizations to remain competitive in the digital world. One area where the impact of digital transformation is particularly evident is in the ability to enhance productivity. Digital transformation allows organizations to streamline their processes, automate repetitive tasks, and improve communication and collaboration. This leads to increased efficiency and productivity, as well as faster decision-making and problem-solving. Furthermore, digital transformation enables organizations to harness the power of data and artificial intelligence. This allows for better analysis and understanding of customer preferences and behaviour, leading to more targeted marketing strategies and personalized products and services.

The link between productivity and competitiveness is clear (Riehl, 1983). Increasing productivity is essential for organizations to remain competitive in the global market (Shehabat, 2020). The effective management of people, the utilization of resources, and the continuous improvement of productivity are all crucial components in enhancing competitiveness. In today's highly competitive global market, organizations that prioritize productivity are more likely to invest in research and development, leading to the development of new products and technologies. These advancements contribute to their competitiveness and ability to meet the changing needs and demands of customers. In today's business environment, improving global competitiveness is a top priority for managers (Stroh & Caligiuri, 1998). They understand that any process or function that enables their organizations to gain a competitive advantage on a global scale is invaluable. One such process that enables organizations to gain a competitive advantage is the effective management of the people side of global business. This includes attracting and retaining talented employees, developing their skills and knowledge, and fostering a positive work culture (Shehabat, 2020). By doing so, organizations can improve productivity and ultimately enhance their competitiveness in the global market.

In summary, productivity and competitiveness are closely interconnected concepts (Soule et al., 2015) in the context of digital transformation (Kuang et al., 2023). Digital transformation is not solely about implementing new technologies; it also requires a strategic approach to organizational design and operations (Vial, 2019). Organizations need to focus on improving productivity through operational efficiency, innovation, collaboration, investment in digital capabilities and infrastructure, adoption of agile methodologies, fostering a culture of continuous learning and skill development, and embracing data-driven decision-making. In today's digital landscape, productivity and competitiveness go hand in hand (Soule et al., 2015). Organizations that are more productive are better equipped to meet customer demands, deliver value, and stay ahead of the competition. With the advancement of digital technology, productivity and competitiveness have become intertwined (Vial, 2019).

1.6 Outlook: productivity and competitiveness in the era of digitalization

Digital transformation has become a driving force behind productivity and competitiveness in today's business landscape. It allows them to streamline their processes, improve coordination and supervision, and create new paths for value creation. Digital transformation significantly enhances productivity and competitiveness in today's economic landscape by incorporating advanced technologies across various aspects of business operations. The evidence from research indicates that digital transformation influences total factor productivity through multiple channels, including technological innovation, reduction in operational costs, improved efficiency in resource allocation, and an upgrade in human capital structure (Li et al., 2020; Kuzior et al., 2023).

Specifically, digital technologies enable a transition from traditional innovation models to more open, collaborative, and networked approaches, significantly improving communication efficiency and facilitating knowledge spillover effects that are crucial for collaborative innovation (Li et al., 2020). Additionally, the integration of digital technologies into production and operational processes not only increases the efficiency of production tools but also significantly reduces manual execution and operational maintenance costs, ultimately enhancing productivity (Li et al., 2020).

Likewise, digital transformation is shown to improve the efficiency of resource allocation within companies by optimizing labour investment decisions and enhancing supply chain resource operation efficiency. This is achieved by leveraging digital technologies to enhance information transparency, which, in turn, facilitates better management decisions regarding labour investments and discourages inefficient investments (Li et al., 2020).

However, the strategic incorporation of digital transformation into organizational strategies is crucial for maintaining or improving processes while ensuring quality, cost-efficiency, and safety. This approach not only positions companies to better compete both locally and internationally but also facilitates growth and expansion into new markets (Yurii et al., 2021).

In the broader economic context, the adoption of Information and Communication Technologies (ICT) is pivotal for national competitiveness, enabling countries to boost productivity, thereby leading to better income, a stronger economy, and an enhanced quality of life for citizens (Duginets & Olena, 2021). Digital technologies play a crucial role in the evolution of economic societies, providing opportunities for traditional companies to reinvent themselves and adapt to dramatic changes across various industrial revolutions (Yurii et al., 2021).

As society continues to embrace digitalization, the outlook for productivity and competitiveness is set to undergo further transformation (Vial, 2019). The evolution of digital technologies and their integration into various aspects of our daily lives will continue to shape the way businesses operate and compete. Organizations that can adapt and leverage digital transformation will likely see increased productivity and a stronger competitive position. These organizations will have the advantage of utilizing advanced technologies and data analytics to optimize their processes, improve efficiency, and drive innovation. Furthermore, digital transformation opens new opportunities for businesses to explore and tap into previously untapped markets.

Traditional metrics are being changed in measuring both concepts and organizations need to consider factors such as customer satisfaction, digital engagement, and the ability to innovate and adapt to changing market dynamics (Izmailova et al., 2021). Digital transformation has revolutionized the way organizations operate and measure productivity and competitiveness (Kuang et al., 2023). Organizations now have access to vast amounts of data that can be used to measure and analyse performance in real time (Vial, 2019). This allows organizations to identify areas of improvement, make data-driven decisions, and continuously optimize their processes for greater productivity and competitiveness.

For example, companies that can deliver personalized and seamless customer experiences through digital channels have a competitive edge over those who cannot, so digital transformation has also expanded the scope of competitiveness beyond traditional industry boundaries. Companies are now competing not only with their direct competitors, but also with digitally savvy start-ups and tech giants that are disrupting traditional industries. Additionally, organizations can use tools like data analytics to measure the efficiency and effectiveness of their digital processes, identify areas for improvement, and make data-driven decisions to enhance productivity and competitiveness (Miklošík & Evans, 2020). Innovation elements are also important. To measure innovation speed organizations can do it by tracking the time it takes to bring new products or features to market (Tung et al., 2020). In addition, organizations can measure digital process efficiency by analysing factors such as automation levels, digitization of workflows, and the use of advanced analytics (Vial, 2019). By incorporating these digital-specific KPIs into their measurement systems, organizations can gain a more comprehensive understanding of their productivity and competitiveness in the digital era.

1.7 Cases and examples – food for thought

Case applications of these principles clearly highlight the significant improvements possible in retail supply chain competence and the resultant competitiveness (Hsu & Fang, 2009). One notable example of the interdependence between productivity and competitiveness can be seen in the retail industry. Productivity and competitiveness are closely intertwined in the business world as we've seen (Mirolyubov et al., 2019). One example is the retail industry, where improvements in supply chain competence can significantly enhance competitiveness. For instance, by leveraging advanced technologies and effective knowledge management practices, retailers can streamline their supply chain operations, reduce costs, and improve customer satisfaction. This can be seen in the case of Amazon, which has invested heavily in technology and innovation to optimize its supply chain.

Another example is the automotive industry, where productivity plays a critical role in maintaining competitiveness. For example, Tesla's success in the electric vehicle market can be attributed to its high productivity levels (Ganesan et al., 2009). They have implemented efficient production processes and automation, allowing them to produce cars faster and at a lower cost than traditional automakers. Therefore, Tesla's ability to achieve high levels of productivity has contributed to its competitiveness in the market. A third example can be found in the manufacturing sector. Many manufacturers rely on productivity improvements to stay competitive in the global market. For instance, companies like Toyota have implemented lean manufacturing principles to enhance productivity and efficiency, allowing them to offer high-quality products at competitive prices.

The implementation of Total Productive Maintenance (TPM) in the Indian process industry serves as a case study that exemplifies the interdependence between productivity and competitiveness. The successful implementation of TPM in the Indian process industry led to improvements in organizational behaviour, equipment availability and utilization, maintenance productivity, and resource utilization (Ahuja et al., 2006). These improvements directly contributed to increased productivity and competitiveness for the companies involved. Furthermore, knowledge management capabilities and the effective implementation of corporate strategies are also crucial for developing a competitive advantage within the supply chain (Pérez-Salazar et al., 2017). Supply chain integration is a key factor in today's competitive landscape, as it allows for tighter cooperation and improved efficiency among enterprises (Ahuja et al., 2006). The intense competition in the business world has shifted from company-to-company to supply chain-to-supply chain (Chen & Papazafeiropoulou, 2013). Overall, these examples and cases highlight the interdependence between productivity and competitiveness in various industries (Chen & Papazafeiropoulou, 2013). Another example is the retail giant Walmart, known for its strong supply chain management practices, which have contributed to its success and competitiveness in the industry. In the case of the Taiwanese IT manufacturing companies, their ability to integrate supply chains and achieve efficiency directly impacted their competitiveness in the market. For example, Foxconn, a Taiwanese IT manufacturer, has implemented efficient supply chain practices and achieved high levels of productivity (Chan et al., 2005). These efforts have allowed them to maintain a competitive edge in the industry and meet the demands of global customers.

References

Ablyazov, T., Asaturova, J., & Koscheyev, V. (2018, January 1). Digital technologies: New forms and tools of business activity. St. Petersburgh. https://doi.org/10.1051/shsconf/20184400004

Acemoglu, D., & Autor, D. (2011). Skills, tasks and technologies: Implications for employment and earnings. *Handbook of Labor Economics*, 4, 1043–1171.

Adagba, T., Ati, J. O., & Makarfi, A. (2021, August 18). An assessment of labour productivity influencing factors in the construction industry: A case study of Zaria, Nigeria. https://doi.org/10.38094/jocef20235

Adamo, G. E., Ferrari, S., & Gilli, M. (2019, January 24). Creativity as a source of differentiation in urban tourism: The case of Torino city. https://doi.org/10.1002/jtr.2261

Ahuja, I. S., Khamba, J. S., & Choudhary, R. (2006, January 1). Improved organizational behavior through strategic total productive maintenance implementation. https://doi.org/10.1115/imece2006-15783

Alghanmi, A. O. (2020, January 1). Innovations as the competitive advantage for small and medium enterprises: The case for the Kingdom of Saudi Arabia. https://doi.org/10.21272/mmi.2020.2-14

Antipov, D., Кузнецова, E., & Aytasova, A. S. (2020, December 1). Digital technologies and QMS of industrial enterprise: Focus on efficiency. https://doi.org/10.1088/1757-899x/986/1/012024

Bahorka, M., Квасова, Л., & Yurchenko, N. (2023, March 31). Comprehensive marketing system as a basis for increasing the competitiveness of trade enterprises in modern conditions of doing business. https://doi.org/10.30525/2661-5169/2023-1-4

Bai, H. (2021, December 23). Role of digital technology in transforming organizational competencies influencing green economy: Moderating role of product knowledge hiding. https://doi.org/10.3389/fpsyg.2021.792550

Becker, G. S. (1964). *Human capital: A theoretical and empirical analysis, with special reference to education*. Chicago: The University of Chicago Press.

Boote, D. N., & Beile, P. (2005). Scholars before researchers: On the centrality of the dissertation literature review in research preparation. *Educational Researcher*, 34(6), 3–15. https://doi.org/10.3102/0013189X034006003

Camp, R. C. (1989). *Benchmarking: The search for industry best practices that lead to superior performance*. Phoenix: Productivity Press.

Castells, M. (1996). *The rise of the network society*. Aberdeen: Blackwell.

Chan, F. T., Lau, H. C. W., Ip, R .W. L., Chan, H., & Kong, S. (2005, January 1). Implementation of total productive maintenance: A case study. https://doi.org/10.1016/j.ijpe.2003.10.021

Chen, H., & Papazafeiropoulou, A. (2013, January 1). Supply chain integration in the IT manufacturing sector: How integration technologies adoption can improve efficiency. https://doi.org/10.1504/ijass.2013.053350

Comin, D., & Mestieri, M. (2018). If technology has arrived everywhere, why has income diverged? *The American Economic Journal: Macroeconomics*, 10(3), 137–178.

Crowhurst, Elizabeth, Amy Finch, and Eleonora Harwich. (2015). Towards a More Productive State. Reform, 2015; London.Dangayach, G., & Deshmukh, S. (2003, March 1). Evidence of manufacturing strategies in Indian industry: A survey. https://doi.org/10.1016/s0925-5273(02)00372-9

Davenport, T. H. (2014). *Big data at work: Dispelling the myths, uncovering the opportunities*. Boston: Harvard Business Review Press.

Dedrick, J., Gurbaxani, V., & Kraemer, K L. (2003, March 1). Information technology and economic performance. https://doi.org/10.1145/641865.641866

Deming, W. E. (1986). *Out of the crisis*. MIT Center for Advanced Engineering Study.

Drucker, P. (1999). Knowledge-worker productivity: The biggest challenge. *California Management Review*, 41(2), 79–94.

Duginets, G., & Olena, K. (2021, June 15). Competitive strategies of companies in the foreign market. Emerald Insight. https://doi.org/10.31617/zt.knute.2021(116)02. https://www.emerald.com/insight/content/doi/10.1108/MD-06-2020-0667/full/html

Fink, A. (2019). *Conducting research literature reviews: From the internet to paper* (4th ed.). Los Angeles: Sage Publications.

Ganesan, S., George, M., Jap, S. D., Palmatier, R. W., & Weitz, B. A. (2009, March 1). Supply chain management and retailer performance: Emerging trends, issues, and implications for research and practice. https://doi.org/10.1016/j.jretai.2008.12.001

Gebayew, C., Hardini, I. R., Panjaitan, G. H. A., Kurniawan, N. B., & Suhardi (2018, October 1). A systematic literature review on digital transformation. https://doi.org/10.1109/icitsi.2018.8695912

Goldstein, H. (2002). Measuring productivity: An overview. *Economica*, 4(16), 32–42.

Grant, M. J., & Booth, A. (2009). A typology of reviews: An analysis of 14 review types and associated methodologies. *Health Information & Libraries Journal*, 26(2), 91–108. https://doi.org/10.1111/j.1471-1842.2009.00848.x

Greenhalgh, T., & Peacock, R. (2005). Effectiveness and efficiency of search methods in systematic reviews of complex evidence: Audit of primary sources. *BMJ*, 331(7524), 1064–1065. https://doi.org/10.1136/bmj.38636.593461.68

Gurbaxani, V., & Dunkle, D. E. (2019, September 1). Gearing up for successful digital transformation. https://doi.org/10.17705/2msqe.00017

Hall, R. E., & Jones, C. I. (1999). Why do some countries produce so much more output per worker than others? *The Quarterly Journal of Economics*, 114(1), 83–116.

Hart, C. (1998). *Doing a literature review: Releasing the social science research imagination*. Los Angeles: Sage.

Harter, J. K., Schmidt, F. L., & Hayes, T. L. (2002). Business-unit-level relationship between employee satisfaction, employee engagement, and business outcomes: A meta-analysis. *Journal of Applied Psychology*, 87(2), 268–279.

Higgins, J. P. T., & Green, S. (Eds.) (2011). *Cochrane handbook for systematic reviews of interventions*. Aberdeen: Wiley-Blackwell.

Hirt, M., & Willmott, P. (2014, May 1). Strategic principles for competing in the digital age. https://www.mckinsey.com/capabilities/strategy-and-corporate-finance/our-insights/strategic-principles-for-competing-in-the-digital-age

Horal, L., Korol, S., Havrylenko, M., Khvostina, I., & Shyiko, V. (2020, January 1). The management of business-processes strategic sectors of economy on digital transformation conditions. https://doi.org/10.2991/aebmr.k.200318.030

Hsu, Y., & Fang, W. (2009, June 1). Intellectual capital and new product development performance: The mediating role of organizational learning capability. https://doi.org/10.1016/j.techfore.2008.03.012

Hulten, C. R. (2001). Total factor productivity: A short biography. *New Developments in Productivity Analysis*, 1–54.

Ianenko, M., Ianenko, M., Kirillova, T., Amakhina, S., & Nikitina, N. (2020, September 1). Digital transformation strategies of trade enterprises: Key areas, development and implementation algorithms. https://doi.org/10.1088/1757-899x/940/1/012051

Izmailova, M. A., Veselovsky, M. Y., & Trifonov, V. (2021, January 1). Digitalization of economy and socio-economic development of Russia: Points of connection. https://doi.org/10.2991/aebmr.k.210222.038

Jesson, J., Matheson, L., & Lacey, F. M. (2011). *Doing your literature review: Traditional and systematic techniques*. Sage.

Joshi, V. S. (2011, November 1). Metrics center of excellence: From idea to implementation of a "meaningful" measurement and analysis process. https://doi.org/10.1109/iwsm-mensura.2011.37

Kaplan, R. S., & Norton, D. P. (1996). Using the balanced scorecard as a strategic management system. *Harvard Business Review*, 74(1), 75–85.

Kraus, S., Schiavone, F., Pluzhnikova, A., & Invernizzi, A C. (2021, February 1). Digital transformation in healthcare: Analyzing the current state-of-research. https://doi.org/10.1016/j.jbusres.2020.10.030

Krugman, P. (1994). Competitiveness: A dangerous obsession. *Foreign Affairs*, 73(2), 28–44.

Kshetri, N. (2013). Cybersecurity needs and market demands. *IEEE Security & Privacy*, 11(4), 12–15.

Kuang, Y., Fan, M., Fan, Y., Jiang, Y., & Bin, J. (2023, March 20). Digitalization, financing constraints and firm performance. https://doi.org/10.3389/fenvs.2023.1090537

Kurilova, A., & Antipov, D. (2020, December 1). Impact of digital innovation on company performance. https://doi.org/10.1088/1757-899x/986/1/012022

Kuzior, A., Krawczyk, D., Onopriienko, K., Petrushenko, Y., Onopriienko, I., & Onopriienko, V. (2023). Lifelong Learning as a Factor in the Country's Competitiveness and Innovative Potential within the Framework of Sustainable Development. *Sustainability*, 15(13), 9968. https://doi.org/10.3390/su15139968.

Li, Y., Chen, P., & Liu, Y. (2020). Digital transformation and total factor productivity: Empirical evidence from China. *PLoS One*. https://journals.plos.org/plosone/article?id=10.1371/journal.pone.0232826

Locke, E. A., & Latham, G. P. (2002). Building a practically useful theory of goal setting and task motivation: A 35-year odyssey. *American Psychologist*, 57(9), 705–717.

MacLure, M. (2005). Clarity bordering on stupidity: Where's the quality in systematic review? *Journal of Education Policy*, 20(4), 393–416. https://doi.org/10.1080/02680930500131801

Магомедов, И. А., Murzaev, H. A., & Bagov, A. M. (2020, May 1). The role of digital technologies in economic development. https://doi.org/10.1088/1757-899x/862/5/052071

Mateus, A., de Brito, J. M. B., & Martins, V. (1995). *Portugal Século XXI: cenários de desenvolvimento*. Lisboa: Bertrand Editora.

Meraghni, O., Bekkouche, L., & Demdoum, Z. (2021, January 1). Impact of digital transformation on accounting information systems – Evidence from Algerian firms. https://doi.org/10.2478/eb-2021-0017

Mergel, I., Edelmann, N., & Haug, N. (2019, October 1). Defining digital transformation: Results from expert interviews. https://doi.org/10.1016/j.giq.2019.06.002

Miklošík, A., & Evans, N. (2020, January 1). Impact of big data and machine learning on digital transformation in marketing: A literature review. https://doi.org/10.1109/access.2020.2998754

Mirolyubov, A. A., Turina, M. I., & Tsekhanovich, A. A. (2019, January 1). Digital transformations in automotive dealer chain – Chances and challenges. https://doi.org/10.2991/icdtli-19.2019.74

Morgan, N., Clark, B. H., & Gooner, R. (2002, May 1). Marketing productivity, marketing audits, and systems for marketing performance assessment: Integrating multiple perspectives. https://doi.org/10.1016/s0148-2963(00)00162-4

OECD. (2017). *Skills for a digital world*. OECD Digital Economy Papers, No. 250.

Office for National Statistics. (n.d.). *Productivity handbook*. London: Office for National Statistics. Retrieved from https://www.ons.gov.uk

Pérez-Salazar, M. D. R., Aguilar-Lasserre, A. A., Cedillo-Campos, M. G., & González, J. C. H. (2017, October 26). The role of knowledge management in supply chain management: A literature review. https://doi.org/10.3926/jiem.2144

Petticrew, M., & Roberts, H. (2006). *Systematic reviews in the social sciences: Techniques and applications*. Aberdeen: Blackwell Publishing.

Porter, M. E. (1980). Industry structure and competitive strategy: Keys to profitability. *Financial Analysts Journal*, 36(4), 30–41.

Porter, M. E. (1990). *The competitive advantage of nations*. Florence, MA: Free Press.

Porter, M. E. (2008, January 1). The five competitive forces that shape strategy. https://pubmed.ncbi.nlm.nih.gov/18271320

Pousttchi, K., Gleiß, A., Buzzi, B., & Kohlhagen, M. (2019, July 1). Technology impact types for digital transformation. https://doi.org/10.1109/cbi.2019.00063

Pritchard, R. D., Harrell, M. M., DiazGranados, D., & Guzman, M. J. (2008). The productivity measurement and enhancement system: A meta-analysis. *Journal of Applied Psychology*, 93(3), 540–567. https://doi.org/10.1037/0021-9010.93.3.540

Priya, R. S., & Aroulmoji, V. (2020, May 29). A review on productivity and its effect in industrial manufacturing. https://doi.org/10.29294/ijase.6.4.2020.1490-1499

Qin, Y., & Gu, Z. (2008, October 1). A study on upgrading competitive advantages for the modern service enterprises based on the customer value. https://doi.org/10.1109/wicom.2008.2069

Randolph, J. J. (2009). A guide to writing the dissertation literature review. *Practical Assessment, Research & Evaluation*, 14(13), 1–13.

Ricafort, M. V. (2021, January 19). Proposed framework for the CALABARZON destination competitiveness. http://consortiacademia.org/wp-content/uploads/2021/m_v9i1/7705_ijrsm_final.pdf

Ricardo, D. (1817). *On the principles of political economy and taxation*. John Murray.
Riehl, J. W. (1983, January 1). Intensive internship. https://doi.org/10.1145/800030.800627
Schmenner, R. W., & Swink, M. L. (1998). On theory in operations management. *Journal of Operations Management*, 17(1), 97–113.
Schneider, S. (2019, January 1). The impacts of digital technologies on innovating for sustainability. https://doi.org/10.1007/978-3-319-97385-2_22
Schumpeter, J. A. (1942). *Capitalism, socialism, and democracy*. New York: Harper & Brothers.
Schwab, K. (2016). *The fourth industrial revolution*. Cologny: World Economic Forum.
Setiawan, A. R. (2020, December 28). A study on the potential of the development of software applications and digital content industrial ecosystem in Indonesia.
Shehabat, I. (2020, May 13). The role of knowledge management in organizational performance and gaining sustainable competitive advantage. https://doi.org/10.1145/3399871.3399878
Sheth, J. N., & Sisodia, R. S. (2002, May 1). Marketing productivity: Issues and analysis. https://doi.org/10.1016/s0148-2963(00)00164-8
Shpak, N., Kuzmin, O., Dvulit, Z., Onysenko, T., & Sroka, W. (2020, February 17). Digitalization of the marketing activities of enterprises: Case study. https://doi.org/10.3390/info11020109
Solow, R. M. (1957). Technical change and the aggregate production function. *The Review of Economics and Statistics*, 39(3), 312–320.
Soule, D. L., Puram, A. D., Westerman, G., & Bonnet, D. (2015, January 1). Becoming a digital organization: The journey to digital dexterity. https://doi.org/10.2139/ssrn.2697688
Stroh, L. K., & Caligiuri, P. (1998, January 1). Increasing global competitiveness through effective people management. https://doi.org/10.1016/s1090-9516(98)80001-1
Tranfield, D., Denyer, D., & Smart, P. (2003). Towards a methodology for developing evidence-informed management knowledge by means of systematic review. *British Journal of Management*, 14(3), 207–222. https://doi.org/10.1111/1467-8551.00375
Tung, T. V., Trung, T. N., Hai, N. H., & Tinh, N. T. (2020, October 30). Digital transformation in oil and gas companies – A case study of Bien Dong POC. https://doi.org/10.47800/pvj.2020.10-07
Vaska, S., Massaro, M., Bagarotto, E. M., & Mas, F. D. (2021, January 7). The digital transformation of business model innovation: A structured literature review. https://doi.org/10.3389/fpsyg.2020.539363
Verhoef, P. C., Broekhuizen, T., Bart, Y., Bhattacharya, A., Dong, J. Q., Fabian, N. E., & Haenlein, M. (2021, January 1). Digital transformation: A multidisciplinary reflection and research agenda. https://doi.org/10.1016/j.jbusres.2019.09.022
Vial, G. (2019, June 1). Understanding digital transformation: A review and a research agenda. https://doi.org/10.1016/j.jsis.2019.01.003
Williams, A., Widayanti, R., Maryanti, T., & Julianingsih, D. (2022, May 27). Effort to win the competition in digital business payment modeling. https://doi.org/10.34306/sabda.v1i1.80
Xiao, Y. (2022, January 1). Effect and influencing factors of digital transformation of manufacturing industry. https://doi.org/10.2991/aebmr.k.220405.072
Zakaria, N. H., Alias, M., & Rani, N. (2020, March 10). Employee's productivity: The most dominant factors. https://doi.org/10.35631/ijemp.39001

2

COMPETITIVE ADVANTAGE

Why and how to evaluate – its importance in competitiveness

Helen E. Salavou

2.1 Introduction

This chapter is structured as follows. After this introductory section, we introduce the concept of competitiveness, which has been and remains a key topic in the organisational performance debate among scholars, practitioners and policymakers for nearly half a century. Next, we discuss how competitiveness relates to the competitive advantage at the firm level and how competitive advantage, one of the most widely used concepts in strategic management, was anchored as a basic theme throughout the periods to date. In the fourth and fifth sections, we contrast the original idea of strategic purity with the revised idea of hybridisation along with some realities of competitive advantage in terms of performance. The fifth section comments on future challenges.

2.2 Competitiveness

Competitiveness as a word originates from the Latin word *competer* meaning 'to engage in business rivalry for markets'. As a concept, it has become synonymous with economic strength at various levels and a buzzword like 'globalisation' (Bhawsar and Chattopadhyay, 2015), which is the reason for the increased importance of competitiveness.[1] Historically, competitiveness bolstered during the early 1980s in the era of Adam Smith and his followers, when European and Asian nations followed the American economic dominance (Banwet et al., 2002; Waheeduzzaman and Ryans, 1996). The concepts of competition and competitiveness gained momentum shortly after Porter's seminal work, *Competitive Strategy*, published in 1980, found widespread use in both business and academia.

DOI: 10.4324/9781032695969-3

Surprisingly, scholars have failed to reach a consensus on the meaning of competitiveness despite the widespread use across a wide range of industries (Flanagan et al., 2007). Even Porter (1990) once stated that it was 'clear to me … that there was no accepted definition of competitiveness'. However, his contribution, as an economist, to the investigation of 'competitiveness' at the level of the firm, industry and nation over the past 50+ years has been fundamental to the development of both the theory and practice of strategy and strategising (Stonehouse and Snowdon, 2007). Especially in terms of firm competitiveness, he initiated new perspectives for scholars, practitioners and policymakers (Sölvell, 2015). All he wanted was to find a framework that would better capture the full complexity of competition (Stonehouse and Snowdon, 2007). His book in 1990 titled *The Competitive Advantage of Nations* created a new model for microeconomic drivers of long-term firm competitiveness, which created new research avenues for scholars and reasons to develop superior strategies and agendas for practitioners and policymakers.

In addition to the abundance of definitions, which serve as an evidence of the diversity, inclusivity and complexity inherent in competitiveness, there are other characteristics that provide valuable insights into this concept. Summarised by (Flanagan et al., 2007), competitiveness may be described as something that is multi-defined, multi-measured, multi-layered, dependent, relative, dynamic and process-related. No doubt throughout the years, this concept is used in different ways by different stakeholders featuring changes with time and context (Flanagan et al., 2007).

In this chapter, we link the concept of competitiveness to firms,[2] as reflected in their ability and competency to compete successfully in a market full of competitors.

2.3 From firm-level competitiveness to competitive advantage

Although the exploration of competition within firms can be traced back as early as 1935, the concept of competitive advantage saw limited application in studies before 1980. During this period, scholars predominantly emphasised the significance of competition in shaping business strategy (Powell, 1992). Nevertheless, competitive advantage has evolved into a cornerstone concept in strategic management, perpetuating an ongoing area of research. The annual scientific production of articles in the field of competitive advantage has exhibited consistent growth, with an annual expansion rate of 9.8% since 1985 (Nayak et al., 2022).

The concept of competitive advantage has been embedded in conceptual models as both a direct and indirect concept (e.g., Drnevich et al., 2020). Interestingly, competitive advantage was anchored as a basic theme across all periods with a high degree of relevance but a comparatively lower degree of development (Nayak et al., 2022). There is still no agreement on a single conceptually clear and ambiguous definition, as scholars believe that the concept is not so easy to identify (e.g., Godfrey and Hill, 1995; Lieberman, 2021).

Nevertheless, competitive advantage achievement for firms has received remarkable attention and is evident in two approaches on firms' competitiveness (see Table 2.1).

The first approach, namely the generic strategy approach, embraces the competitive advantage and competitive strategy models of Professor Michael Porter (1980, 1985), who is recognised as one of the founding fathers of strategy (Snowdon and Stonehouse, 2006). Based on Porter's (1980) initial theory, the typology was composed of two components. First, it categorised competitive strategies at the business level based on the target market's scope (either narrow or broad) and the source of competitive advantage (either cost or differentiation). Second, it put forward a theoretical proposition concerning the impact of business strategy on business performance (Campbell-Hunt, 2000; González-Benito and Suárez-González, 2010).

Despite numerous typologies, including those put forth by Miles and Snow (1978), Hofer and Schendel (1978) and Dess and Davis (1984), as well as various attempts at their integration (Parnell, 1997), Porter's (1980) typology was the most influential within the strategic management literature and inherently tied to firm

TABLE 2.1 Approaches on firms' competitiveness

Approach	*Generic strategy approach*	*Resource-based view and core competence approach*
Basic premise in terms of competitive advantage	Competitive advantage comes from the competitive strategy a firm adopts to neutralise threats or to exploit opportunities within the industry.	Competitive advantage comes from firm-specific resources (valuable, rare, inimitable, non-substitutable), which should be developed and exploited to achieve core competences.
The firm or the industry controls the competitive advantage game?	Emphasises strategic positioning, as the industry structure drives competition and profitability	Emphasises inward focus, as it is possible for the firm to gain and maintain a competitive advantage
Level of analysis	Industry level	Firm level
Superior performance	Comes from competitive advantage developed from market positions.	Comes from competitive advantage created by idiosyncratic firm-specific resources and capabilities.
Main proponents	Porter (1980, 1985)	Barney (1991), Hamel and Prahalad (1990), Penrose (1959) and Wernerfelt (1984)
Criticism	Does not address how a firm converts a promising environment into useful internal abilities	Rarely operationally defined and tested – the inward focus may risk ignoring market conditions

performance (Kim et al., 2004). It stimulated a large body of empirical work on the sources of sustainable competitive advantage that examine conditions under which cost leadership and differentiation strategies produce persistent, supernormal profits (e.g., Hambrick, 1983; White, 1986).

The second approach (henceforth RBV), namely the resource-based view and core competence approach (e.g., Barney, 1991; Hamel and Prahalad, 1990), argues that firms develop unique core competences to outperform rivals by doing things differently and better (Hamel and Prahalad, 1990). This uniqueness precludes general recipes for competitive advantage, such as those implied in the structural approach. Nevertheless, differentiation of products and services remains fundamental to the means, by which firms seek to gain competitive advantage (Stonehouse and Snowdon, 2007). This approach claims an 'inside-out' perspective to strategic management based on the premise that competitive advantage depends on the behaviour of the firm rather than its competitive environment. Consequently, strategy is no longer generic but essentially unique to the firm, as the focus should be on developing knowledge-based core competences through learning and then leveraging them in various markets.

The period from the year 2000 onwards witnessed studies extending the RBV to advance the conversation on competitive advantage. The emergence of the dynamic capabilities, learning and knowledge-based approaches argued that competitive advantage arises from an inward focus based on knowledge developed through continuous organisational learning (Hamel and Prahalad, 1990; Sanchez and Heene, 1997; Nonaka, 1991; Nonaka et al., 2000; Prahalad and Hamel, 1994; Senge, 1990). Technology emerged as an essential part of the firm's processes and became a contributor to firm performance. Technological capabilities were examined as key firm capabilities. Studies in the recent years have focused on business analytics (Côrte-Real et al., 2017; Wamba et al., 2017) and social responsibility (Du et al., 2011; McWilliams and Siegel, 2011) as sources of competitive advantage.

2.4 Competitive advantage: why to evaluate?

Studies in strategic management have mostly dealt with strategies to gain a competitive edge in the market (Linz et al., 2017). The period from the year 1980 to the present demonstrates numerous studies using theories from industrial organisation to dynamic capabilities to explain why and how firms achieve competitive advantage (Nayak et al., 2022).

Porter's (1980) original idea of strategic purity introduced the business level in theorising the strategy-performance relationship and became central in the strategic management literature (Thornhill and White, 2007). The accumulated empirical evidence since 1980 shows that this idea captures part of the reality. In practice, firms adopt a greater variety of competitive strategies that go far beyond the three pure mutually exclusive competitive strategies. The revised idea of hybridisation followed strategic purity to adjust the main research question. More specifically, the research question of strategic purity '*Which one of the three pure strategies lead to higher performance at the business level?*' shifted to the research question of hybridisation '*Does pursuit of a pure business strategy (and which one of the three) or of a hybrid business strategy (and of what structure) lead to superior performance?*' Answering the latter question became the global challenge of dealing with hypercompetition. Scholars have contrasted pure and hybrid strategies (e.g., Thornhill and White, 2007) to better capture reality and revise theory, accordingly, as discussed below.

2.5 Forms of competitive advantage: from strategic purity to hybridisation

Porter's (1980) theory on firm-level competitiveness posited that a competitive advantage arises from the specific competitive, generic or business-level strategy adopted by a company to counter threats or seize opportunities within its industry. In his book *Competitive Strategy*, Porter (1980) introduced the concept of competitive strategies, emphasising an intermediate level, the business level or strategic business unit level. This distinction led to a separation between corporate-level strategy, which dealt with a corporation's choice of businesses and how it managed its business units (Porter, 1989), and business-level strategy, which focused on creating competitive advantages within each business unit of a firm (Salavou, 2015).

Porter's framework outlined three distinct and mutually exclusive strategic options that could enhance a company's performance. The first was the low-cost strategy (cost leadership), which involved delivering products or services with comparable value to competitors but at a lower cost (Porter, 1986). This approach could yield above-average profits since companies could match the prices of their most efficient competitors and still maintain superior profits (Miller and Friesen, 1986). The second strategy, differentiation, required a firm to offer a product or service that was perceived as unique, enabling them to command higher prices. Customer loyalty resulting from this uniqueness made demand less responsive to price changes, leading to higher profit margins (Aulakh et al., 2000). The third strategy, focus, could be based on either low cost, differentiation, or both (Karnani, 1984), and it involved serving a specialised segment in terms of geography, customer type, or product range more effectively or efficiently than broader competitors.

Each of these competitive strategies aimed to help a firm gain an advantage over rivals within the same industry or similar domestic market environments while achieving superior performance. Porter (1980, 1985) asserted that adhering to a single, pure strategy was the key to achieving superior performance, whereas combining generic strategies causes most businesses to be stuck-in-the-middle[3] and have poor performance.

This theory stressing the strategy-performance relationship gained widespread recognition and prompted extensive empirical research across various continents, including Europe, Asia and America (Salavou, 2015). Investigations beyond strategic purity marked hybridisation (see Table 2.2), a new era featuring a shift in emphasis from the pure to the hybrid form of competitive advantage. The dimensional approach, in contrast to the taxonomic, empiricist and nominalist approaches, provided a more comprehensive language for describing competitive strategies. It allowed for the development of complex and multidimensional strategic profiles that could offer not only safety against competitors but also higher profitability (Pertusa-Ortega et al., 2009; Spanos et al., 2004).

Increasing evidence in favour of hybrid strategy combinations, particularly in Europe, suggested that they often outperformed pure and strategy-less choices. Companies that pay particular attention to various competitive advantages, such as different types of differentiation, and creatively combine them may achieve multiple sources of advantage over rival firms.

Table 2.3 illustrates 16 potential hybrid strategies characterised by varying degrees of emphasis on competitive advantages. These strategies span a spectrum, from those highlighting all three competitive advantages concurrently to those concentrating solely on one, while the other two dimensions receive modest

TABLE 2.2 Strategic purity versus hybridisation: Pros and cons

Strategic purity: The original idea	*Hybridisation: The revised idea*
Pros	Pros
Creates strategic options based on theory	Creates strategic options based on facts
Gives a model comprising three pure, mutually exclusive, generic strategies at the business level	Suggests many hybrid strategies at the business level
Offers "black or white" strategic options	Offers "grey shades" strategic options
Defends a taxonomical approach	Defends a dimensional approach
Emphasises the cost/differentiation dichotomy as two basic types of competitive advantage	Emphasises the hybrid form of competitive advantage and benefits from multiple sources of competitive advantage.
Fits to sectorial analysis	Fits either to sectorial or multisectorial analysis
Cons	Cons
Firms that exclusively focus on a single pure strategy might exhibit reduced adaptability and flexibility in market shifts, hindering their ability to provide products that simultaneously emphasise cost-efficiency and specific product features.	Companies focusing on mixed-emphasis strategies may be more responsive to market changes but are difficult to implement and evaluate.
	Hybrid strategies are complex and of multidimensional in nature. They may cause confusion or loss of direction.
Strategic specialisation can result in notable shortcomings in product offerings, overlooking critical customer requirements that could prove detrimental to businesses.	There is a lack of a comprehensive descriptive framework for hybrid strategies. Scholars ought to develop a theoretical spectrum that encompasses the entire range of competitive strategies.
Pure strategies are susceptible to imitation.	

TABLE 2.3 Types of hybrids strategies[a]

	Competitive advantage		
	Differentiation	*Low cost*	*Other competitive advantages*[b]
Hybrid strategy 1	High	High	High
Hybrid strategy 2	High	High	Low
Hybrid strategy 3	Low	High	High
Hybrid strategy 4	High	High	Average
Hybrid strategy 5	Average	High	High
Hybrid strategy 6	Average	High	Average
Hybrid strategy 7	Low	High	Average
Hybrid strategy 8	Average	High	Low
Hybrid strategy 9	High	Average	High
Hybrid strategy 10	High	Average	Low
Hybrid strategy 11	High	Average	Average
Hybrid strategy 12	Average	Average	High
Hybrid strategy 13	Low	Average	High
Hybrid strategy 14	High	Low	High
Hybrid strategy 15	High	Low	Average
Hybrid strategy 16	Average	Low	High

[a] Stuck-in-the-middle strategy type would suggest average emphasis on competitive advantages and no strategy type would suggest low emphasis on competitive advantages.

[b] Other competitive advantages, such as innovation, quality, speed delivery, service base, customer response, etc.

or limited attention. Empirical evidence supports the notion that the greater the complexity and multidimensionality of a hybrid strategy's profile, the more stable and defensible its strategic position becomes (Pertusa-Ortega et al., 2009; Spanos et al., 2004). In simpler terms, a strategy that concurrently prioritises three generic dimensions outperforms one that emphasises only two, and the latter surpasses a strategy where only one dimension is distinct while the others receive average or minimal emphasis.

Since the year 2000, scholars from diverse national contexts and continents like Africa, America, Asia, and particularly Europe have focused on hybridisation as a means to advance research on competitive strategies. Regardless of the structure or the types of hybrid strategies (see, for example, Table 2.3), the hybrid form of competitive advantage is the prevailing form, facilitating higher levels of performance. This is particularly salient in Europe, where nearly half of the studies on competitive strategies have been conducted (Salavou, 2015).

2.6 Competitive advantage: how to evaluate?

It has been argued that competitive advantage is a buzzword that causes confusion to academics, business executives and consultants (Markides, 2000). Confusion comes from the fact that the term is used with different meaning in different contexts (O'Shannassy, 2008). For example, competitive advantage is a relational term between the referent firm and their rivals within a specific context of competition (Ma, 2000). As such, it depends on the referent point, defined when we answer questions such as *against whom?* and *on what?* If we set aside the cost leader, that is, the player holding the industry's lowest cost position, we can focus on any pair of competitors within a particular and distinct dimension of competition that highlights competitive advantage.

As a result, competitive advantage represents the disparity between two competitors across any conceivable dimension that enables one to deliver greater customer value than the other (Ma, 2000). Without clearly identifying the dimension of competition or without comparing a pair of firms within this dimension, confusion is likely to arise. In addition, given that the concept is not well understood, measuring it is not an effective way to understand it. The cliché 'if you cannot measure it, you cannot manage it' offers a rationale for the existing gaps in defining and operationalising competitive advantage.

2.7 Competitive advantage and performance: Some realities

As the operationalisation of competitive advantage is not an easy task, we comment on the relationship patterns between competitive advantage and superior performance (Ma, 2000; Sigalas and Papadakis, 2018). In real business world, a company can find itself in one of four scenarios: possessing both competitive advantage and superior performance, lacking both competitive advantage and superior performance, having competitive advantage without superior performance or achieving superior performance without competitive advantage. To put it differently, there are maximum four relationship patterns, equal to the possible combination of these two concepts (Powell, 2002).

Scholars go beyond the direct effect of competitive advantage on firm performance and raise concerns with additional questions (Ma, 2000). Is competitive advantage the prerequisite for competing, an attribute observed during competition, or a consequence of competition? Below we discuss three realities with the hope to generate the expansion of theory and empirical evidence on this relationship.

Reality #1 *Competitive advantage is not performance*

Contrary to the dominant approaches in strategic management (see Table 2.1), which treat sustainable competitive advantage and performance as interchangeable constructs, competitive advantage is not performance (Ma, 2000). The former is the fundamental concept in the field of strategic management that seeks to explain the variations in performance among firms (Ceccagnoli, 2009; Madsen and Leiblein, 2015; Rumelt, 2003; Zott and Amit, 2008). Some arguments follow. First, the structural approach asserts that a firm's competitive advantage is significantly influenced by its positioning within the industry. This positioning can lead to competitive advantages, either by offering lower prices than competitors for similar benefits (known as cost leadership) or by providing unique benefits that compensate for a higher price (known as differentiation). Competitive advantage is considered an outcome (of positioning) and should be pursued as an end result. Nonetheless, should the response to the query, '*Is either cost advantage or differentiation advantage sufficient and necessary for superior performance?*' be negative, it may lead us to conclude that, in line with Porter's perspective (1980, 1985), competitive advantage does not equate to performance.

Second, in the RBV approach, the association between competitive advantage (unique resources) and performance (economic rent) is more direct, as it does not even have to specify any type of competitive advantage (i.e., cost or differentiation). If a firm has valuable, rare and inimitable resources, then superior performance ensues (Ma, 2000). That is, resources generate, by definition (as the essence of sustained competitive advantage), economic rent. However, if there is no answer to the question '*If two firms A and B have resources X and Y, respectively, that meet the RBV criteria (valuable, rare, etc.), what determines which one possesses a competitive advantage over the other?*' then we may reasonably conclude that using competitive advantage (defined by resources) as a causal substitute for superior performance is not only redundant but also tautological.

Based on the above arguments, the constructs of competitive advantage and performance are not the same (Ma, 2000). Not only these constructs are different, but also sustainable competitive advantage does not necessarily create sustained superior performance (Arend, 2003). Positive causes do not necessarily lead to positive effects. Other forces, such as negative causes or the competitive disadvantages, such as the 'W' in SWOT (Andrews, 1971), inertia (Lieberman and Montgomery, 1988), inefficiency, core rigidities (Leonard-Barton, 1992) and strategic liabilities (Arend, 2003), may counteract the positive causes. Stated differently, negative causes have attributes that fail to have any positive use to a firm; these strategic liabilities are costly, appropriated, and economically inconvertible. They destroy value in a firm rather than simply failing to add any.

Reality #2 *Competitive advantage can be achieved without superior performance*

There are scenarios in which a firm can possess a competitive advantage without attaining superior performance. Such scenarios might be when (1) a firm may have a discrete advantage[4] that fails to develop into a compound advantage,[5] (2) a firm might possess a great competitive advantage over all rivals that fails to fully exploit its potential, (3) a firm may either lack competitive advantage in one critical area or have multiple competitive advantages but lacks the right combination and (4) the management of a firm may intentionally sacrifice a competitive advantage (Ma, 2000). To advance the understanding, one example in each scenario follows. In the first scenario, a firm may have state-of-the-art hardware as a discrete advantage in enhancing operational efficiency but lacks skilled personnel to materialise it into any compound advantage (speed, low cost, flexibility, etc.) to enhance performance. In the second scenario, Apple can be a reference example. The Macintosh line of computers enabled Apple Computer to gain competitive advantages in innovation and differentiation and achieve superior performance. However, not being able to simultaneously establish the industry standard among corporate users that would allow cost advantages, both Apple's market position and performance suffered, especially compared to Microsoft. In the third scenario, we use as an example VCR industry, where success in controlling the industry standard could perhaps account for all competitive disadvantages in other areas. The first-mover, SONY, initially had many competitive advantages (e.g., innovation and differentiation) compared to JVC. Nevertheless, not being able to win in the industry standard war (against JVC's VHS), SONY diminished many competitive advantages. SONY was finally forced to follow the industry standard set by JVC and reduce its own β system into a niche product with all the negative consequences in terms of performance. Finally, in the fourth scenario, let us consider Microsoft's Software Network (MSN). As the only on-line service provided in bundle with Windows 95,[6] MSN managed to gain a huge advantage in reaching customers compared to rivals (e.g., AOL). Nonetheless, Bill Gates opted to accord AOL a similar level of recognition on Windows 95, in return for AOL promoting Internet Explorer. Although this decision aimed to promote both Internet Explorer and its competitor, Netscape, within the web browser industry, it did not only reduce the competitive advantage of MSN but also performance. From Microsoft's perspective, it was a wise decision to boost Internet Explorer's market share, as Internet Explorer was a critical market for the future. Microsoft gained the competitive advantages of response speed, flexibility in manoeuvring, cost advantages (economies of scale) and differentiation advantage (almost monopoly) in the PC operating system business along with the overall firm performance increase, at the expense of the not-so-superior MSN performance potential.

Reality #3 *Superior performance can be achieved without competitive advantage*

Can a firm have superior performance without competitive advantage? It depends on how we define competitive advantage and on the time span of analysis (Ma, 2000). Factors, such as governmental regulation (Bailey, 1997; Baron, 1995), environmental shock (Meyer, 1982) and luck (Barney, 1986), may subvert expectations of the association between competitive advantage and firm performance, as follows.

Regarding governmental regulations, let's consider a scenario where a government decides to provide subsidies to firms within a specific industry to foster innovation. If the government restricts these subsidies to firms whose annual R&D investments exceed a specific threshold based on their annual turnover, then, at least in the short term, it's plausible that firms situated just above the threshold might exhibit superior innovative performance compared to those situated just below it (who do not receive governmental subsidies), even though the latter may possess inherent advantages in innovation over the former. Nevertheless, over the long term, due to the government subsidy, the firms positioned just above the threshold may indeed develop a competitive advantage in innovation over their counterparts situated below the threshold.

Regarding environmental shock, let's examine a scenario where a private national university (A) maintains a competitive advantage and exhibits superior performance compared to a private international university (B) within the same geographical area. Unfortunately, a strike at University A disrupts its operations, particularly during the graduation month, causing significant harm to the institution. In the short term, University B may temporarily outperform University A, even though University A still maintains a competitive advantage over University B. However, in the long term, if University A lacks the necessary organisational resilience, it may risk losing its competitive advantage for various reasons, including demoralisation, the departure of key personnel, and a decline in service quality, reputation and expertise.

Finally, regarding luck, contemplate a scenario where a company, although lacking a competitive advantage, could momentarily outperform a rival firm. This could occur because the former firm receives a one-time serendipitous boost to its profit due to a non-repeatable historical experience (i.e., a booming market).

The above realities in terms of competitive advantage and performance may also be of interest to practitioners and policymakers. To the extent that competitive advantage and performance are not the same; all firms, no matter their number of competitive advantages, have equal opportunities to achieve superior performance. For those seeking to improve firm performance, they should bear in mind that even if they have managed to develop competitive advantages, underperformance is possible in three cases:[7] first, when the future payoff cannot offset the costs of developing them (Coyne, 1986); second, when the economic returns are not generated to a level that justifies a firm's investment in tangible or intangible resources (Ray et al., 2004) and third, when the rents of achieving a competitive advantage are captured by other stakeholders and are not attributed to firm performance (Ambrosini and Bowman, 2010).

2.8 Future Challenges

Interestingly, the discussion surrounding competitive advantage is far from concluded, as noted by Nayak et al. (2022). Nothing about what practitioners do or how they do it at any given moment is likely to ensure sustainable competitive advantage. This chapter has addressed several crucial issues within the realm of competitive advantage, spanning the years from 1985 to 2023. Knowing that 'everything flows',[8] the two tips below can serve as food for thought for scholars willing to delve further into the concept of competitive advantage.

Tip #1 Creating short-term advantages would be easier than one-time deployment of all resources to achieve long-term advantages.

Towards the beginning of this decade, scholars have shifted the traditional centre of attention from competitive advantage that is sustainable over time to a focus on how firms compete by achieving a series of temporary advantages (Dagnino et al., 2021). *Why?* As both the resources and the way firms use them must constantly change, firms are forced towards the creation of continuously changing temporary advantages (Fiol, 2001). Scholars and practitioners have already recognised that transient and short-lived advantages are the only realistic possibility. Already long ago, Leonard-Barton (1992) noted that in highly competitive environments a core competency often becomes a core rigidity. Similarly, Volberda (1996) argued that with hypercompetition, competitive change cannot be predicted but is a more or less efficient response, so superior rents derive from the ability to destroy and rebuild resources over time. Based on the dynamic capabilities approach (Teece et al., 1997), companies may need to give up on seeking the once-coveted 'sustainable competitive advantage' in favour of what some call 'renewable competitive advantage', using one temporary position of strength to hopscotch into another (Useem, 2000, p. 104).

But then what is the value of creating and destroying temporary competitive advantages? To address this question (Fiol, 2001), we need to understand that due to evolutionary changes we can no longer assume that it is possible to gain sustainability of a competitive advantage based on any fixed set of core competencies. Instead, continuous changes may provide temporary competitive advantages. In this context, we may also need to question our prescriptions for competitiveness.

Tip #2 Understanding the multidimensionality of competitive advantage in terms of economic and social aspects is necessary.

After six decades of exploration, it is about time to redefine the competitive advantage in strategic management (Lieberman, 2021; Nayak et al., 2022; Teece, 2020). To be more precise, scholars should elaborate novel dimensions of competitive advantage. They need to expand the boundaries and embrace diverse approaches. Competitive advantage is no doubt a multifaceted concept, which arises out of diverse contextual manifestations and requires theoretical integration across disciplines. For example, scholars have recently started embracing social dimensions in the conceptualisation of competitive advantage (Nayak et al., 2021). There is an emerging thread of conversation integrating the notion of social advantage with competitive advantage (Okafor et al., 2021), which signals a shift towards a more humane transformation of the traditional concept of competitive advantage (Cillo et al., 2019; Porter et al., 2019). In addition, firms need to see beyond the economic aspect of competitive advantage and embrace the societal needs (e.g., Jayashankar et al., 2020) that balance the economic and social goals of organisations (Bapuji et al., 2020). The importance of incorporating sustainable environmental practices into business strategy formulation has become increasingly prominent, as organisations are proactively working to deliver the triple bottom line of economic prosperity, environmental quality and social equity (e.g., Cillo et al., 2019; Singh et al., 2019). In this context, competitive advantage can be viewed as the emerging concept of creating economic value through social value providing a sense of gratitude to managers for their contribution to society through the strategy formulation process (Nayak et al., 2021).

Notes

1 Flanagan et al. (2007) believe that globalisation converted the world into a complex and multifaceted dynamic place, where free competition and free trade thrive and rendered competitiveness the major strategy.
2 We consider competitiveness within the micro context (competition among the firms within a nation) as opposed to the macro (competition among nations) context.
3 For a long time, research had confused hybrid strategies with stuck-in-the-middle strategies (Pertusa-Ortega et al., 2009; Spanos et al., 2004). However, it is now evident that hybrid strategies and stuck-in-the-middle strategies are different. Hybrid strategies involve a competitive approach that emphasises more than one generic strategy, while stuck-in-the-middle strategies signify the absence of a clear emphasis on any specific strategy, essentially representing an average focus on all generic strategies (Salavou, 2015).
4 This advantage is remote enough from performance in the causal chain (Ma, 2000).
5 This advantage has a direct link to performance (Ma, 2000).
6 Automatically shipped with 90% of all new PCs sold in the world.
7 See examples of Apple and Microsoft in Reality #2.
8 Or in Greek *'τα πάντα ῥεῖ' (/*ta *panta rhei)* captures the reality of unending process of change according to Heraclitus of Ephesus (c. 535 BC–475 BC), the Greek philosopher.

References

Ambrosini, V., & Bowman, C. (2010). The impact of causal ambiguity on competitive advantage and rent appropriation. *British Journal of Management*, 21(4), 939–953.

Andrews, K. R. (1971). *The Concept of Corporate Strategy*. Dow-Jones-Irwin, Homewood, IL.

Arend, R. J. (2003). Revisiting the logical and research considerations of competitive advantage. *Strategic Management Journal*, 24(3), 279–284.

Aulakh, P. S., Kotabe, M., & Teegen, H. (2000). Export strategies and performance of firms from emerging economies: Evidence from Brazil, Chile, and Mexico. *Academy of Management Journal*, 43(3), 342–361.

Bailey, E. E. (1997). Integrating policy trends into dynamic advantage. *Wharton on Dynamic Competitive Strategy*, 76–98.

Banwet, D. K., Momaya, K., & Shee, H. K. (2002). Competitiveness: Perceptions, reflections and directions. *IIMB Management Review*, 14(3), 105–116.

Bapuji, H., Ertug, G., & Shaw, J. D. (2020). Organizations and societal economic inequality: A review and way forward. *Academy of Management Annals*, 14(1), 60–91.

Barney, J. (1991). Firm resources and sustained competitive advantage. *Journal of Management*, 17(1), 99–120.

Barney, J. B. (1986). Strategic factor markets: Expectations, luck, and business strategy. *Management Science*, 32(10), 1231–1241.

Baron, D. P. (1995). Integrated strategy: Market and nonmarket components. *California Management Review*, 37(2), 47–65.

Bhawsar, P., & Chattopadhyay, U. (2015). Competitiveness: Review, reflections and directions. *Global Business Review*, 16(4), 665–679.

Campbell-Hunt, C. (2000). What have we learned about generic competitive strategy? A meta-analysis. *Strategic Management Journal*, 21(2), 127–154.

Ceccagnoli, M. (2009). Appropriability, preemption, and firm performance. *Strategic Management Journal*, 30(1), 81–98.

Cillo, V., Petruzzelli, A. M., Ardito, L., & Del Giudice, M. (2019). Understanding sustainable innovation: A systematic literature review. *Corporate Social Responsibility and Environmental Management*, 26(5), 1012–1025.

Côrte-Real, N., Oliveira, T., & Ruivo, P. (2017). Assessing business value of big data analytics in European firms. *Journal of Business Research*, 70, 379–390.

Coyne, K. P. (1986). Sustainable competitive advantage—What it is, what it isn't. *Business Horizons*, 29(1), 54–61.

Dagnino, G. B., Picone, P. M., & Ferrigno, G. (2021). Temporary competitive advantage: A state-of-the-art literature review and research directions. *International Journal of Management Reviews*, 23(1), 85–115.

Dess, G. G., & Davis, P. S. (1984). Porter's (1980) generic strategies as determinants of strategic group membership and organizational performance. *Academy of Management Journal*, 27(3), 467–488.

Drnevich, P. L., Mahoney, J. T., & Schendel, D. (2020). Has strategic management research lost its way? *Strategic Management Review*, 1(1), 35–73.

Du, S., Bhattacharya, C. B., & Sen, S. (2011). Corporate social responsibility and competitive advantage: Overcoming the trust barrier. *Management Science*, 57(9), 1528–1545.

Fiol, C. M. (2001). Revisiting an identity-based view of sustainable competitive advantage. *Journal of Management*, 27(6), 691–699.

Flanagan, R., Lu, W., Shen, L., & Jewell, C. (2007). Competitiveness in construction: A critical review of research. *Construction Management and Economics*, 25(9), 989–1000.

Godfrey, P. C., & Hill, C. W. (1995). The problem of unobservables in strategic management research. *Strategic management journal*, *16*(7), 519–533.

González-Benito, J., & Suárez-González, I. (2010). A study of the role played by manufacturing strategic objectives and capabilities in understanding the relationship between Porter's generic strategies and business performance. *British Journal of Management*, 21(4), 1027–1043.

Hambrick, D. C. (1983). An empirical typology of mature industrial-product environments. *Academy of Management Journal*, 26(2), 213–230.

Hamel, G., & Prahalad, C. K. (1990). The core competence of the corporation. *Harvard Business Review*, 68(3), 79–91.

Hofer, C.W., & Schendel, D. (1978). *Strategy Formulation: Analytical Concepts*. West Publishing Company, St Paul, MN.

Jayashankar, P., Nilakanta, S., Mohan, G., & Johnston, W. J. (2020). *The Case of the Hand in Hand Rice Value Chain Initiative in India: How Can Social Enterprises Catalyze Inclusive Market Development?* SAGE Publications: SAGE Business Cases Originals.

Karnani, A. (1984). Generic competitive strategies—An analytical approach. *Strategic Management Journal*, 5(4), 367–380.

Kim, E., Nam, D. I., & Stimpert, J. L. (2004). The applicability of Porter's generic strategies in the digital age: assumptions, conjectures, and suggestions. *Journal of Management*, *30*(5), 569–589.

Leonard-Barton, D. (1992). Core capabilities and core rigidities: A paradox in managing new product development. *Strategic Management Journal*, 13(S1), 111–125.

Lieberman, M. (2021). Is competitive advantage intellectually sustainable. *Strategic Management Review*, 2(1), 29–46.

Lieberman, M. B., & Montgomery, D. B. (1988). First-mover advantages. *Strategic Management Journal*, 9(S1), 41–58.

Linz, C., Müller-Stewens, G., & Zimmermann, A. (2017). *Radical Business Model Transformation: Gaining the Competitive Edge in a Disruptive World*. London: Kogan Page Publishers.

Ma, H. (2000). Competitive advantage and firm performance. *Competitiveness Review: An International Business Journal*, 10(2), 15–32.

Madsen, T. L., & Leiblein, M. J. (2015). What factors affect the persistence of an innovation advantage? *Journal of Management Studies*, 52(8), 1097–1127.

Markides, C. (2000), Cross talk: Strategy and management: Constantinos Markides discusses strategic innovation, an interview by Peter Mang. *European Management Journal*, 18(4), 357–366.

McWilliams, A., & Siegel, D. S. (2011). Creating and capturing value: Strategic corporate social responsibility, resource-based theory, and sustainable competitive advantage. *Journal of Management*, 37(5), 1480–1495.

Meyer, A. D. (1982). Adapting to environmental jolts. *Administrative Science Quarterly*, 515–537.

Miles, R. E., & Snow, C. C. (1978). *Organizational Strategy, Structure and Process*. McGraw-Hill, New York.

Miller, D., & Friesen, P. H. (1986). Porter's (1980) generic strategies and performance: An empirical examination with American data: Part I: Testing Porter. *Organization Studies*, 7(1), 37–55.

Nayak, B., Bhattacharyya, S. S., & Krishnamoorthy, B. (2021). Strategic advantage through social inclusivity: An empirical study on resource based view in health insurance firms in India. *Journal of Cleaner Production*, 298, 126805.

Nayak, B., Bhattacharyya, S. S., & Krishnamoorthy, B. (2022). Exploring the black box of competitive advantage–An integrated bibliometric and chronological literature review approach. *Journal of Business Research*, 139, 964–982.

Nonaka, I. (1991). The knowledge-creating company. *Harvard Business Review*, 6(8), 96–104.

Nonaka, I., Toyama, R., & Konno, N. (2000). SECI, Ba and leadership: A unified model of dynamic knowledge creation. *Long Range Planning*, 33(1), 5–34.

Okafor, A., Adeleye, B. N., & Adusei, M. (2021). Corporate social responsibility and financial performance: Evidence from US tech firms. *Journal of Cleaner Production*, 292, 126078.

O'Shannassy, T. (2008). Sustainable competitive advantage or temporary competitive advantage: Improving understanding of an important strategy construct. *Journal of Strategy and Management*, 1(2), 168–180.

Parnell, J. A. (1997). New evidence in the generic strategy and business performance debate: A research note. *British Journal of Management*, 8(2), 175–181.

Penrose E. T. (1959). *The Theory of Growth of the Firm*. Wiley, New York.

Pertusa-Ortega, E. M., Molina-Azorín, J. F., & Claver-Cortés, E. (2009). Competitive strategies and firm performance: A comparative analysis of pure, hybrid and 'stuck-in-the-middle' strategies in Spanish firms. *British Journal of Management*, 20(4), 508–523.

Porter M. (1980). *Competitive Strategy*. Free Press, New York.

Porter, M. E. (1985). *Competitive Advantage: Creating and Sustaining Superior Performance*. Free Press, New York.

Porter, M. E. (1986). *Competition in Global Industries*. Harvard Business Press, New York.

Porter, M. E. (1989). *From Competitive Advantage to Corporate Strategy* (pp. 234–255). Macmillan Education UK.

Porter, M. E. (1990). *The Competitive Advantage of Nations*. MacMillan, London.
Porter, M. E., Kramer, M. R., Lenssen, G., & Smith, N. (2019). Creating shared value. Managing sustainable business. *Harvard Business Review*, 1–17.
Powell, T. C. (1992). Organizational alignment as competitive advantage. *Strategic management journal*, *13*(2), 119–134.
Powell, T. C. (2002). The philosophy of strategy. *Strategic Management Journal*, 23(9), 873–880.
Prahalad, C. K., & Hamel, G. (1994). *Competing for the Future* (Vol. 25). Harvard Business School Press, Boston, MA.
Ray, G., Barney, J. B., & Muhanna, W. A. (2004). Capabilities, business processes, and competitive advantage: Choosing the dependent variable in empirical tests of the resource-based view. *Strategic Management Journal*, 25(1), 23–37.
Rumelt, R. P. (2003). What in the world is competitive advantage. *Policy Working Paper*, 105(3), 1–5.
Salavou, H. E. (2015). Competitive strategies and their shift to the future. *European Business Review*, 27(1), 80–99.
Sanchez, R., & Heene, A. (1997). Reinventing strategic management: New theory and practice for competence-based competition. *European Management Journal*, 15(3), 303–317.
Senge, P. (1990, Fall). Building learning organizations. *Sloan Management Review*, 16(3), 48–56.
Sigalas, C., & Papadakis, V. M. (2018). Empirical investigation of relationship patterns between competitive advantage and superior performance. *Journal of Strategy and Management*, 11(1), 81–111.
Singh, S. K., Chen, J., Del Giudice, M., & El-Kassar, A. N. (2019). Environmental ethics, environmental performance, and competitive advantage: Role of environmental training. *Technological Forecasting and Social Change*, 146, 203–211.
Snowdon, B., & Stonehouse, G. (2006). Competitiveness in a globalised world: Michael Porter on the microeconomic foundations of the competitiveness of nations, regions, and firms. *Journal of International Business Studies*, 37, 163–175.
Sölvell, Ö. (2015). The competitive advantage of nations 25 years–opening up new perspectives on competitiveness. *Competitiveness Review*, 25(5), 471–481.
Spanos, Y. E., Zaralis, G., & Lioukas, S. (2004), Strategy and industry effects on profitability: Evidence from Greece. *Strategic Management Journal*, 25(2), 139–165.
Stonehouse, G., & Snowdon, B. (2007). Competitive advantage revisited: Michael Porter on strategy and competitiveness. *Journal of Management Inquiry*, 16(3), 256–273.
Teece, D. J. (2020). Fundamental issues in strategy: Time to reassess. *Strategic Management Review*, 1(1), 103–144.
Teece, D. J., Pisano, G., & Shuen, A. (1997). Dynamic capabilities and strategic management. *Strategic Management Journal*, 18(7), 509–533.
Thornhill, S., & White, R. E. (2007). Strategic purity: A multi-industry evaluation of pure vs. hybrid business strategies. *Strategic Management Journal*, 28(5), 553–561.
Useem, J. (2000). Dot-coms: What have we learned? Dot-coms soared. Dot-coms crashed. Somewhere in between we uncovered 12 truths about how the Net really changes business. *Fortune-European Edition-*, 142(10), 54–73.
Volberda, H. W. (1996). Toward the flexible form: How to remain vital in hypercompetitive environments. *Organization Science*, 7(4), 359–374.
Waheeduzzaman, A. N. M., & Ryans Jr, J. K. (1996). Definition, perspectives, and understanding of international competitiveness: A quest for a common ground. *Competitiveness Review: An International Business Journal*, 6(2), 7–26.

Wamba, S. F., Gunasekaran, A., Akter, S., Ren, S. J. F., Dubey, R., & Childe, S. J. (2017). Big data analytics and firm performance: Effects of dynamic capabilities. *Journal of Business Research*, 70, 356–365.

Wernerfelt, B. (1984). A resource-based view of the firm. *Strategic Management Journal*, 5(2), 171–180.

White, R. E. (1986). Generic business strategies, organizational context and performance: An empirical investigation. *Strategic Management Journal*, 7(3), 217–231.

Zott, C., & Amit, R. (2008). The fit between product market strategy and business model: Implications for firm performance. *Strategic Management Journal*, 29(1), 1–26.

3

ORGANIZATION DNA

Vision, purpose, and values – its importance in competitiveness

José António Porfírio, Carlos Rey Peña, and Ricardo Rodrigues

3.1 Introduction

The current chapter deals with Organizational Purpose (OP).

It starts with a brief introduction where we present a brief overview setting the stage for our discourse on 'Corporate Purpose' and giving a short history of the use and importance of Purpose in corporate management, and how it has evolved, highlighting its current consideration, and explaining the reason for its importance in terms of corporate success, and employee engagement and motivation.

Further on, we embark on a journey to explore the concept of 'Purpose' within the corporate landscape. We begin by setting the stage for a deeper inquiry into why 'Corporate Purpose' is essential in today's business environment. This leads us to a comprehensive examination of what 'Purpose' truly means, drawing from the main definitions that have shaped its understanding over time.

As we delve further, we consider what makes 'Corporate Purpose' so distinctive, especially when compared to recent business concepts and trends like ESG, CSR, and the various experiences that companies strive to offer their employees and customers. The narrative then transitions to a critical analysis of how 'Purpose' differentiates itself from vision, mission, and strategy—three pillars that have traditionally guided organizational direction.

Despite the compelling evidence supporting the value of 'Corporate Purpose', we investigate why it remains underutilized in the modern corporate world. This inquiry naturally leads to a discussion on the practical aspects of implementing 'Corporate Purpose' within an organization and the role of leadership in creating a 'Ripple Effect of Purpose' that resonates throughout the company.

DOI: 10.4324/9781032695969-4

In summary, in this chapter, we propose to answer, briefly, some specific research questions that represent the outline of the current chapter:

- The Why of Corporate Purpose?
- What is Purpose? What are the main definitions of Corporate Purpose?
- What makes Corporate Purpose so special? (Compared to recent concepts like ESG, CSR, Employee Experience, Customer Experience, etc.)
- What differentiates Corporate Purpose, Vision, Mission, and Strategy?
- Why Corporate Purpose is not so much used nowadays?
- How to implement Corporate Purpose?
- Leadership and the "Ripple Effect of Corporate Purpose"
- What's beyond Corporate Purpose?

Our main conclusions support that 'Corporate Purpose' is integral to contemporary management practices, encapsulating key trends, such as sustainability and ESG. It is vital for corporate success, fostering full engagement and motivation across the workforce, notably among new market entrants. Yet, realizing purpose-driven organizations necessitates surmounting numerous challenges to establish 'Corporate Purpose' as the bedrock for organizational Mission and strategic development.

3.2 The why of corporate purpose?

Purpose is at the heart of everything we do (or do not) and is critical for management's success. It is related with the answer to the main questions regarding the reason for the existence of a business and its creation, as well as its vision and aspirations. Simultaneously, purpose is related to changes to the business practices and policies required to its adequate performance to achieve better social outcomes and an enhanced functioning of firms and, ultimately, markets (Mayer, 2021).

The world seems to support a strong desire for change in the way companies are managed and the economy is conducted. Although that is not necessarily new, more and more voices are claiming the end of capitalism and the development and implementation of a "new world order." Porter and Kramer (2019) consider that Purpose can be the solution to the current capitalism crisis and even as the future of capitalism.

In fact, corporations are more than mere business entities; they are central institutions in society, endowed with significant resources and knowledge. As such, they bear a considerable responsibility for generating wealth through productivity and competitiveness, as well as for being agents of social change (Bartlett and Ghoshal, 1994). This dual role positions companies as forums for social interaction and personal fulfillment, impacting both the macro and micro levels of society.

At the same time, Corporate Purpose is increasingly recognized as a fundamental aspect of modern business, extending beyond the traditional goal of profit maximization. This concept is rooted in the belief that a company's raison d'être involves a quest for meaning and identity (Henderson & Van den Steen, 2015). It's not just the actions of a company that matter, but its core identity—"*who you are*" as opposed to "*what you do*"—which is integral to its reason for existence (Leider, 1998).

This purpose-driven approach integrates a company's operational elements—vision, strategy, and priorities that drive performance (Mourkogiannis, 2008)—with its softer elements, such as brand, values, and culture, whose elements contribute to a distinctive organizational climate that fosters engagement and identity (Ready & Truelove, 2011; Mayer, 2021).

The societal demand for companies to serve a social purpose is echoed by influential voices like Larry Fink of BlackRock (Fink, 2018), who emphasize the need for companies to benefit all stakeholders, including shareholders, employees, customers, and the communities they operate in.

Fink's perspective was recognized and reinforced by the Business Roundtable (BRT) in their 2019 statement, having as a result what we may call the definitive shift of management's focus from the shareholder's primacy to a stakeholder-centric model of management.

In fact, the "Statement on the Purpose of the Corporation" by the BRT in August 2019 marked a significant departure from the previous shareholder-focused doctrine that had prevailed since at least 1987. By endorsing the stakeholder view, the statement—signed by leaders of some of the world's largest companies—highlights the evolving priorities in corporate management. While profit remains essential for survival, the modern corporate ethos considers profit to be a result of a commitment to delivering value to all stakeholders (BainBridge, 2021).

At the same time, although differently, the BRT's declaration reflects a broader trend toward embracing Environmental, Social, and Governance (ESG) criteria, Corporate Social Responsibility (CSR), and sustainability as key considerations in business operations (BainBridge, 2021: 285), through Corporate Purpose.

More recently, IESE, one of the world's most important business schools, has declared 2020 as the so-called Year of Purpose.

Another crucial push for the development of Corporate Purpose has been provided by Simon Sinek (2011) with the so-called Golden Circle Model, which we may consider to be routed in the broader scientific line of behavioral economics (see Figure 3.1).

Sinek's (2011) proposed model offers a transformative view of organizational leadership and communication. At the heart of this model lies the 'Why'—the purpose, cause, or belief that drives every organization. Sinek posits that understanding this core 'Why' is essential for inspiring action, as it connects with the limbic brain, the part of our brain that influences emotions and decision-making (Sinek, 2011).

Surrounding the 'Why' is the 'How'—the specific actions or processes that organizations undertake to realize their core purpose.

According to Sinek, these issues are the unique strengths or values that allow an organization to stand out from the competition. Finally, the 'What' represents

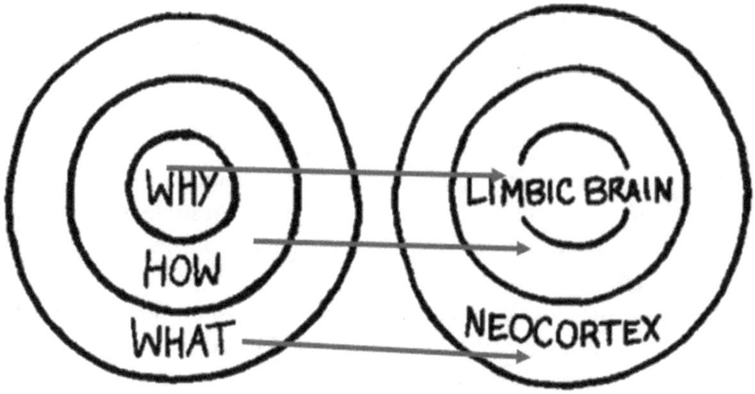

FIGURE 3.1 The golden circle model and our brain.

Source: Adapted from Sinek (2011: 61).

the tangible output of the organization: the products, services, or results that they deliver as proof of their 'Why'.

Sinek's model correlates with the neuroanatomy of the human brain. The limbic brain, associated with feelings such as trust and loyalty, is linked to the 'Why'. In contrast, the neocortex is responsible for rational thought, analytical thinking, and language, aligning with the 'How' and 'What' (Sinek, 2011).

By starting with 'Why', leaders can inspire their teams to achieve more, as they resonate with the fundamental human need to belong and contribute to something greater than themselves. This approach not only fosters a strong organizational culture but also drives innovation and excellence.

Gyori, Kazakova, and Gyori (2019) present a compelling argument for the centrality of corporate purpose in redefining the capitalist paradigm. The research underscores that a well-articulated corporate purpose is the linchpin that aligns strategy, leadership, values, and operations toward a common goal. It is the driving force that impregnates every facet of an organization—from its vision and mission to its products and services—with a sense of meaning and direction.

The study reveals that when corporate purpose is deeply integrated into the leadership and employee ethos, it fosters an environment where values are lived rather than merely stated. This purposeful alignment extends to the development of ecosystems and stakeholder relationships, ensuring that the company's strategic objectives harmonize with broader societal needs, thus, with its different stakeholders.

Moreover, the iterative process of developing a corporate purpose statement is not a static declaration but a dynamic engagement that evolves with the organization's journey.

It is through this continuous refinement that companies can truly embody their role as agents of positive social change, creating value that transcends the traditional profit-centric model of business.

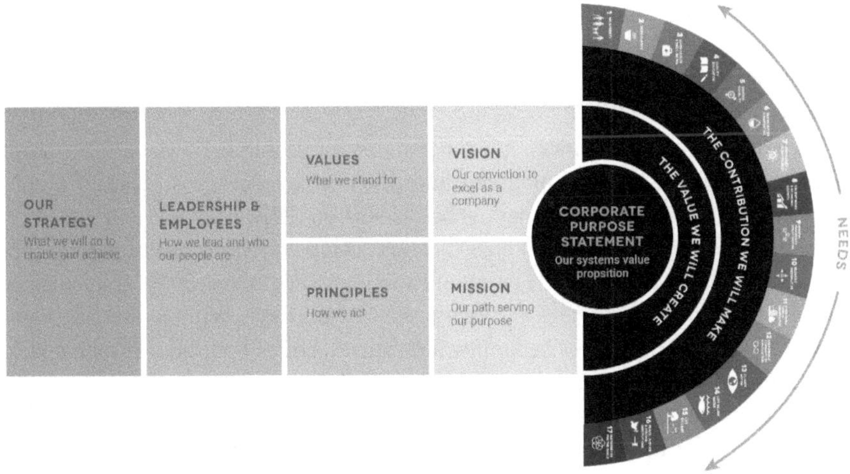

FIGURE 3.2 From strategy to purpose, and vice-versa.

Source: Gyori et al. (2019: 13).

In essence, research on corporate purpose supports that a purpose-driven approach is not just a moral imperative but a strategic one, enabling companies to navigate the complexities of the 21st-century business landscape with agility and integrity (see Figure 3.2).

3.3 What is purpose? What are the main definitions of corporate purpose?

The idea of purpose and its importance for a company is not truly new.

Levitt (1983) emphasizes the importance of customers to the business, stating that without them, no amount of technical or operational expertise can sustain a company. This perspective has been influential in shaping modern marketing and business strategies, focusing on customer acquisition and retention as key drivers of business success.

Levitt's perspective on the purpose of organization emphasized the need of order and conformity to efficiently accomplish tasks and avoid chaos. This viewpoint is consistent with Levitt's broader work on management and marketing, where he often discussed the importance of understanding and shaping consumer behavior, as well as the structure and function of organizations (Levitt, 2006a, 2006b).

Levitt (2006a, 2006b) considered that purpose, as the essence of any organization, should be related with its ability to impose a certain level of structure and uniformity. The company's structure was not merely for the sake of orderliness but served a functional purpose: to ensure that specific tasks are accomplished with precision and punctuality. He argued that without this organizational framework, individual efforts could become erratic and uncoordinated, leading to disarray and inefficiency. Therefore, organizations are designed to introduce a necessary degree of rigidity, channeling individual behaviors into a cohesive and predictable pattern, as the cornerstone of achieving operational efficiency and meeting critical deadlines (Levitt, 2006a, 2006b).

To generate loyal customers, a business must adopt a holistic view, functioning as an entity dedicated to creating and fulfilling customer needs. Instead of merely manufacturing goods, management should focus on delivering value that leads to customer satisfaction. Levitt contends that this customer-centric philosophy must be ingrained in every segment of the organization, pursued relentlessly, and executed with enthusiasm that motivates and energizes the workforce. Without this integrated approach, the company risks becoming a disjointed collection of departments lacking a unified mission or clear strategic orientation (Levitt, 2006a, 2006b).

Although this systemic view of a company may have been adequate for its time, and despite its deep routes are still crucial, it might now be considered old-fashioned, given the current dynamics of innovation, management and economics, consumer behavior, and employee relations within companies.

In the existing framework, organizations are characterized by moving within a scenario of chaos theory[1] where order and planning are replaced by agility, flexibility, and creativity (Peters, 1987).

For Peters (1987), a management system characterized by the rigidity of classical hierarchical systems represented a critical challenge for those companies. Such inflexible structures were considered disadvantageous since they would compromise a company's agility in dealing with the current unpredictable nature of business. These issues accentuated the importance of companies being attuned to customer demands, which demands a dynamic approach to organizational change, that is characterized by three core elements: adaptability, initiative, and entrepreneurial creativity.

Consequently, Peters' philosophy advocates for a fluid organizational model that embraces change and fosters a culture of innovation and proactive problem-solving.

In summary, the classic model of structure-strategy-processes has given way to the alternative Purpose-People-Strategy model. This is also a consequence of what Kaplan and Norton call the end of the so-called industrial era, and the beginning, at the end of the 20th century, of the so-called Information Age.

Probably, at the hedge of the 21st century, we are already in another era, that we may call the knowledge era, where, like never before, change occurs at an unprecedented speed, and where companies need to be agile, people flexible, and the market needs to understand organizations' Purpose.

In this new scenario, if corporate ambition focus is on the company's narrow self-interest, it will eventually lose the excitement, support, and commitment that emerge when objectives are linked to broader human aspirations (Bartlett & Ghoshal, 1994).

This calls for a broader management focus that occurs through a shift from the shareholders to the stakeholders' perspective.

The importance of stakeholders for long-term sustainability is not, however, new or innovative. Flatin (2019) remembers that in 1947, Forest Mars Jr., president of Mars, recognized that "Mars hasn't been in business for over 100 years by accident," having been able to reinvent themselves many times, decade after decade." According to a memo distributed by Forest Mars, "the objective of our businesses is to create mutual benefit for all stakeholders." (Flatin, 2019)

The evolution from the shareholders to stakeholders' focus of management underscores the importance of core values and stakeholder inclusivity as essential components of strategic management and is dully translated in the so-called stakeholders' theory.

In his seminal work from 1971, "Modern Entreprise Management in Mechanical Engineering," Klaus Schwab and Kroos (Schwab and Kroos, 1971) championed the idea that businesses should prioritize the interests of all stakeholders, not just shareholders, to secure enduring success and growth. This holistic approach to business management led him to establish the World Economic Forum that same year, as a platform to further the stakeholder concept. According to Klaus Schwab, stakeholders involve the following agents (Figure 3.3):

Collins and Porras (1994) shed new light on the debate between shareholders and stakeholders by suggesting that the secret to a company's lasting success lies in its core values, which should infuse every aspect of the organization, much like

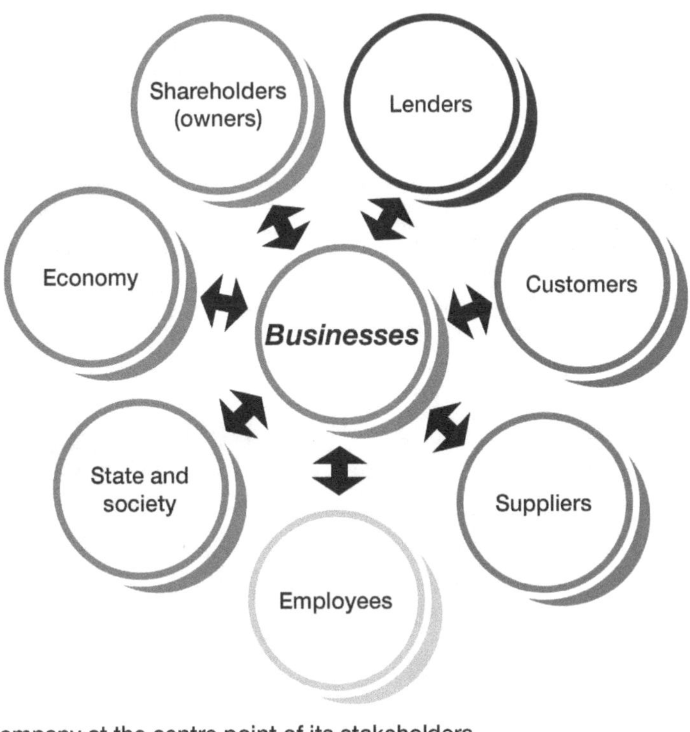

FIGURE 3.3 Who are our stakeholders?

Source: "Modern Entreprise Management in Mechanics Engineering"; Klaus S. and Kroos, H. (1971: 20).

a person's life philosophy or an organism's DNA. Their theory is backed by a thorough financial analysis comparing prosperous companies with their less successful counterparts over the past 100 years.

Svendsen (1998) examines companies that have integrated stakeholder collaboration into their business strategies and predicts that the ability to equitably manage stakeholder interests will be a hallmark of successful companies in the future. He acknowledges that while it's impossible to always please all parties, firms with robust values and clear communication of their business objectives will continue to enjoy stakeholder support, even when outcomes are not as expected.

Wheeler and Sillanpaa (1998) highlight the historical context, rationale, and practical application of stakeholder principles, advocating for a business narrative that extends beyond mere profit maximization.

Mercer (2020) emphasizes that the stakeholder approach is derived from a practical examination of management challenges, advocating for a pragmatic approach to strategic management, which involves detailed studies of specific business scenarios, paving the way for the eventual emergence of general theories, rather than relying on abstract theoretical development (Mercer (2020: 8); Figure 3.4).

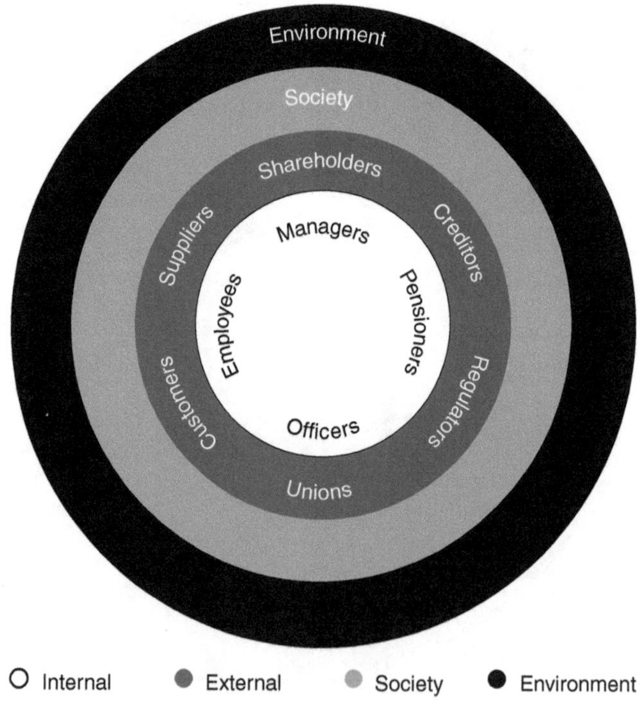

FIGURE 3.4 The stakeholders' ecosystem.

Source: Mercer (2020: 8).

3.4 So, what is, in fact, corporate purpose? How can we define it?

The exploration of corporate purpose has become increasingly significant in contemporary business discourse. The concept, while popular, suffers from a lack of clear definition and empirical testing, as noted by Jasinenko and Steuber (2023: 1415). The ambiguity surrounding corporate purpose is echoed by Henderson (2021: 5481), who observes the plethora of definitions available in the literature.

There are many definitions and possible angles of analysis about corporate purpose, some of them more accurate than others, with each author providing a unique perspective that reflects their understanding of the role and impact of corporations in society (Jimenez, Franco & Smith, 2021).

Beyond the discussions about whether corporate purpose is found, emergent, or previously defined, each perspective through which we analyze corporate purpose provides a unique lens to understand and apply this concept within the context of corporate strategy and stakeholder engagement. They collectively underscore the multifaceted nature of corporate purpose, highlighting its role in guiding companies toward not only financial success but also societal contribution and stakeholders' well-being, encompassing a commitment to creating a positive impact on the world.

George et al. (2021: 1847) offer a definition that encapsulates the essence of an organization's existence, focusing on the value created for stakeholders. They argue that corporate purpose should provide a clear intent, inspire stakeholders with the firm's mission, vision, and values, and establish actionable pathways for the firm's actions. However, this raises questions about the compatibility of such purpose with the traditional.

Ebert and Hurth (2022) expand on this by suggesting that corporate purpose should include public purposes that contribute to societal goals, moving beyond profit as the sole purpose. This perspective aligns with the principles of CSR, which encourages companies to improve their environmental and social impacts with the promise of increased profits (Carroll & Shabana, 2010).

Gulati (2022: 46) discusses purpose as long-term organizational goals with an idealistic bent, emphasizing broader social duties. The notion that doing good must also lead to financial gain persists, reflecting a pragmatic approach to corporate ethics.

These modern definitions of corporate purpose bear resemblance to the mission statements of the past.

As Duska (1997) explains,

> the purpose of something is the 'what a thing is for,' and how a full understanding of something requires knowing what its purpose is. Motives, however, are quite different from purposes. Motives are individual psychological forces which "move" (hence, "emotive") individuals to behave in certain ways.
>
> *(Duska, 1997: 1404)*

The distinction between purpose and motive could not be more applicable to business organizations. In this vein, the key question is: what is the purpose of business organizations? Those who argue that the primary purpose of corporations is to seek profits, or to maximize shareholder wealth, have confused purpose with motive (Duska, 1997). Businesses as human institutions are established to better society through producing goods and services and advancing knowledge. However, as some philosophers such as Davidson have suggested, things like "purpose" which gives us reasons for acting can also be "motives" or causes of our actions. In other words, companies with a purpose enable people to live better lives; they positively contribute to society in one way or another.

Drucker and Maciariello (2008: 97) also contend that although profits are a test for the validity of a business, they cannot be "the explanation, cause, or rationale of business behavior and business decisions.

For Bartlett and Ghoshal (1994: 88), "purpose is the statement of a company's moral response to its broadly defined responsibilities, not an amoral plan for exploiting commercial opportunity." So, Purpose is mostly related to the organization's recognition that its relationships with its diverse stakeholders are interdependent.

Drucker (2012: 361) considers that "The purpose of an organization is to enable ordinary human beings to do extraordinary things."

Mourkogiannis (2006: 25) support that "Purpose is what makes employees feel their work is worthwhile maintaining their morale and energy levels. If effectively managed, it also guides their work, leading them to do things that create competitive advantage for the company."

Purpose, then, represents the essential cause for the establishment of a company and serves as a profound motivational force for its members, despite its challenging attainment (Collins & Porras, 1994).

The corporate purpose embodies the organization's intended impact on its stakeholders (Ellsworth, 2002), underpinning organizational stability and simultaneously encouraging transformation by maintaining a consistent focus on evolving customer demands, which are central to the firm's collective values (Ellsworth, 2002).

It is purpose that allows individuals to align individually with the collective goals that must change society for the better, while the potential of Purpose becomes more effective when it is aligned with the nature of man (Ellsworth, 2002), being considered a primary key to success (Mourkogiannis, 2006).

In other words, companies with a purpose enable people to live better lives; they positively contribute to society in one way or another (Freeman & Ginena, 2015).

Several definitions of Purpose may be found in Jimenez, Franco, and Smith (2021). Those definitions can also be considered related to the Purpose's impact and coverage.

Mayer (2018) emphasizes the broad impact of a company's purpose on society and stakeholders. Mayer focuses on the company's reason for being and its societal contributions, suggesting that a company's purpose is not limited to profit but includes creating value for a wider community.

In line with the idea about the importance of Purpose for the larger community surrounding the organizations, Porter and Kramer (2019) associate corporate purpose with addressing societal needs and speaking of creating societal value through economic value.

In a more stakeholders' perspective, Hollensbe et al. (2014) define purpose as the reason for an organization's existence concerning stakeholders and Thakor and Quinn (2013) introduce the idea of a 'Higher purpose' that transcends financial payoffs, focusing on social benefits. Both definitions imply that purpose serves as a guiding principle for organizational existence and actions.

Hurst (2014) introduces the term 'purpose economy,' which is distinct in its focus on the value created by establishing a purpose for employees and customers. This definition is unique in its emphasis on personal growth and community building.

Lastly, Porter and Kramer (2019) provide a definition that encapsulates the aspirational aspect of purpose, which inspires and provides a call to action, benefiting society at large. This definition aligns with the others in its recognition of purpose as a motivational force but stands out in its emphasis on inspiration and a call to action.

The concept of corporate purpose is evolving, with a growing emphasis on stakeholder value and societal contributions. While the idea is not new, its current iteration seeks to integrate ethical considerations into the core of business strategy, advocating for a balance between profitability and social responsibility, and connecting it to the higher values of the corporation, and its stakeholders. The challenge lies in translating these lofty ideals into tangible actions that genuinely benefit society without sacrificing business viability.

In summary, while there are differences in emphasis, impact and scope, the definitions converge on the idea that corporate purpose goes beyond financial gain and puts the overall society ahead of the proper corporate immediate goals. It encompasses creating societal value, addressing societal needs, inspiring members, and contributing to the broader community. The similarities lie in the recognition of purpose as a motivational and simultaneously stabilizing force that guides companies towards societal contribution and stakeholder well-being, while the differences are mainly in the specific aspects each author chooses to highlight, such as stakeholder engagement, societal contribution, or internal organizational alignment. This comparative analysis underscores the complexity and richness of the concept of 'Purpose' in the corporate world.

Griffin (2020) supports that Purpose is at the heart of four crucial issues of any organization: (i) passion, (ii) meaning, (iii) mission, and (iv) value.

As so, to reach its Purpose, any organization must answer at least the four crucial questions (see Figure 3.5):

a What do we love?
b What are we best at?

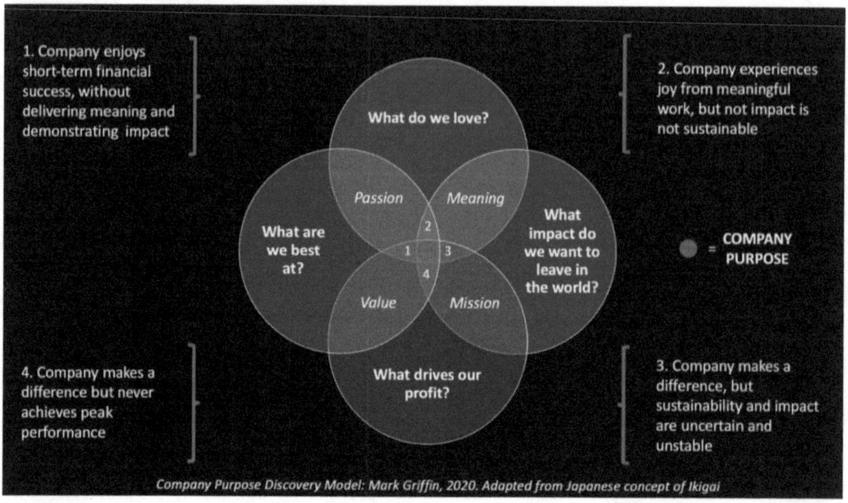

FIGURE 3.5 The crucial questions of purpose.

Source: Griffin (2020). How to discover and articulate organizational purpose, Wharton, available at: https://whartonbc.co.uk/insights/how-do-you-discover-and-articulate-your-organisational-purpose/.

c What drives our profit?
d What impact do we want to leave in the world?

3.5 The business case for corporate purpose

Purpose is inevitably linked to people, planet, and profits (4Ps). The business case for purpose shows that Purpose affects the relationship of organizations with their stakeholders, promoting profits' sustainability, and shareholders' value.

Half of the organizations driven by a clear purpose report a higher likelihood of complete employee engagement within their company and 47% of these organizations are perceived as more likely to invest in the professional growth of their employees (Freeman & Ginena, 2015).

The presence of a defined purpose is also pivotal for fostering trust: 46% of companies that deem purpose essential are more likely to enjoy employee trust in their cultural values and beliefs.

Twenty-three percent of organizations with a strong sense of purpose report a greater likelihood of establishing enduring customer relationships, supported by higher levels of trust in their commitment to delivering superior quality products and services. Moreover, 35% are more likely to be recognized as responsible and beneficial corporate entities by their community, regulatory bodies, and investors. There's an 18% higher likelihood of reporting a favorable regulatory record over the previous year, and a 22% increased chance that investors are optimistic about the organization's growth potential in the forthcoming year and beyond.

Employees serving in organizations with a well-defined purpose experience a 27% greater degree of stakeholder trust in their leadership compared to those working for organizations lacking a strong sense of purpose (Freeman & Ginena, 2015).

These ideas were also supported on a 2014 survey conducted by Deloitte, involving 300 executives and 753 employees from sizable organizations that ascertained that a robust sense of purpose correlates with a 34% increase in confidence regarding organizational growth within the year. Furthermore, these purpose-aligned individuals were 20% more likely to report surpassing their competitors in growth the previous year. This underscores the role of a strong sense of purpose in bolstering confidence in an organization's short-term growth (Deloitte, 2014).

Looking at long-term growth prospects within a five- to ten-year horizon, those who identified with their organization's strong sense of purpose reported higher expectations than their peers. They were 42% more likely to believe in the maintenance or enhancement of brand reputation and loyalty, 34% more confident in delivering robust growth, 41% more optimistic about staying ahead of industry disruptions, and 32% more assured that their organization would lead or continue to lead its industry, as well as outshine the competition.

The commitment to delivering superior quality products and services was the foremost reason for confidence among those who felt their organization had a strong sense of purpose, with 65% of respondents agreeing. This was followed by a dedication to long-term sustainable growth (55%) and a clear grasp of the organization's purpose and core values (48%). On the other hand, those who did not perceive a strong sense of purpose in their organization cited financial objectives, with 69% pointing to the bottom line as their confidence driver and 52% attributing it to short-term financial returns. Nevertheless, the quality of products and services was also a significant factor for this group, with 54% acknowledging it as a basis for their confidence in growth prospects (Freeman & Ginena, 2015).

In summary, companies managed with purpose enjoy the trust of others which manifests itself in the form of greater loyalty on the part of customers, more engaged employees, more reliable suppliers, and more supportive societies and shareholders. These in turn generate greater revenue, lower costs, and more profits. But they only occur where there is sufficient clarity about corporate purpose and demonstrably credible commitments to fulfilling them (Mayer, 2021: 890).

3.6 What makes corporate purpose so special?

Historically, senior managers have aimed to intellectually involve employees by using the persuasive rationale of strategic analyses. However, relationships that are clinically structured and contractually driven fail to ignite the exceptional effort and enduring dedication necessary to consistently achieve superior performance. To achieve this, organizations require employees who are emotionally invested and have a deep connection with the company.

Senior executives in modern large corporations must transition from the traditional emphasis on strategy, structure, and systems to a more flexible, holistic, and organic approach that prioritizes the cultivation of purpose, process, and people (Bartlett & Ghoshal, 1994). Or, as Drucker (2012: 97) puts it:

> Profit and profitability are crucial for society even more than for the individual business. Yet profitability is, not the purpose of, but a limiting factor on business enterprise and business activity. Profit is not the explanation, cause, or rationale of business behavior and business decisions, but the test of their validity.
>
> *(Drucker, 2012: 97)*

EY (2022) found that the inclusion of Purpose as a corporate end has increased fivefold since 1994. Purpose and sustainability are closely linked as both expand the long-term vision, sharing a focus on social well-being, with the main difference being that the goal of sustainability is primarily concentrated on natural capital (Ebert et al., 2018).

In France, the Ministry of Economy clearly states in no. 9 of the entitled "Plan d' action pour la croissance et la transformation des entreprises" (PACTE), of 11 September 2019, the need for companies to redefine their "raison d'être." According to what is stated:

> Companies are not limited to the pursuit of profit. The company must be a place of creation and sharing of its value. The PACTE allows for the redefinition of the raison d'être of companies and strengthens the consideration of social and environmental issues related to their activity.' (https://www.economie.gouv.fr/loi-pacte-redefinir-raison-etre-entreprises)

A study conducted by Malnight et al., using a set of high growth large companies from various countries, brought an innovative conclusion in the analysis of the concept of Purpose: it concluded that all the successful companies examined had placed their Purpose at the center of the organization's Strategy and not just as an indirect guide to it (Malnight et al., 2019).

3.7 What differentiates corporate purpose, vision, mission, and strategy?

Corporate purpose is related with the fundamental mission of a corporation, or its core reason for existence (Collins & Porras, 1994; Basu, 1999; Ellsworth, 2002, Freeman & Ginena, 2015). This mission goes beyond the mere production of goods or services and the identification of its consumer base and must not be confused with motives associated with seeking profits, or the maximization of shareholder wealth (Duska, 1997).

Cynthia Montgomery (2012) states in her book entitled *The Strategist* that strategy and leadership must be reunited at the highest level of an organization.

The CEO, according to Montgomery, should be the guardian of organizational purpose. It is the CEO who must make sure that the purpose is clearly stated, and everyone in the organization knows and understands it.

As previously stated, Corporate Purpose is possibly the best way of conciliating profit with the planet and people, contributing to improving the potential of the organizations for social change and establishing the reason why a company exists and the impact it can make (Jimenez, Franco & Smith, 2021).

Considering that opportunities of purpose-driven business models have a transformative effect on both business and the world, companies have an obligation not just to articulate a sense of purpose but to enact and embed that purpose (Gyori and Kazakova, 2020). This may occur from the company's Mission.

The problem arises usually, as Drucker (2012: 361) puts it, from the fact that "business purpose and business mission are so rarely given adequate thought is perhaps the most important cause of business frustration and failure."

To overcome these problems, Porfírio (2022) proposes a model (the so-called Golden-fish Model of Purpose) where Purpose is at the heart of each management cycle of the organization, corresponding to about a generation lifetime. According to Porfírio (2022), each cycle of Purpose comprehends several cycles of a company's Mission, and each cycle of Mission contains several cycles of strategy which, in its turn, encompass several cycles of Operational Management (see Figure 3.6):

To accommodate these principles, and to include corporate purpose at the core of the strategic management of the organization, Porfírio (2022) suggests the former Strategic Planning Model proposed by Wheelen and Hunger (2015) (see Figure 3.7).

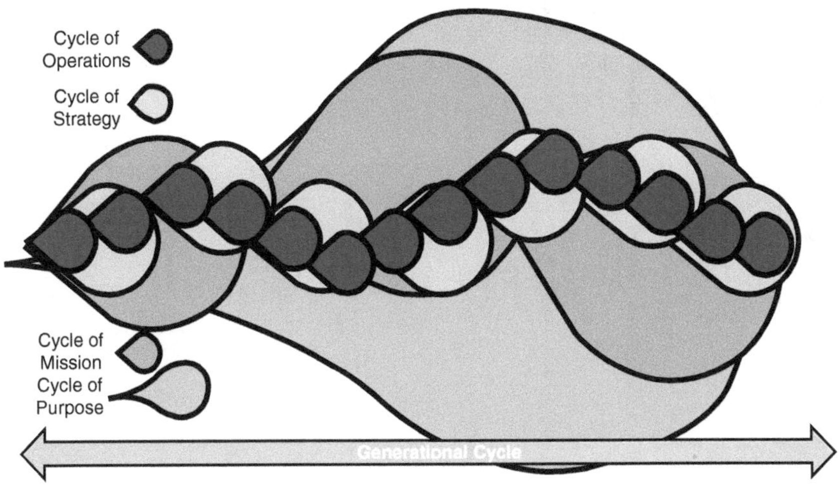

FIGURE 3.6 The big fish of purpose.

Source: Porfírio (2022).

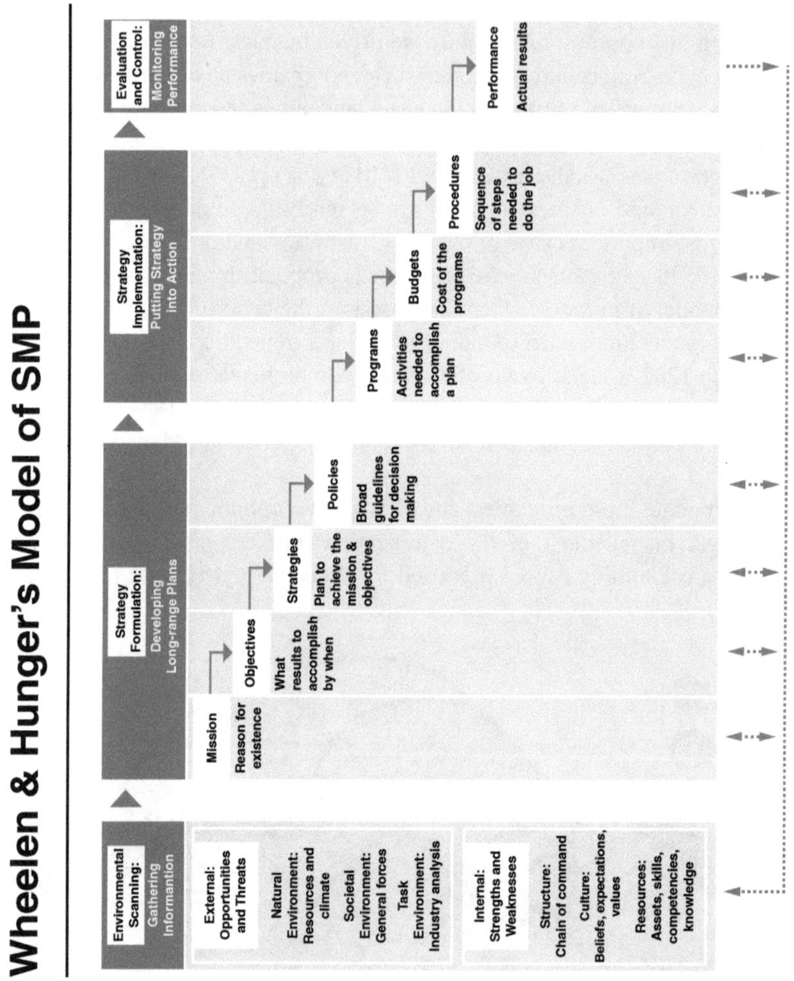

(Source: Wheelen & Hunger, "Strategic Management and Business Policy: Toward Global Sustainability,")

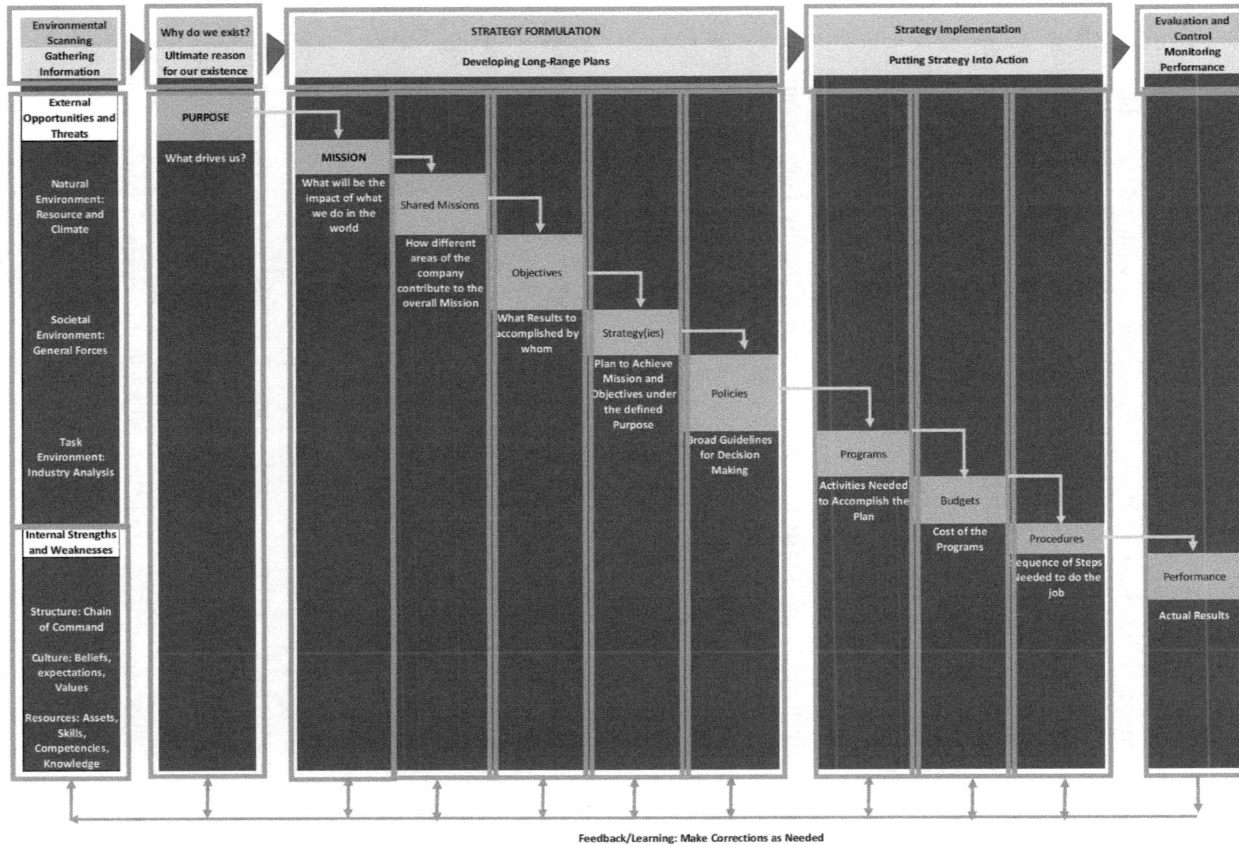

FIGURE 3.7 (a) The traditional Wheelen and Hunger's Model of Strategic Management. (b) The newly adapted Wheelen and Hunger's Model of Strategic Management.

Source: Wheelen and Hunger (2015: 48).

Must be redesigned to the new proposed model of strategic planning:

By promoting these adaptations, corporate purpose can truly ensure its role to promote corporate transformation, as proposed by EY (2016), considering:

1 Corporate purpose impacts strategic clarity, serving as a guide for short-term decisions and long-term strategies at all levels of the organization. When corporate purpose is welldefined, it directs the company in what it does and how it does it.
2 Corporate purpose empowers people to seek innovative solutions that provide increased value, establishes clear boundaries for the area in which the company wishes to operate, and keeps energy focused on innovation that truly brings benefits to the organization.
3 The impact of corporate purpose on the motivation of people, by promoting a leadership that improves meaning instead of fear and inspires creativity instead of mechanization of actions.
4 Corporate purpose appeals to a fundamental human need, regardless of individual motivations. In this sense, it promotes inclusion and diversity, by uniting people through the desire to contribute to a greater cause.
5 Corporate purpose facilitates the creation of alliances between organizations, improving relationships (for example, with suppliers) through collaboration for a common social good.

To formulate strategies centered on corporate purpose, leadership of organizations must first clarify and disseminate a sense of purpose while testing the business model to promote disruptive innovation management and co-creating strategies with stakeholders to create a quantified vision that must support the announced purpose of the company while contributing to the achievement of the organization's mission.

3.8 Despite all the evidence, why corporate purpose is not so much used nowadays, and how to implement it?

Understanding the idea of an organization's purpose is critical for the sustainability of a business or organization (Hollensbe et al., 2014: 1233).

The British Academy's Future of the Corporation Programme (BAFCP), as discussed by Mayer (2021), advocates for a business model centered on corporate purpose. The 2018 report of the BAFCP introduced this concept, while the 2019 report presented eight principles for business reform. These principles encompass changes in law, regulation, ownership, governance, measurement, performance, finance, and investment to support purpose-driven business.

Many other authors supported the need to promote the use of Corporate Purpose by all organizations. However, despite all these efforts, it is a paradox to see that, notwithstanding all the developments on the use and importance of corporate purpose, this is not a widely used concept nor practice.

Some of the reasons why this happens are related to the following problems arising when implementing Purpose:

- The idea that corporate purpose is something vague… not directly applicable to the business or the way the organization operates
- Thinking of corporate purpose as a marketing slogan
- Inadequate definition of corporate purpose
- Management inconsistency
- Difficulty in feeling and living the corporate purpose
- Difference between motive and purpose
- Sense of searching for the corporate purpose (and not living the corporate purpose)

Having in mind those issues, concurrently, there has been an expansion of frameworks designed to facilitate the adoption of Organizational Purpose. These frameworks offer a structured approach to the key dimensions and variables essential for embedding and actualizing an organization's corporate purpose, ensuring its systematic implementation and integration into daily operations. Among the most notable is the Purpose Strength Model, crafted by Lleo, Rey, and Chinchilla (2019), which stands out for its comprehensive methodology in guiding purpose-driven organizational strategy.

The "Purpose Strength Model" (see Figure 3.8) is a strategic framework that guides organizations in developing and implementing a shared purpose. In summary, this model proposes the following:

First, the framework for corporate purpose implementation (considered as the development of a shared purpose) can be divided roughly into three main dimensions: (i) the Drivers of corporate purpose; (ii) the Accelerators of corporate purpose and, after reaching a certain shared corporate purpose; (iii) the outcomes of a shared corporate purpose.

Regarding the first Dimension—the Drivers of Corporate Purpose—the organization needs to look into its Strategy, Leadership, Systems, and Communication to devise whether those systems are driven (or not) by Corporate Purpose. If work is needed to reach that stage, it is important to undertake it to avoid hindering the potential development of a Shared Corporate Purpose.

After considering the Drivers of Purpose—the foundational elements that initiate the development of a shared corporate purpose within an organization—the organization must turn into the so-called Accelerators of Corporate Purpose, that is, the

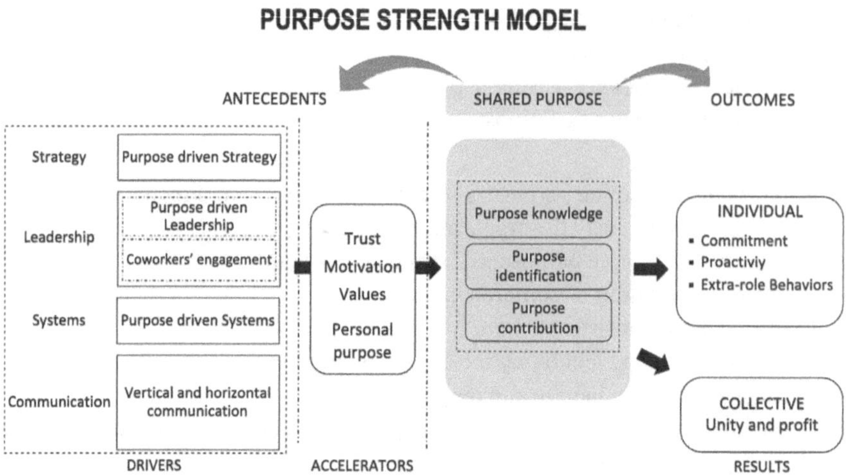

FIGURE 3.8 The purpose strength model.

Source: Lleo, Rey and Chinchilla (2019: 120) and Rey et al. (2019: 119–130).

elements that will propel the shared corporate purpose forward. These elements, already a result of the observed drivers, consist broadly on the following issues:

- Trust: Building trust within the organization encourages alignment with the shared corporate purpose.
- Motivation: Motivating employees to engage with the corporate purpose leads to better integration and implementation.
- Values: Shared values reinforce the corporate purpose and guide behavior within the organization.

Finally, after the consideration of the first two Dimensions, the organization must look into the expected Outcomes of Corporate Purpose, comprehending:

- Individual Outcomes: Such as increased commitment, proactivity, and extra-role behaviors among employees.
- Collective Outcomes: Including unity among team members and, ultimately, profit for the organization.

Each stage of the model builds upon the previous one, indicating that a well-established corporate purpose can drive organizational success through a systematic and holistic approach, although not necessarily sequential. The model suggests that when an organization's purpose is clearly defined and supported by its leadership, systems, and communication, and when it is accelerated by trust, motivation, and values, it leads to positive individual and collective outcomes. This reinforces the importance of a strong, shared corporate purpose as a central pillar of organizational identity and performance.

Lleó et al. (2021),[2] however, alert to the fact that the three manifestations of a shared corporate purpose within the organization—Knowledge of Purpose, Internalization of Purpose, and Contribution to Purpose—do not necessarily occur at the same time.

Rey and Bastons (2019) considered three complimentary independent dimensions of Corporate Purpose that also help the development and implementation of Purpose in any organization. Those dimensions (see Figure 3.9) are:

a Knowledge, usually represented by a head with a brain, and related to strategy, and its relationship with the company's Purpose.
b Action, represented by a world atlas inside two hands, usually associated with the management systems of the company, and their relation to Purpose;
c Motivation, represented by a Heart, associated to the leadership style, methods, and coherence and its relation to Corporate Purpose.

Considering that these three dimensions do not always occur at the same time, nor as a sequence, they propose basically two possible models for the implementation of Corporate Purpose: a linear approach, and an Oblique approach (see Figure 3.10):

In the study conducted by Rey et al. (2019), whose goal was to identify the level of significance of seven factors that interfere with the internalization of corporate purpose, the authors concluded that the level of Commitment to corporate purpose by leadership, commitment to corporate purpose by coworkers, and the coherence between corporate purpose and the organization's practices are the three most relevant factors. Following these, the variables Knowledge of corporate purpose,

FIGURE 3.9 The three dimensions of corporate mission and purpose.

Source: Adapted from Rey and Bastons (2018)/Graphic Design, In: Rey et al. (2019).

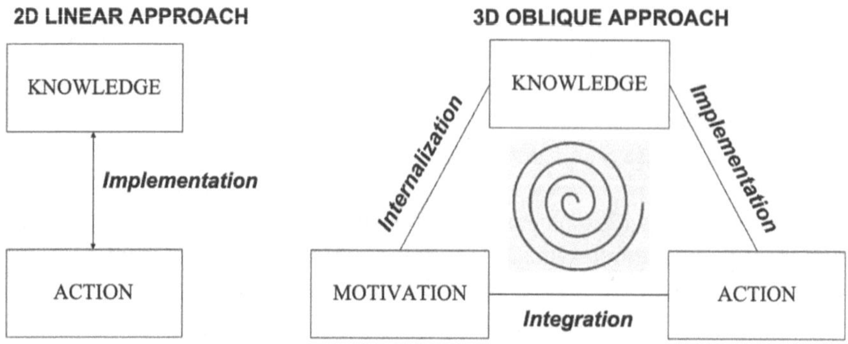

FIGURE 3.10 Possible approaches to corporate purpose.

Fonte: Adapted from Rey and Bastons (2019: 37).

Understanding of corporate purpose, and Reflection on corporate purpose by the workers emerge as factors that significantly interfere with the internalization of corporate purpose. Lastly, the variable related to the communication of corporate purpose by the organization through billboards, videos, speeches, and other means of communication proved to be non-significant, not being relevant for the internalization of corporate purpose.

More recently, Rey developed the so-called Purpose 3D Model, which integrates the various research projects carried out by the chair Management by Missions and Corporate Purpose (UIC) that was created in 2012. This model establishes the conceptualization of Corporate Purpose and Mission in three dimensions (2012): knowledge, motivation, and action under the graphic representation of head, heart, and hands (2017). In turn, it reflects the consistency relationships between the dimensions (2018): authenticity, coherence and integrity, and the key processes for their development (2019): internalization, implementation, and integration (see Figure 3.11):

According to the proposed model, the coherence of the purpose management system occurs every time that the company does what it is announced. There is Authenticity, if managers live what they announce, and finally there's Integrity if managers and staff feel what they do.

When the dimensions of corporate purpose are connected, corporate purpose is internally sustained. The connection between the dimensions is made through Coherence, Authenticity, and Integrity, and the set of these connections and the dimensions of corporate purpose represent its strength and quality (Rey & Prat, 2019; Rey & Bastons, 2019).

The Implementation of corporate purpose involves the connection between the knowledge of corporate purpose and action, and it's mostly related to the organization's Stakeholders. Implementation involves conducting a prospective analysis in which the definition of Strategy, communication of objectives, and tactics to be implemented arise.

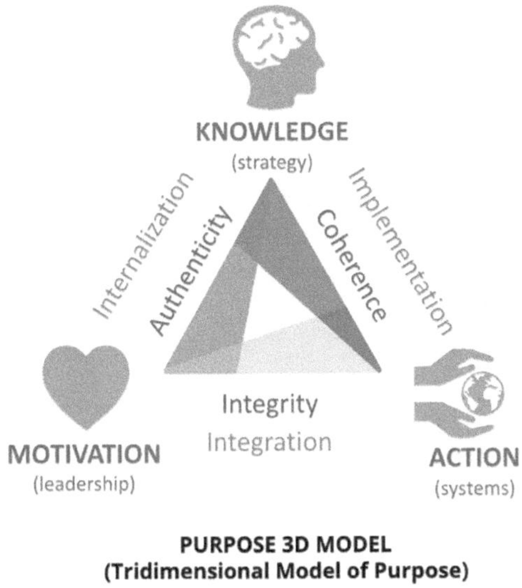

FIGURE 3.11 The coherence, integrity and authenticity of purpose.

Source: https://direccionpormisiones.uic.es/en/.

Regarding the Integration of corporate purpose, it can be considered a natural connection between the workers' motivation and sense of action promoted by the transformation of corporate purpose into a daily present action. This translates the quality of Purpose in what workers develop within their organization.

Finally, the Internalization of Purpose is made through the connection between the knowledge of corporate purpose and people's motivation. It reveals the process through which members of the organization incorporate corporate purpose into their beliefs, promoting it beyond economic incentives and self-satisfaction (Rey & Bastons, 2019).

3.9 Leadership and the "Ripple Effect of corporate purpose"

Purpose involves all the staff of the organization but is critically linked to leadership. Leaders are the prime responsible for the setting-up, development, and implementation of corporate purpose, and ultimately their guardians (Porfírio et al., 2024).

Freeman and Ginena (2015) found a gap between the scores of employees and executives on various dimensions relating to corporate purpose. Employees were 19% less likely to identify with the organization's purpose, 13% less likely to consider the organization's purpose in major business decisions, 8% less likely to say that the organization's purpose is part of employees' performance evaluations, and 7% less likely to report that the organization's purpose is conveyed to all employees, when compared to executive C-levels. On the one hand, it is possible that executives overestimated the effect of corporate purpose on each of these dimensions and that the scores are closer to those of employees. On the other hand, it may be the case that executives did overestimate the effect but that employees truly feel that their organization's culture could be improved by becoming more purpose-driven.

Baldoni (2011) conducted a study with 1.100 employees and leaders to assess the importance of corporate purpose in the workplace. The author found that more than 90% of respondents believe that leaders convey corporate purpose when they carry out the following set of actions:

- Communicate the Vision.
- Link work to the results obtained.
- Show how customers benefit from the work done by workers.
- Do what they promise.
- Instill trust.

Gartenberg et al. (2019) conducted a study on organizational purpose with a sample of about 500,000 workers and 429 organizations, with responses collected over six years. In their analysis, they identified two types of organizations with purpose.

The first type, termed by the authors as "high purpose companionship organizations" (Gartenberg et al., 2019: 3), includes organizations that have a strong feeling about their purpose and a high degree of camaraderie among employees, associated with high scores on questions such as "my workplace is fun" and "there is a sense of friendship and team." The second type of organizations, "high purpose-clarity organizations," also has a strong feeling about its purpose but recognizes a strong influence from leadership, scoring high on questions such as "Leadership clarifies its expectations" and "Leadership has a clear vision of where the organization wants to go and how to do it." These latter showed better financial performance when compared to the first group.

Interestingly, these authors discovered that top management had a better perception of the organization's purpose, which diminished with hierarchical levels. However, evidence from their study also showed that it is the workers at a middle hierarchical level who, when knowledgeable and inspired by corporate purpose, connect "high purpose-clarity organizations" to superior financial performance. This may occur because this level of workers is closer to the market, able to affect customer loyalty and satisfaction, also have more contact with other stakeholders of the organization, with greater opportunity to disseminate corporate purpose, as well as having relationships with higher and lower hierarchical levels, besides being the main responsible for translating Strategy ideas into actions (Gartenberg et al., 2019).

A study conducted by Porfírio and Magalhães (see Magalhães, 2022) in a subsidiary of an international chemical company operating in Portugal, showed what Porfírio (2022), and Porfírio et al. (2024) call the Ripple Effect of Purpose on leadership (see Figure 3.12).

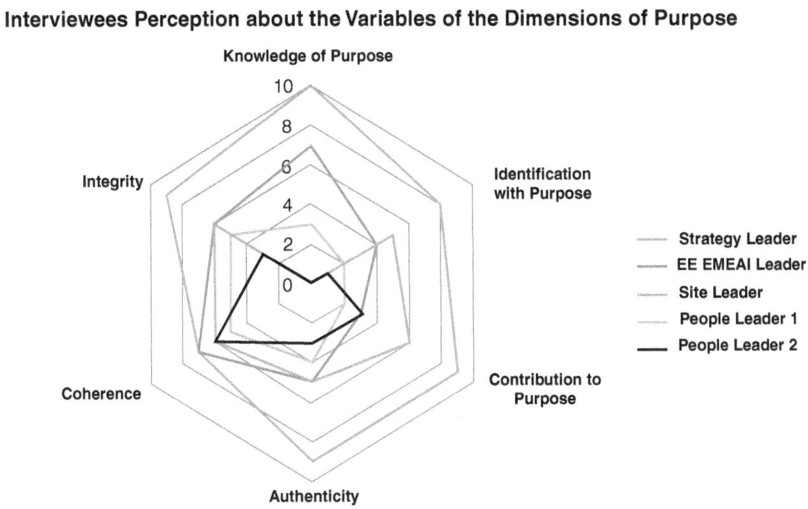

FIGURE 3.12 Leadership and ripple effect of purpose.

Fonte: Magalhães (2022).

Basically we've noticed that, if we set aside from the higher levels of management, the strength of corporate purpose seems to diminish (is getting cold), and simultaneously, it spreads like concentric waves, unless some random situation stops it, that is, corporate purpose creates ripple effects on leadership (Smith et al., 2018a, 2018b).

From our point of view, this occurs because the ownership of a company's purpose should start with the CEO or chief strategy officer who are uniquely positioned to balance stakeholder outcomes.

After being defined, the Purpose must subsequently be known, checked, validated, and implemented by executives across the C-suite. Every executive has its team (larger or smaller) to manage, perform a certain role to play, and can benefit from the effective implementation of purpose strategy—measured through the returns it generates for the company, and the legacy of impact left behind (Schönwälder & Weber, 2023).

This is related with the idea that corporate purpose provides a unifying operating framework that starts at the top and cascades through. It sits at the core of the organization's values and serves to cut through the noise. Corporate purpose clarifies the strategic direction the company should take, and it must consistently be communicated to all stakeholders across the organizational ecosystem—top-down, bottom-up, and to the side (Smith et al., 2018a, 2018b).

Leadership should, therefore, build a Purpose taking into account three interdependent aspects: corporate ambition supported by commitment and human aspirations, attractive organizational values that evoke a sense of pride in all involved, and employee commitment and motivation by creating strategic practices that respect their ideas and contributions (Bartlett & Ghoshal, 1994).

And, to promote Purpose, Leadership should, therefore, build a Purpose taking into account four interrelated aspects: discovering purpose, understanding purpose, test consistency of Purpose, and finally Enunciate Purpose (Mercurio, 2017; Figure 3.13).

Purpose-Driven Leaders (PDLs) understand the inner game of leadership (Anderson & Adams, 2015). While the outer game of leadership comprises processes and competencies, the inner game is about consciousness and character traits like humility, self-awareness, courage, and compassion.

FIGURE 3.13 The stages of corporate purpose.

Source: Mercurio (2017: 12).

FIGURE 3.14 Purpose and corporate union.

Notwithstanding, ripple effects deriving from purpose-driven leadership (like previously observed in the so-called social ripple effects) seem to be critical to understand the potential of Purpose for Management.

And those ripple effects are also crucial to generate Union. As so, Purpose supports unified companies that are stronger and more resilient than a company where there's no Purpose, or Mission whereas leadership has a critical role in reaching that stage of Union (see Figure 3.14).

3.10 Conclusions and remarks

There is nothing predetermined about how the role of business in society will evolve in coming years and decades, unless that it must involve moral and social choices (Hollensbe et al., 2014), and that is the natural field for Corporate Purpose.

From new business models, until the reformulation of the capitalist system, Corporate Purpose has paved its way, and evolved naturally, gaining importance within corporate management.

Purpose is beyond Mission and Strategy, empowering Management and corporate staff to promote development in a balanced way, while aggregating the interests of multiple stakeholders without losing the focus on profitability.

Corporate Purpose is based on the idea of making the World a Better Place, since purpose-driven organizations focus on positive impact beyond profits, aiming to contribute to societal well-being, sustainability, and positive change.

Purpose is, also, an important way for being Sustainable, since it involves environmental responsibility, improving the Supply Chain by adopting ethical sourcing practices, fair labor, and supply chain transparency. Simultaneously, Corporate Purpose tends to consider people at the core of business management. As so, it must depart from improving staff well-being and may be also considered one of the best ways to recruit and retain talent, especially the new generations, aligned with the company's values. So, Purpose fosters loyalty and engagement, promotes better risk management, and builds trust with stakeholders.

By assuring all these issues, probably Purpose is the best way to sustainably drive a company's financial performance aligned with societal needs.

It is unthinkable to consider future businesses without Purpose. Consequently, the narrative surrounding purpose in business involves transitioning it from a specialized discretionary element to a fundamental aspect of the overall business strategy—a shift that society is likely to require (Gyori et al., 2020: 24).

Notes

1 It is important to notice that the Chaos Theory follows the principles of the so-called Butterfly Effect described by Edward Lorenz, MIT Meteorologist that, in 1969 developed the Lorenz System that originated Chaos Theory.
2 Translated from Lleo et al. (2021: 4).

References

Anderson, R. J., & Adams, W. A. (2015). *Mastering Leadership: An Integrated for Breakthrough Performance and Extraordinary Business Results.* John Wiley & Sons. New Jersey. ISBN: 978-1-119-14719-0

Bainbridge, Stephen Mark, Making Sense of The Business Roundtable's Reversal on Corporate Purpose. 46 Journal of Corporation Law 285 (2021), UCLA School of Law, Law-Econ Research Paper No. 20-03, Available at SSRN: https://ssrn.com/abstract=3664078

Baldoni, J. (2011), Lead With Purpose (1ª ed.). AMACOM

Bartlett, C., & Ghoshal, S. (1994). Changing the role of top management: Beyond strategy to purpose. *Harvard Business Review*, 11–12, 79–88

Basu, S. (1999), *Corporate Purpose: Why it Matters More Than Strategy.* Garland Pub., New York. http://search.lib.virginia.edu/catalog/u3519762

Carroll, A. B., & Shabana, K. M. (2010). The business case for corporate social responsibility: A review of concepts, research and practice. *International Journal of Management Reviews*, 12(1), 85–105.

Collins, J., & Porras, J. I. (1994). *Built to Last: Successful Habits of Visionary Companies.* Harper Collins Publishing, New York.

Deloitte (2014). *Culture of Purpose — Building Business Confidence; Driving Growth, 2014 Core Beliefs & Culture Survey.* Deloitte.

Drucker, P. (2012). *Management.* Routledge, New York, USA.

Drucker, P. F., & Maciariello, J. A. (2008). *Management.* Rev. ed. Collins, New York.

Duska, R. F. (1997). The why's of business revisited. *Journal of Business Ethics*, 16, 1401–1409. https://doi.org/10.1023/A:1005731008313

Ebert, C., & Hurth, V. (2022). Principles of purposeful business: Illustrative examples. *Journal of the British Academy*, 10(s5), 163–207.

Ebert, C, Hurth, V, & Prabhu, J. (2018). *The What, The Why and The How of Purpose*, Chartered Management Institute, July 2018, available online at: https://www.managers.org.uk/~/media/Files/Reports/Guide-for-Leaders-White-Paper.pdf

Ellsworth, R. R. (2002). *Leading with Purpose: The New Corporate Realities.* Stanford University Press, Stanford, CA.

Ernst & Young (2022). *From Ambition to Action: How to Attain Purpose-Led Transformation A Guide on How to Get Practical about Purpose, EY Lane4 Work Force Transformation*, EY LLP, London.

Freeman, R., & Ginena, K. (2015). Rethinking the purpose of the corporation: Challenges from stakeholder theory. *Notizie di Politeia*, 31, 9–18.

Fink, Larry (2018). *A Sense of Purpose - Letter to CEO's*, BlackRock, Inc., Wednesday, January 17, 2018, posted by Larry Fink, BlackRock, Inc., available at Harvard Law School Forum on Corporate Governance, at: https://corpgov.law.harvard.edu/2018/01/17/a-sense-of-purpose/

Flatin, J-C (2019). *"The Power of Purpose in Business", 2019 Responsible Business Forum's "Economics of Mutuality: Putting Purpose into Practice."*, available at: https://www.youtube.com/watch?v=jyCJ2MpXxa8 (available at: https://www.mars.com/news-and-stories/articles/how-mars-puts-purpose-into-practice)

Gartenberg, C., Prat, A., & Serafeim, G. (2019). Corporate purpose and financial performance. *Organization Science*, 30(1), 1–18.

George, G., Haas, M. R., McGahan, A. M., Schillebeeckx, S. J., & Tracey, P. (2021). Purpose in the for-profit firm: A review and framework for management research. *Journal of Management*, 49, 1841–1869.

Griffin, M. (2020). How to discover and articulate organizational purpose. Wharton, available at: https://whartonbc.co.uk/insights/how-do-you-discover-and-articulate-your-organisational-purpose/

Gulati, R. (2022). *Deep Purpose: The Heart and Soul of High-Performance Companies*. Harper Collins, New York, February 2022.

Gyori, C., Kazakova, T., & Gyori, B. (Eds.) (2019). *Purpose-Driven Leadership for the 21st Century: How Corporate Purpose Is Fundamental to Reimagining Capitalism -2017–2019 Global Multi-Year Ceo Study*. Leaders on Purpose, London, available online at: https://eprints.bournemouth.ac.uk/35013/1/CEO%20Study%202020%20-%20final%20online%2026122020.pdf

Gyori, C. & Kazakova, T. (Eds.) (2020). *Purpose-Driven Leadership for the 21st Century: Transitioning to a Purpose-First Economy Through the New Business Logic – 2020 Global Multi-Year CEO Study, Leaders on Purpose*, available at: https://www.leadersonpurpose.com/2020-ceo-study

Henderson, R. (2021). Changing the purpose of the corporation to rebalance capitalism. *Oxford Review of Economic Policy*, 37(4), 838–850.

Henderson, R., & Van den Steen, Eric. (2015). Why do firms have "purpose"? The firm's role as a carrier of identity and reputation. *American Economic Review*, 105, 326–330. https://doi.org/10.1257/aer.p20151072

Hollensbe, E., Wookey, C., Hickey, L., George, G., & Nichols, C. V. (2014). Organizations with purpose. *Academy of Management Journal*, 57(5), 1227–1234.

Hurst, A. (2014). The purpose economy: How your desire for impact, personal growth and community is changing the world. *Stanford Social Innovation Review*. https://doi.org/10.48558/H164-HX79

Jasinenko, A. & Steuber, J. (2023), Perceived organizational purpose: Systematic literature review, construct definition, measurement and potential employee outcomes. *Journal of Management Studies*, 60, 1415–1447. https://doi.org/10.1111/joms.12852

Jimenez, D., Franco, I. B., & Smith, T. A. (2021). Review of corporate purpose: An approach to actioning the Sustainable Development Goals (SDGs). *Sustainability*, 13, 3899.

Leider, R.J. (1998), *Leading Our Organizations on Purpose*. Leader to Leader, 1998: 10–12. https://doi.org/10.1002/ltl.40619980905

Levitt, T. (1983). The Globalization of Markets. *Harvard Business Reviews*, 61, 92–102.

Levitt, T. (2006a). *The Marketing Imagination*. Copyright © 1983 by The Free Press, New York/London.

Levitt, T. (2006b). What business are you in? Classic advice from Theodore Levitt. *Harvard Business Review*, 84, 126–137, 150.

Lleo, A., Rey, C., & Chinchilla, N. (2019). Measuring the purpose strength. Ch 10 (pp. 119–130) In: Rey, C., Bastons, M., & Sotok, P. (Eds.) *Purpose-Driven Organizations*. Palgrave Macmillan, Cham. https://doi.org/10.1007/978-3-030-17674-7_10

Lleó, A., Bastons, M., Rey, C., Ruiz-Perez, F. (2021). Purpose Implementation: Conceptualization and Measurement. *Sustainability*, 13, 1921. https://doi.org/10.3390/su13041921

Magalhães, F. (2022). O propósito enquanto fator determinante na motivação dos trabalhadores. [S.l.]: [s.n.], 2022. 116 p., Master Thesis in Management oriented by José Porfírio, available online at: https://repositorioaberto.uab.pt/handle/10400.2/11796

Malnight, T. W., Buche, I., & Dhanaraj, C. (2019). Put purpose at the core of your strategy. *Harvard Business Review*, 97(5), 70–78.

Mayer, C. (2021). The future of the corporation and the economics of purpose. *Journal of* Management *Studies*, 58, 887–901. https://doi.org/10.1111/joms.12660

Mayer, C. (2018). *Prosperity: Better Business Makes the Greater Good.* Oxford University Press, Oxford.

Mercer (2020): *The Purpose of the Corporations: A Tale of Two Theories.* Mercer LLC, February 2020.

Mercurio, Z. (2017). *The Invisible Leader: Transform your Life, Work, and Organization with the Power of Authentic Purpose.* Advantage, Charleston, South Carolina USA, ISBN: 978-1-59932-851-5

Montgomery, C. A. (2012). *The Strategist: Be the Leader Your Business Needs.* Collins, New York.

Mourkogiannis, N. (2008). HR's return to purpose-focused organizations. *Employment Relations Today*, 35, 25–30

Mourkogiannis, N. (2006). *Purpose—The Starting Point of Great Companies.* Palgrave/Macmillan, New York. ISBN 1-4039-7581-7

Peters, T. (1987). *Thriving on Chaos: Handbook for a Management Revolution.* Alfred A. Knopf, Inc., New York

Porfírio, J. (2022). *Provas de Agregação em Ciências Sociais.* Lisboa: [s.n.], 3 vol, online at: http://hdl.handle.net/10400.2/12120

Porfírio, J.; Rodrigues, R.; Magalhães, F.; Carrilho, T. (2024). Organizational Purpose and Employee Motivation: a fsQCA analysis, *Journal of Organizational Effectiveness: People and Performance*, August 2024 (in printing).

Porter, M. E., & Kramer, M. R. (2019). Creating shared value. In: Lenssen, G. & Smith, N., (Eds.), *Managing Sustainable Business*, Springer, Dordrecht, 323–346. https://doi.org/10.1007/978-94-024-1144-7_16. Springer, Berlin/Heidelberg.

Ready, D., & Truelove, E. (2011). The power of collective ambition. *Harvard Business Review*, 22, 17–23.

Rey, C., & Bastons, M. (2018). Three dimensions of effective mission implementation. *Long Range Planning*, 51(4), 580–585.

Rey, C., & Bastons, M. (2019). Three dimensions of purpose—Knowledge, motivation and action. Ch 3 (pp. 29–42). In: Rey, C., Bastons, M., & Sotok, P. (Eds.) *Purpose-Driven Organizations.* Palgrave Macmillan, Cham. https://doi.org/10.1007/978-3-030-17674-7_10

Rey, C., Almandoz, J., & Montaner, A. (2019). Nurturing personal purpose at work. Ch 8 (pp. 97–106). In: Rey, C., Bastons, M., & Sotok, P. (Eds.) *Purpose-Driven Organizations.* Palgrave Macmillan, Cham, https://doi.org/10.1007/978-3-030-17674-7_10

Rey, C. & Prat, M. (2019). Three Dimensions of Purpose: Knowledge, Motivation, and Action. In: Rey, C., Bastons, M., & Sotok, P. (Eds.) *Purpose-Driven Organizations.* Palgrave Macmillan, Cham, (pp. 29–41) https://doi.org/10.1007/978-3-030-17674-7_10

Schönwälder, J., & Weber, A. (2023). Maturity levels of sustainable corporate entrepreneurship: The role of collaboration between a firm's corporate venture and corporate sustainability departments. *Business Strategy and the Environment*, 32(2), 976–990.

Schwab, K. & Kroos, H. (1971). *"Modern Company Management in Mechanical Engineering" working group*, Verein Deutscher Maschinenbau Anstalten e.V. Frankfurt/Main Niederrad

Sinek, S. (2011). *Start with Why: How Great Leaders Inspire Everyone to Take Action.* Penguin Books. New York.

Smith, T., Kirkman, B., Chen, G., & Lemoine, G. (2018a). *Leading Teams Research: When Employees Work on Multiple Teams.* Good Bosses can have Ripple Effects, HBR, 2018, New York.

Smith, T., Kirkman, B., Chen, G., & Lemoine, G. J. (2018b). When employees work on multiple teams, good bosses can have ripple effects. *Harvard Business Review Digital Articles*, 1–5.

Svendsen, A. (1998). *The Stakeholder Strategy* ([edition unavailable]). Berrett-Koehler Publishers. Retrieved from https://www.perlego.com/book/116507/the-stakeholder-strategy-profiting-from-collaborative-business-relationships-pdf (Original work published 1998).

Thakor, A. & Quinn, R., The Economics of Higher Purpose (December 2, 2013). ECGI - Finance Working Paper No. 395/2013, Available at SSRN: https://ssrn.com/abstract=2362454 or http://dx.doi.org/10.2139/ssrn.2362454

Wheeler, D. & Sillanpa, M. (1998). Including the stakeholders: The business case, *Long Range Planning*, 31(2), 201–210, https://doi.org/10.1016/S0024-6301(98)00004-1

Wheelen, T. L., & Hunger, J. D. (2015). *Strategic Management and Business Policy*. Pearson. 14th Edition. New York.

4

IS INCLUSIVE LEADERSHIP A RENEWED HOPE FOR THE BUILDING OF PEOPLE-CENTRIC ORGANIZATIONS?

Daniel Roque Gomes and Neuza Ribeiro

4.1 Introduction

Unveiling effective ways of managing people in organizations has been an enduring challenge both for researchers and managers, as the determinants, the processes, and the contexts surrounding people management issues are very wide (e.g., Gomes & Neves, 2010; Gaudencio *et al.*, 2020; Yucel *et al.*, 2020; Gomes et al., 2023; Ribeiro *et al.*, 2023) as well as far from being systematically understood.

The last century brought different approaches concerning the effectiveness of leadership (e.g., Quinn & Rohrbaugh, 1983; Schein, 1985) as well as the effectiveness of human resources management models encompassing a vast plethora of approaches (e.g., Beer *et al.*, 1984; Schuler, 1992; Ulrich, 1997) to the handling of the human side of organizations. As a result of the long and persistent efforts of understanding what determines effective ways of managing people in organizations, researchers have produced a significant body of knowledge providing inspiring considerations over the idiosyncrasies of the challenge considered here.

The last few years of research over leadership issues have brought different trends and approaches over the way how leaders may effectively deal with workers in organizational scenarios (e.g., Avolio *et al.*, 2004; Ilies *et al.*, 2005; Alilyyani *et al.*, 2018; Romão *et al.*, 2022). Globally, several kinds of leadership models and leadership approaches have been presented and tested for its robustness with respect to the desired influence expected to be generated by the leader over the corresponding group of workers to have leadership effectiveness.

Its due to this global alignment of concerns that it is possible to identify, over the last decades, leadership models based on the importance of traits for achieving influence over employees (e.g., Gardner, 1989; Fleenor, 2006), or models in which the main concern is to identify the contingencies through which leaders can become

DOI: 10.4324/9781032695969-5

more effective when managing their workers (e.g., Fiedler, 1964; Vroom & Yetton, 1973). It is also due to this alignment that researchers have proposed for the impact of alternative forms of leadership to achieve the long during desire of leadership effectiveness, such as ethical leadership (e.g., Bedi *et al.*, 2016; Bai *et al.*, 2019), transformational leadership (ex.: Braun *et al.*, 2013; Khan *et al.*, 2019), authentic leadership (e.g., Semedo *et al.*, 2018; Ribeiro *et al.*, 2022), virtuous leadership (e.g., Flynn, 2008; Hendriks *et al.*, 2020), Inclusive Leadership (e.g., Choi *et al.*, 2017; Ashikali *et al.*, 2021).

At the same time, researchers have also been trying to understand in what way can managers build human-guided models of developing and managing organizations. These types of concerns have been build based on several management trends and approaches, testing for effective ways of valuing workers in working environment and as a way of enhancing work-related attitudes predicting performance, as well as performance itself (e.g., Cropanzano & Mitchell, 2005; Tourigny *et al.*, 2013; Pellegrini *et al.*, 2020). It's mainly due to this reason that it is possible to identify human resources management trends during (globally) the 1920s and 1930s and through the 1970s valuing for the importance of personnel management as a function to deal with the unions' representatives, and on labor conditions of employment negotiation (Wright *et al.*, 1990), or during the 1990s, under the umbrella of the resource-based view theory of the firm (Barney, 1991), promoting the vision of the strategic side of human resources management in organizations. This strategic value consideration of the human side of organizations has grown in significance especially during the 1980s and the 1990s, in which several theoretical perspectives have pointed for the importance of promoting commitment (e.g., Meyer & Allen, 1991), organizational perceived justice (e.g., Greenberg, 1987), or organizational citizenship behavior (e.g., Bateman & Organ, 1983).

Presently under discussion in various scientific forums is the impact of inclusive leadership over the people-centric organizations approach. The inclusive leadership approach on leadership enhances the abilities of the leader to effectively manage diversity and the inclusion of workers, in such way that researchers assume that it can be seen as "an extension of diversity management" (Booysen, 2014, p. 297). It fosters equity and social justice in workplaces and builds the idea of engagement of workers through inclusion (Ferdman, 2010), and invites for organizations to manage their people with strategic orientation toward the sense of valuing workplaces "with individual and intergroup differences within its workforce", or with a strong sense of "collaboration with individuals, groups and organizations across national and cultural boundaries" (Mor Barak, 2015, p. 8).

Current agendas on people management issues provide enthralling avenues of research, including (but not limited to) happiness in workplaces, diversity, well-being, innovative behavior of employees, and employee commitment. As the bearing of people-centric approach seems highly adjusted to the content foreseen in inclusive leadership way of managing people in workplace scenarios, it seems pertinent to forecast in these agendas the impact of inclusive leadership over the people-centric organizations approach, notably, due to the prospective impacts on aspects such as happiness, innovative behavior, and inclusion in workplace scenarios.

As effective responses concerning the influence of inclusive leadership on the referred organizational outcomes are still awaited from researchers, promoting the discussion of the impact of inclusive leadership on people-centric organizations may very well deliver an important impact over the enduring scientific challenge of how to manage people in today's working environments.

4.2 Inclusive leadership and people-centric organizations

4.2.1 Leadership and inclusive leadership

Managers and leaders are perceived as organizational agents, and the actions they take are viewed as the organization's actions by the employees (Eisenberger *et al.*, 1986). Leaders play a pivotal role in organizations, as they bear the responsibility for decision-making and fostering a supportive environment (Nishii, 2013). This aligns with the social exchange theory, where employees perceive leaders' behaviors as an exchange to reciprocate. When leaders demonstrate openness, support, and flexibility in their interactions with employees, it fosters a positive exchange perception, leading employees to respond accordingly.

Inclusive leadership is a leadership style that provides an inclusive and supportive environment that values the unique qualities of each employee, actively manages diversity, and acknowledges and appreciates the input of all team members (Mor Barak, 2015). Compared with other leadership styles, inclusive leadership places greater emphasis on individuals by supporting and facilitating a sense of belonging, while also expressing appreciation for uniqueness to encourage diverse contributions and abilities (Guo *et al.*, 2023). Inclusive leadership is defined as the words and actions employed by a leader to recognize and promote the contributions of others (Buskirk, 2020). In this sense, an inclusive leader accepts and appreciates the differences among the employees, while also integrating their opinions and perspectives into discussions and decision-making processes (Cohen, 2022).

This style of leadership not only reveals respect for individuals but also creates a system to ensure justice and equity (Randel *et al.*, 2018). Three important dimensions of inclusive leadership include (1) availability, (2) accessibility, and (3) openness. Availability denotes the degree to which the leaders are present for their employees. Accessibility pertains to the extent to which employees can reach the leader at any given time. Meanwhile, openness refers to the extent to which the leader encourages employees to express their ideas and opinions (Sung, 2021). Through demonstrating availability, accessibility, and openness, inclusive leaders help and support employees in problem-solving, and fostering a belief that mistakes are not criticized, but rather viewed as opportunities for learning (Ye *et al.*, 2019). Inclusive leaders additionally cultivate a sense of belonging and individuality among employees, providing developmental support for them to voice their opinions, learn from others, and enhance their work performance (Shafaei & Nejati, 2023).

Inclusive leadership style makes the employees feel respected and recognized by the organization, therefore, it promotes well-being and reduces their work-related stress (Jha *et al.*, 2023). These positive feelings and the perceived support encourage employees to handle the demands of their job (Qi *et al.*, 2019).

Drawing upon self-determination theory, it is possible to understand how inclusive leadership enhances employees' positive outcomes. The self-determination theory posits that individuals, when autonomously motivated and feeling competent, will undergo various positive psychological outcomes (Deci & Ryan, 1985). Furthermore, the self-determination theory suggests that relationships built on meaningful interactions are essential for employees' well-being and optimal functioning (Baumeister & Leary, 1995). This underlines the critical role of leadership in establishing a work environment that prioritizes respect, trust, support, and high-quality relationships (Trépanier *et al.*, 2012).

Therefore, if organizations understand, implement, and sustain an inclusive culture and inclusive practices of leadership, they ultimately reap the benefits of these practices (Kuknor & Bhattacharya, 2021).

4.2.2 Human capital management and the people-centric debate

Over the years, diverse scientific fields have been dedicated to advancing knowledge across distinct subjects related to the strategic management of organizations. Numerous organizational researchers and managers have extensively explored specific facets of strategic management, such as resource planning and strategic development, as well as organizational outcomes like effectiveness, financial performance (e.g., value contribution), and human resource management, which includes aspects like employee training, recruitment, and selection (Barber, 1998). Given that research exploring the interrelationships among these areas transcends a single discipline, the spectrum of scientific domains addressing strategic management issues is broad, encompassing disciplines such as organizational psychology, industrial management, and marketing management. In the midst of this diversification of disciplines, a shared emphasis emerges on the search for effective management practices and the strategic advancement of organizations, and in which human capital management has been linked to relevant organizational outputs (e.g., Beer *et al.*, 1984; Schuler, 1992; Harter *et al.*, 2002; Pawee *et al.*, 2013; Bondarouk & Brewster, 2016).

Human capital management has become a main target of attention by managers and researchers, who view the human side of organizations as a strategic path of response for the challenges brought by global competitive markets (e.g., Rose & Kumar, 2006; Friedman, 2007). This line of reasoning has evolved over the years, strongly supported by evidence highlighting the positive impact of strategic human resources management in work settings (e.g., Parker *et al.*, 2001). With effect, copious studies have consistently demonstrated that organizational performance is significantly influenced by human resource management practices (e.g., Harris & Ogbonna, 2001; Stavrou & Brewster, 2005). Moreover, the specific contributions of employees' knowledge, competencies, and abilities to organizational development have been corroborated (Breaugh & Starke, 2000; Luthans & Sommer, 2005). This awareness has prompted organizations to implement various human resource management practices to efficiently oversee their human resources as a capital worthy of investment.

These current assumptions over the positive impacts of human capital in organizations are a result of various historical contexts in the evolution of society and diverse economic development trends that have significantly influenced the evolutionary course of human resource management. Initially, this area of management encompassed technical aspects related to production and cost control, reflecting a distinct Tayloristic influence (Pina e Cunha *et al.*, 2010).

The establishment of HRM functions can be traced back to the industrial expansion of the 1900s and the appearance of labor unions (Wright *et al.*, 1990), even though in contemporary times the area is a strategic organizational domain addressing all human capital issues impacting the organization's internal and external development. The functions aimed at addressing pressures from union environments served as the primary substance for creating the first personnel departments, leading to the appearance of the welfare officer role in this context. The primary objectives of personnel management included to persuade employees that unions were unnecessary and to manage the pressures from union representatives related to wage demands, as well as negotiations on labor conditions (Wright *et al.*, 1990). In the subsequent decades, these personnel departments have had their responsibilities expanded with the human relations movement, making possible to assure that workers have strong social needs and have acceptance and belonging desires. The movement has significantly emphasized the growing importance of personnel management in organizations.

In the 1970s and in the 1980s, there was a growing support for the importance of human resources in organizational strategy to effectively respond to the external environment (Neves, 2002). From this period onward, the management of organizations could narrowly be considered without due attention of its human factor (e.g., Thompson, 1967; Pfeffer & Salancik, 1978; Davenport & Prusak, 1998). Fueled by the imperative to boost competitiveness in organizations during this era, the perception of human resources began to be considered as strategic. This shift prompted a critical reevaluation of the human aspect in organizations. The traditional cost-based perspective of human resources, rooted in the operational focus of personnel management, gave way to an investment-based perspective embodied in human resources management practices (Neves, 2002).

The 1990s period gave rise to various empirical models aligned with a more strategic perspective on organizations' human assets. Recommendations included urging managers to implement commitment-seeking human resources policies for their employees and emphasizing the importance of promoting positive working environments (Bach & Sisson, 2000). For instance, the significance of the relationship between employees and employers has been prominent, especially since the introduction of Meyer and Allen's (1991) commitment model, endorsing the notion of the necessity for organizational commitment-seeking practices (e.g., Wasti, 2003).

The new millennium has ushered a broadened understanding of the centrality of the human side of organizations, emphasizing its pivotal role in search for unique edges for the purpose of fostering business development and performance. Nowadays, the debate concerning the significance of people in organizations surrounding the "people are our best asset" (Jones, 2014) idea is at the center of a renewed attention regarding the importance of people for organizational success with the people-centric concept considerations, as well as the challenges brought by workforce diversity and inclusion management.

Organizations with people-centric orientations struggle to produce positive work experiences and impactful employee journeys. Organizations with this kind of culture nurture the notion that all people are relevant and that happy people working together perform at a higher level (Black & Venture, 2017).

The concept itself is hardly an unanimously accepted concept, although the idea that these kinds of organizations prioritize employee's well-being, happiness, employee motivation, and commitment is well established. Interesting to see is that the concept seems to be fostered by the entrepreneurial sector, apparently, to be up bringing the it on the entrepreneurial language. With effect, business leaders are becoming more interested in enhancing the organizational cultural trait that employees should not be subservient to customers, as they should be treated in equal standards (Bonsu, 2020). To do so, they are investing in a wide array of HR programs (highly compatible to people-centric organizations' concerns) of benefits as ways of valuing the human side of the organization, such as medical incentives, vacation trips, extensive maternal leaves, community involvement, flexible work involvement, transparent internal communication, and developing a solid motivational atmosphere in work environments.

Managing inclusion of diverse workforce has become a foremost concern and striking challenge in organizations across all business sectors and constitutes an ongoing concern for HR managers (Choi, 2017; Ohunakin *et al.*, 2019). In addition, promoting effective ways of dealing with internal diversity of organizations, and in consequence, dealing with the challenge of inclusion promotion is associated to positive competitive differentiation of organizations (Veli Korkmaz, et al., 2022). It is interesting to see that the content of people-centric organizations' orientations seems highly fitted with the concerns of the management of diversity and inclusion in workplaces.

When considering the content over this current trend of dialogue regarding the people-centric concept over the way how can organizations manage their people and their inherent diversity and inclusion on workplace locations, it seems interesting to try to establish if inclusive leadership stimulate the people-centric foreseen outputs. With effect, when the content of this specific kind of leadership is in consideration, as well as the bearing of people-centric organizations concept, and diversity management, one comes to question if there are positive and significant associations between themselves. In addition, there are empirical evidence that seem encouraging over the relation between inclusive leadership, diversity management, and people-centric foreseen outputs. Through the literature review, the impact of inclusive leadership on employees' positive outcomes is known, such as psychological empowerment (Javed *et al.*, 2019a), self-efficacy (Qi *et al.*, 2019), engagement (Bao *et al.*, 2022), creativity (Zhu *et al.*, 2020), innovative behavior (Guo *et al.*, 2023), proactive behavior (Chang *et al.*, 2022), organizational citizenship behavior (Younas *et al.*, 2021), voice (Chen *et al.*, 2023), and task performance (Xiaotao *et al.*, 2018).

These evidences offer compelling interest in extending research over the impact of inclusive leadership on these outputs, as existing research is still recent and prone to supplementary assessments and, thus, open to contradictory findings. With effect, current subjects regarding diversity management and inclusion in work locations, workplace happiness, or innovative behavior are quite impactful for managers and justify additional research investment.

4.3 Empirical research over the inclusive leadership and people-centric organizations bond

In the following point of this chapter, we will present a methodological approach regarding the idea of the research opportunity of further understanding the relation between inclusive leadership and the bearing of the people-centric organizations relation.

4.3.1 Sample and procedure

Regarding procedure, data collection has occurred in the first trimester of 2023 using Google forms widespread with the help of social media, such as Facebook, Instagram, and LinkedIn. The instrument used (questionnaire) gathered data using measures of inclusive leadership, as well as people-centric study variables (happiness in the organization and innovative behavior), and sociodemographic questions, such as gender, age, qualifications, hierarchical position, or tenure.

Regarding sample, it is formed with 110 individuals (57% female and 43% male), majorly ranging from 20 to 60 years old, and 71% have a graduation level at higher education. Most respondents work in the central region of Portugal (70%), and in the tertiary sector (48%). Fifty-nine percent of employees have permanent employment contract, and 25% have fixed-term or temporary contracts. In what concerns hierarchical position, almost half of the sample constitute operational staff, and managers and middle management positions are held by 20% of the respondents. In terms of tenure, the majority of the sample respondents have tenure between one and five years (47%).

4.3.2 *Variable measures*

Regarding variable measures, the study variables were measured using a 5-point Likert scale (1 – strongly disagree to 5 – strongly agree), and were treated as follows:

a *Inclusive leadership* – ten items were used based on the instrument validated by Carmeli, Reiter-Palmon, and Ziev (2010). In the current study, this measure has reported 97 Cronbach alpha value.
b *Innovative behavior* – eight items were used based on the instruments validated by J. P. De Jong and Kemp (2003), and Kleysen and Street (2001). In the current study, this measure has reported 93 Cronbach alpha value.
c *Happiness in the organization* – seven items were used based on the instrument validated by Daniels (2000). In the current study, this measure has reported 94 Cronbach alpha value.

4.3.3 *Results*

4.3.3.1 Descriptive statistics

Regarding mean and standard deviation of the study variables (Table 4.1), it was possible to see that respondents are presenting a high level of inclusive leadership reported value ($M = 3.93$ on a 1–5 scale), and also a high level of innovative behavior perception ($M = 3.82$ on a 1–5 scale), and high level of happiness in the organization ($M = 3.73$ on a 1–5 scale). Based on these means, it seems that participants in the study tend to perceive their work environments as prone for inclusive leadership, as well as innovative behavior and happiness in the organization. Regarding standard deviation levels, the reported value for inclusive leadership is 1.01, for innovative behavior is 0.80, and for happiness in the organization is 0.82. These values indicate variance regarding the means and demonstrating different individual positionings facing the measures used.

4.3.3.2 Relation between variables

According to Table 4.1, inclusive leadership shows a positive and significant correlation with innovative behavior ($r = 549$) and with happiness in the organization ($r = 630$). In a similar way, it was possible to find a positive and significant association between organizational happiness and innovative behavior ($r = 766$).

TABLE 4.1 Means, SDs, correlations, Cronbach's alpha values

	M	*SD*	*1*	*2*	*3*
1 Inclusive Leadership	3.93	1.01	(0.97)	–	
2 Org. Happiness	3.73	0.82	0.630**	(0.94)	–
3 Innovative Behavior	3.82	0.80	0.549**	0.766**	(0.93)

**The correlation is significant at level 0.01 (2 ends); Cronbach coefficients in parentheses.

According to these results, when theoretical reasoning is applied to the reading of the data, results seem to imply that inclusive leadership leads to the stimulation of innovative behavior and happiness in the organization. This means that inclusive leaders should be expected to generate better work environments compatible with people-centric organizations. With effect, results seem to imply that this type of leadership enhances the way how workers feel stimulated to participate and to promote innovative processes on work locations, as well as a sense of enthusiasm, energy, and optimist at work locations.

Results also seem to imply that research over the impact of inclusive leadership over people-centric organization behavioral outputs seem to have research interest and merit and stimulate debate and practical considerations for the management of people in organizations, notably, if considering the current importance given on people-centric approaches on organizational management.

4.4 Conclusions

The people-centric organizations' debate has brought a renewed discussion to the human-side valuation on the way how people are managed in organizations. Both boosted by managers and by researchers, the debate concerning the human value in organizations is passing by challenges regarding new agendas to which the people-centric debate may offer relevant insights, notably, workforce diversity, inclusion, and the way how leaders should perform in these renewed workplace environments.

Organizations with people-centric culture are oriented toward the importance of people for organizational performance, and that organizations should strive to have happy people working together, due to higher performance levels exhibited by happy people at work locations (Black & Venture, 2017). In addition, more recent forms of leadership, such as inclusive leadership, seem to be well suited to these current people-centric challenges, with the bearing that inclusive leadership can be a powerful facilitator of effective management of workplace diversity, happiness at work locations, or innovative behavior. Following these considerations, an exploratory empirical study was conducted to better understand if inclusive leadership is significantly and positively related with happiness at work location and innovative behavior, both relevant indicators of people-centric organizations.

Main results show that inclusive leadership is positively and significantly associated with organizational happiness and innovative behavior. These results empower the main idea surrounding the core values of the people-centric debate concerning the importance of this specific kind of leadership in enabling these relevant organizational outputs. Based on these results, and on the discussion raised on this chapter, it is possible to outline theoretical, empirical, and practical contributions of this study.

Regarding the main theoretical and empirical contributions, this work brings to the center of the theoretical debate on people-centric organizations, the idea that inclusive leadership may work as an interesting predictor of relevant people-centric outputs, such as organizational happiness and innovative behavior. Inclusive leadership has shown to be positively and significantly associated with these indicators, which allow to enrich the current theoretical debate over the significance of inclusive leadership as a way of managing effectively the challenge of diversity and inclusion in work locations using people-centric theoretical reference of alignment.

Regarding main practical contributions, this work enhances an underlying logic on people management more oriented toward the new millennium challenges on workforce diversity, workers' inclusion, and the way leaders should behave to have effective people management practices. Considering our results, it seems advisable for organizations to develop training programs directed toward top and middle managers regarding the content of inclusive leadership and the use of ways to increase the presence of inclusive leaders and forms of inclusive leadership in organizations. Main results also seem to advise that inclusion should be regarded as part of the current dictionary of workforces, and that diversity, inclusion, and well-being are key arguments for the building of effective teams in organizations. Fostering inclusive leadership plans of action with the purpose of enhancing the presence of these contents on a daily basis in organizations should be seen as a relevant way to go for the purpose of having modern and up-to-date attractive organizations as a good place to work.

References

Alilyyani, B., Wong, C. A., & Cummings, G. G. (2018). Antecedents, mediators, and outcomes of authentic leadership in healthcare: a systematic review. *International Journal of Nursing Studies*, *83*, 34–64. DOI: 10.1016/j.ijnurstu.2018.04.001

Ashikali, T., Groeneved, S., & Kuipers, B. (2021). The role of inclusive leadership in supporting an inclusive climate in diverse public sector teams. *Review of Public Personnel Administration*, *42*, 497–519. https://doi.org/10.1177/0734371X19899722

Avolio, B., Gardner, W., Walumbwa, F. O., Luthans, F., & May, D. R. (2004). Unlocking the mask: a look at the process by which authentic leaders impact follower attitudes and behaviors. *Leadership Quarterly, 15*, 801–823. https://doi.org/10.1016/j.leaqua.2004.09.003

Bach, S. & Sisson, K. (2000). *Personnel management: a comprehensive guide to theory and practice.* Oxford: Blackwell Business.

Bai, Y., Lin, L., & Liu, J. T. (2019). Leveraging the employee voice: a multilevel social learning perspective of ethical leadership. *The International Journal of Human Resource Management, 30*(12), 1869–1901.

Bao, P., Xiao, Z., Bao, G., & Noorderhaven, N. (2022). Inclusive leadership and employee work engagement: A moderated mediation model. *Baltic Journal of Management, 17*(1), 124–139. https://doi.org/10.1108/BJM-06-2021-0219

Barber, A. (1998). *Recruiting employees: individual and organizational perspectives.* Thousand Oaks, CA: Sage Publications.

Barney, J. (1991). Firm resources and sustained competitive advantage. *Journal of Management, 1*, 99–120.

Bateman, J. & Organ, D. (1983). Job satisfaction and the good soldier: the relationship between affect and employee "citizenship". *Academy of management Journal, 26*, 587–595.

Baumeister, R. F., & Leary, M. R. (1995). The need to belong: desire for interpersonal attachments as a fundamental human motivation. *Psychological Bulletin, 117*(3), 497–529.

Bedi, A., Alpaslan, C. M., & Green, S. (2016). A meta-analytic review of ethical leadership outcomes and moderators. *Journal of Business Ethics, 139*(3), 517–536. https://doi.org/10.1007/s10551-015-2625-1

Beer, M., Spector, B., Lawrence, P., Mills, D. Q., & Walton, R. (1984). *Human resource management: a general manager's perspective.* New York: Free Press.

Black, J. & Venture, K. (2017). The human factor to profitability: people-centered cultures as meaningful organizations. *Journal of Organizational Psychology, 17*(2), 24–34.

Bondarouk, T., & Brewster, C. (2016). Conceptualising the future of HRM and technology research. *The International Journal of Human Resources Management, 27*, 2652–2671. https://doi.org10.1080/09585192.2016.1232296

Bonsu, S. (2020). Creating an employee-centric culture in organizations. *International Journal of Business Management and Economic Review, 3*, 276–284.

Booysen, L. (2014). The development of inclusive leadership practice and processes. In B. M. Ferdman & B. R. Deane (Eds.), *Diversity at Work: The Practice of Inclusion* (pp. 296–329). Jossey-Bass/Wiley. https://doi.org/10.1002/9781118764282.ch10

Braun, S., Peus, C., Weisweiler, S., & Frey, D. (2013). Transformational leadership, job satisfaction, and team performance: a multilevel mediation model of trust. *Leadership Quarterly, 24*, 270–283. https://doi.org/ 10.1016/j.ijproman.2012.09. 003

Breaugh, J. & Starke, M. (2000). Research on employee recruitment: so many studies, so many remaining questions. *Journal of Management, 26*, 405–434.

Buskirk, M. (2020). *Inclusive leadership, psychological empowerment, and affective organizational commitment: a mediated model.* M.Sc. Thesis, San Jose State University.

Carmeli, A., Reiter-Palmon, R., & Ziv, E. (2010). Inclusive leadership and employee involvement in creative tasks in the workplace: The mediating role of psychological Safety. *Creativity Research Journal, 22*(3), 250–260. https://doi.org/10.1080/10400419.2010.504654

Chang P., Ma G, Lin Y. (2022). Inclusive leadership and employee proactive behavior: A cross-level moderated mediation model. *Psychology Research and Behavior Management.* doi: 10.2147/PRBM.S363434.

Chen, H., Liang, Q., Feng, C., & Zhang, Y. (2023). Leadership and follower voice: The role of inclusive leadership and group faultlines in promoting collective voice behavior. *Journal of Applied Behavioral Science, 59*(1), 61–87. https://doi.org/10.1177/00218863211035243

Choi, S. (2017). Workforce diversity and job satisfaction of the majority and the minority: analyzing the asymmetrical effects of relational demography on whites and racial/ethnic minorities. *Review of Public Personnel Administration, 37*(1), 84–107. https://doi.org/10.1177/0734371X15623617

Choi, S. B., Tran, T. B. H., & Kang, S.-W. (2017). Inclusive leadership and employee well-being: The mediating role of person-job fit. *Journal of Happiness Studies, 18*, 1877–1901. https://doi.org/10.1007/s10902-016-9801-6

Cohen, R. (2022). *The Relationships between Dimensions of Inclusive Leadership and Aspects of Employee Engagement: Crucial Connections for Organizational Success*. Ph.D. Dissertation, Antioch University.

Cropanzano, R. & Mitchell, M. S. (2005). Social exchange theory: an interdisciplinary review. *Journal of Management, 31*(6), 874–900.

Daniels, K. (2000). Measures of five aspects of affective well-being at work. *Human Relations, 53*(2), 275–294

Davenport, T. & Prusak, L. (1998). *Working knowledge*. Boston, MA: Harvard Business School Press.

Deci, E. L. & Ryan, R. M. (1985). *Intrinsic motivation and self-determination in human behavior*. New York: Plenum Press.

De Jong, Jeroen; KEMP, Ron. (2003). Determinants of co-workers' innovative behaviour: An investigation into knowledge intensive services. *International Journal of Innovation Management, 7*(2), 189–212. DOI https://doi.org/10.1142/S1363919603000787

Eisenberger, R., Huntington, R., Hutchison, S., & Sowa, D. (1986). Perceived organizational support. *Journal of Applied Psychology, 71*, 500–507.

Ferdman, B., Avigdor, A., Braun, D., Konkin, J., Kuzmycz, D. (2010). Collective experience of inclusion, diversity, and performance in work groups. *RAM, Rev. Adm. Mackenzie 11*, 6–26. https://doi.org/10.1590/S1678-69712010000300003

Fiedler, F. E. (1964). A contingency model of leadership effectiveness. *Advances in Experimental Social Psychology, 1*, 149–190.

Fleenor, J. (2006). *Trait approach to leadership*. Encyclopedia of industrial and Organizational Psychology. Thousand Oaks: Sage Publications.

Flynn, G. (2008). The virtuous manager: a vision for leadership in business. *Journal of Business Ethics, 78*(3), 359–372.

Friedman, B. (2007). Globalization implications for human resource management roles. *Employees Responsibilities and Rights Journal, 19*, 157–171.

Gardner, J. W. (1989). *On leadership*. New York: Free Press.

Gaudencio, P., Coelho, A., & Ribeiro, N. (2020). The impact of CSR perceptions on workers' turnover intentions: exploring the supervisor exchange process and the role of perceived external prestige. *Social Responsibility Journal, 17*, 543–561. https://doi.org/10.1108/SRJ-12-2018-0330

Gomes, D. & Neves, J. (2010). Do applicants' prior experiences influence organizational attractiveness prediction? *Management Research, 8*, 203–220. https://doi.org/10.1108/1536-541011089420

Gomes, D., Ribeiro, N. & Santos, M. (2023). "Searching for gold" with sustainable human resources management and internal communication: evaluating the mediating role of employer attractiveness for explaining turnover intention and performance. *Administrative Sciences, 13*, 24. https://doi.org/10.3390/ admsci13010024

Greenberg, J. (1987). A taxonomy of organizational justice theories. *Academy of management Review, 12*, 9–22.

Guo, Y., Junge, J., & Sang-Hyuk, Y. (2023). Impact of inclusive leadership on innovative work behavior: the mediating role of job crafting. *Administrative Sciences, 13*, 4. https://doi.org/10.3390/admsci13010004

Harris, L., & Ogbonna, E. (2001). Strategic human resource management, market orientation, and organizational performance. *Journal of Business Research, 51*, 157–166.

Harter, J., Schmidt, F., & Hayes, T. (2002). Business-unit-level relationship between employee satisfaction, employee engagement and business outcomes: a meta-analysis. *Journal of Applied Psychology, 87*, 268–279.

Hendriks, M., Burger, M., Rijsenbilt, A., Pleeging, E., & Commandeur, H. (2020). Virtuous leadership: a source of employee well-being and trust. *Management Research Review, 43*(8), 951–970. https://doi.org/10.1108/MRR-07-2019-0326

Ilies, R., Morgeson, F. P., & Nahrgang, J. D. (2005). Authentic leadership and eudaemonic well-being: understanding leader-follower outcomes. *Leadership Quarterly, 16*, 373–394. https://doi.org/10.1016/j.leaqua.2005.03.002

Jha, I. N., Pal D., & Sarkar, S. (2023). Unlocking the secret to happiness at work: the power of inclusive leadership, organizational justice and workplace inclusion. *Journal of Management Development*. Vol. ahead-of-print No. ahead-of-print. https://doi.org/10.1108/JMD-04-2023-0136

Jones, K. (2014). Research Bulletin 2014. *Wooing the Workforce: Creating an Employee-Centric Organization*. Retrieved from https://webcdn.ultimatesoftware.com/static/pdf/miscellaneous/bersin-wooing-the-workforce.pdf, Accessed on January 22, 2024

Khan, A. M., Jantan, A. H. B., Salleh, L. B. M., Dato'Mansor, Z., Islam, M. A., & Hosen, S. (2019). The impact of transformational leadership effects on innovative work behavior by the moderating role of psychological empowerment. *Journal of Reviews on Global Economics, 8*, 925–938. https://doi.org/10.6000/1929-7092.2019.08.79

Kleysen, R. F., & Street, C. T. (2001). Toward a multidimensional measure of individual innovative behaviour. *Journal of Intellectual Capital, 2*, 284–296. https://doi.org/10.1108/EUM0000000005660

Kuknor, S. & Bhattacharya, S. (2021). Exploring organizational inclusion and inclusive leadership in Indian companies. *European Business Review, 33*(3), 450–464. https://doi.org/10.1108/EBR-04-2020-0089

Luthans, K. & Sommer, S. (2005). The impact of high-performance work on industry-level outcomes. *Journal of Managerial Issues, 17*, 327–345.

Meyer, J. P. & Allen, N. J. (1991). A three component conceptualization of organizational commitment. *Human Resource Management Review, 1*, 61–89.

Mor Barak, M. (2015). Inclusion is the key to diversity management, but what is inclusion? *Human Service Organizations Management, Leadership and Governance, 39*(2), 83–88.

Neves, J. (2002). Gestão de recursos humanos: evolução do problema em termos dos conceitos e das práticas. In Caetano, A. & Vala, J. (Org.) (pp. 3–30). *Gestão de Recursos Humanos*. Lisboa: RH Editora.

Nishii, L. H. (2013). The benefits of climate for inclusion for gender-diverse groups. *Academy of Management Journal, 56*(6), 1754e1774.

Ohunakin, F., Adeniji, A., Ogunnaike, O. O., Igbadume, F., & Akintayo, D. I. (2019). The effects of diversity management and inclusion on organisational outcomes: a case of multinational corporation. *Business: Theory and Practice, 20*, 93–102. https://doi.org/10.3846/btp.2019.09

Parker, S., Wall, T., & Corderly, J. (2001). Future work design research and practice: towards and elaborated model of work design. *Journal of Occupational and Organizational Psychology, 74*, 413–440.

Pawee, J., Guest, D., & Wright, P. (Eds) (2013). *HRM and performance: achievements and challenges*. Chichester: John Wiley & Sons.

Pellegrini, M., Ciampi, F., Marzi, G., & Orlando, B. (2020). The relationship between knowledge management and leadership: mapping the field and providing future research avenues. *Journal of Knowledge Management 24*, 1445–1492. https://doi.org/10.1108/JKM-01-2020-0034

Pfeffer, J. & Salancik, G. (1978). *The external control of organizations*. New York: Harper and Row.

Pina e Cunha, M., Rego, A., Campos e Cunha, R., Cabral-Cardoso, C., & Gomes, J. (2010). O que é a gestão de pessoas/ recursos humanos? In Pina e Cunha, M., Rego, A., Campos e Cunha, R., Cabral-Cardoso, C., & Gomes, J. *Manual de Gestão de Pessoas e do Capital Humano* (pp. 54–92). Lisboa: Edições Sílabo.

Qi, L., Liu, B., Wei, X., & Hu, Y. (2019). Impact of inclusive leadership on employee innovative behavior: perceived organizational support as a mediator. *PLoS One, 14*(2), e0212091.

Quinn, R. E. & Rohrbaugh, J. (1983). A spatial model of effectiveness criteria: towards a competing values approach to organizational analysis. *Management Science, 29*, 363–377.

Randel, A., Galvin, B., Shore, L., Ehrhart, K., Chung, B., Dean, M., & Kedharnath, U. (2018). Inclusive leadership: realizing positive outcomes through belongingness and being valued for uniqueness. *Human Resource Management Review, 28*(2), 190–203.

Ribeiro, N., Duarte, A., Filipe, R., & David, R. (2022). Does authentic leadership stimulate citizenship behaviors? The importance of affective commitment as a mediator. *Sustainability Accounting, Management and Policy Journal, 13*, 320–340.

Ribeiro, N., Gomes, D., & Oliveira, A. (2023). The impact of the work-family conflict on employee engagement, performance and turnover intention. *International Journal of Organizational Analysis, 31*, 533–549.

Romão, S., Ribeiro, N., Gomes, D. R., & Singh, S. (2022). The impact of leaders' coaching skills on employees' happiness and turnover intention. *Administrative Sciences, 12*, 84.

Rose, R. & Kumar, N. (2006). The influence of organizational and human resource management strategies on performance. *Performance Improvement, 45*, 18–24.

Schein, E. H. (1985). *Organizational culture and leadership*. San Francisco, CA: Jossey-Bass.

Schuler, R. S. (1992). Strategic human resourcc management: linking the people with the strategic needs of the business. *Organizational Dynamics*, *21*, 18–32.

Semedo, A., Coelho, A., & Ribeiro, N. (2018). The relationship between authentic leaders and employees' creativity: what are the roles of affective commitment and job resourcefulness? *International Journal of Workplace Health Management, 11*, 58–73.

Shafaei, A. & Nejati, M. (2023). Creating meaningful work for employees: the role of inclusive leadership. *Human Resource Development Quarterly*, 1–23. https://doi.org/10.1002/hrdq.21512

Stavrou, E. & Brewster, C. (2005). The configurational approach to linking strategic human resource management bundles with business performance: myth or reality? *Management Revue, 16,* 186–201.

Sung, S. (2021). *Effects of inclusive leadership on job satisfaction: the mediating role of organizational justice*, Ph.D. Dissertation, Alliant International University.

Thompson, J. (1967). *Organizations in action*. New York: McGraw-Hill.

Tourigny, L., Baba, V. V., Han, J., & Wang, X. (2013). Emotional exhaustion and job performance: the mediating role of organizational commitment. *The International Journal of Human Resource Management, 24*(3), 514–532.

Trépanier, S.-G., Fernet, C., & Austin, S. (2012). Social and motivational antecedents of perceptions of transformational leadership: a self-determination theory perspective. *Canadian Journal of Behavioural Science/Revue canadienne des sciences du comportement, 44*(4), 272–277. https://doi.org/10.1037/a0028699

Ulrich, D. (1997). *Human resource champions: the next agenda for adding value and delivery results*. Harvard: Harvard Business School Press.

Veli Korkmaz, A.S., R., Knappert, L. and van Engen, M. (2022). About and beyond leading uniqueness and belongingness: a systematic review of inclusive leadership research. *Human Resource Management Review, 23*(4), 100894, doi: 10.1016/j.hrmr.2022.100894.

Vroom, V. H. & Yetton, P. W. (1973). Leadership and decision making. Pittsburgh, PA: University of Pittsburgh Press.

Wasti, S. (2003). Organizational commitment, turnover intentions and the influence of cultural values. *Journal of Occupational and Organizational Psychology, 76*, 303–321.

Wright, P., Rowland, K., & Ferris, G. (1990). Perspectives on human resources management (pp. 4–16). *Human resource management: perspectives and issues* (2nd ed). MA, California: Allyn and Bacon, inc Publisher.

Xiaotao, Z., Yang, X., Diaz, I., & Yu, M. (2018). Is too much inclusive leadership a good thing? An examination of curvilinear relationship between inclusive leadership and employees' task performance. *International Journal of Manpower, 39*(7), 882–895.

Ye, Q., Wang, D., & Guo, W. (2019). Inclusive leadership and team innovation: the role of team voice and performance pressure. *European Management Journal, 37*(4), 468–480.

Younas A, Wang D, Javed B, Zaffar MA. Moving beyond the mechanistic structures: The role of inclusive leadership in developing change-oriented organizational citizenship behaviour. Can J Adm Sci. 2021; 38: 42–52. https://doi.org/10.1002/cjas.1586

Yucel, I., Ribeiro, N., & Gomes, D. (2020). Perceived organizational support and employees' performance: the mediating role of affective commitment. *International Journal of Management and Enterprise Development, 19*, 187–202.

Zhu, J., Xu, S., & Zhang, B. (2020). The paradoxical effect of inclusive leadership on subordinates' creativity. *Frontiers of Psychology, 10*, 2960. https://doi.org/10.3389/fpsyg.2019.02960

5

WORK PASSION AND INNOVATIVE BEHAVIOURS

The anchor for success

Clara Margaça, Elisabeth Figueiredo, and José Carlos Sánchez-García

5.1 Introduction

Continuous innovation is the key to a company's competitiveness and sustainability, in a world devastated by several crises and, in particular, with changing economic conditions. Self-evidently, people are the actors to carry out innovative behaviours, through the generation and implementation of new ideas, and face this challenging global panorama. Several studies point out that innovative behaviour depends on external variables, such as organizational identity (e.g., Niu et al., 2018), but also on internal variables, such as happiness (Fuller & Marler, 2009). Subsequently, maintaining work passion can improve both personal performance and innovative behavioural intention (Fuller & Marler, 2009).

Work passion, according to Zigarmi et al. (2009), can be defined as "persistent, emotionally positive, based on a feeling of well-being, resulting from cognitive and affective evaluations of various professional and organizational situations, which result in consistent and constructive work intentions and behaviours" (p. 310). These evaluations generally concern three dimensions related to the work environment: (i) organizational characteristics (e.g., performance expectations), (ii) work characteristics (e.g., autonomy) and (iii) relationship characteristics (e.g., feedback) (Nimon & Zigarmi, 2015; Zigarmi et al., 2009). From the perspective of Vallerand et al. (2003), this construct can be defined as a desire or strength towards something that one likes and believes is important, which is why one decides to invest time and energy, and they proposed a dualistic model: obsessive passion and harmonious passion. In obsessive passion, individuals are controlled by the desire to engage in the activities performed, which leads to the experience of anxiety, as well as the manifestation of inflexible behaviours, which triggers consequences at intrapersonal and interpersonal levels (Vallerand, 2012). At opposite poles, harmonious passion is

DOI: 10.4324/9781032695969-6

aligned with the individual's personal desires, which leads them to maintain control over the desire to engage in the activities they perform and to experience feelings of interest and motivation. This means that internalization is autonomous, that is, the individual controls their experiences, which become part of their identity. Based on appraisal theory, Nimon and Zigarmi (2015) proposed the Employee Work Passion Appraisal model, which is composed of environmental (e.g., work characteristics) and personal (e.g., beliefs and values) antecedents with a view to understanding how work passion is formed. By applying this theory, the authors reinforce the idea that the environment influences a person's well-being and the way they deal with these impacts depends on their personal values and characteristics. Also Fang et al. (2020) offer their perspective, highlighting that passionate individuals see work issues as a characteristic of their identity, a process associated with autonomous internalization (Ho et al., 2018). In turn, Mustafa et al. (2020) and Gong et al. (2020) refer to work passion as a form of intrinsic motivation, the self-determined drive in time and energy towards meaningful activities, mainly because it is characterized by an autonomous and flexible involvement (Malchelosse et al., 2023). Finally, work passion can also be understood as an affective and conscious evaluation related to labour activity, which provides the individual with a persistent state of well-being and constructive work-related behaviours (Ho et al., 2018).

Scientific research on work passion is relatively recent, but it has evolved over the last few years, mainly as a psychological process that, on the one hand, brings meaning and balance to people's lives (Malchelosse et al., 2023; Vallerand et al., 2003) and, on the other, trigger an obsessive process and guilty (Vallerand, 2015). When compared with obsessive passion, studies on harmonious passion show its positive influence on job satisfaction (Chen et al., 2020), individual value and meaning at work (Liu et al., 2020), less turnover (Gong et al., 2020; Muneeb et al., 2017), sense of autonomy (Chummar et al., 2019), enrichment experience and psychological needs satisfaction (Malchelosse et al., 2023) and civic behaviour (Muneeb et al., 2017). In sum, a worker who is obsessively passionate about his work will feel internal pressure and will find it difficult to disengage, leading to compromised psychological functioning (Vallerand, 2015). While harmonious passion allows for an adaptive and positive experience, through a process of self-internalization, leading to full psychological functioning.

Innovative behaviour is a multistep process and refers to the introduction, promotion and implementation of new ideas (Janssen, 2000; Lambriex-Schmitz et al., 2020), which offer utility and the resolution of a given problem and added value (Kleysen & Street, 2001). Also presupposes that the individual is able to identify a problem, develops a set of solutions and chooses the one that best suits for resolution, which means that the individual also has an entrepreneurial orientation (Noreña-Chavez & Guevara, 2020). While creativity concerns the generation of original ideas, innovation concerns the application of these ideas aiming for business success and sustainability, which comprises a socio-psychological process (Anderson et al., 2014) and goal planning. Hence, this type of behaviour depends on personal characteristics, circumstantial and contextual factors and the personal/professional attitude (Kwon & Kim, 2020), where work passion would be represented. The natural engagement of work passion can trigger innovative behaviours, as passionate employees are cognitively flexible and involved, which promotes the generation of meaningful and valuable ideas. In a similar manner, when tough times come, passion sustains individual belief and is oftentimes the deciding factor for organizational success, including from the customer's perspective. Consumer can spot when a businessperson is passionate about their products/services, and this may dictate that the personal brand is respected, improving the company's competitive advantage.

Based on the definition of Birkeland and Nerstad (2016), work passion triggers positive emotional experiences and high motivation at work. Undoubtedly, work passion as a personal resource and a motivational mechanism, by providing a feeling of job satisfaction, can also influence the workers' creative process, which is revealed through the proposal of innovative solutions (Luu, 2019). In contrast, the negative side of work passion drives employees to work for external rewards and motivations (e.g., social status), and this can also push them to innovative behaviours (Liu et al., 2020).

In recent years, research on work passion has received increasing attention from academics due to its potential impact on organizational performance. However, few studies have explored how work passion relates to innovation capacity and to competitive advantage. In short, work passion and innovative behaviour are not independent phenomena, but intrinsically related, since passion can serve as a catalyst for the creation of new ideas and for the search and implementation of creative solutions. Subsequently, a sustainable competitive advantage is achieved when work passion and innovation are cultivated and sustained over time.

Therefore, this study seeks to explore the role that these variables play in the organizational context, highlighting their importance in obtaining competitive advantage. To achieve this objective, a critical review of the literature was carried out, analysing studies published between 2000 and 2023 and pointing out the most relevant theoretical approaches. This chapter represents a contribution for business leaders who, by effectively understanding the different influences of passion in the work context, can implement strategies to cultivate a more efficient, stimulating and rewarding work environment that encourages innovation, guaranteeing the company an advantageous position in a volatile market. Hence, this chapter highlights the importance of considering work passion as an essential factor for organizational success and offers important contributions to future research and management practices.

5.2 Work passion and innovative behaviours: dominant approaches

5.2.1 Entrepreneurial behaviour and work passion

Considering the relevance of passion and innovative behaviour in the work context, several authors have analysed a set of factors that drive this behaviour, both at an individual and organizational level. Udin (2022) emphasizes the knowledge sharing and, based on the Social Exchange Theory, argues that sharing between managers and employees positively influences entrepreneurial passion, creating favourable conditions for innovation. This research showed that the synergy resulting from knowledge exchange generates a collaborative environment, which encourages the sharing of experiences, know-how and new ideas among employees, which encourages the creation of creative resources and stimulates innovation, while leads a favourable position and offers a differentiating value. In a similar line of research, Flores-Pérez and Guevara (2023) discuss the impact of entrepreneurial passion on the relationship between entrepreneurial orientation and innovative behaviour. They conclude that employees' entrepreneurial passion plays an important role in this relationship, suggesting that the intensity of positive emotions and the strong attraction to entrepreneurial initiatives are critical factors for promoting innovation in the workplace.

Escamilla-Fajardo et al. (2021), for their part, found that entrepreneurial orientation, under the influence of work passion, influences service quality and performance. Therefore, from this perspective, entrepreneurial orientation, which reflects a company's ability to identify innovative business opportunities, represents a fundamental resource for the survival of these organizations that face competitive environments. In this way, the promotion of an entrepreneurial organizational culture and work passion among employees are crucial strategies for these structures, guaranteeing their success and sustainability.

A study carried out by Alhumoudi et al. (2022a), in the United Arab Emirates, with 508 generation Y nurses, concluded that the positive perception of Corporate Social Responsibility (CSR) led to an increase in work passion, which, consequently, positively influenced their innovative behaviour. In this particular context, harmonious passion was emphasized, and it was found that nurses who demonstrated a balanced enjoyment of their work activities showed greater aptitude for carrying out challenging innovative initiatives. In contrast, workers with higher levels of obsessive passion demonstrated more controversial behaviour, avoiding taking on initiatives that were not strictly aligned with their personal interests. Similarly, Alhumoudi et al. (2022b), based on an exploratory literature review, analysed the role of organizational commitment and work passion in the relationship between the perception of CSR and innovative behaviour. From the results it can be concluded that the way employees position themselves and interpret the organization's CSR directly influences their work passion and tendencies to take on creative and innovative challenges.

Han et al. (2023), based on the Conservation of Resources Theory, analysed the implications of superior-subordinate Guanxi (SSG) on the employees' work passion and entrepreneurial behaviour. SSG, an organizational practice originating in China, focuses on relationships between superiors and subordinates, prioritizing values such as reciprocity, loyalty, communication and mutual trust. In a business context, these values are crucial with regard to work dynamics, due to facilitate exchange of ideas, creating favourable conditions for entrepreneurial attitudes. In this sense, a positive hierarchical relationship based on Guanxi can influence operational effectiveness and organizational culture, reducing follower dependence on superiors and creating a more harmonious and productive work environment, which encourages work passion and values entrepreneurial behaviour and innovation.

Luu (2019) highlighted the importance of a climate of diversity in promoting innovation in the organizational context, pointing out the practical implications for company management. The application of Self-Determination Theory is substantially relevant, as it allows to understand how work passion, in particular harmonious passion, can influence employees' innovative behaviour. This study attests that diversity, within the organization, drives innovation, creating a positive space where all employees are valued and treated fairly, regardless of their origins or perspectives. The structure of Social Exchange Theory in this context is a valuable aid to understanding the dynamics of social interaction, focusing on its impact and contribution to innovative behaviour.

Koumproglou and Biginas (2022) underlined the importance of start-ups in the field of entrepreneurship, highlighting the importance of work passion and innovative behaviour for the success and sustainability in a dynamic and challenging business environment. Innovation is a fundamental pillar for these companies and, therefore, requires great dedication. Based on Social Identity Theory, the authors argue that motivated employees who are highly committed to the company's values increase their levels of work passion when they realize that entrepreneurial identity is central to self-image, demonstrating greater enthusiasm and dedication to carrying out their professional activities.

Finally, based on the Dualistic Model of Passion and Self-Determination Theory, Jan and Zainal (2020) focus on harmonious passion, considering it a motivating force that drives employees to stand out and adopt innovative behaviours. Undoubtedly, the application of these two theories is relevant, as it provides a solid framework for understanding the relationship between cooperative psychological climate, harmonious passion and innovative behaviours at work. Hence, this study concludes that in a cooperative and supportive work environment, in which social interaction between colleagues and managers prevails, employees tend to develop a harmonious passion for their work, which increases commitment and dedication and, consequently, promotes innovative approaches.

5.2.2 Employees leadership

Employee leadership emerges as a vital element in an organizational context, which facilitates the expression of work passion and the manifestation of innovative behaviour in the workplace.

Xiao et al. (2022) highlighted the importance of temporal leadership in employees' innovative behaviour, emphasizing its potential effectiveness in contexts where employees' preference for synchronicity is more pronounced, which implies adapting the pace of work and activities depending on colleagues and/or temporal limitations. According to these authors, effective time management by leaders, the definition of tasks and deadlines aligned with organizational objectives, has a significant influence on promoting a passionate work culture. This approach provides an organized environment, and positively contributes to improving the efficiency and posture of employees in workplace.

Similarly, Dalain (2023) and Jan et al. (2022) observed the positive influence of servant leadership in the context of business innovation, arguing that leaders who prioritize the needs of subordinates rather than the organization's objectives or their own needs foster harmonious passion among employees, which favours innovative views. In both studies, work passion was assumed to be an important factor due to its positive impact on employees' involvement and dedication, positively affecting the practice of leadership. Therefore, it became clear that companies can improve employee engagement and innovative behaviour by focusing on developing servant leaders, with a view to promoting harmonious passion and stimulating creative self-efficacy (Caza & Posner, 2022; Jan et al., 2022).

Jan et al. (2021) and Luu (2021) showed that specific Human Resource Management (HRM) practices (e.g., skills development, autonomy, participation in decision-making, flexibility), through harmonious passion, play a relevant role in promoting innovative behaviour among employees. The authors are unanimous regarding the fact that the prevalence of harmonious passion, combined with HRM practices, exerts a positive influence on employee leadership. This impact is reflected not only in commitment, motivation and performance, but also in the way these individuals interact with colleagues, which positively influences their efficiency as leaders.

In the same vein, Koednok and Sungsanit (2018) and Salas-Vallina et al. (2020) draw particular attention to HRM practices that focus specifically on the well-being of employees, highlighting these instead of practices exclusively oriented towards organizational objectives. For these authors, it is important to prioritize a leadership style that values well-being and development of employees, which can positively influence the way and style of leadership, as they are encouraged to adopt a more human-centred approach. The study by Salas-Vallina et al. (2020) also highlights the positive effect of ethical leadership on employees' intrinsic motivation, which opens up space for innovative behaviours.

Finally, Gorgievski et al. (2014) reinforce the perspective that work passion can lead to different results in terms of entrepreneurial performance, varying depending on the type of passion experienced and the affect associated with it. Thus, engagement at work, managed by positive affect, encourages better entrepreneurial performance, while workaholism, more associated with negative affect, results in less favourable entrepreneurial performance. In this sense, Gorgievski and his collaborators call on leaders to pay attention to these possible states, suggesting that emotional regulation can constitute an important strategy for improving entrepreneurial and innovative performance, especially in the case of workaholics.

5.3 Work passion and innovation: differentiating factors for competitive advantage

Aiming for organizational excellence is a constant in today's business environment. Among the several factors that influence an organization's competitiveness, work passion and innovative behaviour emerge as central resources (Alhumoudi et al., 2022b; Jan et al., 2021; Udin, 2022). Therefore, companies are increasingly seeking to integrate dedicated and passionate employees, with a view to better organizational performance (Gorgievski et al., 2014). Several authors have explored the intrinsic relationship between employees' work passion, their innovative behaviour and the organization's ability to stand out in a competitive scenario. In this sense, it is possible to find a close relationship between innovation and work passion for work and competitiveness, as work passion can influence innovative and entrepreneurial behaviour (Gorgievski et al., 2014). Han et al. (2023) highlight the breadth of these factors for the success and sustainability of organizations. Subsequently, in the face of an increasingly challenging business world, innovative behaviour and work passion stand out as two critical factors, which emerge not only as pillars to boost business competitiveness, but are also considered the essential driver to boost all organizational development, being able to positively influence innovation and, consequently, create competitive value for the organization. When studying the relationship between CSR, work passion and innovative behaviour, Alhumoudi et al. (2022b) found that the positive perception of CSR by workers leads to an increase in work passion, which positively influence the innovative approach, which, in itself, represents a competitive advantage for organizations. It is possible to determine that employees who are passionate about their work tend to be more involved, creative and innovative, elements that contribute positively to the organization's competitiveness.

In essence, work passion is a broad and multifaceted phenomenon, which transcends simple professional motivation (Escamilla-Fajardo et al., 2021), which means that this type of passion is intrinsically linked to the constant search for improvements and innovations. Passionate teams often transcend productivity expectations and are often driven by the desire to find creative and ground-breaking solutions (Jan & Zainal, 2020), which contributes to strengthening competitiveness (Han et al., 2023). The high performance and commitment of employees who are passionate about their work result in a tangible increase in operational efficiency. Consequently, the intention and capacity to innovate is potentially developed and becomes a competitive differentiator for organizations seeking to stand out in dynamic markets. A company in which work teams not only carry out tasks but are also positively committed to structural objectives achieves more efficient results, charts paths of innovation and improves its ability to overcome market conditions (Luu, 2019), as well as gaining competitive advantage.

Innovative behaviour is a fundamental resource for the survival and success of modern organizations. The cognitive dynamics behind innovation, creativity,

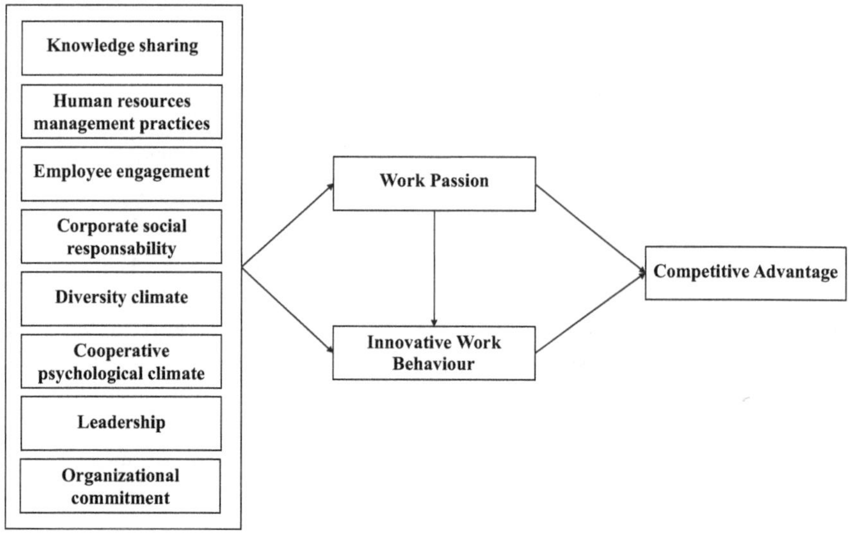

FIGURE 5.1 Conceptual model

critical thinking and openness to experimentation converge to create an environment conducive to the creation of innovative ideas (Escamilla-Fajardo et al., 2021; Han et al., 2023). In this connection, innovative behaviour can be considered a state of mind that permeates the entire organization, involving several areas and hierarchical levels (Salas-Vallina et al., 2020; Xiao et al., 2022). Also, it can be seen as an essential tool for operating in competitive markets (Escamilla-Fajardo et al., 2021). Hence, it is possible to assert that from the leadership of hierarchical elements to base employees, the innovative mentality and work passion are the elements that truly binds work teams in favour of the company's common objectives, leading them to overcome limits and challenges and maximize competitiveness and unique positioning in the business world.

Based on carefully scrutinized literature and as a systematization, the following conceptual model was created (Figure 5.1), which describes the relationship between the variables under study and the various factors listed.

Additionally, and based on the review of the set of publications included in this study, several theoretical frameworks were explored that elucidate the mechanisms through which passion for work influences innovative behaviours and competitive advantage. For enhanced organization and comprehension, the main theories were compiled in Table 5.1.

5.4 Discussion

Several theoretical approaches explore the relationship between work passion and innovative behaviours. Among these, the Dualist Model of Passion predominates, which identifies two types of passion, harmonious and obsessive, recognizing that

TABLE 5.1 Main theories

N	*Theory*	*Article example*
5	Dualistic Model of Passion (Vallerand et al., 2003) – postulates that passion can be divided into two distinct forms: harmonious passion and obsessive passion. This theory allows to analyse how different types of work passion can influence entrepreneurial performance and innovative behaviour.	Gong et al. (2020)
4	Self-determination theory (SDT) (Ryan & Deci, 2000) – this theory argues that intrinsic motivation, which arises from the satisfaction of basic psychological needs, such as autonomy, competence and relationships, leads to positive results such as well-being and work performance. Within the context of work passion and innovative behaviour, SDT highlights harmonious passion as an element of intrinsic motivation and emphasizes the importance of autonomy in promoting creativity and innovation.	Luu (2019)
2	Conservation of Resources Theory (Hobfoll, 1989) – supports the idea that employees use resources such as knowledge, skills and experience to improve their work performance. This theory determines that work passion can promote the performance of demanding tasks, expanding employees' cognitive abilities.	Udin (2022)
2	Social Exchange Theory (Thibaut & Kelley, 1959) – suggests that individuals seek to maximize benefits and minimize costs in their social interactions, acting based on a cost-benefit approach. In the current thematic framework, this theory provides an explanation of how employees, who develop passion for their work and show themselves to be innovative, can boost the organization's efficiency, quality, creativity and adaptability, making it more competitive.	Salas-Vallina et al. (2020)
1	Social Cognitive Theory (Bandura, 1986) – This theory highlights the interaction between personal, behavioural and environmental factors in human behaviour. Some of the fundamental principles defended by this theoretical model include self-efficacy, observational learning and self-regulation.	Jan et al. (2022)
1	Job Demands and Resources Model (Demerouti et al., 2001) – This model represents one of the main analytical structures that allows investigating the relationship between management practices aimed at employee well-being and innovative behaviour. The model highlights the importance of harmonizing work demands with available resources to promote employee well-being and performance.	Salas-Vallina et al. (2020)

not all passion is similar, and its effects on innovative behaviour may vary based on the nature of the passion experienced by the individual. Three other theories are among the most cited: (i) the Self-Determination Theory, which argues that passion results from the satisfaction of fundamental psychological needs, such as autonomy, competence and social relationships; (ii) the Conservation of Resources

Theory which, applied to work passion, highlights the importance of resources that foster passion and, consequently, innovative behaviours and (iii) the Social Exchange Theory, which argues that the quality of social relationships in the workplace can influence work passion and, consequently, innovative behaviour.

The analysis of the results enable to identify several factors that positively influence the relationship between work passion and innovative behaviours, namely knowledge sharing (Udin, 2022), CSR (Alhumoudi et al., 2022a), the climate of diversity (Luu, 2019), the cooperative psychological climate (Jan & Zainal, 2020), servant (Dalain, 2023; Jan et al., 2022), temporal (Xiao et al., 2022) and ethical leadership (Salas-Vallina et al., 2020), SSG (Han et al., 2023), HRM practices (e.g., performance recognition, autonomy, well-being, flexibility) (Koednok & Sungsanit, 2018; Salas-Vallina et al., 2020), work engagement (Gorgievski et al., 2014), organizational commitment (Alhumoudi et al., 2022b) and also the valuing innovation (Han et al., 2023) and entrepreneurial thinking (Flores-Pérez & Guevara, 2023; Koumproglou & Biginas, 2022). This set of factors allows to foresee the complexity and importance of multiple variables in this context with a view to innovation, a strategic tool to create competitive advantage.

In a broader approach, the reviewed literature, although scarce, provided a comprehensive framework of the dimensions of work passion and innovative behaviour, involving behavioural, affective, social and contextual dimensions. Therefore, the studies analysed become particularly relevant, as they deepen the understanding of innovative behaviour and explore the intrinsic factors associated with work passion. What is clear is that work passion is directly linked to a positive attitude, both of which are fundamental pillars for innovation.

Entrepreneurial behaviour is understood to be a stimulus that drives innovation, converting challenges into opportunities. Entrepreneurial behaviour is characterized by the search for opportune contexts, innovation and acceptance and transformation of risks, and appears as a direct manifestation of passion in the professional environment (Flores-Pérez & Guevara, 2023). Several entrepreneurship researchers argue that at the heart of this behaviour, work passion plays a substantial role, an intrinsic motivational force that encourages the search for new and creative ideas in the workplace and increases readiness to overcome obstacles (Alhumoudi et al., 2022a; Caza & Posner, 2022; Han et al., 2023; Jan & Zainal, 2020). Therefore, by being harmoniously passionate (Alhumoudi et al., 2022a; Jan & Zainal, 2020; Luu, 2019), employees achieve the necessary resources to boost and guide entrepreneurial thinking (Escamilla-Fajardo et al., 2021; Flores-Pérez & Guevara, 2023), feeding a continuous flow of positive emotional and cognitive resources (Xiao et al., 2022), which leads them to implement innovative projects (Han et al., 2023), and also optimizing their performance in daily work tasks. The reviewed literature is consensual on this point, recognizing that individuals who nurture a harmonious passion in performing their duties establish a deep emotional connection to their work (Jan & Zainal, 2020; Xiao et al., 2022) and demonstrate greater propensity to adopt an innovative stance in the workplace (Koednok & Sungsanit, 2018).

It is manifest that organizational dynamics are substantially influenced by leadership practices, which are determinant in the flourish of work passion, as well as in the emergence of innovative behaviours. By deepening the analysis in this conceptual domain, it is possible to verify that the leaders' work passion can be widespread among employees through emotional contagiousness (Xiao et al., 2022), consolidating their determining position as fundamental models of work passion. The literature stresses the premise that a leadership style that provides a fair and egalitarian relationship between leader and team members encourages the expression of innovative behaviours (Han et al., 2023). Consequently, there is also scientific consensus that both work passion and innovative attitudes in the workplace are distinctive attributes of successful leaders. Leaders who promote a dynamic and positive work environment, adopting a temporal (Xiao et al., 2022), servant (Dalain, 2023) or ethical (Salas-Vallina et al., 2020) perspective, are able, on the one hand, to create a breeding ground for expanding work passion with greater effectiveness and, on the other hand, encouraging work teams to more easily get involved and embark on challenging innovative projects. Also, autonomy, proactivity and resilience are dominant characteristics of passionate leaders (Dalain, 2023), which are decisive for the organization's competitive advantage. The determination and persistence of these professionals when faced with new challenges lead their teams to adopt the same behaviour, promoting experimentation and transforming organizational culture while simultaneously stimulating the sharing and implementation of new ideas. In other words, the emphasis on timing, service to others, ethics or resilience provides a solid basis for innovation, promoting an organizational culture that enhances creativity and the search for new and effective solutions, with a view to sustainable growth. These results suggest that the relationship between work passion, innovative behaviour and employee leadership creates a synergy that drives modern companies towards innovation and the future, as a way of ensuring a competitive advantage in the market.

5.5 Conclusion

In the contemporary business era, work passion and innovative behaviour are seen as essential pillars that support organizational success (Koednok & Sungsanit, 2018) and an increase in its competitive advantage. In doing so, as organizations face an increasingly dynamic business landscape, innovation capacity becomes an essential competitive differentiator (Alhumoudi et al., 2022b; Udin, 2022).

This chapter brings to light evidence supporting that work passion, specifically harmonious passion (e.g., Jan & Zainal, 2020; Xiao et al., 2022), can act as a powerful catalyst to foster a culture of innovation, motivating employees to be creative, to collaborate efficiently, to be more resilient and proactive in the face of challenges and to maintain a strong focus on the customer (Flores-Pérez & Guevara, 2023). Although there are still no robust studies that highlight which contextual and/or situational factors influence the development of harmonious and obsessive work passion, it is known that their effects can vary depending on a specific context (Jung & Sohn, 2022). What is known is that, according to Jan and Zainal (2020), an empowering organizational environment triggers harmonious passion and, consequently, innovative behaviour on the part of employees.

Dominant approaches, such as the Dualistic Model of Passion, Self-Determination Theory, Social Exchange Theory and Conservation of Resources Theory provide essential theoretical frameworks to understand the complex relationship between work passion, innovative behaviour and, consequently, develop and enhance organizational competitive advantage. Subsequently, several factors (e.g., knowledge sharing, human resources management practices, employee engagement, self-efficacy, corporate social responsibility, diversity climate, cooperative psychological climate, leadership, organizational commitment) were combined within the scope of this relationship, and recognized as an important influence on creativity and innovation. Of these, HRM practices predominated, followed by servant leadership and knowledge sharing. Therefore, understanding the multifaceted nature of work passion and identifying the variables that positively influence the relationship between this component and innovative behaviour has practical implications for organizations that are concerned with promoting a positive, creative and continuous improvement of environment with a view to contributing to competitive advantage.

The intrinsic relationship between passion, innovation and competitiveness is clear. Companies that cultivate environments where work passion is fostered and innovative behaviour is encouraged are those that emerge as leaders in their sectors. They not only respond to market demands but anticipate their needs (Flores-Pérez and Guevara, 2023). In an increasingly complex and volatile business scenario, work passion and innovative behaviour emerge as essential tools for organizational competitiveness, offering companies an advantage in achieving high performance in the market. In other words, business competitiveness, defined by an organization's potential to surpass competitors, is directly influenced by work passion and innovation (Han et al., 2023). These two driving forces, which interact synergistically, create an environment conducive to growth, differentiation and adaptation to constant change.

By way of conclusion, the results set out in this chapter highlight the critical importance of the strategic management of passion in the workplace, outlining practices that can be adopted by leaders to promote an advantageous context to innovation, entrepreneurship and employee well-being. In this context, leaders and managers are seen as a model and play a preponderant role in creating an organizational culture that fosters the emergence and consolidation of harmonious passion, which is an absolute essential and delivers a concrete competitive advantage. In doing so, they not only stimulate innovation and entrepreneurship but also significantly contribute to reducing the risks associated with obsessive passion, which can otherwise compromise the well-being and effectiveness (Alhumoudi et al., 2022a; Flores-Pérez & Guevara, 2023). Work passion influences employees' intrinsic interest in the work itself, as well as their performance and, consequently, the company's productivity will increase. In this sense, an organization that considers the plea for connectedness at work is paving the way for employees to show their skills and commit to the company's objectives, with a view to increasing the innovation and competitiveness of business.

5.5.1 Theoretical implications

This chapter suggests some theoretical implications. First, we further clarify the importance of the catalysing influence of work passion to promote innovative behaviour. Although the structure of knowledge is still not very robust, a systematization of the concepts and processes underlying the set of variables was developed, in order to deepen and expand understanding of the topic. In doing so, we add to the literature by offering a conceptual model composed of a structure that allows us to understand how elements (e.g., knowledge sharing, HRM practices, employee engagement, CSR, diversity climate, cooperative psychological climate, leadership and organizational commitment) can influence the relationship between work passion and innovative behaviour and contributing to the competitive advantage of organizations. Therefore, it is considered that the proposed model can constitute a valid starting point for carrying out future researches. In addition, by demonstrating the importance of these resources for the long-term value of companies, and by highlighting the positive effects aimed at competitive advantage, this chapter points to the need for work passion to be integrated as an important variable in theoretical models of organizational innovation.

Second, we explore an important pathway between work passion and innovative behaviour, whose goal is competitive advantage. The success and sustainability of organizations depend, to a large extent, on the organizational behaviours of employees, who work not only to obtain financial rewards, but to find something that is psychologically rewarding for them. To the best of authors' knowledge, this is the first work to present a theoretical model that integrates passion at work and innovation as strategies that drive competitive advantage. This finding enriches the literature, on the one hand, concerning the variables that a priori influence work passion and innovative behaviours and, on the other, how these variables determine business competitive advantage. The attempt to delve deeper into these complex interactions offers a more complete understanding of the mechanisms underlying work passion and through which it contributes to organizational success, as well as enabling the identification of effective strategies to promote a dynamic and innovative work environment.

5.5.2 Practical implications

From a practical perspective, this chapter is valuable because it allows organizational leaders and managers to better understand their decisions and its impact, in order to create a work environment that encourages work passion and stimulates innovation. First, the insights indicate that investing in an organizational culture that promotes passion and values new and creative ideas is considered an important resource for the long-term success of organizations in the current competitive scenario. Second, we suggest that companies' human resources play a preponderant role in obtaining competitive advantage. For instance, companies that value and encourage values such as harmonious passion can use it as a leadership practice aimed at achieving the company's goals. Third, we propose that a company should foster passionate workers. Passionate teams have differentiated resources to achieve success, both individual and organizational. Being harmoniously passionate about work offers bilateral advantages: on an individual level, on the one hand, such as well-being, motivation, recognition, progression, material and non-material rewards, and at the business level on the other, such as increased productivity and performance, development of innovation to maintain competitive advantage, long-term value.

References

Alhumoudi, R., Singh, S., & Ahmad, S. (2022a). Perceived corporate social responsibility and innovative work behavior: the role of passion at work. *International Journal of Organizational Analysis, 31*(6), 2239–2251. https://doi.org/10.1108/IJOA-11-2021-3042

Alhumoudi, R., Singh, S., Caputo, F., Riso, T., & Iandolo, F. (2022b). Corporate social responsibility and innovative work behavior: is it a matter of perceptions? *Corporate Social Responsibility and Environmental Management, 29*(6), 2030–2037. https://doi.org/10.1002/csr.2299

Anderson, N., Potočnik, K., & Zhou, J. (2014). Innovation and creativity in organizations: a state-of-the-science review, prospective commentary, and guiding framework. *Journal of Management, 40*(5), 1297–1333.

Bandura, A., & National Inst of Mental Health. (1986). *Social Foundations of Thought and Action: A Social Cognitive Theory*. Englewood Cliffs: Prentice-Hall, Inc.

Birkeland, I., & Nerstad, C. (2016). Incivility is (not) the very essence of love: passion for work and incivility instigation. *Journal of Occupational Health Psychology, 21*(1), 77–90.

Caza, A., & Posner, B. (2022). How and when does grit influence leaders' behavior? *Leadership & Organization Development Journal, 40*(1), 124–134. https://doi.org/10.1108/LODJ-06-2018-0209

Chen, C., Chen, S., & Tsai, P. (2020). Job passion in the context of green restaurant: environmental stewardship orientation and job autonomy as antecedents. *Journal of General Management, 46*(1), 16–25. https://doi.org/10.1177/0306307020911177

Chummar, S., Singh, P., & Ezzedeen, S. R. (2019). Exploring the differential impact of work passion on life satisfaction and job performance via the work–family interface. *Personnel Review, 48*(5), 1110–1119. https://doi.org/10.1108/PR-02-2017-0033

Dalain, A. (2023). Nurturing employee engagement at workplace and organizational innovation in time of crisis with moderating effect of servant leadership. *SAGE Open, 13*(2). https://doi.org/10.1177/21582440231175150

Demerouti, E., Bakker, A. B., Nachreiner, F., & Schaufeli, W. B. (2001). The job demands-resources model of burnout. *Journal of Applied Psychology, 86*(3), 499–512. https://doi.org/10.1037/0021-9010.86.3.499

Escamilla-Fajardo, P., Alguacil, M., & Gómez-Tafalla, A. (2021). Effects of entrepreneurial orientation and passion for work on performance variables in sports clubs. *Sustainability, 13*(5). https://doi.org/10.3390/su13052920

Fang, Y., Chen, J., Zhang, X., Dai, X., & Tsai, F. (2020). The impact of inclusive talent development model on turnover intention of new generation employees: the mediation of work passion. *International Journal of Environmental Research and Public Health, 17*. https://doi.org/10.3390/ijerph17176054

Flores-Pérez, J., & Guevara, R. (2023). Mediating effect of entrepreneurial passion in the relationship between entrepreneurial orientation and innovative work behavior. *Measuring Business Excellence, 27*(3), 483–500. http://doi.org/10.1108/MBE-10-2022-0126

Fuller, J., & Marler, L. (2009). Change driven by nature: a meta-analytic review of the proactive personality literature. *Journal of Vocational Behavior, 75*(3), 329–345. http://doi.org/10.1016/j.jvb.2009.05.008

Gong, Z., Zhang, Y., Ma, J., Liu, Y., & Zhao, Y. (2020). Effects of work passion on turnover intention for Chinese government employees: the dualistic model of passion perspective. *Journal of Management and Organization, 26*(4), 502–518. https://doi.org/10.1017/jmo.2017.71

Gorgievski, M., Moriano, J., & Baker, A. (2014). Relating work engagement and workaholism to entrepreneurial performance. *Journal of Managerial Psychology, 29*(2), 106–121. http://doi.org/10.1108/JMP-06-2012-0169

Han, Z., Ni, M., Hou, C., & Zhang, Y. (2023). Effects of superior-subordinate Guanxi on employee innovative behavior: the role of follower dependency and work passion. *Behavioral Sciences, 13*(8). https://doi.org/10.3390/bs13080645

Ho, V., Kong, D., Lee, C., Dubrcuil, P., & Forest, J. (2018). Promoting harmonious work passion among unmotivated employees: a two-nation investigation of the compensatory function of cooperative psychological climate. *Journal of Vocational Behavior, 106*, 112–125. https://doi.org/10.1016/j.jvb.2018.01.005

Hobfoll, S. E. (1989). Conservation of resources: A new attempt at conceptualizing stress. *American Psychologist, 44*(3), 513–524. https://doi.org/10.1037/0003-066X.44.3.513

Jan, G., & Zainal, S. (2020). Linking cooperative psychological climate, harmonious passion, and servicing empowerment with innovative work behavior. *Asian Academy of Management Journal, 25*(2). https://doi.org/10.21315/aamj2020.25.2.8

Jan, G., Zainal, S., & Lee, M. (2021). HRM practices and innovative work behavior within the hotel industry in Pakistan: harmonious passion as a mediator. *Journal of Human Resources in Hospitality & Tourism, 20*(4), 512–541. https://doi.org/10.1080/15332845.2021.1959803

Jan, G., Zainal, S. R. M., & Panezai, B. A. (2022). Service innovative work behavior in the hotel firms: the role of servant leadership and harmonious passion. *Journal of Human Behavior in the Social Environment, 32*(5), 646–662. https://doi.org/10.1080/10911359.2021.1944419

Janssen, O. (2000). Job demands, perceptions of effort-reward fairness and innovative work behaviour. *Journal of Occupational and Organizational Psychology, 73*, 287–302. http://doi.org/10.1348/096317900167038

Jung, Y., & Sohn, Y. (2022). Does work passion benefit or hinder employee's career commitment? The mediating role of work-family interface and the moderating role of autonomy support. *PLoS One, 17*. https://doi.org/10.1371/journal.pone.0269298

Kleysen, R., & Street, C. (2001). Toward a multi-dimensional measure of individual innovative behavior. *Journal of Intellectual Capital, 2*(3), 284–296. https://doi.org/10.1108/EUM0000000005660

Koednok, S., & Sungsanit, M. (2018). The influence of multilevel factors of human resource practices on innovative work behavior. *International Journal of Behavioral Science, 13*(1), 37–55.

Koumproglou, A., & Biginas, K. (2022). Exploring the unique start-up organisational culture. In Biginas, K., Sindakis, S., Koumproglou, A., Sarantinos, V., & Wyer, P. (Eds.), *Small business management and control of the uncertain external environment (advanced strategies in entrepreneurship, education and ecology)* (pp. 59–67). Leeds: Emerald Publishing Limited. https://doi.org/10.1108/978-1-83909-624-220211004

Kwon, K., & Kim, T. (2020). An integrative literature review of employee engagement and innovative behaviour: revisiting the JD-R model. *Human Resource Management Review, 30*(2). https://doi.org/10.1016/j.hrmr.2019.100704

Lambriex-Schmitz, P., Van der Klink, M., Beausaert, S., Bijker, M., & Segers, M. (2020). Towards successful innovations in education: development and validation of a multi-dimensional innovative work behaviour instrument. *Vocations and Learning 13*, 313–340. https://doi.org/10.1007/s12186-020-09242-4

Liu, Z., Jiang, Y., Yao, Z., Liu, X., Zhao, L., & Zhang, X. (2020). Congruence in career calling and employees' innovation performance: work passion as a mediator. *Chinese Management Studies.* http://doi.org/10.1108/CMS-12-2019-0427

Luu, T. (2019). Can diversity climate shape service innovative behavior in Vietnamese and Brazilian tour companies? The role of work passion. *Tourism Management, 72*, 326–339. https://doi.org/10.1016/j.tourman.2018.12.011

Luu, T. (2021). Can human resource flexibility disentangle innovative work behavior among hospitality employees? The roles of harmonious passion and regulatory foci. *International Journal of Contemporary Hospitality Management, 33*(12), 4258–4285. https://doi.org/10.1108/IJCHM-02-2021-0276

Malchelosse, K., Houlfort, N., Lavoie, C.-E., & Masson, R. (2023). The role of resilience and psychological needs satisfaction in the relationship between passion for work and work-life enrichment. *Current Psychology.* http://doi.org/10.1007/s12144-023-04846-0

Muneeb, H., Akhtar, N., Moazzam, A., SobiaTufail, H., Shahid, A., & Shahid, J. (2017). The impact of harmonious passion on intention to leave through work engagement in banking sector of Lahore, Pakistan. *European Online Journal of Natural and Social Sciences, 6*(2), 169–177.

Mustafa, M., Ramos, H., & Zainal, S. (2020). Determining nonfamily employees' job satisfaction and turnover intentions: the roles of job autonomy and work passion. *Journal of Family Business Management.* https://doi.org/10.1108/JFBM-08-2020-0079

Nimon, K., & Zigarmi, D. (2015). The work cognition inventory: initial evidence of construct validity for the revised form. *Journal of Career Assessment, 23*(1), 117–136. http://doi.org/10.1177/1069072714523241

Niu, W., Yuan, Q., Qian, S., & Liu, Z. (2018). Authentic leadership and employee job behaviors: the mediating role of relational and organizational identification and the moderating role of LMX. *Current Psychology, 37*(4), 982–994. https://doi.org/10.1007/s12144-018-9937-0

Noreña-Chavez, D., & Guevara, R. (2020). Entrepreneurial passion and self-efficacy as factors explaining innovative behavior: a mediation model. *International Journal of Economics and Business Administration, 8*(3), 352–373.

Ryan, R.M., & Deci, E.L. (2000). Self-determination theory and the facilitation of intrinsic motivation, social development, and well-being. *American Psychologist, 55*(1), 68–78. https://doi.org/10.1037/0003-066X.55.1.68

Salas-Vallina, A., Pozo, M., & Fernandez-Guerrero, R. (2020). New times for HRM? Well-being oriented management (WOM), harmonious work passion and innovative work behaviour. *Employee Relations, 42*(3), 561–581. https://doi.org/10.1108/ER-04-2019-0185

Thibaut, J. W., & Kelley, H. H. (1959). *The Social Psychology of Groups*. New York: John Wiley.

Udin, U. (2022). Knowledge sharing and innovative work behaviour: testing the role of entrepreneurial passion in distribution channel. *Journal of Distribution Science, 20*(2), 79–89. http://dx.doi.org/10.15722/jds.20.02.202202.79

Vallerand, R. (2012). The role of passion in sustainable psychological well-being. *Research and Practice, 2*, 1–21. http://doi.org/10.1186/2211-1522-2-1

Vallerand, R. (2015). *The psychology of passion*. New York: Oxford University Pres.

Vallerand, R., Blanchard, C., Mageau, G., Koestner, R., Ratelle, C., & Léonard, M. (2003). Les passions de l'âme: on obsessive and harmonious passion. *Journal of Personality and Social Psychology, 85*, 756–767. http://doi.org/10.1037/0022-3514.85.4.756

Xiao, H., Zhang, Z., & Zhang, L. (2022). Is temporal leadership always beneficial? The role of job passion and synchrony preference. *Personnel Review, 51*(1), 299–316. https://doi.org/10.1108/PR-02-2020-0078

Zigarmi, D., Nimon, K., Houson, D., Witt, D., & Diehl, J. (2009). Beyond engagement: toward a framework and operational definition for employee work passion. *Human Resource Development Review, 8*(3), 300–326. http://doi.org/10.1177/1534484309338171

6

CUSTOMER-CENTRIC ORGANIZATION

Creating customer value for competitive advantage

Mika Yrjölä and Harri Hokkanen

6.1 Introduction

Competitiveness emerges as interplay of customer needs, competitor offerings, and the organization's unique capabilities (Collis & Rukstad, 2008; Ferreira et al., 2022). While these factors and many others shape the competitiveness of an organization, it is eventually the customers who make the critical choice of whether to purchase the offering and enter a customer relationship with the organization. If the customer does not perceive meaningful differences between competing offerings, then they will not be willing to pay more for such offerings and likely choose the cheapest one or the one they purchased last time (Day & Moorman, 2010; Do & Mai, 2020). In other words, customer perceptions ultimately decide the competitiveness of an organization (Yrjölä, 2021). Customer-centricity, an organization's tendency and capability to emphasize the importance of customers with the assumption that creating customer value is a priority for organizational success in the long term (Grizzle et al., 2009; Korunka et al., 2007; Lamberti, 2013; Morgan et al., 2018; Yrjölä et al., 2023), therefore, is a key concept for understanding organizational performance and competitiveness.

Customer-centricity is in the vogue with many companies highlighting customer-oriented values and customer experience in their communications. Nonetheless, many organizations remain at the buzzword level without being able to connect customer-centricity to how the organization operates (Yrjölä, 2021). This is dangerous, as it can leave customers, employees, and other stakeholders feeling betrayed. Moreover, inadequate understanding of customers will mean that the organization is at risk of becoming irrelevant in the eyes of its customers and ultimately lose its ability to operate in the market (Day & Moorman, 2013). Hence, in this chapter we outline and discuss the ways in which customer-centricity can

DOI: 10.4324/9781032695969-7

improve the competitiveness of organizations. We argue that customer-centricity moves the focus of organizations towards customer value creation, because the objective of customer-centricity is to create a competitive advantage for the business or to ensure long-term profitability in general (e.g., Deshpandé et al., 1993; Narver & Slater, 1990; Shah et al., 2006).

Unsurprisingly, customer-centricity has spurred much research (Morgan et al., 2018). Multiple conceptualizations and definitions exist in the literature. For example, authors have proposed terms such as customer-centricity (e.g., Chang et al., 2010; Gurău et al., 2003; Lamberti, 2013; Shah et al., 2006; Sheth et al., 2000; Trainor et al., 2014), customer orientation (e.g., Angulo-Ruiz et al., 2014; Bettencourt & Brown, 2003; Deshpandé et al., 1993; Hartline et al., 2000; Homburg et al., 2000; Hortinha et al., 2011; Kohli & Jaworski, 1990; Narver & Slater, 1990; Schwepker, 2003), customer intimacy (e.g., Treacy & Wiersema, 1993), and customer focus (e.g., Lindic & DaSilva, 2011; Said et al., 2009; Zhao et al., 2001) to refer to an organization's or individual's tendency to stress the importance of customers for success. It should be noted that customer-centricity can refer to an individual or organization (Whelan et al., 2010). Individual customer-centricity is an employees' or managers' tendency to think and act in ways that recognize and meet individual customer needs (Brown et al., 2002), while organizational customer-centricity involves the conditions (e.g., atmosphere, culture, and practices) that either promote or hinder individuals' customer-oriented attitudes and behaviours (Grizzle et al., 2009). For the purposes of this chapter, we use the term 'customer-centricity' to denote an organization's tendency to emphasize the importance of customers in their decisions, practices, and ways of thinking.

Customer-centric organizations have different practices, vocabularies, and culture than their product or firm-centric counterparts (Ramani & Kumar, 2008). Namely, customer-centric organizations are characterized by structures, cultures, and processes that emphasize the importance of customers. First, a customer-centric structure is one that is structured around the needs of different customer groups or segments (Homburg et al., 2000; Mukerjee, 2013). Such a structure enables firms to overcome functional silos and share customer information (Wang & Feng, 2012). Second, organizational culture can also be customer-centric. This refers to managers' and employees' shared beliefs (mental models) and practices involving customers (Chang et al., 2010; Hult et al., 2005; Narver & Slater, 1990; Slater & Narver, 2000; Strong & Harris, 2004). Third, customer-centricity allows organizations to gather and manage customer and market information more efficiently (Hult et al., 2005), thus improving customer relationship management processes (Trainor et al., 2014), enabling more durable customer relationships (Rapp et al., 2010), and improving overall performance (Vorhies & Morgan, 2005).

The rest of this chapter is organized as follows. We first discuss the relationship between customer-centricity and competitiveness. We discuss studies that have shown how customer-centricity is linked to improved organizational performance, while also trying to outline some boundary conditions of this relationship.

Next, we argue that customer-centricity improves organizational competitiveness and performance through two mechanisms: (1) through enabling organizations to create superior value in relation to competition, and (2) through enabling organizations to better adapt to market changes. After describing these mechanisms, we put forward suggestions for managers that aim to adopt customer-centricity in their organizations before moving on to spot the possible dangers and risks of customer-centricity. A final section concludes the chapter.

6.2 Customer-centricity and performance

Previous studies show that customer-centric organizations orientation tend to be rewarded with superior financial performance (e.g., Hortinha et al., 2011; Narver & Slater, 1990; Shah et al., 2006; Ziggers & Henseler, 2016), although with some caveats (e.g., Noble et al., 2002). This performance is due to an improved ability of customer-centric organizations to create customer value. Thus, the logic is that organizations that are better at understanding customers and turning this insight into offerings that better match customer needs are thus able to create more value for customers, which is rewarded by improved financial performance (e.g., Kohli & Jaworski, 1990; Korunka et al., 2007; Lamberti, 2013; Lindic & DaSilva, 2011; Narver & Slater, 1990; Sheth et al., 2000; Slater & Narver, 2000; Treacy & Wiersema, 1993; Zhao et al., 2001; Zhou & Li, 2010).

Customer-centricity brings multiple benefits to organizations. Companies, who are judged more customer-centric by their customers, have better financial performance (Deshpandé et al., 1993). It should be emphasized that the evaluations made by customers mattered here: the authors found significant differences between customers and suppliers on evaluations about the supplier's level of customer-centricity (Deshpandé et al., 1993). Financial performance effects are found both on the short and long terms (Angulo-Ruiz et al., 2014) with those organizations that adopt customer-centricity earlier benefitting the most (Kumar et al., 2011). Moreover, companies that are better able to quickly respond to changes benefit more from the positive performance effects of customer-centricity (Hult et al., 2005). In the banking sector, customer-centricity and the resulting value created for customers increase customer satisfaction, customer acquisition, retention, and cross-selling (Sahi et al., 2018). Customer-centricity can also improve marketing performance (Vorhies et al., 2011), for example, return on advertising (ROA) (Morgan et al., 2009). Beyond financial performance, customer-centricity can also allow the organization to improve service quality (Said et al., 2009) and innovation capabilities (Hortinha et al., 2011). In surveys on the computer and electronics industries, customer-centricity improves customer perceptions of value, and this effect was stronger in conditions where customer demands were higher (Bharadwaj & Dong, 2014).

It should be noted that customer-centricity isn't a fix-all, but rather there is an optimal level of customer-centricity. Crick et al. (2022) point out in relation to their analysis that maintaining customer-centricity is expensive, especially for SMEs, as it involves large investments in market research, advertising, and giving product samples to customers. Previous studies have shown that the optimal mix of customer-centricity and firm-centricity likely to vary by industry, economic conditions, and country (Saeed et al., 2015; Zhou & Li, 2010). For instance, customer-centricity can contribute to better innovation outcomes in high-tech industries, while firm centricity is more effective in low-tech industries (Saeed et al., 2015). In conditions of uncertain demand, companies might be wiser to invest in technology-centric initiatives rather than customer-centric ones, whereas customer-centricity becomes more important when demand is high (Zhou & Li, 2010). Similarly, Noble et al. (2002) have also found evidence of competitor orientation sometimes being the better strategy for improving financial and market performance. Further, Zhou et al. (2007) examine the relative payoffs associated with either being oriented towards customers or competitors. In their analysis of global hotel firms, they find that customer-centricity has better payoffs in contexts characterized as economically developed and featuring good business conditions, greater resource availability, and demanding customers. Being competitor-oriented, on the other hand, is a better strategy in markets that are developing and face resource scarcity. In a follow-up study, Dev et al. (2009) also find that in cases where investing in customer-centricity has a higher payoff, focusing on competitors would lead to a decrease in performance. Moreover, investments in customer-centricity can lower performance if the conditions otherwise favour a competitor-based strategy (Dev et al., 2009). However, in a study on the banking sector, a mixture of customer and competitor-centricity was found beneficial for performance (Sahi et al., 2016).

Thus, the link between customer-centricity and performance involves important nuances and boundaries, including industry, economic conditions, and other market characteristics. We next turn to two key mechanisms through which customer-centricity allows organizations to achieve competitiveness and superior performance. These are customer value creation and adaptation.

6.3 Customer-centricity and customer value

Customer-centricity improves organizational competitiveness and performance via enabling organizations to create superior value in relation to competition. Customer-centric organizations are geared towards customer value creation via being able to translate customer needs into effective value propositions. Thus, customer-centric organizations think in terms of customer value. Customer value involves aspects that customers perceive as meaningful and important. Customer value therefore addresses how and why customers choose certain products over others, and why they become loyal to organizations, enabling them to succeed (Kumar & Reinartz, 2016). Strategically, customer value is used as a frame of reference and useful language. It allows managers to shift their attention from internal quality standards to how customers eventually perceive the organization in relation to its competitors.

Rather than relying on easy-to-measure metrics, such as number of defects per unit, occurrences of process errors, or ratio of shipments made on time, it forces organizational members to consider how customers actually make inferences about product quality (Yrjölä et al., 2018). This could lead to insights about how to improve various factors, such as customer service, market positioning, and price image.

Companies propose value to their customers in the form of customer value propositions (CVPs). A CVP is defined as "a competitive statement of the dimension of value offered to a specific group of customers, the ways in which the firm creates value, and reasons for customers to select the firms' offering" (Yrjölä, 2015, p. 30). It thus involves the decision of what kind of value the firm creates for its customers (Anderson et al., 2006; Rintamäki et al., 2007). Moreover, a CVP is a key element of any business model. It specifies the intended customer segment or market, the offering, and types of customer relationships that the organization wants to achieve (Battistella et al., 2017; Osterwalder & Pigneur, 2013).

Successful CVPs involve benefits and sacrifices that are most relevant to customers and uniquely different from competition. For instance, many companies are tapping into the rapidly growing markets for second-hand products, and these companies highlight the unique value associated with these items compared to newly purchased goods. The unique benefits include lower price points, large assortments, and a chance to promote a sustainable lifestyle. Further, competition between second-hand companies is harsh as more and more companies enter the market. To achieve competitiveness, a second-hand fashion company, Zadaa, has introduced their "Connecting wardrobes" CVP to underline the peer-to-peer and social aspects of second-hand commerce. Their app lets users browse fashion items by size and secures the payments between buyers and sellers, thus reducing the risk perceptions commonly associated with peer-to-peer transactions. As an alternative approach, Netflea.com is focusing on sellers of second-hand clothes via their CVP. They enable the sellers to ship items to their logistics warehouse in bulk and the company handles the selling, thus increasing the convenience of peer-to-peer transactions.

CVPs have both internal and external functions. Externally, CVPs are used to position the brand in relation to competitors and customer needs (Day & Moorman, 2010; Johnson et al., 2008). Based on managers' assumptions, expectations, and choices regarding, for instance, revenue, customer behaviour, and competitive aspects (Casadesus-Masanell & Ricart, 2010; Teece, 2009), CVPs allow managers to explore market opportunities and consider how internal capabilities can be matched with these opportunities (Doganova & Eyquem-Renault, 2009; Teece, 2010). Internally, the proposition made to customers is used to guide organizational efforts and investments to guarantee that the promise can be kept. Customer-centric organizations invest in initiatives that promise to improve value for customers, while eliminating any elements that do not impact customer perceptions of value (Maklan et al., 2017). In sum, customer-centric organizations think and act in terms of customer value, which enables them to formulate effective CVPs that customers are willing to pay for and that are out of reach of competitors.

6.4 Customer-centricity and market adaptation

Customer-centricity improves organizational competitiveness and performance via enabling organizations to better adapt to market changes, such as evolving customer needs, than their competitors. Literature on strategic management stresses the importance of organizations to constantly change and adapt to ensure their survival. Many organizational transformations are indeed driven by external rather than internal pressure. These external drivers create internal pressure on organizations to develop new capabilities. From this perspective, customer-centricity is about transforming the organization to be more in line with the marketplace reality, especially customer preferences (Day & Moorman, 2010).

Without customer-centricity, organizations focus on their products and internal matters, neglecting customers, and the market more broadly. While product – or firm-centric thinking in the form of considering the organization's unique strengths, such as valuable resources, superior goods or distinct capabilities is necessary (Hooley et al., 2001), it typically dominates organizational decision-making, leaving customers often neglected. This is problematic because a one-sided focus on current strengths may lead the organization astray. Possible negative outcomes include unawareness of own competitive vulnerabilities, lateness in spotting emerging marketplace changes, and path dependency that can hinder the ability to adapt to change.

Customer-centric thinking shifts attention towards the organization's external environment and includes activities such as sensing and interpreting market signals, identifying emerging consumer trends, and anticipating competitor behaviour (Payne et al., 2008; Saeed et al., 2015). Customer insight, knowledge about the customer that is valuable for the firm (Said et al., 2015; Smith et al., 2006), is seen as a valuable resource for customer-centric organizations (Day, 1994; Greenley et al., 2005; Hooley et al., 2001; Saeed et al., 2015). It allows the organization to anticipate, influence, and meet marketplace changes by developing new capabilities and offerings (Day & Moorman, 2010). In other words, customer insight will allow organizations to understand how their customers perceive its current CVP (Day & Moorman, 2013) and to develop new CVPs so that the organization is better positioned in relation to customers' actual needs (Day & Moorman, 2010). Further, knowledge and understanding about customers is typically tacit and closely held in companies, making it immune to competitive imitation and acquisition (Krasnikov & Jayachandran, 2008).

The Danish toy manufacturer Lego serves as an illustrative example of customer insight used to develop new offerings. For their Lego Friends product line aimed at girls five years and older, they undertook extended market research including ethnographic studies of play and hundreds of testing and feedback sessions with kids and their parents. This learning process generated important insights, such as the importance of storytelling, role-playing, and social interaction for how girls play with toys. These insights had major impacts on the design of Lego toys, including re-design of the minifigure characters, sets with more detailed interiors and customization opportunities. Thus, customer insight enabled the company to expand their customer base with new offerings.

Finally, customer-centric organizations typically see customer and market insight processes as strategically important capabilities that should rarely be outsourced or conducted in by a function far removed from strategic decision-making. An overreliance on outsourced intelligence or readily available data might be problematic. If organizations solely rely on information that is easy to measure and apply, their decisions are likely to become biased over time (Du et al., 2021). For instance, organizational learning can be limited if the commission for market research is made to answer a predetermined question. Day and Moorman (2010) warn that such practices will only reinforce existing managerial mental models of customers.

6.5 Adopting customer-centricity

Adopting customer-centricity in their own organizations is no easy task for managers. Indeed, previous research has demonstrated that managers face difficulties in putting themselves in their customers' shoes. These efforts are hindered by: (1) existing mental models, (2) lack of exposure to customers, and (3) prevailing organizational norms and practices related to structure and metrics.

First, managers' mental models – their internal representations and assumptions of the world – are likely to be biased and slow down adoption of customer-centricity. Mental models determine how individuals make choices and investment decisions (Adner & Helfat, 2003; Narayanan et al., 2011; Strandvik et al., 2014), and thus also influence how managers make sense of such strategic issues as customer value creation (Holmlund et al., 2017) and how they eventually design and communicate CVPs (Yrjölä et al., 2018). As an example, mental models influence organizational priorities, such as whether to pursue customer satisfaction and retention or cost reduction (Rust et al., 2016). As these mental models are difficult to articulate and are generally taken for granted, it is difficult to change a firm-centric mental model into a customer-centric one (Day & Moorman, 2010). Accordingly, studies have shown that managers struggle to understand their customers (Hult et al., 2017). In one study, managers were shown to project their own preferences instead of the customers' preferences into marketing decisions (Hattula et al., 2015). In another study, managers both overestimated the level of their customers' satisfaction and loyalty, while underestimating how much customers' perceptions of quality influence their satisfaction (Hult et al., 2017).

Second, one likely cause for the findings related to managerial difficulties in adopting a customer-centric viewpoint is the limited top management spends on interacting with customers. In effect, other stakeholders might be more visible and closer to executives than customers. In many cases, there are multiple organizational layers between top management and customers, meaning that any signals from customers will become filtered and distorted on their way to strategic discussions. Alarmingly, an American study reported that, on average, chief executive officers (CEOs) spend as little as 3% of their time with customers, although the time spent with customers varied greatly among CEOs (Porter & Nohria, 2018). Thus, top management spends more time talking to consultants than customers (Yrjölä, 2021). Direct contact with customers would ensure an independent and less biased source of information about market conditions and the organization's competitiveness (Porter & Nohria, 2018). To remedy the issue, both practitioners and scholars recommend managerial immersion into the market reality, observing and talking to customers (e.g., Porter & Nohria, 2018; Rust et al., 2010). To illustrate, the global logistics operator DHL introduced a co-creation process with customers, where customers helped to generate new innovations and concepts. One outcome was the "Parcelcopter" drone that delivers parcels to remote and geographically challenging areas. Although the customer co-creation concept initially met with scepticism internally, DHL has not only improved customer satisfaction but also reduced research and development costs.

Third, Rust et al. (2010, p. 2) note aptly that "companies are set up to market products rather than cultivate customers." This is evident from organizational structure and titles that reflect products rather than customer needs. Companies organized around products instead of customer segments will be tuned to optimize product profitability at the cost of customer relationship profitability. Moreover, customer-centric organizations are less hesitant to partner with competitors if it will help them create more value for their customers. In firm-centric organizations, such initiatives would be unthinkable as competitors are regarded with suspicion and jealousy (Yrjölä, 2021). Perhaps the most troubling practices relate to the metrics used in organizations (Shah et al., 2006). A key question to reflect upon is what is being measured: the product (e.g., features and quality), the competitors (e.g., market share), or the customers (e.g., satisfaction)? We therefore encourage organizations to adopt customer-centric metrics complemented with 'thick data' (i.e., contextual and nuanced data on observed customer behaviour), such as ethnographic studies.

In sum, customer-centricity is a strategic issue that should be addressed by top management. Previous research has widely demonstrated that top management commitment is the single most important predictor of customer-centricity in an organization (e.g., Kirca et al., 2005; Lamberti, 2013; Shah et al., 2006). Nonetheless, implementing customer-centricity cannot be done solely as a top-down, hierarchical process. An effective approach is to rely on frontline employees who are interacting with customers, as these employees typically have vital knowledge and observations about what customers value (Hartline et al., 2000; Lam et al., 2010). Moreover, managers need to carefully communicate expectations regarding employee behaviour and goals, because vague expressions related to acting in a customer-centric way while also pushing to increase revenue might lead to role conflict or ambiguity for employees (Bettencourt & Brown, 2003).

6.6 The dangers of customer-centricity

While the benefits of customer-centricity for organizational competitiveness are well documented, it naturally also involves risks and other caveats. Thus, at the end of the day, managers are left to decide how customer-centric their organization should be (Yrjölä, 2021). First, customer-centricity might be inefficient, if too many resources and capabilities are devoted to gathering market intelligence and understanding customer preferences (Yrjölä et al., 2018). Customer heterogeneity can thus lead to inefficiencies, if the organization cannot prioritize some customer groups over others and ends up trying to serve a wide range of outside stakeholders. Second, choosing the right customers to focus on might prove difficult, as customers can vary greatly in terms of profitability and service costs. Moreover, focusing solely on customers might create problems if other stakeholders suffer as a result (Simons, 2014). Excessive customer-centricity can cause firms to overemphasize current customer needs instead of analysing long-term market trends (Grewal & Tansuhai, 2001) or monitor competitor behaviour (O'Dwyer & Gilmore, 2019). Third, neglecting of unique resources and capabilities can endanger the organization's competitive advantage (Yrjölä, 2021). All of these are also complicated by the fact that managerial mental models are difficult to detect (Day & Moorman, 2010).

6.7 Summary and conclusion

6.7.1 An integrative framework of customer-centricity

In this chapter, we have introduced customer-centricity as a key construct for understanding the competitiveness of organizations. We have discussed studies that have shown how customer-centricity is linked to improved organizational performance, while also outlining some boundary conditions of this relationship. We argue that customer-centricity improves organizational competitiveness and performance through two mechanisms: (1) through enabling organizations to create superior value in relation to competition, and (2) through enabling organizations to better adapt to market changes. We also put forth suggestions for managers aiming to adopt customer-centricity in their organizations, while also reminding of the potential pitfalls of customer-centricity.

In Figure 6.1, we integrate the above discussion into a framework of customer-centricity. First, the framework summarizes the findings of previous studies on the factors affecting the adoption of customer-centricity: mental models, exposure to customers, organizational norms, and top management commitment. Second, the framework outlines how customer-centricity improves organizational competitiveness through the two aforementioned mechanisms of value creation and market adaptation. Finally, we also propose a number of moderators to the relationship between customer-centricity and competitiveness. These moderators are based on our reading and interpretation of previous research results.

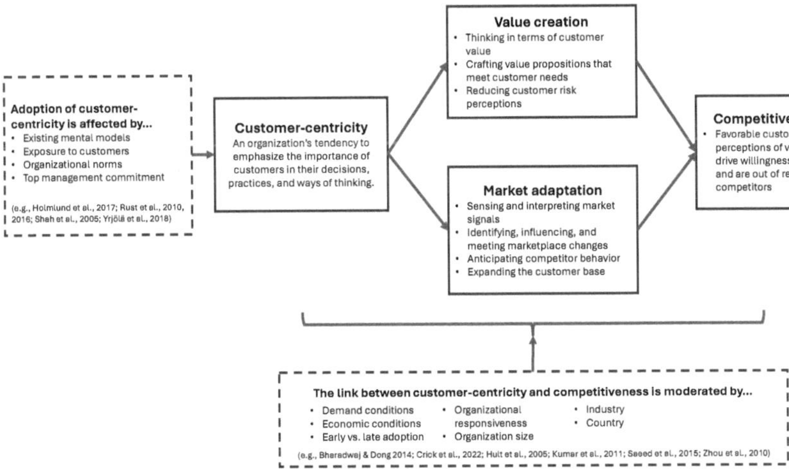

FIGURE 6.1 An integrative framework of customer-centricity.

Source: Authors' own elaboration.

6.7.2 Theoretical and practical implications

We put forth a number of theoretical implications. First, while previous research has identified factors that affect the adoption and implementation of customer-centricity (e.g., mental models, exposure to customers, top management commitment), little is known about the actual process through which organizations eventually change their decision-making, practices, and ways of thinking to be more customer-centric. Therefore, we call for in-depth studies on different organizations going through this transformation to map out the mechanisms and processes of customer-centricity adoption. Second, our framework identifies two key mechanisms (i.e., customer value creation and adaptation) through which customer-centricity allows organizations to achieve competitiveness and superior performance. While these mechanisms were identified and established from previous research, more research is needed to verify their relative impact on competitiveness as well as their dynamics. For example, can too much adaptation be harmful for value creation or are these two mechanisms complementary? Third, our framework identifies several moderators for the impact of customer-centricity on competitiveness. While this list of moderators is extensive, it is not meant to be exhaustive and future research could therefore aim to identify other key variables, such as technological turbulence, competitive intensity, and organizational strategy. Moreover, future studies could compare the relative importance of these moderators (e.g., comparisons of organizational factors, market factors, and macro factors). Fourth, this chapter has focused on organization-level customer-centricity which is in line with the aim of this book. As noted in the introduction, however, customer-centricity can also be analysed at the individual-level (Whelan et al., 2010). To complement our integrative framework, we therefore suggest that future research would find a way to link individual customer-centricity to organizational customer-centricity. We call for research on how individuals' attitudes and behaviours that recognize and meet individual customer needs (Brown et al., 2002; Grizzle et al., 2009) aggregate to an organization's customer-centric decision-making, practices, and ways of thinking.

This chapter also offers implications for managers aiming to adopt customer-centricity in their organizations, while also steering clear of the potential pitfalls of customer-centricity. First, customer-centricity begins with how individuals in organizations think about customers. Hence, a transition towards customer-centricity starts from challenging the existing, dominant mental models held in the organization. Both learning and unlearning (e.g., Mattila et al., 2021) are needed to change the deep-rooted knowledge structures concerning customers. One starting point here would be to pay attention to the word choices and terminology used in the company – are they more product or customer-oriented (Yrjölä et al., 2023)? Second, managers will benefit from ensuring that all organizational decision-makers are exposed to customers. Thus, finding ways to increase the time spend with customers is encouraged. Moreover, while firms can host events for their customers, an even more insightful approach would be to observe and meet customers in their natural settings. For example, managers can visit the customers' homes or factories to see how their products are actually being used. In some cases, customers can even become co-designers of new products and services. Third, customer-centric behaviour should be recognized and rewarded in the organization. Especially in the beginning of adopting customer-centricity in an organization, employees might face role conflicts if customer-centric behaviours are seemingly at odds with their other goals, such as efficiency. Thus, managers should clearly communicate the expected behaviours to employees and guarantee they will not be reprimanded for sacrificing other goals in favour of creating more value for customers.

To conclude, we hope our discussions has sparked inspiration for both managers and academics in this strategically important area.

References

Adner, R., & Helfat, C. E. (2003). Corporate effects and dynamic managerial capabilities. *Strategic Management Journal*, 24(10), 1011–1025.

Anderson, J. C., Narus, J. A., & Van Rossum, W. (2006). Customer value propositions in business markets. *Harvard Business Review*, 84(3), 90–99.

Angulo-Ruiz, F., Donthu, N., Prior, D., & Rialp, J. (2014). The financial contribution of customer-oriented marketing capability. *Journal of the Academy of Marketing Science*, 42(4), 380–399.

Battistella, C., De Toni, A. F., De Zan, G., & Pessot, E. (2017). Cultivating business model agility through focused capabilities: A multiple case study. *Journal of Business Research*, 73, 65–82.

Bettencourt, L. A., & Brown, S. W. (2003). Role stressors and customer-oriented boundary-spanning behaviors in service organizations. *Journal of the Academy of Marketing Science*, 31(4), 394–408.

Bharadwaj, N., & Dong, Y. (2014). Toward further understanding the market-sensing capability–value creation relationship. *Journal of Product Innovation Management*, 31(4), 799–813.

Brown, T. J., Mowen, J. C., Donavan, D. T., & Licata, J. W. (2002). The customer orientation of service workers: Personality trait effects on self-and supervisor performance ratings. *Journal of Marketing Research*, 39(1), 110–119.

Casadesus-Masanell, R., & Ricart, J. E. (2010). From strategy to business models and onto tactics. *Long Range Planning*, 43(2–3), 195–215.

Chang, W., Park, J. E., & Chaiy, S. (2010). How does CRM technology transform into organizational performance? A mediating role of marketing capability. *Journal of Business Research*, 63(8), 849–855.

Collis, D. J., & Rukstad, M. G. (2008). Can you say what your strategy is? *Harvard Business Review*, 86(4), 82–90.

Crick, J. M., Karami, M., & Crick, D. (2022). Is it enough to be market-oriented? How coopetition and industry experience affect the relationship between a market orientation and customer satisfaction performance. *Industrial Marketing Management*, 100, 62–75.

Day, G. S. (1994). The capabilities of market-driven organizations. *Journal of Marketing*, 58(4), 37–52.

Day, G., & Moorman, C. (2010). *Strategy from the Outside-In: Profiting from Customer Value*. New York: McGraw Hill Professional.

Day, G., & Moorman, C. (2013). Regaining customer relevance: The outside-in turnaround. *Strategy & Leadership*, 41(4), 17–23.

Deshpandé, R., Farley, J. U., & Webster Jr, F. E. (1993). Corporate culture, customer orientation and innovativeness in Japanese firms: A quadrad analysis. *Journal of Marketing*, 57(January), 23–37.

Dev, C., Zhou, K. Z., Brown, J., & Agarwal, S. (2009). Customer orientation or competitor orientation: Which marketing strategy has a higher payoff for hotel brands? *Cornell Hospitality Quarterly*, 50(1), 19–28.

Do, T. T., & Mai, N. K. (2020). High-performance organization: A literature review. *Journal of Strategy and Management*, 13(2), 297–309.

Doganova, L., & Eyquem-Renault, M. (2009). What do business models do?: Innovation devices in technology entrepreneurship. *Research Policy*, 38(10), 1559–1570.

Du, R. Y., Netzer, O., Schweidel, D. A., & Mitra, D. (2021). Capturing marketing information to fuel growth. *Journal of Marketing*, 85(1), 163–183.

Ferreira, J. J. M., Fernandes, C. I., & Ferreira, F. A. F. (2022). What makes organizations unique? Looking inside the box. *Journal of Business Research*, 139(C), 664–674.

Greenley, G. E., Hooley, G. J., & Rudd, J. M. (2005). Market orientation in a multiple stakeholder orientation context: Implications for marketing capabilities and assets. *Journal of Business Research*, 58(11), 1483–1494.

Grewal, R., & Tansuhaj, P. (2001). Building organizational capabilities for managing economic crisis: The role of market orientation and strategic flexibility. *Journal of Marketing*, 65(2), 67–80.

Grizzle, J. W., Zablah, A. R., Brown, T. J., Mowen, J. C., & Lee, J. M. (2009). Employee customer orientation in context: How the environment moderates the influence of customer orientation on performance outcomes. *Journal of Applied Psychology*, 94(5), 1227.

Gurău, C., Ranchhod, A., & Hackney, R. (2003). Customer-centric strategic planning: Integrating CRM in online business systems. *Information Technology and Management*, 4, 199–214.

Hartline, M. D., Maxham III, J. G., & McKee, D. O. (2000). Corridors of influence in the dissemination of customer-oriented strategy to customer contact service employees. *Journal of Marketing*, 64(2), 35–50.

Hattula, J. D., Herzog, W., Dahl, D. W., & Reinecke, S. (2015). Managerial empathy facilitates egocentric predictions of consumer preferences. *Journal of Marketing Research*, 52(2), 235–252.

Holmlund, M., Strandvik, T., & Lähteenmäki, I. (2017). Digitalization challenging institutional logics: Top executive sensemaking of service business change. *Journal of Service Theory and Practice*, 27(1), 219–236.

Homburg, C., Workman Jr, J. P., & Jensen, O. (2000). Fundamental changes in marketing organization: The movement toward a customer-focused organizational structure. *Journal of the Academy of Marketing Science*, 28(4), 459–478.

Hooley, G., Greenley, G., Fahy, J., & Cadogan, J. (2001). Market-focused resources, competitive positioning and firm performance. *Journal of Marketing Management*, 17(5–6), 503–520.

Hortinha, P., Lages, C., & Lages, L. F. (2011). The trade-off between customer and technology orientations: Impact on innovation capabilities and export performance. *Journal of International Marketing*, 19(3), 36–58.

Hult, G. T. M., Ketchen, D. J., & Slater, S. F. (2005). Market orientation and performance: An integration of disparate approaches. *Strategic Management Journal*, 26(12), 1173–1181.

Hult, G. T. M., Morgeson, F. V., Morgan, N. A., Mithas, S., & Fornell, C. (2017). Do managers know what their customers think and why? *Journal of the Academy of Marketing Science*, 45(1), 37–54.

Johnson, M. W., Christensen, C. M., & Kagermann, H. (2008). Reinventing your business model. *Harvard Business Review*, 86(12), 50–59.

Kirca, A. H., Jayachandran, S., & Bearden, W. O. (2005). Market orientation: A meta-analytic review and assessment of its antecedents and impact on performance. *Journal of Marketing*, 69(2), 24–41.

Kohli, A. K., & Jaworski, B. J. (1990). Market orientation: The construct, research propositions, and managerial implications. *Journal of Marketing*, 54(2), 1–18.

Korunka, C., Scharitzer, D., Carayon, P., Hoonakker, P., Sonnek, A., & Sainfort, F. (2007). Customer orientation among employees in public administration: A transnational, longitudinal study. *Applied Ergonomics*, 38(3), 307–315.

Krasnikov, A., & Jayachandran, S. (2008). The relative impact of marketing, research-and-development, and operations capabilities on firm performance. *Journal of Marketing*, 72(4), 1–11.

Kumar, V., & Reinartz, W. (2016). Creating enduring customer value. *Journal of Marketing*, 80(6), 36–68.

Kumar, V., Jones, E., Venkatesan, R., & Leone, R. P. (2011). Is market orientation a source of sustainable competitive advantage or simply the cost of competing? *Journal of Marketing*, 75(1), 16–30.

Lamberti, L. (2013). Customer centricity: The construct and the operational antecedents. *Journal of Strategic Marketing*, 21(7), 588–612.

Lindic, J., & DaSilva, C. M. (2011). Value proposition as a catalyst for a customer focused innovation. *Management Decision*, 49(10), 1694–1708.

Maklan, S., Antonetti, P., & Whitty, S. (2017). A better way to manage customer experience: Lessons from the royal bank of Scotland. *California Management Review*, 59(2), 92–115.

Mattila, M., Yrjölä, M., & Hautamäki, P. (2021). Digital transformation of business-to-business sales: What needs to be unlearned? *Journal of Personal Selling & Sales Management*, 41(2), 113–129.

Morgan, N. A., Slotegraaf, R. J., & Vorhies, D. W. (2009). Linking marketing capabilities with profit growth. *International Journal of Research in Marketing*, 26(4), 284–293.

Morgan, N. A., Whitler, K. A., Feng, H., & Chari, S. (2018). Research in marketing strategy. *Journal of the Academy of Marketing Science*, 47(1), 4–29.

Mukerjee, K. (2013). Customer-oriented organizations: A framework for innovation. *Journal of Business Strategy*, 34(3), 49–56.

Narayanan, V. K., Zane, L. J., & Kemmerer, B. (2011). The cognitive perspective in strategy: An integrative review. *Journal of Management*, 37(1), 305–351.

Narver, J. C., & Slater, S. F. (1990). The effect of a market orientation on business profitability. *Journal of Marketing*, 54(4), 20–35.

Noble, C. H., Sinha, R. K., & Kumar, A. (2002). Market orientation and alternative strategic orientations: A longitudinal assessment of performance implications. *Journal of Marketing*, 66(4), 25–39.

O'Dwyer, M., & Gilmore, A. (2019). Competitor orientation in successful SMEs: An exploration of the impact on innovation. *Journal of Strategic Marketing*, 27(1), 21–37.

Osterwalder, A., & Pigneur, Y. (2013). *Business Model Generation: A Handbook for Visionaries, Game Changers, and Challengers*. John Wiley & Sons: Hoboken, New Jersey, USA.

Payne, A. F., Storbacka, K., & Frow, P. (2008). Managing the co-creation of value. *Journal of the Academy of Marketing Science*, 36, 83–96.

Porter, M. E., & Nohria, N. (2018). How CEOs manage time. *Harvard Business Review*, 96(4), 42–51.

Ramani, G., & Kumar, V. (2008). Interaction orientation and firm performance. *Journal of Marketing*, 72(1), 27–45.

Rapp, A., Trainor, K. J., & Agnihotri, R. (2010). Performance implications of customer-linking capabilities: Examining the complementary role of customer orientation and CRM technology. *Journal of Business Research*, 63(11), 1229–1236.

Rintamäki, T., Kuusela, H., & Mitronen, L. (2007). Identifying competitive customer value propositions in retailing. *Managing Service Quality: An International Journal*, 17(6), 621–634.

Rust, R. T., Moorman, C., & Bhalla, G. (2010). Rethinking marketing. *Harvard Business Review*, 88(1/2), 94–101.

Rust, R. T., Moorman, C., & van Beuningen, J. (2016). Quality mental model convergence and business performance. *International Journal of Research in Marketing*, 33(1), 155–171.

Saeed, S., Yousafzai, S., Paladino, A., & De Luca, L. M. (2015). Inside-out and outside-in orientations: A meta-analysis of orientation's effects on innovation and firm performance. *Industrial Marketing Management*, 47, 121–133.

Sahi, G. K., Gupta, M. C., & Lonial, S. C. (2018). Relating strategic market orientation and market performance: Role of customer value types. *Journal of Strategic Marketing*, 26(4), 318–338.

Said, J., Hui, W. S., Taylor, D., & Othman, R. (2009). Customer-focused strategies and information technology capabilities: Implications for service quality of Malaysian local authorities. *International Review of Business Research Papers*, 5(3), 241–256.

Said, E., Macdonald, E. K., Wilson, H. N., & Marcos, J. (2015). How organisations generate and use customer insight. *Journal of Marketing Management*, 31(9–10), 1158–1179.

Schwepker Jr, C. H. (2003). Customer-oriented selling: A review, extension, and directions for future research. *Journal of Personal Selling & Sales Management*, 23(2), 151–171.
Shah, D., Rust, R. T., Parasuraman, A., Staelin, R., & Day, G. S. (2006). The path to customer centricity. *Journal of Service Research*, 9(2), 113–124.
Sheth, J. N., Sisodia, R. S., & Sharma, A. (2000). The antecedents and consequences of customer-centric marketing. *Journal of the Academy of Marketing Science*, 28(1), 55–66.
Simons, R. (2014). Choosing the right customer. *Harvard Business Review*, 92(3), 48–55.
Slater, S. F., & Narver, J. C. (2000). The positive effect of a market orientation on business profitability: A balanced replication. *Journal of Business Research*, 48(1), 69–73.
Smith, B., Wilson, H., & Clark, M. (2006). Creating and using customer insight: 12 rules of best practice. *Journal of Medical Marketing*, 6(2), 135–139.
Strandvik, T., Holmlund, M., & Grönroos, C. (2014). The mental footprint of marketing in the boardroom. *Journal of Service Management*, 25(2), 241–252.
Strong, C. A., & Harris, L. C. (2004). The drivers of customer orientation: an exploration of relational, human resource and procedural tactics. *Journal of Strategic Marketing*, 12(3), 183–204.
Teece, D. J. (2009). *Dynamic Capabilities and Strategic Management: Organizing for Innovation and Growth*. Oxford University Press, New York, USA.
Teece, D. J. (2010). Business models, business strategy and innovation. *Long Range Planning*, 43(2–3), 172–194.
Trainor, K. J., Andzulis, J. M., Rapp, A., & Agnihotri, R. (2014). Social media technology usage and customer relationship performance: A capabilities-based examination of social CRM. *Journal of Business Research*, 67(6), 1201–1208.
Treacy, M., & Wiersema, F. (1993). Customer intimacy and other value disciplines. *Harvard Business Review*, 71(1), 84–93.
Vorhies, D. W., & Morgan, N. A. (2005). Benchmarking marketing capabilities for sustainable competitive advantage. *Journal of Marketing*, 69(1), 80–94.
Vorhies, D. W., Orr, L. M., & Bush, V. D. (2011). Improving customer-focused marketing capabilities and firm financial performance via marketing exploration and exploitation. *Journal of the Academy of Marketing Science*, 39, 736–756.
Wang, Y., & Feng, H. (2012). Customer relationship management capabilities: Measurement, antecedents and consequences. *Management Decision*, 50(1), 115–129.
Whelan, S., Davies, G., Walsh, M., & Bourke, R. (2010). Public sector corporate branding and customer orientation. *Journal of Business Research*, 63(11), 1164–1171.
Yrjölä, M. (2015). Departures to executive decision making in omni-channel retailing [Doctoral dissertation, Tampere University], *Acta Universitatis Tamperensis 2107*. Tampere University Press: Tampere, Finland.
Yrjölä, M. (2021). Eye on the customer: Breaking away from the inside-out mindset. *Journal of Business Strategy*, 42(3), 206–214.
Yrjölä, M., Kuusela, H., Neilimo, K., & Saarijärvi, H. (2018). Inside-out and outside-in mental models: A top executive perspective. *European Business Review*, 30(5), 529–553.
Yrjölä, M., Niittymies, A., & Tabas, A. M. (2023). Customer orientation: The case of creating value in ecosystems. In S. T. Marinova, & M. A. Marinov (Eds.), *Reconfiguration of Business Models and Ecosystems* (pp. 163–184). Routledge: New York, NY, USA.
Zhao, M., Dröge, C., & Stank, T. P. (2001). The effects of logistics capabilities on firm performance: Customer-focused versus information-focused capabilities. *Journal of Business Logistics*, 22(2), 91–107.

Zhou, K. Z., & Li, C. B. (2010). How strategic orientations influence the building of dynamic capability in emerging economies. *Journal of Business Research*, 63(3), 224–231.

Zhou, K. Z., Brown, J. R., Dev, C. S., & Agarwal, S. (2007). The effects of customer and competitor orientations on performance in global markets: A contingency analysis. *Journal of International Business Studies*, 38(2), 303–319.

Ziggers, G. W., & Henseler, J. (2016). The reinforcing effect of a firm's customer orientation and supply-base orientation on performance. *Industrial Marketing Management*, 52, 18–26.

7

CORE INFRASTRUCTURE

The company's backbone and its importance in business competitiveness

Marco Arraya

7.1 Introduction

The business world currently faces considerable volatility, uncertainty, complexity, and ambiguity, which affect markets, transform business models, and change the nature of competition (Doheny et al., 2012). To succeed in this environment, companies need to develop new characteristics, behaviors, and attitudes that allow them to adapt to changing reality (Eriksson et al., 2022). Managers' primary objective is to enhance global competitiveness through strategic leadership (Stroh & Caligiuri, 1998) by identifying, diagnosing, and projecting the resources and organizational capabilities of emerging and competitive business models as necessary tools for companies' action strategies (Inigo et al., 2017).

Resources, organizational capabilities, and their microfoundations[1] (distinctive skills, processes, and routines) serve as foundations for a company's strategy and give rise to systems that emerge within a company because of the unique and difficult-to-replicate configuration that integrates them in a symbiotic relationship with available human capital (Salvato & Vassolo, 2018). These foundations and microfoundations (F&MF) provide clarity for higher-level analyses. This is achieved by their configuration, which creates a core infrastructure that supports the evolution of the strategy and the company over time (Arraya, 2024; Bojesson & Fundin, 2021). This is because both identify the underlying causes of a phenomenon at a lower level than that of the phenomenon itself (Foss & Pedersen, 2016).

Consequently, by identifying and managing essential F&MF, managers can gain a competitive advantage. This requires a system capability-driven approach that focuses on building and optimizing the company's core infrastructure to create value. Figure 7.1 presents a visual summary of the core infrastructure framework.

DOI:10.4324/9781032695969-8

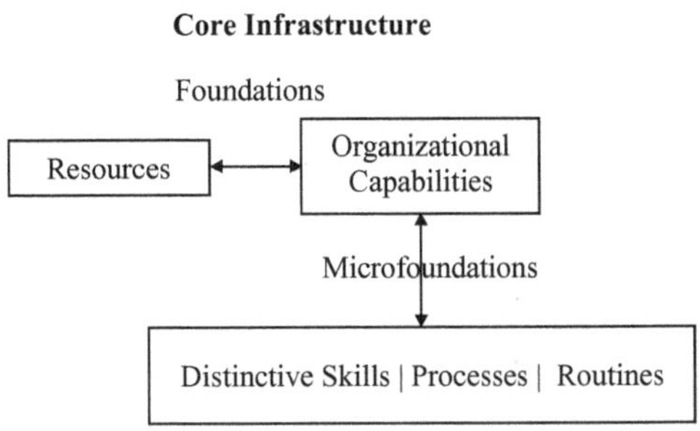

FIGURE 7.1 Core infrastructure framework.

7.2 Core infrastructure

The core infrastructure is the central axis of a company and is responsible for its equilibrium and sustainability. Its configuration offers the groundwork for sustainable, scalable, and sellable business. The core infrastructure of a company refers to how it is organized, including resources, organizational capabilities, and its microfoundations: microsystems, processes, routines, workflow, and practices that align with its vision and goals, supporting a customer-centric culture (Carew et al., 2009; Grant, 2010). Furthermore, these microfoundations can be easily replicated with minimal additional investment.

A company's core infrastructure is its functional component, encompassing a diverse range of elements such as technology, departments, and teams supported by human innovation and leadership. It is essential for company managers to inquire about the existence of this infrastructure and assess its adequacy for the task at hand. Furthermore, they must determine the measures to be taken to establish an effective infrastructure that can facilitate the completion of each task.

Core infrastructure should facilitate a company's ability to change and innovate quickly in response to the external environment, simplify work processes, enhance product and service quality and customer experience, accelerate coordination between people and work areas, and make work easier (Carew et al., 2009; Lamberti, 2013).

Managers must run their companies on core infrastructure, and if one pillar is out of alignment, the business will run insufficiently, sluggish, and lack profits. Although a solid core infrastructure configuration is crucial, it is insufficient on its own. This must be coordinated with the other formal and informal components. It should typically serve as the basis, rather than the culmination, of a company's competitive advantage. In the following sections, we discuss the core infrastructure components.

7.3 Resources

Why do companies in the same industry perform differently? What makes a company unique? An appropriate response can be obtained by examining the characteristics of organizational resources, including value, rarity, imitability, and organization (the VRIO framework). Successful business strategies require an understanding of a company's assets and competencies (Barney et al., 2021; Ferreira & Fernandes, 2017).

The resource-based view (RBV) was first introduced by Penrose (1959) in her research, who emphasized the importance of efficiently utilizing available resources to stimulate and restrict a company's growth (Ferreira et al., 2022). These resources encompass a company's assets, capabilities, processes, attributes, knowledge, and know-how, which are crucial for developing and implementing competitive strategies (Barney, 1991; Teece et al., 1997).

According to Warnier et al. (2013), a company possesses two types of resources, strategic and ordinary. A strategic resource is typically viewed as a valuable asset in the market because of its ability to enhance performance and generate productivity higher than the cost of acquisition or development. Consequently, they are often seen as sources of potential profit or rent. An ordinary resource is a widely available commodity typically perceived to have a neutral performance level, meaning that its expected productivity is equal to its cost (acquired or developed). This type of resource is generally regarded as providing competitive parity only.

The diversity of resources available to competitors can result in some companies having access to more strategic resources than others, which can generate rent and enable the development or expansion of competitive advantages (Hoopes et al., 2003). The ordinary resources possessed by a company are considered assets. These resources, which are frequently utilized and widely available, are typically regarded as commodities and their productivity is equivalent to the cost of acquiring or developing them (Warnier et al., 2013). As a strategic line of thought, the RBV helps a company analyze its strengths and weaknesses (Ferreira et al., 2022).

Both types have internal resources that can be considered in three categories (Barney & Hesterly, 2009; Simon, 2010): tangible, personnel-based, and intangible. As noted by Barney and Hesterly (2009), each of these categories is significant in generating a company's value.

According to Kamasak (2017), *tangible resources* refer to the financial or physical assets included in an organization's balance sheet. These resources can be physical inputs for production or service delivery, facilities, equipment, patents, or other properties that provide value. These resources can be protected from unauthorized use by copyright law, as noted by Miller and Shamsie (1996).

Personnel-based resources refer to the attributes of an organization associated with its human capital, such as employees' know-how, collective aptitudes, culture, and training (Barney & Arikan, 2002). These resources encompass the company's internal systems, structures, and routines, including internal social capital resources; organizational culture; planning, controlling, and coordinating systems; reporting structures; operating routines; and all other factors that are dependent on people. Although personnel-based resources are generally considered ordinary and do not typically drive organizational growth, their coordination mechanisms are critical for maintaining expansion.

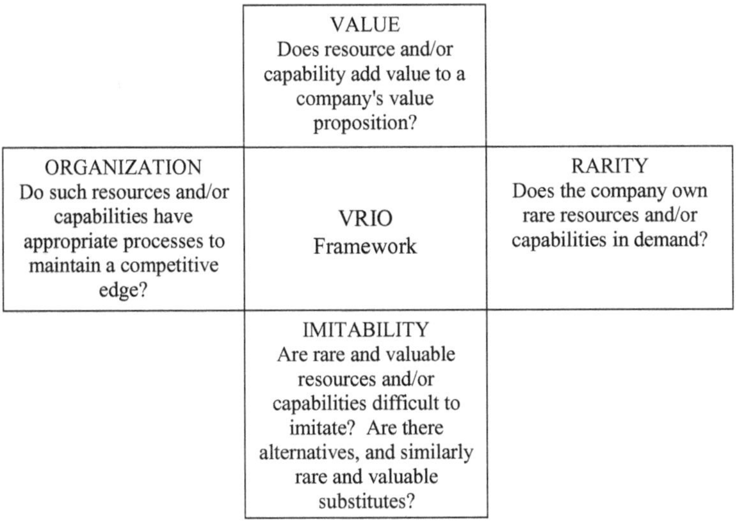

FIGURE 7.2 The VRIO framework. Adapted from Barney and Arikan (2001).

Intangible resources, as defined by Kamasak (2017), are difficult to quantify and acquire and are often unique to a particular company. They are considered assets, such as intellectual property, including patents, trademarks, trade secrets, and databases. These resources exhibit complementary characteristics and are independent of individuals (Rivkin, 2000). Consequently, it is often difficult for competitors to replicate or understand, which potentially leads to superior performance. Additionally, intangible resources enable companies to enhance the value of tangible assets (Jancenelle, 2021). These resources are nonphysical, nonfinancial, and nonpersonnel (Andersen & Kheam, 1998).

Barney's (1991) study linked these resources to competitive advantages in the realm of business management and found that competitive advantage is related to competitiveness, performance, and financial returns (Newbert, 2007). Grant (1991) elevates RBV to the central concept of crafting corporate strategies. Consequently, the importance of gathering VRIO resources to gain a competitive advantage has become a crucial aspect of both academic and managerial strategic thinking. Figure 7.2 presents a visual summary of the VRIO framework.

The RBV argues that when a resource simultaneously has four characteristics, it is VRIO (Barney & Hesterly, 2009):

Valuable: Scholars widely agree that a resource or capability is considered valuable if it enables a company to capitalize on opportunities or mitigate threats in its environment. However, if a resource or capability fails to help a firm minimize threats or seize opportunities, it is deemed ineffective and does not enhance the company's competitive position. It is important to mention that certain authors contend that possessing resources that do not pass the VRIO value test can disadvantage a firm in terms of competition.

Rare: A resource or capability is considered rare if it is not widely possessed by competitors. A company that possesses valuable resources or capabilities is on par with its competitors. However, if a company possesses resources or capabilities rare in the industry, it has a competitive advantage over other companies. This advantage allows a company to exploit opportunities and negate threats in ways that competitors without resources or capabilities cannot. The criterion of rarity requires that resources or capabilities not be widely used in the industry. The more exclusive a company's access to a valuable resource or capability is, the greater its benefit. It is not necessary for a company to have exclusive ownership of resources or capabilities, as long as only a few companies possess them.

Inimitability: An inimitable resource or capability cannot be replicated or substituted easily. Such a resource or capability is considered inimitable when it is difficult for another company to acquire or replace it. Imitation refers to acquiring a lacking resource or capability, or replacing it with a similar one that offers equivalent benefits. An important question is whether competitors face a disadvantage when acquiring or replacing resources or capabilities that are lacking. Companies can acquire the resources or capabilities they lack in various ways, but this is the hardest criterion to evaluate because, given sufficient time and money, almost any resource or capability can be replicated. Therefore, one way to think about this is to compare how long it will take for competitors to imitate or replace resources, and compare it to the product's useful life. Another way to determine whether a resource or capability is inimitable is by considering how it is acquired. Inimitable resources and capabilities often result from historical, ambiguous, or socially complex factors. Generally, intangible resources or capabilities, such as corporate culture or reputation, are difficult to imitate and therefore inimitable.

Organization: The final criterion for evaluating resources and capabilities as sources of competitive advantage is that possession or control is insufficient. To gain an advantage, the company must also have organizational competency to capture any value that the resource or capability may generate. This encompasses various aspects of the company such as control systems, reporting relationships, compensation policies, and management interfaces with both internal and external stakeholders. It is important to note that the concept of an organization is similar to that of planning, organizing, leading, and controlling frameworks.

The graphical representation in Figure 7.3 provides a comprehensive overview of the VRIO configuration and its impact on competitive dynamics.

The configuration of strategic and ordinary VRIO resources ensures superior performance. This resource configuration is characterized as an adaptive system that has evolved from the coordination of strategic and ordinary resources (Arraya,

<table>
<tr><th>Valuable?</th><th>Rare?</th><th>Inimitability?</th><th>Supported by Organization?</th><th>Competitive Implications</th><th>Performance</th></tr>
<tr><td>No</td><td>—</td><td>—</td><td rowspan="4">Yes</td><td>Competitive Disadvantage</td><td>Below Normal</td></tr>
<tr><td>Yes</td><td>No</td><td>—</td><td>Competitive Parity</td><td>Normal</td></tr>
<tr><td>Yes</td><td>Yes</td><td>No</td><td>Temporary Competitive Advantage</td><td>Above Normal</td></tr>
<tr><td>Yes</td><td>Yes</td><td>Yes</td><td>Sustained Competitive Advantage</td><td>Above Normal</td></tr>
</table>

FIGURE 7.3 VRIO and relative company performance. Adapted from Barney and Arikan (2001).

2024; Warnier et al., 2013). It also exhibits holistic behavior. Therefore, a company must concentrate its efforts on bundles of embedded resources that can serve as a source of competitive advantage (Baía et al., 2020).

Nonetheless, it is essential for managers to determine the optimal allocation of resources to effectively navigate the market and develop more efficient strategies (Amit & Schoemaker, 1993; Arraya, 2024). However, resources are highly context-dependent and are subject to change, thus subjecting the company to change in continuity. Moreover, value creation can be achieved only by utilizing a company's capability system (Arraya, 2024; Makadok, 2001). The dynamic capabilities system is a transformer that converts resources into an enhanced performance. By leveraging the VRIO features, the system can effectively extract the best competitive configurations to improve a company's performance. Thus, dynamic capabilities serve as mediators between VRIO resources and performance improvements.

7.4 Organizational capabilities

Organizational capabilities are high-level systems of routines that, when combined with appropriate input flows, provide management with a range of decision-making options to generate substantial outcomes of a specific nature (Winter, 2000). They refer to a group of acquired abilities and functions that empowers a company to achieve a specific objective. It encompasses the knowledge and skills necessary to deliver desired outcomes (Teece, 2023). These are the collaborative interactions of individuals, technology, skills, systems, knowledge, and mindsets that work synergistically in a company's processes, transforming available resources into valuable outcomes relative to rivals (Morgan, 2012).

Organizational capabilities involve efficient allocation and deployment of resources for a specific goal (Cavusgil et al., 2007; Dutta et al., 2005). They facilitate problem-solving and decision-making by providing a collective process of coordination, learning, and transformation that fits various company environments. Without them, a resource may lose value over time (Coates & McDermott, 2002; Harreld et al., 2007; Schreyogg & Kliesch-Eberl, 2007).

They are also a social process that is dependent on context, strategic and tactical decisions, and competitor responses that are influenced by diverse factors, such as the company's history, culture, and learning and execution skills. Furthermore, along with the business model, the market and its dynamics dictate a company's organizational capabilities. Contrary to common beliefs, companies in the same sector or industry do not always require the same capabilities for their success. If a company matches only its competitors' capabilities, it will never be able to create or maintain competitive advantage. Thus, a company's ability to possess VRIO organizational capabilities is crucial for effective resource management and competitive advantage. These capabilities must be skillfully integrated to leverage their strengths and position them for success (Arraya, 2024; Ordanini & Rubera, 2008; Sirmon et al., 2007).

To summarize, organizational capabilities (Wu et al., 2010) are company-specific, emerge gradually over time, are tacit, participants may be unaware of their existence, are path-dependent, influenced by a company's history and the actions of its decision-makers, and empirically validated through their application to problems faced by a company.

To approach a core infrastructure-driven company, managers can begin by confronting different types of organizational capabilities. At the first level, ordinary capabilities, also known as operational capabilities, are vital for a company's survival, because they offer unity, integration, and direction to resources and operational practices. These capabilities encompass both explicit elements, such as resources and practices, as well as tacit elements, such as know-how and skill sets, which are necessary for addressing a diverse range of problems or dealing with uncertainty (Wu et al., 2010). They encompass specialized tasks, such as creating external alliances, developing innovative products, or delivering value creation (Newey et al., 2016, 2016; Teece, 2023). Although they are undeniably strategic and catalytic, they often involve repetitive and imitable processes.

Their configuration may vary depending on the activities of the company's business model and value proposition, which is a unique combination of the products, services, and experiences that a company offers to its customers (Arraya, 2024). The ordinary capabilities that a company possesses may provide it with a transient competitive advantage because they allow the company to carry out these activities more efficiently than its competitors (Dutta et al., 2005; Karna et al., 2016). However, for a company that relies heavily on conventional labor and physical resources, their ordinary capabilities do not provide an advantage. These capabilities can often be outsourced, especially in situations where there is intense competition and a sound legal system that facilitates market functioning (George & Kerai, 2022; Teece, 2023).

Nevertheless, they can increase a company's revenue and/or reduce costs, thus contributing to its performance (George & Kerai, 2022). Although the configuration of ordinary capabilities may change, they are associated with "focused non-change" or essentially with their inertia or stability (Barreto, 2010; Hine et al,

2014). Consequently, they have difficulty adapting to dynamic environments (Drnevich & Kriauciunas, 2011).

Unlike ordinary capabilities, dynamic capabilities are future oriented. Instead of simply detailing a company's present activities, they focus on charting the course for future actions, securing essential resources, and establishing optimal organizational structures (Teece, 2023). However, dynamic capabilities are unique to each company, and cannot be purchased. Thus, the second level of organizational capabilities is intimately linked to dynamic capabilities because it directly reflects the ability of a company to adapt to changing environments and the concept of the continuous improvement of business processes. Dynamic capabilities are not static entities; rather, they evolve and adapt to changing circumstances, allowing a company to respond effectively to changing environments. By concentrating on dynamic capabilities, a company can position itself for long-term success and sustainable growth, ensuring that it is well prepared to meet future challenges and capitalize on emerging opportunities. The development of dynamic capabilities is essential for a company to thrive in today's rapidly changing business landscape.

Dynamic capabilities are characterized by their innovation-driven nature and responsible for creating, expanding, and altering a company's resources and/or ordinary capability bases (Helfat et al., 2007). Teece (2007) argues that dynamic capabilities can be classified as (i) *sensing* opportunities and threats, (ii) *seizing* opportunities, and (iii) *transforming* a company's resource base. These clusters are supported by microfoundations which consist of distinctive skills, processes, and routines (Teece, 2007).

The development of *sensing* capabilities is a crucial aspect of market research that involves digitalization, learning, and interpretation to recognize new opportunities (Khan et al., 2020). Managers typically begin the innovation design process by identifying and analyzing customer needs and latent demand and then use and recombine new and existing knowledge in the company in association with new technologies to respond to the opportunities detected (Katila & Ahuja, 2002). However, these sensing capabilities must also detect threats to the internal and external environments of a company (Protogerou et al., 2012). Thus, it is critical for companies to have the ability to sense or recognize market opportunities and threats to maintain their competitiveness in the face of environmental changes.

Seizing capabilities involve a series of activities focusing on the execution of newly discovered prospects (Khan et al., 2020). Seizing can also be referred to as a process that mobilizes internal and external resources and/or expertise to pursue identified opportunities, resulting in a competitive advantage. According to Teece (2007), to effectively leverage the identified opportunities, a company must be capable of (i) enhancing technological proficiency, (ii) maintaining its assets, (iii) selecting or developing suitable business models, and (iv) making the decision to move forward with the necessary investments. Consequently, seizing involves making strategic choices, investing in tangible and intangible assets to create value, and shaping markets (Helfat & Peteraf, 2009).

Adopting new strategies to enter the market with new products or services could involve the implementation of a new business model. To capitalize on an identified opportunity, it is crucial to identify and address gaps in resources and capabilities. This can be achieved through internal development, procurement, and alliances. The ability to transform or reconfigure existing resources and capabilities is critical for a successful innovation (Khan et al. 2020; Teece 2023).

Dynamic *transformative* capabilities, also known as reconfiguration (i.e., improving competitiveness through the reconfiguration of organizational assets), refer to a company's ability to keep resources, organizational capabilities, and competencies internally coherent, aligned with its strategy, and competitive in the ecosystem in which it operates (Teece, 2018). Reconfiguration is an iterative process that relies on the internal and external environments that influence a company's business processes (Jantunen et al., 2018; Yoshikuni & Dwivedi, 2023). They are supported primarily by internal processes and routines. Sometimes, small adjustments in resource and capability bases can be sufficient to explore opportunities or new purposes in response to changing business priorities (Mikalef & Pateli, 2017). However, when the external environment is disrupted, broader renovation may be necessary (Helfat & Peteraf, 2009).

New configurations of resources and capabilities, whether old or new, general or specialized, allow for the acquisition and integration of critical knowledge that is essential for superior performance (Matarazzo et al., 2021). Thus, transformative capability depends on an organizational culture that supports openness, flexibility, and experimentation as the basis for success and future advantages.

The third level of the hierarchy of capabilities encompasses a unique ability, characterized by valuable ordinary or dynamic capabilities that are difficult to imitate or replicate, value-added, and dependent on scarce resources (Barney, 1991). In essence, this capability is typically implicit, exceptional, and challenging to replicate and build on unique organizational relationships that are intrinsically difficult to transfer between multiple companies. The literature calls this capability distinctive (Arraya, 2022), as it strategically differentiates the company and creates a competitive advantage recognized by customers in the creation of value.

Distinctive capability refers to an ordinary or dynamic capability with a superior attribute, strength, or quality that sets the company apart from its competitors and determines how efficiently and effectively it creates value for stakeholders (Arraya, 2022). This is a source of a company's ability to create and deliver value to customers and ensure superior performance. In other words, it confers tangible value to customers and contributes to a company's transient competitive advantage (McGrath, 2019).

The cornerstone of this distinctive capability lies in the knowledge-based competencies, skills, and tacit knowledge of the employees who feed on technical systems. To remain competitive in the market, technical systems require continuous adaptation, which leads to the development of management systems that facilitate knowledge creation and dissemination. Ultimately, these dimensions (knowledge, technical, and management systems) must align with the company's purpose and culture. Moreover, a distinctive capability is a system of knowledge that is interrelated, interdependent, idiosyncratic, and with signature, because it reflects the way things are done in the company.

7.5 Building capabilities for outperform competitors

A company's prosperity is closely connected to its capabilities for organizational effectiveness and utilization of these capabilities. For a business to optimize its model, it is crucial to consolidate, refine, and enhance its organizational capabilities (Teece, 2023). However, merely retaining the current configuration of capabilities is insufficient for a company to flourish (Arraya, 2024). Thus, it is essential to closely monitor the market and initiate the following configuration. To accomplish this, the forward path involves continuously enhancing the capability base based on customer requirements, evaluating current performance using metrics, and devising future strategies for market penetration. Metrics are critical components for proactively adjusting and constructing capabilities (Bocken & Geradts, 2020). Metrics such as individual performance, employee and manager feedback, return on investment, and the overall economic performance of the company contribute to the selection and definition of capabilities that need to be developed or improved.

Implementing a strategy depends heavily on its capabilities, as it provides crucial input. However, given the volatile nature of the market, it is essential to continuously modify the strategy, and consequently, the capabilities required to generate customer value and promote economic growth (Rashidirad & Salimian, 2020).

As previously stated, the essential element of organizational capabilities is human knowledge, both individual and collective. Therefore, it is crucial to construct intellectual capital through an ongoing learning and development process that is closely aligned with the company's existing and future objectives. This continuous cycle empowers individuals and organizations to perform tasks efficiently, adjust to evolving situations, attain objectives, and realize their full potential. It emphasizes the cultivation of specific abilities, competencies, behaviors, skills, knowledge, and desirable traits that have demonstrated their impact on the business model.

The logical question is, where should one begin? The answer to this question depends on the company's position and thorough assessment of its business strategy components.

A company can only establish benchmark organizational capabilities when it systematically evaluates the components of its strategy, including corporate purpose, corporate culture, where to play, how to win, resources and capabilities, management systems, and future shape (Drucker, 1974; Lafley & Martin, 2013). These components possess inherent value, and when they complement each other, they mutually reinforce each other, resulting in strategic coherence. Strategic coherence stems from the company's ability to integrate all components, thereby providing

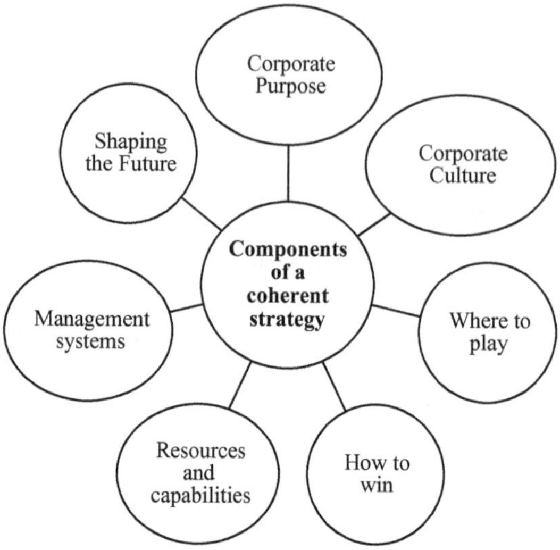

FIGURE 7.4 Components of the coherent strategy.

greater differentiation from competitors, focusing on what is truly important, and achieving an extremely beneficial alignment of the entire company with a common and consistent purpose (Leinwand & Mainardi, 2011). The schematic in Figure 7.4 provides a comprehensive summary of the constituent elements of the coherent strategy.

Strategic coherence contributes to a company's competitive advantage by enabling it to outperform its competitors and generate value for customers through consistent application of a capability-adaptive system. The initial step in achieving strategic coherence involves distinguishing these unique sources of differentiation and value from strategic components (Lafley & Martin, 2013; Leinwand & Mainardi, 2011). The following is a concise overview of these components.

The primary *purpose* of a business is to create customers, deliver value, and enhance their overall well-being (Drucker, 1974). This mission ought to be embraced by every member of the organization (Reichheld et al., 2021) and serve as a driving force for teams and individuals to collaborate and execute tasks that ultimately benefit all stakeholders (Hollensbe et al., 2014). Corporate purposes ought to guide all company decisions, serving as the starting point for aligning strategic choices (Lafley & Martin, 2013).

Corporate culture refers to a set of beliefs and attitudes dictating how operations are conducted within a company. A positive corporate culture not only fosters employee confidence, motivation, and inspiration but also enhances customer satisfaction and loyalty (Ali et al., 2015; Walsh & Beatty, 2007) and provides a competitive advantage (Gray & Balmer, 1998). Conversely, a toxic culture leads to increased employee turnover (Sull et al., 2022) and diminished competitiveness.

Selecting the optimal playing field—*where to play*—which includes determining customer segments, geographic locations, and all dimensions of marketing, as well as considering competition, is crucial for defining a business model that enables a company to compete effectively and achieve its purpose and objectives (Lafley & Martin, 2013). Defining areas in which a company will not compete is essential (Leinwand & Mainardi, 2011). Attempting to be simultaneously present in all segments and locations is a failure recipe.

Following the identification of where to play, the next step is to determine *how to win* the customer; that is, to articulate the value proposition and other strengths that will enable the company to secure customer loyalty (Lafley & Martin, 2013). The choice of where to play and how to win must align and complement one another in a coherent and integrated manner.

Organizational capabilities and resources are demonstrated through a range of activities and forms of support that enable a company to make decisions about where to focus its efforts and how to achieve success (Lafley & Martin, 2013). The objective is to establish a capability-adaptive system that reinforces one another and underpins strategic choices that are feasible, distinctive, and defendable (Leinwand & Mainardi, 2011).

A company requires *management systems* that facilitate the creation, evaluation, and dissemination of strategic plans (Drucker, 2001), including (a) devising a brainstorming strategy, (b) enhancing organizational innovation, (c) refining the value proposition, (d) discussing the operational plan, (e) discussing the operational budget and budget for future-shaping activities, (f) conducting talent assessments, and (g) reviewing the company's development, among others. These systems are essential for the effective operation, survival, and growth of a company.

Change is an unavoidable aspect of the universe that cannot be controlled. As Drucker (2001) notes, this can only be anticipated. A company must adapt to either disruptive or incremental changes to remain competitive, which presents an opportunity for managers to practice entrepreneurial management (Teece, 2023). To *shape the future*, managers must implement policies that facilitate the creation of the future, employ systematic methods to identify and anticipate change, and determine the most effective approach to introducing change within the organization. Drucker (2001) emphasized the importance of balancing change and continuity through policies. Managers must monitor new market trends, develop and test innovative business models, and coordinate internal and external resources. Ultimately, entrepreneurial and forward-thinking management should be integrated throughout the company.

The coherent strategic model, along with its various components, guarantees operational effectiveness and supports change (Lafley & Martin, 2013). It offers a comprehensive roadmap for achieving final objectives and provides employees with a central point of motivation. As a strategic frame of reference, it serves as a guiding light for both the implementation and achievement of good work practices and attainment of organizational goals. Notably, the seven components are inextricably linked, necessitating their collective adoption in the model to prove their effectiveness. If any of these components is disregarded, the model tends to falter.

To achieve success, a coherent strategic model must be specific and measurable. This allows a company to identify and assess the capabilities and competencies incorporated into its processes, systems, and routines that create value for stakeholders and impact the business model. Evaluations and metrics play a crucial role in this process, helping diagnose the model by identifying strengths, weaknesses, and gaps in capabilities and competencies in comparison to competitors. By addressing these weaknesses and gaps, companies can create effective learning programs that align with their strategy, market, and value-creation goals, ultimately linking acquired knowledge to the model's economic impact on the business.

How will a company proceed? This is essential for building the capability of a coherent strategic model.

The initial step of the process involves the development of exceptional capabilities. Companies that consistently perform at a high level focus their efforts on making certain capabilities stand out—distinctive—as those that are most valued by customers and differentiate them from competitors. Establishing distinctive capabilities demands a concentrated focus and significant investment in areas where the company possesses exceptional skills and competencies, as well as the potential for a competitive advantage. However, this does not imply that the company neglects or underestimates the importance of other capabilities that contribute to the overall adaptive system, including the ordinary ones. To be effective, all capabilities must adhere to good practice. These distinctive capabilities can be developed through the use of a company's own technologies or external partnerships and practices that integrate tacit and explicit knowledge, both individually and collectively. It should be noted that, as Leinwand and Mainardi (2011) point out, companies typically have between three and six distinguishing capabilities due to considerations of focus, resources, and time.

New distinctive capabilities typically necessitate either empowerment of existing personnel or development of new personnel. In either case, the company must provide individuals and teams with sufficient time to establish new processes and work routines as well as cultivate fresh relationships among them. Conversely, these new capabilities often confer a competitive advantage on a company, even in the early stages of development. However, they typically require time to reach their maximum potential and effectiveness (Lafley & Martin, 2013).

The second step is *to design and deliver learning programs* that cater to both individual and collective needs to enhance organizational capabilities. The unique characteristics of the company and the market facilitate the customization of learning programs to suit the specific context and particularities of the business model, while simultaneously addressing the strengths and specific needs of employees. Customization should focus on capabilities that have the greatest impact on a company's competitiveness, without neglecting other important capabilities. It is essential to align the learning objectives with the strategic interests of the business model. Co-responsibility for skill development between the company and its employees and integrating learning outcomes into assessment metrics are effective strategies for achieving this alignment.

The main factor that sets companies apart in the market is the third stage, which involves a *capability-adaptive system* configuration. While distinctive capabilities alone do not necessarily result in superior performance, the attributes, complementarities, and effects of these capabilities, which work together in an adaptive system to enhance and compensate for one another, can lead to improved performance-related benefits (Altintas & Ambrosini, 2019; Baía & Ferreira, 2019; Fainshmidt et al., 2018; Leinwand & Mainardi, 2011).

A capability-adaptive system refers to a company's management's ability to integrate distinctive and ordinary capabilities in a cohesive manner, resulting in a strategically differentiating and mutually reinforcing system. This system delivers value creation to stakeholders, and competitors are unable to replicate it, thereby contributing to a company's competitive advantage (Arraya, 2022, 2024). Thus, when a capability-adaptive system successfully and efficiently combines organizational capabilities, it enhances the competitiveness of a company's processes and routines (Ireland & Webb, 2007). Ultimately, this system plays a crucial role in achieving company performance (Leinwand & Mainardi, 2011).

The development of a capability-adaptive system requires individualized attention from each company, as the configuration is contingent on the company's strategic model. Thus, the configuration of a capability-adaptive system is crucial for maintaining a company's competitiveness. Apart from the technical analysis and decision-making rules pertaining to an adaptive system (Sullivan, 2011), it is substantially influenced by managers' creative perceptions, intuition, and managerial skills (Teece, 2023). The adaptive system of "appropriate" capabilities facilitates the alignment of the business model around a corporate purpose, creates synergies as it surpasses the sum of its capabilities and even the constituent elements of the comprehensive strategy, and differentiates between managing the intricacy of the business model and excelling in it.

The final step involves linking a company's capabilities to the performance of its business model. To ensure that learning programs and the adjustment, adaptation, or development of organizational capabilities have a meaningful impact on a business model, it is essential to focus on *performance metrics*. Metrics that offer early warning signs, whether things are going well, or when actions are necessary. Hence, a comprehensive performance management system should be implemented with several subsystems primarily focused on organizational capabilities. Ultimately, a capability-adaptive system, with robust metrics and progress against defined goals, should be evaluated to determine where and how gaps in capabilities, skills, and competencies are addressed.

The schematic in Figure 7.5 illustrates a thorough perspective of the organizational capability-building cycle.

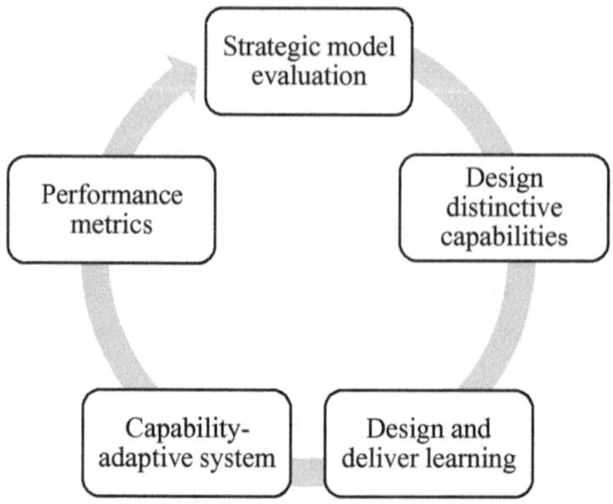

FIGURE 7.5 Organizational capability building cycle.

The five stages of the organizational capability-building cycle are crucial, and a single oversight can lead to a chain reaction of misinterpretations that hinder the company's performance. As Lorenz (1972) posited, the efficiency of the cycle is highly sensitive to initial conditions, which implies that the company is intricately connected, such that a minor occurrence can significantly impact the larger system at various points in time or space. Although a small change may have no effect in some instances, it can result in a proportional change in the final outcome, or in other cases, has a profound impact on the overall process.

It is not sufficient to merely assess the whereabouts of a company; it is imperative for most companies to possess excellent organizational capabilities, competencies, and skills for success. Tailor-made training is now widely available, and success is directly proportional to a company's unique process that managers establish through interaction with peers and external and internal environments. This process involves the configuration and management of organizational capabilities in the capability-adaptive system, making it VRIO, as well as company-wide practices that involve all employees in the application of these capabilities to create value for customers. However, this requires a management entrepreneurial mindset, a focus on value creation, and an understanding of the company's functioning as a coherent whole, which reinforces its larger and stronger components through a coherent strategic model and organizational capability-building cycle. When a company successfully configures a capability-adaptive system in a systematic and sustainable manner, it can differentiate itself and consistently outperform its competitors by achieving a competitive advantage.

7.6 Processes

Processes comprise a structured, interactive set of activities designed to enable a company to deliver value to customers or achieve other strategic objectives (Guha et al., 1997; Strnadl, 2006). This approach emphasizes the manner in which work is conducted within the company and represents a defined sequence of tasks organized over time and space, with clear commencement and conclusion points, as well as defined inputs and outputs: a framework for action (Lemanska-Majdzik & Okreglicka, 2015). Adopting a process-oriented approach requires adopting a customer-centric perspective.

This process is composed of events and activities (Goel et al., 2023). Market events occur naturally and prompt initiation of the process. An activity refers to a single unit of work or task (Dumas et al., 2018). A characteristic of these processes is that they consist of logically ordered activities with well-defined inputs and outputs to achieve a business objective (Weske, 2019). Processes are generally established as control systems to ensure that errors are avoided, variations in task performance are minimized, and efficiency is attained (Lager & Simms, 2023). The informal process is typically characterized by undocumented, tacit information and emerging work patterns that may be carried out intuitively and on an ad hoc basis (Lager & Simms, 2023). By contrast, a formally structured process involves a detailed description of how work should be performed, including defined inputs and outputs, flowcharts with supporting decision structures, and checklists (Andersen et al., 2008).

Well-defined processes play a crucial role in maintaining efficiency and ensuring consistent quality in a company's operations (Romero et al., 2015). By establishing clear task guidelines, the processes can prevent errors and reduce the time required to complete them. The absence of defined processes can lead to inconsistent results, affecting the quality of products or services and accuracy of data collection (Tregear, 2015). Furthermore, this may result in legal documentation failing to meet regulatory standards (Mahmoodzadeh et al., 2009). When employees are aware of the procedures they must follow, they can complete tasks more efficiently with fewer errors. Implementing well-designed processes not only enhances consistency but also enables companies to achieve greater efficiency, deliver higher-quality products and services, and provide better customer service (Dumas et al., 2018). Ultimately, effective business processes contribute to a company's overall success (Godin, 2020).

Building well-designed processes has several advantages including increased efficiency and quality. In addition to these benefits, the processes should be repeatable, transparent, adaptable, and cost-effective. Repeatability ensures that processes can be repeated without redundancy (Tregear, 2015). Transparency is essential for tracking and comparing performance and efficacy over time (Kettenbohrer et al., 2013). Agility allows processes to adapt to multiple situations, ensuring that changes in the work environment do not cause delays (Muenstermann, 2015). Finally, cost-effectiveness helps companies reduce their expenses by developing faster and more efficient processes (Muenstermann et al., 2010). When a company's processes meet these criteria, they are more likely to support the company's goals and positively impact its business performance (Muenstermann, 2015).

A process is essentially a set of structured actions that are repeatedly undertaken by a company to achieve a specific objective. It is essential that these processes are efficient and effective in making steady progress toward goals and in enhancing the overall functioning of the business.

7.7 Routines

In the context of the dynamic capabilities vision, organizational capabilities are defined as bundles of organizational routines[2] that impact a company's performance (Dosi et al., 2008; Peng et al., 2008). As such, the success of organizational capabilities is heavily dependent on the refined routines that companies have established over time to evaluate their environment, recognize potential opportunities and threats, assess and select the most favorable opportunities for investment, and leverage the resources and capabilities necessary to seize these opportunities (Helfat & Winter, 2011; Schilke et al., 2018; Schreyögg & Kliesch-Eberl 2007). Dynamic capabilities are considered meta-routines that monitor and modify ordinary capabilities (Winter, 2003), that is, the capabilities that enable a company to generate revenue. According to some authors, such as Di Stefano et al. (2014), dynamic capabilities are situated at the strategic level, while ordinary capabilities are the focus of action at the operational level. Wohlgemuth and Wenzel (2016) revealed that there are higher levels of routinization[3] at the strategic level and lower levels of routinization at the operational level.

Routine refers to a habitual, recurrent, or established manner of performing an action that emerges from the repetitive execution of a specific behavior by specific individuals at specific places and times (Feldman & Pentland, 2003; Koumakhov & Marengo, 2023). This may be because of rules, methods, techniques, or the practice of a skill (Bingham et al., 2015; Howard-Grenville & Rerup, 2016; Ohly et al., 2006; Schreyögg & Kliesch-Eberl, 2007). Routine involves accomplishing an endeavor aimed at a specific task in which the objective is known, and individuals are aware of the resources needed to carry out the task (Dittrich & Seidl, 2018; Feldman, 2016). According to Feldman and Pentland (2022), the defining quality of a routine is its ability to convert inputs into outputs efficiently.

Routines can be influenced by various factors, and their stability is derived from their ability to adapt to changes (Winter, 2013). The interplay between stability and change is essential for maintaining efficiency and balance within an organization's capabilities, both intentionally and unintentionally (Dittrich & Seidl, 2018; Eisenhardt & Piezunka, 2011). Hence, practical experience demonstrates that change is inextricably linked to the execution of organizational routines. Therefore, these routines provide valuable insights into how organizational capabilities lead to results, and how dynamic capabilities can be sustained (Wenzel et al., 2021).

Routines play a vital role in establishing coherent strategies and developing organizational capabilities. They are essential for promoting efficiency and can serve as competitive assets when aligned with strategic objectives (Feldman &

Pentland, 2022; Salvato, 2021). Furthermore, routines enable companies to adapt and reconfigure their capabilities in response to market changes, thereby becoming important strategic assets (Salvato, 2021). Additionally, routines generate cognitive slack during task performance, which can be used to address non-routine events or allocate more mental resources to strategic decision-making (Morgan & Hancock, 2011; Quinn et al., 2012; Voss et al., 2008). This cognitive slack is crucial for strategic thinking, which requires considerable mental energy and availability to examine various alternatives and approach challenges in a divergent manner. Routines can significantly influence the success or failure of an organization by determining its ability to survive and grow.

7.8 Core infrastructure practical benefits

In our view, core infrastructure is a vital component of a company's survival, as it encompasses all aspects of the organization's daily operations and long-term success. This includes fostering collaboration among employees to achieve corporate objectives. As the foundation that underlies all resources, organizational capabilities, routines, and processes, the core infrastructure serves as the backbone of the company. It can drive growth, adaptability, and economic returns when properly aligned and coordinated with a business model. Core infrastructure offers five key advantages in terms of practical benefits.

Developing clear and achievable skills and work routines can significantly *increase the productivity and efficiency* within a company. By concentrating on what a company does best and focusing on specific tasks and goals, it is possible to achieve the best value proposition for customers. Configured properly, these capabilities can improve people's skills, simplify workflows, reduce the time and effort required to complete tasks, and foster collaboration and efficiency. Consequently, productivity and profitability are significantly enhanced.

Second, core infrastructure helps *decrease uncertainty*, *ambiguity*, and *misconceptions*. By establishing clear and well-defined workflows that are consistent with the model and business objectives, employees are better able to manage their daily activities and prioritize their tasks. This approach also promotes a healthy work-life balance, enables employees to think critically about opportunities for improvement, and encourages them to propose innovative solutions. Moreover, this approach fosters a sense of purpose and direction, allowing employees to understand the "why," "what," "how," and "when" of their tasks and activities.

Third, the core infrastructure guarantees *consistent* task execution, thereby ensuring that similar outcomes are achieved by different team members when performing the same task. Consistency fosters quality control, facilitates identification of the underlying factors responsible for any issues that may arise, and ultimately results in enhanced customer satisfaction and loyalty.

Fourth, core infrastructure plays a crucial role in facilitating the execution of strategic initiatives. A competent workforce possesses the necessary skills and competencies that are instrumental in supporting processes and directly contributing to the company's strategic goals. If personnel or processes are found to be inefficient, it is likely that infrastructure will be inefficient.

Ultimately, an individual is the most critical component of core infrastructure. To construct a robust and successful infrastructure, as well as a high-performing company, the quality of personnel and leadership is of paramount importance. A healthy and innovative organizational culture and hiring practices that ensure that the right individuals are in place to support the infrastructure and support employees to maintain the systems and processes are all essential for enhancing human capital.

7.9 Conclusion

Constructing a robust core infrastructure is essential for developing scalable, efficient, and profitable enterprises. Nonetheless, it is crucial to recognize that each business is distinct in terms of its industry, market, dimensions, and specific requirements. Therefore, a personalized approach is required for infrastructure optimization.

Recognizing the significance of core infrastructure offers companies the opportunity to enhance their processes, streamline their operations, and boost their responsiveness to change, thereby enabling them to remain competitive in volatile markets. Establishing an optimal infrastructure that caters to the market is not only a basic requirement, but also a crucial strategic move for long-term viability. Thus, constructing and maintaining robust core infrastructure is indispensable for businesses, and we believe that incorporating the four pillars outlined in this chapter is the most effective approach.

Notes

1 Microfoundations are defined as specific actions and interactions that occur at both the individual and group levels, which ultimately influence strategy development and organizational performance. The aforementioned actions involve the use of resources and capabilities, which are collectively facilitated by specific micro-level routines, skills, and competencies that collaborate to bring about the desired outcome (Eisenhardt et al., 2010; Foss & Linder, 2019).

2 In this work, the term "organizational routines" is interpreted as constructions of the collective level, thus, throughout the text, the term "routines" is understood as "organizational routines."

3 The discussion of the routinization levels of organizational capabilities goes beyond the scope of this chapter; however, it is an excellent avenue for future investigations.

References

Ali, R., Lynch, R., Melewar, T., & Jin, Z. (2015). The moderating influences on the relationship of corporate reputation with its antecedents and consequences: A meta-analytic review. *Journal of Business Research, 68*, 1105–1117.

Amit, R., & Schoemaker, P. (1993). Strategic assets and organisational rent. *Strategic Management Journal, 14*(1), 33–46.

Andersen, B., Fagerhaug, T., Henriksen, B., & Onsoyen, L. E. (2008). *Mapping Work Processes*. Milwaukee, WI: American Society for Quality; Quality Press.

Andersen, O., & Kheam, L. S. (1998). Resource-based theory and international growth strategies: An exploratory study. *International Business Review*, 7(2), 163–184.

Arraya, M. (2022). The relationship between distinctive capabilities system, learning orientation, leadership and performance. *European Journal of Management Studies*, *27*(2), 205–227.

Arraya, M. (2024). Capabilities configurational method for organizations' sustainability: antecedents and consequences. *International Journal of Management Concepts and Philosophy*, *17*(2), 215-233.

Altintas, G. & Ambrosini, V. (2019). Dynamic managerial capabilities. In R. J. Aldag (Ed.) *Oxford Research Encyclopedia of Business and Management*, pp. 1–18. Oxford University Press.

Baía, E., & Ferreira, J.J. (2019). Dynamic capabilities and performance: How has the relationship been assessed? *Journal of Management & Organization*, *30*(1),188–217.

Baía, E., Ferreira, J., & Rodrigues, R. (2020). Value and rareness of resources and capabilities as sources of competitive advantage and superior performance. *Knowledge Management Research & Practice, 18*(3), 249–262.

Barney, J. B. (1991). Firm resources and sustained competitive advantage. *Journal of Management*, *17*(1), 99–120.

Barney, J.B. and Arikan, A.M. (2001). The Resource-based view: origins and implications. In: Hitt, M.A., Freeman, R.E. and Harrison, J.S., (Eds.), *The Blackwell Handbook of Strategic Management*. pp. 124–188. Hoboken: Wiley-Blackwell.

Barney, J. B., & Hesterly, W. S. (2009). *Strategic Management and Competitive Advantage: Concepts and Cases*, 3rd edition. Hoboken, New Jersey, United States: Prentice Hall.

Barney, J. B., Ketchen, D., & Wright, M. (2021). Resource-based theory and the value creation framework. *Journal of Management*, *47*(7), 1936–1955.

Barreto, I. (2010). Dynamic capabilities: A review of past research and an agenda for the future. *Journal of Management, 36*, 256–280.

Bingham, C. B., Heimeriks, K. H., Schijven, M., & Gates, S. (2015). Concurrent learning: How firms develop multiple dynamic capabilities in parallel. *Strategic Management Journal, 36*, 1802–1825.

Bocken, N. M., & Geradts, T. (2020). Barriers and drivers to sustainable business model innovation: Organization design and dynamic capabilities. *Long Range Planning, 53*(4), 101950.

Bojesson, C., & Fundin, A. (2021). Exploring microfoundations of dynamic capabilities – challenges, barriers and enablers of organizational change. *Journal of Organizational Change Management, 34*(1), 206–222.

Carew, D., Kandarian, F., Parisi-Carew, E., and Stoner, J. (2009). Is your organization high performing? In Ken Blanchard (Ed.). *Leading at a higher level, revised and expanded edition: Blanchard on leadership and creating high performing organizations,* 2nd Edition, (pp. 3–16). Pearson.

Cavusgil, E., Seggie, S. H., & Talay, M. B. (2007). Dynamic capabilities view: Foundations and research agenda. *Journal of Marketing Theory and Practice, 15*(2), 159–166.

Coates, T. T., & McDermott, C. M. (2002). An exploratory analysis of new competencies: A resource based view perspective. *Journal of Operations Management, 20*(5), 435–450.

Di Stefano, G., Peteraf, M., & Verona, G. (2014). The organizational drivetrain: A road to integration of dynamic capabilities research. *Academy of Management Perspectives, 28*(4), 307–327.

Dittrich, K., & Seidl, D. (2018). Emerging intentionality in routine dynamics: A pragmatist view. *Academy of Management Journal, 61*(1), 111–138.

Doheny, M., Nagali, V., & Weig, F. (2012). Agile operations for volatile times. *McKinsey Quarterly*. Retrieved from https://www.mckinsey.com/capabilities/operations/our-insights/agile-operations-for-volatile-times

Dosi, G., Faillo, M., & Marengo, L. (2008). Organizational capabilities, patterns of knowledge accumulation and governance structures in business firms: An introduction. *Organization Studies, 29*(8–9), 1165–1185.

Drnevich, P. L., & Kriauciunas, A. P. (2011). Clarifying the conditions and limits of the contributions of ordinary and dynamic capabilities to relative firm performance. *Strategic Management Journal, 32*, 254–279.

Drucker, P. F. (1974). *Management: Tasks, Responsibilities, Practices*. New York: Harper & Row.

Drucker, P. F. (2001). *Management Challenges for the 21st Century*. New York: HarperBusiness.

Dumas, M., Rosa, M. L., Mendling, J., & Reijers, H. A. (2018). *Fundamentals of Business Process Management*, 2nd edition pp. 75–115. Berlin, Heidelberg: Springer.

Dutta, S., Narasimhan, O., & Rajiv, S. (2005). Conceptualizing and measuring capabilities: Methodology and empirical application. *Strategic Management Journal, 26*, 277–285.

Eisenhardt, K. M., Furr, N. R., & Bingham, C. B. (2010). Microfoundations of performance: Balancing efficiency and flexibility in dynamic environments. *Organization Science, 21*, 1263–1273.

Eisenhardt, K. & Piezunka, H. (2011). *Complexity and Corporate Strategy*. Sage Handbook of Complexity and Management, 506–523.

Eriksson, T., Heikkilä, M., & Nummela, N. (2022). Business model innovation for resilient international growth. *Small Enterprise Research, 29*(3), 205–226.

Feldman, M. S. (2016). Routines as process: Past, present, and future. In Howard-Grenville, J., Rerup, C., Langley, A., & Tsoukas, H. (Eds), *Organizational Routines: How They Are Created, Maintained, and Changed*, pp. 23–46, (Oxford, 2016; online edn, Oxford Academic, 19 May 2016), https://doi.org/10.1093/acprof:oso/9780198759485.003.0002, accessed 26 March, 2024

Fainshmidt; S., Judge, W. Q., Aguilera, R. V., & Smith, A. (2018). Varieties of institutional systems: A contextual taxonomy of understudied countries. *Journal of World Business, 51*(1), 40–49.

Feldman, M. S., & Pentland, B. T. (2003). Reconceptualizing organisational routines as a source of flexibility and change. *Administrative Science Quarterly, 48*, 94–118.

Feldman, M. S., & Pentland, B. T. (2022). Routine dynamics: Toward a critical conversation. *Strategic Organization, 20*(4), 846–859.Ferreira, J., & Fernandes, C. (2017). Resources and capabilities' effects on firm performance: What are they? *Journal of Knowledge Management, 21*(5), 1202–1217.

Ferreira, J. J. M., Fernandes, C. I., & Ferreira, F. A. F. (2022). What makes organizations unique? Looking inside the box. *Journal of Business Research, 139*, 664–674.

Foss, N. J., & Linder, S. (2019). *Microfoundations. Nature, Debate, and Promise*. Cambridge University Press, UK.

Foss, N. J., & Pedersen, T. (2016). Microfoundations in strategy research. *Strategic Management Journal, 37*, E22–E34.

George, N., & Kerai, A. (2022). Ordinary capabilities and firm performance: The role of capital market development. *Asia Pacific Journal of Management*. Retrieved from https://doi.org/10.1007/s10490-022-09848-3

Godin, S. (2020). *The Practice: Shipping Creative Work*. New York, United States: Penguin Random House.

Goel, K., Bandara, W., & Gable, G. (2023). Conceptualizing business process standardization: A review and synthesis. *Schmalenbach Journal of Business Research, 75*, 195–237.

Grant, R. (1991). The resource-based theory of competitive advantage. *California Management Review, 33*, 114–488.

Grant, R. M. (2010). *Contemporary Strategy Analysis*, 7th edition. Wiley.

Gray, E. R., & Balmer, J. M. (1998). Managing corporate image and corporate reputation. *Long Range Planning, 31*, 695–702.

Guha, S., Grover, V., Kettinger, W. J., & Teng, J. T. C. (1997). Business process change and organizational performance: Exploring an antecedent model. *Journal of Management Information Systems, 14*(1), 119–154.

Harreld, J. B., O'Reilly, C. A., & Tushman, M. L. (2007). Dynamic capabilities at IBM: Driving strategy into action. *California Management Review, 49*(4), 21–43.

Helfat, C. E., Finkelstein, S., Mitchell, W., Peteraf, M. A., Singh, H., Teece, D. J., et al. (2007). *Dynamic Capabilities: Understanding Strategic Change in Organizations*. Malden, MA: Blackwell.

Helfat, C. E., & Peteraf, M. A. (2009). Understanding dynamic capabilities: Progress along a developmental path. *Strategic Organization, 7*, 91–102.

Helfat, C. E., & Winter, S. G. (2011). Untangling dynamic and operational capabilities: Strategy for the (N) ever-changing world. *Strategic Management Journal, 32*, 1243–1250.

Hine, D., Parker, R., Pregelj, L., & Verreynne, M. L. (2014). Deconstructing and reconstructing the capability hierarchy. *Industrial and Corporate Change, 23*, 1299–1325.

Hollensbe, E., Wookey, C., Hickey, L., & George, G. (2014). Organizations with purpose. *Academy of Management, 57*(5), 1227e1234.

Hoopes D. G., Madsen T. L., & Walker, G. (2003). Guest editors' introduction to the special issue: Why is there a resource-based view? Toward a theory of competitive heterogeneity. *Strategic Management Journal, Special Issue 24*(10), 889–902.

Howard-Grenville, J., & Rerup, C. (2016). A process perspective on organisational routines. In Langley, A., & Tsoukas, H. (Eds), *The SAGE Handbook of Organisation Process Studies*, pp. 323–337. London: Sage.

Inigo, E. A., Albareda, L., & Ritala, P. (2017). Business model innovation for sustainability: Exploring evolutionary and radical approaches through dynamic capabilities. *Industry and Innovation, 24*(5), 515–542.

Ireland, R.D., & Webb, J.W. (2007) Strategic entrepreneurship: creating competitive advantage through streams of innovation. *Business Horizons, 50*(1), 49–59.

Jancenelle, V. E. (2021). Tangible–Intangible resource composition and firm success. *Technovation, 108*(C), 102337.

Jantunen, A., Tarkiainen, A., Chari, S., & Oghazi, P. (2018). Dynamic capabilities, operational changes, and performance outcomes in the media industry. *Journal of Business Research, 89*(C), 251–257.

Kamasak, R. (2017). The contribution of tangible and intangible resources, and capabilities to a firm's profitability and market performance. *European Journal of Management and Business Economics*, *26*(2), 252–275.

Karna, A., Richter, A., & Riesenkampff, E. (2016). Revisiting the role of the environment in the capabilities-financial performance relationship: A meta-analysis. *Strategic Management Journal, 37*, 1154–1173.

Katila, R., & Ahuja, G. (2002). Something old, something new: A longitudinal study of search behavior and new product introduction. *Academy of Management Journal, 45*(6), 1183–1194.

Kettenbohrer, J., Beimborn, D., & Kloppenburg, M. (2013). Developing a governance model for successful business process standardization. In *Proceedings of the Nineteenth Americas Conference on Information Systems,* Chicago, IL: AIS Electronic Library (AISeL).

Khan, O., Daddi, T., & Iraldo, F. (2020). Microfoundations of dynamic capabilities: insights from circular economy business cases. *Business Strategy and the Environment, 29*, 1479e1493.

Koumakhov, R., & Marengo, L. (2023). Organizational routines: Between change and stability—Introduction to the special section. *Industrial and Corporate Change, 32*(6), 1305–1318.

Lafley, A. G., & Martin, R. L. (2013). *Playing to Win: How Strategy Really Works*. Boston, MA: Harvard Business School Publishing.

Lager, T., & Simms, C. D. (2023). From customer understanding to design for processability: Reconceptualizing the formal product innovation work process for non-assembled products. *Technovation, 125*, 102750.

Lamberti, L. (2013). Customer centricity: The construct and the operational antecedents. *Journal of Strategic Marketing, 21*, 588–612.

Leinwand, P., & Mainardi, C. (2011). *The Essential Advantage: How to Win with Capabilities-Driven Strategy*. Boston, MA: Harvard Business Review Press.

Lemanska-Majdzik, A., & Okreglicka, M. (2015). Identification of business processes in an enterprise management. *Procedia Economics and Finance, 27*, 394–403.

Lorenz, E. N. (1972). *Predictability: Does the Flap of a Butterfly's Wings in Brazil Set off a Tornado in Texas*. Washington, DC: American Association for the Advancement of Science.

Mahmoodzadeh, E., Jalalinia, S., & Yazdi, F. N. (2009). A business process outsourcing framework based on business process management and knowledge management. *Business Process Management Journal, 15*(6), 845–864.

Makadok, R. (2001). Toward a synthesis of the resource-based and dynamic-capability views of rent creation. *Strategic Management Journal, 22*(5), 387–401.

Matarazzo, M., Penco, L., Profumo, G., & Quaglia, R. (2021). Digital transformation and customer value creation in Made in Italy SMEs: A dynamic capabilities perspective. *Journal of Business Research, 123*(C), 642–656.

McGrath, R. G. (2019). *Seeing Around Corners: How to Spot Inflection Points in Business Before They Happen*. New York: Houghton Mifflin Harcourt Publishing Company.

Mikalef, P., & Pateli, A. (2017). Information technology-enabled dynamic capabilities and their indirect effect on competitive performance: Findings from PLS-SEM and fsQCA. *Journal of Business Research, 70*, 1–16.

Miller, D., & Shamsie, J. (1996). The resource-based view of the firm in two environments: The Hollywood firm studios from 1936 to 1965. *Academy of Management Journal, 39*(3), 519–543.

Morgan, J. F., & Hancock, P. A. (2011). The effect of prior task loading on mental workload: An example of hysteresis in driving. *Human Factors, 53*(1), 75–86.

Morgan, N. A. (2012). Marketing and business performance. *Journal of the Academy of Marketing Science*, *40*(1), 102–119.

Muenstermann, B. (2015). State of the art of BPS research. In *Business Process Standardization: A Multi-Methodological Analysis of Drivers and Consequences*, pp. 29–118. Hershey: IGI Global. *Proceedings*. 64. https://aisel.aisnet.org/confirm2008/64

Muenstermann, B., Eckhardt, A., & Weitzel, T. (2010). The performance impact of business process standardization. *Business Process Management Journal, 16*(1), 29–56.

Newbert, S. (2007). Empirical research on the resource? Based view of the firm: An assessment and suggestions for future research. *Strategic Management Journal, 28*(2), 121–146.

Newey, L. R., Verreynne, M.-L., & Griffiths, A. (2012). The relationship between dynamic and operating capabilities as a stage-gate process: Insights from radical innovation. *Journal of Management and Organization, 18*(1), 123–140.

Ohly, S., Sonnentag, S., & Pluntke, F. (2006). Routinization, work characteristics and their relationships with creative and proactive behaviors. *Journal of Organizational Behavior, 27*(3), 257–279.

Ordanini, A., & Rubera, G. (2008). Strategic capabilities and internet resources in procurement: A resource-based view of B-to-B buying processes. *International Journal of Operations and Production Management, 28*(1), 27–52.

Peng, D. X., Schroeder, R. G., & Shah, R. (2008). Linking routines to operations capabilities: A new perspective. *Journal of Operations Management, 26*(6), 730–748.

Penrose, E. (1959). *The Theory of the Growth of the Firm*. Basil Blackwell, Oxford.

Protogerou, A., Caloghirou, Y., & Lioukas, S. (2012). Dynamic capabilities and their indirect impact on firm performance. *Industrial and Corporate Change, 21*(3), 615–647.

Quinn, R. W., Spreitzer, G. M., & Lam, C. F. (2012). Building a sustainable model of human energy in organizations: Exploring the critical role of resources. *Academy of Management Annals, 6*(1), 337–396.

Rashidirad, M., & Salimian, H. (2020). SMEs' dynamic capabilities and value creation: The mediating role of competitive strategy. *European Business Review, 32*(4), 591–613.

Reichheld, F. F., Darnell, D., & Burns, M. (2021). *Winning on Purpose: The Unbeatable Strategy of Loving Customers*. Harvard Business Review Press, Massachusetts, United States.

Rivkin, J. (2000). Imitation of complex strategies. *Management Science*, *46*, 824–844.

Romero, H. L., Dijkman, R. M., Grefen, P. W. P. J., & van Weele, A. J. (2015). Factors that determine the extent of business process standardization and the subsequent effect on business performance. *Business & Information Systems Engineering, 57*(4), 261–270.

Salvato, C. (2021). Dynamic capabilities and routine dynamics. In: Feldman, M. S., Pentland, B. T., D'Adderio, L., et al. (Eds), *Cambridge Handbook of Routine Dynamics*, pp. 460–480. Cambridge: Cambridge University Press.

Salvato, C., & Vassolo, R. (2018). The sources of dynamism in dynamic capabilities. *Strategic Management Journal, 39*, pp. 1728–1752.

Schilke, O., Hu, S., & Helfat, C. E. (2018). Quo vadis, dynamic capabilities? A content-analytic review of the current state of knowledge and recommendations for future research. *Academy of Management Annals, 12*, 390–439.

Schreyogg, G., & Kliesch-Eberl, M. (2007). How dynamic can organizational capabilities be? Towards a dual-process model of capability dynamization. *Strategic Management Journal, 28*(9), 913–933.

Simon, A. (2010). Resources, dynamic capabilities and Australian business success. *Journal of Global Business and Technology*, *6*(2), 12–31.

Sirmon, D. G., Gove, S., & Hitt, M. A. (2008). Resource management in dyadic competitive rivalry: The effects of resource bundling and deployment. *Academy of Management Journal*, *51*(5), 919–935.

Strnadl, C. F. (2006). Aligning business and it: The process-driven architecture model. *Information Systems Management, 23*(4), 67–77.

Stroh, L. K., & Caligiuri, P. M. (1998). Increasing global competitiveness through effective people management. *Journal of World Business, 33*(1), 1–16.

Sull, D., Sull, C., & Zweig. B. (2022). Toxic culture is driving the great resignation. *MIT Sloan Management Review*. Retrieved from https://sloanreview.mit.edu/article/toxic-culture-is-driving-the-great-resignation/

Sullivan, G. M. (2011). A primer on the validity of assessment instruments. *Journal of Graduate Medical Education,3*(2), 119–120.

Sullivan, T. (2011). Embracing complexity. *Harvard Business Review*, September.

Teece, D.J., Pisano, G. & Shuen, A. (1997). Dynamic capabilities and strategic management. *Strategic Management Journal, 18*(7), 509–533.

Teece, D. J. (2007). Explicating dynamic capabilities: The nature and microfoundations of (sustainable) enterprise performance. *Strategic Management Journal, 28*, 1319e1350.

Teece, D. J. (2018). Business models and dynamic capabilities. *Long Range Planning, 51*(1), 40–49.

Teece, D. J. (2023). The evolution of the dynamic capabilities framework. FGF Studies in Small Business and Entrepreneurship. In Adams, R., Grichnik, D., Pundziene, A., & Volkmann, C. (Eds), *Artificiality and Sustainability in Entrepreneurship*, pp. 113–129. Berlim, Germany: Springer.

Tregear, R. (2015). Business process standardization. In J. vom Brocke, M. Rosemann (Eds), *Strategic Alignment, Governance, People and Culture Handbook on Business Process Management*, Vol. 2pp. 421–442. Berlin, Heidelberg: Springer.

Voss, G. B., Sirdeshmukh, D., & Voss, Z. G. (2008). The effects of slack resources and environmental threat on product exploration and exploitation. *Academy of Management Journal, 51*, 147–164.

Walsh, G., & Beatty, S. E. (2007). Customer-based corporate reputation of a service firm: Scale development and validation. *Journal of the Academy of Marketing Science, 35*, 127–143.

Warnier, V., Weppe, X., & Lecocq, X. (2013). Extending resource-based theory: Considering strategic, ordinary and junk resources. *Management Decision, 51*(7), 1359–1379.

Wenzel, M., Danner-Schröder, A., & Spee, A. P. (2021). Dynamic capabilities? Unleashing their dynamics through a practice perspective on organisational routines. *Journal of Management Inquiry, 30*, 395–406.

Weske, M. (2019). Business process modelling foundation. In Weske, M. (Ed.) *Business Process Management*, pp. 71–122. Springer, Berlin, Heidelberg. https://doi.org/10.1007/978-3-540-73522-9_3

Winter, S. G. (2000). The satisfying principle in capability learning. *Strategic Management Journal, 21*(10/11), 981–996.

Winter, S. G. (2003). Understanding dynamic capabilities. *Strategic Management Journal, 24*(10), 991–995.

Winter, S. G. (2013). Habit, deliberation, and action: Strengthening the microfoundations of routines and capabilities. *Academy of Management Perspectives, 27*, 120–137.

Wohlgemuth, V., & Wenzel, M. (2016). Dynamic capabilities and routinization. *Journal of Business Research, 69*, 1944–1948.

Wu, S. J., Melnyk, S. A., & Flynn, B. B. (2010). Operational capabilities: The secret ingredient. *Decision Sciences, 41*, 721–754.

Yoshikuni, A. C., & Dwivedi, R. (2023). The role of enterprise information systems strategies enabled strategy-making on organizational innovativeness: A resource orchestration perspective. *Journal of Enterprise Information Management, 36*(1), 172–196.

8

SUPPORTING BUSINESS VIABILITY AND COMPETITIVENESS THROUGH SUSTAINABILITY-BASED ADAPTATION

Rodolfo Damiano, Marcantonio Ruisi, and Federico Cosenz

8.1 Introduction

An ever-evolving array of challenges and opportunities characterizes the modern business landscape. Among these, sustainability has emerged as a pivotal driver of innovation, particularly in the realm of business models. As organizations navigate the complexities of today's competitive and socially conscious markets, adaptation to sustainability plays a central role in shaping their strategies and ensuring long-term viability.

In the domain of business development and survival, innovation is not merely a buzzword; it is nowadays an imperative. The ability to innovate business models is crucial to guaranteeing their resilience and, ultimately, the survival of the organizations they represent. Failure to adapt business models in response to the demands of the competitive and social environments within which businesses operate can signify a grim prognosis for long-term success.

Recent studies have underscored the significance of sustainability in guiding businesses toward the achievement of economic, social, and environmental goals. By embracing sustainability, organizations not only enhance their resource utilization but also bolster their competitiveness by harnessing sustainability-based competitive advantages. In an era marked by global sustainability efforts, epitomized by initiatives like Agenda 2030 (UN, 2015) and the associated Sustainable Development Goals (SDGs), the role of sustainability in shaping business models and competitive strategies becomes even more pronounced.

This chapter delves into the symbiotic relationship between sustainability, adaptability, innovation, and competitiveness in the context of business models. By examining the extant contributions to this dynamic domain, we aim to shed light on how organizations can leverage the adaptability brought about by sustainability

DOI: 10.4324/9781032695969-9

to foster innovation and gain competitive advantages. Our endeavor is to present a framework that guides sustainability-based business model innovation, facilitating the realization of competitive advantages in today's dynamic marketplace.

As we embark on this exploration, it is essential to acknowledge the wealth of research and insights that have paved the way for our understanding of this subject. By building upon the works of researchers such as Lüdeke-Freund (2020) and Bocken et al. (2014), we aim to synthesize the current state of knowledge in this domain and offer a comprehensive framework that both academics and professionals can apply.

In this chapter, we dissect the multifaceted relationship between sustainability, business model innovation, and competitive advantages. We explore the various dimensions of sustainability, analyze the dynamics of innovation within business models, and elucidate how these elements collectively propel organizations toward a more sustainable and competitive future.

8.2 Business model innovation in search for competitive advantages

Maintaining a competitive edge is a formidable challenge in the rapidly evolving landscape of contemporary business. Business model innovation (BMI) has emerged as an essential strategic activity to adapt and thrive in this dynamic environment. This section focuses on the concept of BMI, explores its underlying principles, and describes how it serves as a catalyst for creating and sustaining competitive advantages within organizations.

8.2.1 Defining business model innovation

BMI entails a fundamental re-evaluation and redesign of the way an organization creates, delivers, and captures value (Johnson et al., 2008). Unlike conventional product or service innovation, which focuses on incremental improvements, BMI seeks to redefine core aspects of how a company operates, interacts with its stakeholders, and generates revenue over time. As such, it entails one or more relevant changes in the original business model of the firm (Foss & Saebi, 2018).

8.2.2 The dynamics of competitive advantage

Competitive advantage is the capability of an organization to outperform rivals by offering distinct products, services, or solutions that provide superior value to customers (Porter, 1985). BMI becomes instrumental in achieving and sustaining competitive advantage for various reasons. Firstly, BMI allows organizations to stand out in the market by offering something unique from competitors. This differentiation can show up in pricing strategies, customer experiences, distribution channels, or revenue models. For example, the subscription-based model introduced by Netflix disrupted the traditional video rental industry (Wasserman,

2013). Additionally, innovative business models can yield cost efficiencies that competitors find challenging to replicate. By optimizing processes, leveraging technology, or sharing resources, organizations can reduce operational costs and offer more competitive pricing to customers. Amazon's utilization of its extensive fulfillment network exemplifies this (Hill, 2014). Yet, BMI empowers organizations to align more closely with evolving customer needs and preferences. Customer-centric models enhance loyalty, increase retention rates, and attract new customers, all contributing to a competitive advantage. Apple's integrated ecosystem of hardware, software, services, and content characterizes customer-centric innovation (Hinterhuber & Liozu, 2016). In terms of market expansion strategies, innovative business models can open up new markets and customer segments that were previously untapped. For instance, Airbnb's peer-to-peer home-sharing model not only transformed the hospitality industry but also created new opportunities for homeowners to monetize their properties (Zervas et al., 2017). Ultimately, in a volatile business environment, adaptability is critical. BMI equips organizations with the agility to respond swiftly to changes in technology, regulations, or market conditions. This adaptability can be a powerful source of competitive advantage (Markides, 2013).

8.2.3 Examples of business model innovation

Several prominent examples illustrate how BMI has driven competitive advantages. For example, Apple's transition from a product-centric model to an ecosystem-based model, encompassing hardware, software, services, and content, has fostered customer loyalty, recurring revenue streams, and a dominant market position (Cusumano & Gawer, 2002). As for Tesla, its direct-to-consumer sales model, coupled with continuous over-the-air software updates, challenges traditional automakers and enables rapid adaptation to changing market demands. Yet, Uber's platform-based model disrupted the taxi industry by providing a more convenient and cost-effective transportation solution, backed by real-time data analytics (Cramer & Krueger, 2016).

In an intensely competitive business landscape, organizations must continually seek ways to differentiate themselves and maintain relevance. BMI emerges as a dynamic pathway to foster competitive advantages. By reimagining how they create, deliver, and capture value, organizations can differentiate themselves, reduce costs, enhance customer-centricity, expand their markets, and adapt more effectively to change. Through these means, BMI is a powerful driver of competitive advantage in modern markets.

8.3 Sustainability-driven adaptability

The global business landscape is undergoing a profound transformation, shaped by environmental, social, and economic challenges. Climate change, resource scarcity, social inequality, and regulatory shifts are redefining the rules of the game. In this context, sustainability-driven adaptability has emerged as a crucial concept for organizations seeking to thrive in an uncertain future. This section explores the concept of sustainability-driven adaptability, its significance, underlying principles, and how organizations can harness it to navigate an evolving world successfully.

8.3.1 Defining sustainability-driven adaptability

Sustainability-driven adaptability refers to an organization's capacity to respond effectively to sustainability challenges and opportunities by adjusting its strategies, processes, and behaviors in a timely and agile manner. It goes beyond mere compliance with sustainability regulations; instead, it entails a proactive stance to align an organization's operations with sustainable principles (Lozano, 2015).

Sustainability-driven adaptability is significant for several reasons:

- Resilience to environmental risks: Organizations that proactively adapt to sustainability challenges, such as climate change and resource depletion, are better positioned to mitigate environmental risks. By reducing their ecological footprint, they safeguard their operations from the increasing volatility of resource prices and supply chain disruptions (Sullivan & Gouldson, 2019).
- Enhanced reputation and stakeholder engagement: Demonstrating a commitment to sustainability fosters trust among stakeholders, including customers, investors, and employees. Sustainability-driven adaptability can enhance an organization's reputation, attract ethical investors, and improve employee retention rates (Sharma & Henriques, 2005).
- Innovation and competitiveness: Sustainable adaptability fuels innovation. Organizations that embrace sustainability-driven adaptability are more likely to uncover new market opportunities, develop eco-friendly products, and adopt circular business models, which, in turn, can lead to competitive advantages (Schaltegger et al., 2012).
- Compliance and risk mitigation: As global regulations related to sustainability become more stringent, organizations that fail to adapt may face legal and financial repercussions. Sustainability-driven adaptability ensures compliance and minimizes legal and reputational risks (Delmas & Toffel, 2008).

To nurture sustainability-driven adaptability, organizations should consider some principles suggested by the prevailing literature. In this regard, Schuler and Jackson (1987) remark that senior leadership must champion sustainability-driven adaptability initiatives, setting the tone for the entire organization. Commitment at the top fosters a culture of sustainability and aligns business strategies with sustainability goals. In addition, as Waddock and Bodwell (2004) suggest, organizations should promote a culture of continuous learning and adaptation. This involves regular assessment of sustainability risks and opportunities, feedback loops, and the willingness to adjust strategies based on emerging challenges.

Yet, Freeman (1984) stresses that engaging stakeholders, including customers, employees, suppliers, and communities, is crucial. Their insights and expectations can inform sustainability strategies and initiatives, enhancing their relevance and effectiveness. Ultimately, Eisenhardt and Martin (2000) argue that sustainability-driven adaptability often relies on innovative solutions and technology. Therefore, organizations should invest in research and development to identify sustainable technologies and practices that can transform their operations.

8.3.2 *Harnessing sustainability-driven adaptability*

Organizations can harness sustainability-driven adaptability through various strategies. Table 8.1 summarizes those strategies that have recently emerged as the most promising for pursuing sustainability-driven adaptability.

Organizations embrace sustainability-driven adaptability to remain resilient and competitive in an era of increasing environmental and social challenges. Proactive adaptation to sustainability principles not only minimizes risks but also fosters innovation, enhances reputation, and positions organizations for long-term success. Sustainability-driven adaptability is not merely a response to external pressures but a strategic imperative for organizations aiming to thrive in a rapidly changing world.

TABLE 8.1 Examples of sustainability-driven adaptability strategies

Strategy	*Description*	*Authors*
Circular economy	Embracing circular economy principles, such as reusing, remanufacturing, and recycling, can improve resource use and minimize waste, contributing to both sustainability and cost-efficiency	Kirchherr et al. (2017)
Eco-design	Integrating sustainability considerations into product design and development processes can lead to innovative, eco-friendly products that resonate with environmentally conscious consumers	Mont and Plepys (2012)
Regulatory compliance	Staying informed about evolving sustainability regulations and proactively adjusting operations to align with these standards can prevent costly legal and reputational issues (e.g., ESG, SDGs)	Delmas and Toffel (2010)
Supply chain optimization	Organizations can promote sustainability-driven adaptability by working closely with suppliers to reduce environmental impacts, enhance transparency, and ensure responsible sourcing (e.g., industrial symbiosis)	Seuring and Müller (2008)

8.4 Pursuing sustainability-driven adaptability through BMI

8.4.1 *In search of a sustainable business model*

In such a dynamic era characterized by a major consciousness and attention by civil society, public authorities, and the market on the complexity of social and environmental issues, organizations must become part of the solution, not the problem. This is not simply a call for the planet but for organizations' survival. Indeed, organizations operate in a complex institutional system characterized by societal pressures capable of determining their success or failure (see DiMaggio & Powell, 1983; Morioka et al., 2017). Therefore, they should align their performances with society's expectations and contribute to a more sustainable economic system. The question is: how can companies follow this path?

Morioka et al. (2017) attempt to provide a concrete understanding of how companies should act in this regard. The authors highlight that commercializing sustainable products is not sufficient. Indeed, they posit that organizations should strategically align all their processes to sustainable principles. Therefore, organizations should shift their activities into sustainable business models (SBM). However, Morioka and colleagues point out that the literature on SBM is still in its infancy and necessitates major research efforts to reveal organizations' potentiality for helping our society and preserving natural environment resources while staying profitable. For instance, the authors emphasize that there is still no consensus on the components of an SBM. Notably, the authors posit that while several archetypes of possible SBMs can be currently identified (e.g., "create value from waste" and "maximize energy efficiency"), these archetypes risk not generating a business that can be systematically sustainable. They suggest that organizations could focus on isolated initiatives regarding these archetypes by not integrating them into their business's core. Similarly, in 2007, Porter and Kramer had already posed that although organizations have become aware of the social and environmental risks of their operations, they often respond to these risks through uncoordinated lists of "sustainable initiatives" lacking an underlying strategic vision.

Such behavior from organizations' decision-makers risks not leading to the creation of the so-called "shared value" (see Porter & Kramer, 2011) but masking BMs merely oriented by the financial paradigm of value as SBMs.

However, Morioka and colleagues precise that SBMs should systematically integrate sustainability principles into organizational strategy and operations to create and deliver not only financial but also "sustainable value" and achieve objectives that "traditional business models" cannot. Further, in line with the "shared value" concept (Porter & Kramer, 2011), they specify that SBMs are not attempts to revoke the business-as-usual perspective, but to complement it using a more systemic approach to business. Therefore, SBMs are about broadening the traditionally financially oriented paradigm of business to address sustainability challenges. According to Morioka et al. (2017), SBM should enable corporate sustainability performance to produce sustainable value exchange with stakeholders. Specifically, corporate sustainability performance can be conceived as the organization's capacity to meet societal or stakeholder expectations regarding corporate behavior (Di Vaio et al., 2022).

In this regard, the authors highlight the complexity related to the generation of such a value. Indeed, they remind us that while well-defined metrics exist for financial performance, the same is not true for generating sustainable value. However, in highlighting that this kind of value is related to stakeholders' expectations, they specify that organizations should be aware of sustainability trade-offs and stakeholder conflicts to comply with SBM challenges. In particular, Morioka and colleagues highlight that the value generation for stakeholders can be associated with the organization's resource-based view. This is because previous studies show a positive relationship between investing in resources and capabilities for corporate sustainability and improving organizations' competitive advantages (Hart, 1995; Bansal, 2005), suggesting the integration of sustainability challenges into organizations' strategies (Engert et al., 2016).

On this basis, Morioka et al. (2017) results show that organizations carrying out an SBM are characterized by a value proposition composed by, on the one hand, the classic offering of products and services and, on the other, by the business purpose as an entrepreneurial dream based on sharable values and believes. This intangible part of the value proposition materializes competitive advantages that Morioka et al. (2017), relying on the resource-based view, identify in: (i) being authentic to the declared environmental and/or social cause, and having faith in the organization's objectives; (ii) employees' innovative problem-solving approaches, family atmosphere, and knowledge; (iii) networks of contacts and the combination of competition and cooperation with competitors capable of generating harmony.

All these elements should be taken into account when searching for the SBM.

8.4.2 Sustainable business model, dynamics, and innovation

While highly illuminating, the work of Morioka et al. (2017), as admitted by the authors, depicts a static picture of organizations' SBM, not offering evolutionary guidelines for its implementation. In this respect, other works have focused on the dynamicity needed to implement SBM and, particularly, to achieve SBM innovation through "sustainable business modeling." However, as Geissdoerfer et al. (2016) highlighted, SBM innovation is another emerging topic in business literature. Such a topic needs and deserves more research focus. Similarly, Roome and Louche (2016) notice that most of the research in this field is largely conceptual and offers a static view of a dynamic and complex reality.

Among the works that coped with this topic using a dynamic perspective, there are Girotra and Netessine (2013), Roome and Louche (2016), Geissdoerfer et al. (2016), and Cosenz et al. (2020).

Girotra and Netessine (2013) suggest that understanding the context of decision-making in existing business models and the related inefficiencies is pivotal to identifying new and more SBMs. They propose a dynamic three-step approach to achieve this task. The first step is to audit the current business model to identify those drivers capable of destroying value. The second step is to change the context of the decisions associated with the identified inefficiencies by stimulating brainstorming on new sustainable business models. Then, the final step suggested by the authors is to analyze and experiment with the identified business models to choose the most promising ones. Overall, the work of Girotra and Netessine (2013) emphasizes the importance of increasing organizations' consciousness of their decision-making processes and experimenting with new ideas.

In their work, Roome and Louche (2016) emphasize how new SBMs can be shaped by interactions between individuals and groups inside and outside organizations. Girotra and Netessine (2013) highlight the importance of considering value destruction and creation to define SBMs. However, their findings suggest to focus more on "sharing" to innovate. Specifically, they posit that the transformation of BMs toward SBMs relies on: (i) learning by building collaborations and acting around a new and improved vision, (ii) applying new concepts from outside the organization, (iii) implementing and reconfiguring networks.

Geissdoerfer et al. (2016) propose a workshop framework based on "design thinking" helping organizations to improve their performance while becoming more sustainable dynamically. Their work particularly emphasizes the pivotal importance of harmonizing conflicting stakeholder interests.

Lastly, Cosenz et al. (2020) propose a system dynamics approach – that we will deepen in the next sections of this work – to overcome organizations' difficulties in shifting from traditional BMs to SBMs.

Overall, these works highlight the call for supporting organizations in implementing SBMs. In investigating the SBMs' implementation process, these authors suggest focusing on organizations' dynamicity because of their nature of complex systems embedded in the societal context. Improving decision-making, staying open to collaborations, listening to stakeholders (internal and external), and trying to create harmony with them are fundamental steps to achieve SBM.

8.4.3 *Dynamic business modeling to achieve sustainability-related competitive advantages*

In light of the considerations above, sustainability-driven adaptability can offer enhanced support in innovating value creation processes (Hart, 1995; Bansal, 2005; Engert et al., 2016; Morioka et al., 2017). Therefore, inspired by previous literature (e.g., Bocken et al., 2014; Lüdeke-Freund, 2020), the results and suggestions of Girotra and Netessine (2013), Roome and Louche (2016), Geissdoerfer et al. (2016), Morioka et al. (2017), and by the research of Cosenz et al. (2020), we propose an approach for dynamic business modeling for sustainability (DBMfS) that may further boost the support to organizations to move toward

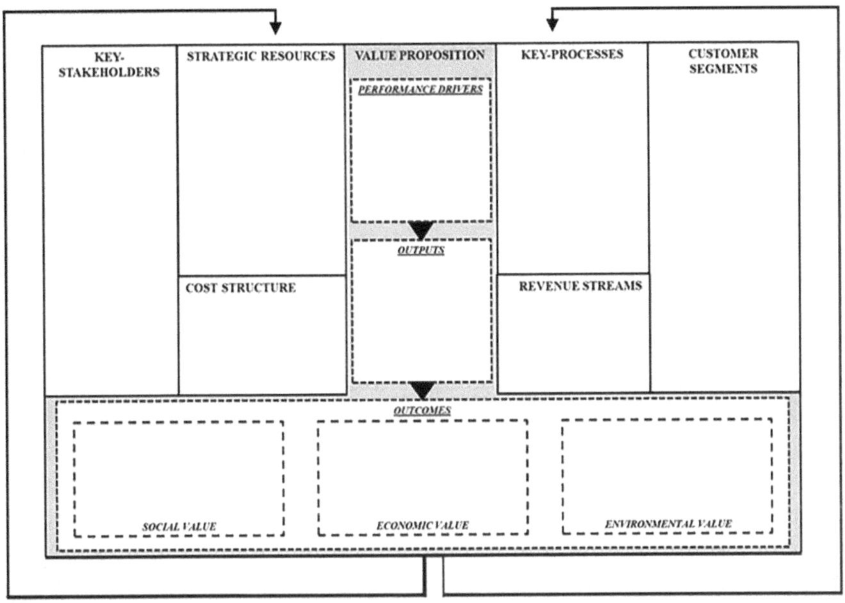

FIGURE 8.1 Our adaptation of the Dynamic Business Model for Sustainability structure by Cosenz et al. (2020). We added the two arrows at the edges of the canvas to emphasize the circular relationship between outcomes and the attraction of strategic resources and the improvement of key processes.

SBMs by expanding beyond organizational boundaries and encompassing supplementary elements in the business model to frame the inter-organizational dynamics allowing for the creation of sustainable value. As highlighted by Geissdoerfer et al. (2016), currently, only a few tools exist to help organizations in sustainable business modeling. Among these, the DBMfS proposed by Cosenz et al. (2020) is a method that employs a modified version of the business model canvas (Osterwalder & Pigneur, 2010) that integrates a systemic perspective, enabling the examination of the causal relationships among the key variables of the business model (Cosenz, 2017; Cosenz and Noto, 2018). Its structural framework, depicted in Figure 8.1, comprises seven primary building blocks that detail how sustainable value is generated, distributed, and captured. These building blocks encompass key stakeholders, strategic resources, essential processes, customer segments, sustainable value propositions, cost structures, and revenue streams.

Of particular significance is the value proposition, subdivided to incorporate outputs and their corresponding value drivers, as well as outcomes associated with the economic, social, and environmental aspects of the organization's value. Outputs refer to short-term achievements by an individual organization, while outcomes encompass the impact that the organization and its stakeholders foster in the long term.

This impact encompasses social, environmental, and economic outcomes, finally shaping the construct of sustainable value (Elkington, 1997). The representation of the outcome component aligns with the intangible dimension of the value proposition highlighted by Morioka et al. (2017).

When the key variables are identified and placed within their respective building blocks, their causal connections are examined to understand their relative influence (i.e., indirect and direct causal relationships) in shaping a causal feedback loops system (Sterman, 2000). These feedback loops can significantly contribute to promoting a common understanding of how to generate sustainable value and the areas where strategic changes and innovations can and should be implemented (Bocken et al., 2015) thanks to value exchange with internal and external stakeholders (Geissdoerfer et al., 2016; Roome & Louche, 2016). In such a context, locating and evaluating sustainable outcomes permits decision-makers to backtrack and pinpoint the outputs and the performance factors that contributed to these impacts. As Girotra and Netessine (2013) suggested, these characteristics of DBMfS should enhance critical reflection from decision-makers. Additionally, this systemic perspective pinpoints the strategic resources whose utilization impacts the sustainable performance drivers, thus simplifying the enactment of corrective measures. The creation of sustainable value is subsequently highlighted by outlining the processes of depletion and accumulation of resources due to the outputs and outcomes influences.

Sustainable value capture and the associated assessment are categorized into outputs and outcomes. Outputs encompass metrics related to the specific organizational results (e.g., sales volume, new customers). On the other hand, outcomes are focused on a comprehensive perspective of sustainable value, in line with Elkington's "triple bottom line" concept from 1997. These three elements incorporate and establish connections between measures that pertain to the environmental, social and economic value that the organization generates. In contrast to outputs, which are solely influenced by the single organization's actions, outcomes depend on the various actors that operate within the same reference value ecosystem.

Typically, representations of business models do not combine measurements of sustainable value (Lüdeke-Freund, 2020). While some tools for designing business models successfully consider sustainability (Bocken et al., 2014; Coffay & Bocken, 2023), they often overlook the interconnections among variables that impact the performance of a sustainable ecosystem. Nevertheless, integrating these interactions is essential for coping with complex sustainability-related challenges. In contrast, the DBMfS structure places great importance on this aspect. Consequently, it identifies the interactions between variables and the feedback loops that govern the functional framework of creating value sustainably (Cosenz et al., 2020). Further, in our proposition, we emphasize the resource-based view perspective, since previous studies show the highly positive impact of investing in resources and capabilities for corporate sustainability has on the generation of organizations' competitive advantages (Hart, 1995; Bansal, 2005; Engert et al., 2016; Morioka et al., 2017).

Therefore, in Figure 8.1, we emphasize the connection between the blocks "strategic resources" and "key processes" with the outcomes to remark on how the latter should be considered essential elements for continuously enhancing the former. For instance, part of the planned social outcomes – even if not achieved – should create a positive atmosphere within the organization, where workers, as fundamental strategic resources, should feel stimulated, accepted, and capable of contributing to societal value creation. Similarly, environmental outcomes should be the basis for improving the organization's productive key processes in acting efficiently and respecting the natural environment. In summary, this framework seeks to go beyond the limits of other business model designs, specifically the lack of consideration for sustainability objectives and the necessity to uncover the underlying dynamics and processes. Therefore, the development of DBMfS offers a way to move beyond previous models, allowing for the drawing of processes of generation of sustainable value by examining the causal relationships among key variables. It emphasizes multifaceted dynamics and the triple bottom line of sustainability. As a result, it provides an agile tool for strategy design that can be used to readily pinpoint critical variables and map the causal connections among them.

8.5 Sustainability-based business model innovation and competitive advantages

According to Kramer and Porter (2006) and Porter and Kramer (2011), acting as a sustainable and responsible organization can be more than just a cost or charitable deed for business organizations. Such behavior can serve as a source of competitive advantages. In this chapter, we highlighted the potential role of sustainability adaptation for organizations' viability but without deepening its effects on their competitiveness. Hence, this section emphasizes the link between the proposed method and business competitiveness. To this end, we introduce a modified version of DBMfS. While DBMfS is suitable for planning SBMs, it lacks focus on the competitive arena and, therefore, on competitive advantages.

We added a further building block to the DBMfS to address this issue. As shown in Figure 8.2, this block includes key competitors. The rationale for adding this block is to consider how the competitors, whose specific target is similar to our target, try to qualify and differentiate their offer; it is useful, before developing our value proposition, to be aware of the other products available in the market in order to be different, to be better, more effective in terms of customer satisfaction. It is remarkable for a company to be aware of its competitors' strategic resources and processes and how much they are compliant with the sustainability issue. Environmental and social sensitivity should become a "mantra" in defining these key processes and related products and services (Ruisi, 2022: 262).

Following Porter and Kramer's suggestions, capitalism should be partially reinterpreted to allow organizations to be fundamental players in social and environmental progress. This consideration can guide toward a redefinition of who the

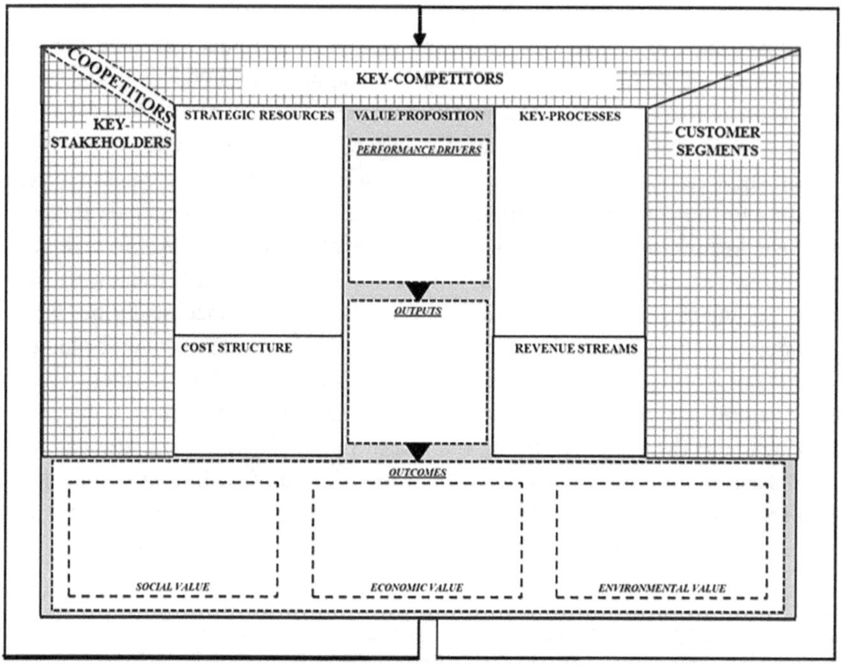

FIGURE 8.2 Our adaptation of the Dynamic Business Model for Sustainability structure of Cosenz et al. (2020). In this adaptation, we add the key competitor block. These can be converted into coopetitors to generate superior social, environmental, and economic outcomes or remain competitors with whom to compete for such outcomes.

competitors of the organizations are in pursuing sustainable goals and profits. Indeed, according to the call of Agenda 2030, sustainable development objectives cannot be achieved in isolation. Organizations should not just adapt to sustainability; they have to prosper in sustainability by spotting opportunities for alliances and competition.

A continuous comparison among the competitors' offers and the pillars on which they build up their products and services (resources and processes) is crucial to get a dynamic (temporary) competitive advantage. Being aware of the state of competitive resources (or lack thereof) could stimulate a company to work toward a collaborative approach with some of its rivals; it could push a company toward coopetition (on coopetition, or collaborative competition, see Brandenburger & Nalebuff, 1996; Dagnino, 2009).

In this representation, we emphasize the importance of considering key competitors in business modeling. Further, the gray lines area indicates that key competitors can also act as coopetitors based on the environmental, economic, or social value the organizations can provide.

Adding this block aligns with Girotra and Netessine's (2013) proposal of increasing organizations' consciousness in decision-making processes and experimenting with new ideas for SBMs. As in previous alternative propositions of the BMC that directly or indirectly coped with the competitive dimension (see Kim & Mauborgne; 2014; Maurya, 2012, 2022), we suggest drawing a list of the organization's possible main competitors. We propose writing down a small number of key competitors, as characterized by Porter's classic five forces model (1979). Once the model users have detailed the competitors in this block, they should understand whether they are pure or convertible competitors. Namely, it is crucial to determine the feasibility of creating new partnerships. Performing such a distinction follows the perspective of Girotra and Netessine (2013), Roome and Louche (2016), and Geissdoerfer et al. (2016), who argue that SBMs should be shaped relying on the interactions between individuals and groups inside and outside organizations, building collaborations and generating harmony with stakeholders. Morioka et al. (2017) maintain that sustainable business purposes should be conceived as shareable entrepreneurial dreams.

However, to understand whether a competitor is "pure" or "convertible," managers should focus on the value the organizations can offer them. The organization could provide economic value through commercial agreements, co-branding initiatives, and other commercial solutions. In addition, it is possible to offer social value in terms of solid relationships and cultural growth or environmental value by offering or using greener outsourcing production services, joining efforts for R&D activities or obtaining economies of scale in turning infrastructures into greener solutions. Working on such levers could make organizations' BMs more sustainable and partially reduce the competitive pressure in the arena, thereby favoring the viability of organizations.

All these elements should be added as drivers to monitor within the classic DBMfS. For instance, the users of the dynamic canvas can monitor the number of commercial agreements, meetings, or co-branding initiatives and attempt to forecast their effects on the economic, social, and environmental results of the organization.

This synergic way of conceiving organizational boundaries and interactions addresses the importance of constantly reinventing them to stay ahead of the competition (Osterwalder et al., 2020) by simultaneously mastering organizations' present and preempting the future (Abell, 1993). Framing and working with convertible competitors may empower competitive advantages against pure competitors. We can define this type of cooperative advantage deriving from the harmony created by an SBM (Geissdoerfer et al., 2016) as a relational competitive advantage or competitive advantage from a relationship (see Dyer & Singh, 1998; Hu et al., 2015). We posit that this relational competitive advantage is a useful type of competitive advantage an SBM can generate.

Thus, relational competitive (coopetitive) advantages are significant against pure competitors, i.e., those competitors that cannot be converted into partners. Indeed, coopetitive advantages generate three other competitive advantages: environmental, social, and economic. In addition, these advantages must be enhanced and, where possible, also innovated in a disruptive manner to distance the organization from its pure competitors in order to provide, where possible, a unique value proposition (see Kim & Mauborgne; 2014, Ramfelt et al., 2014; Maurya, 2012, 2022). This is the rationale for connecting the key competitors' block of the proposed DBMfS to the value proposition block. Lastly, according to Girotra and Netessine (2013), the model should be constantly audited to identify drivers capable of destroying value and, if necessary, experiment with alternative solutions.

Acting in such a way within the competitive arena should make the organization a sustainable and responsible entity, as hypothesized by Porter and Kramer (2011), capable of reconceiving and redefining products, markets, and the value chain, allowing society development by reconnecting its success with the progress of the society overall. By following the suggestions above, results such as reducing ecological footprint (Sullivan & Gouldson, 2019), enhancing reputation and stakeholders' engagement (Sharma & Henriques, 2005), creating new market opportunities, eco-friendly products, and circular business models (Schaltegger et al., 2012), minimizing legal and reputational risks (Delmas & Toffel, 2008) would become an integral and structural part of organizations' competitive behavior.

8.6 Conclusions

8.6.1 Theoretical and practical implications

This chapter focused on the interplay between sustainability and business model innovation, offering a wide array of theoretical and practical insights. It emphasizes sustainability's pivotal role in shaping business strategies, urging a redefinition of how organizations perceive and integrate sustainability into their core operations. This integration not only responds to the increasing environmental and societal challenges but also unlocks new avenues for innovation and competitive differentiation.

From a theoretical viewpoint, the chapter enriches the sustainability discourse by positioning it as a central pillar in business model innovation. This perspective extends beyond traditional views that often sideline sustainability as a peripheral concern, suggesting that it is fundamental to modern strategic management. The synthesis of sustainability and business model innovation theories provides a fresh lens through which to examine business practices, challenging companies to rethink how they create, deliver, and capture value in a way that aligns with broader societal and environmental objectives.

Moreover, the research contributes to the competitive advantage literature by illustrating how sustainability-driven adaptability can be a source of strategic differentiation. This aligns with the resource-based view, suggesting that unique sustainability practices can serve as critical resources and capabilities that set firms apart in the marketplace (Barney, 1991).

From a practical perspective, the chapter offers a tangible framework for organizations to weave sustainability into the fabric of their business models. The Dynamic Business Modeling for Sustainability (DBMfS) proposed in the research provides a structured methodology for firms to systematically evaluate and integrate sustainability considerations into their strategic and operational decisions. This framework not only aids in identifying sustainable innovation opportunities but also helps firms articulate a clear value proposition that resonates with increasingly environmentally and socially conscious markets.

The research also underscores the importance of collaboration and cooperation in the context of sustainability. It suggests a paradigm shift where competitors can become collaborators in pursuit of shared sustainability goals, advocating for a more nuanced understanding of competitive dynamics where shared value creation becomes a focal point (Porter & Kramer, 2011). For strategic decision-makers, the paper serves as a clarion call to embed sustainability at the heart of business strategy. It argues that sustainability should not be an afterthought but a key driver of innovation, competitive advantage, and long-term success. By adopting the framework and perspectives outlined in the research, companies can not only navigate the complexities of the modern business landscape more effectively but also contribute to the broader goal of sustainable development.

In sum, the research provides a robust framework that combines theoretical depth with practical applicability, offering a comprehensive guide for academics and practitioners alike to understand and implement sustainability-driven business model innovation.

8.6.2 Concluding remarks

This chapter has explored the relationship between sustainability, adaptability, innovation, and competitiveness, focusing on BM, SBM, and BMI. The dynamic nature of today's corporate environment necessitates constant adaptation, and sustainability-driven flexibility is one key component. For an organization to succeed, it must be able to develop or convert its BM according to sustainability principles. This result can be obtained through business model innovation (BMI).

The work has underscored the role of sustainability in steering enterprises toward financial, societal, and ecological objectives and improving resource allocation and organizations' competitiveness. Overall, this chapter seeks to offer a thorough manual for sustainability-based business model innovation and competitive advantages by relying on previous contributions in this field.

Business model innovation has been offered as a crucial tactic for organizations to keep a competitive advantage. Using creative business models, organizations could stand out from the competition, cut costs, improve customer focus, and penetrate new markets.

While these insights are already acknowledged for non-sustainability matters, the chapter has particularly delved into sustainability-driven adaptability.

It emphasizes how organizations should respond proactively to possibilities and problems related to sustainability. Adaptability driven by sustainability strengthens resistance against environmental hazards, improves stakeholder engagement and reputation, encourages innovation, and guarantees adherence to changing legal requirements. The tactics suggested for utilizing sustainability to drive flexibility, such as eco-design and circular economy concepts, highlight the diverse approaches that organizations might adopt.

Furthermore, the integration of sustainability-driven adaptability with business model innovation has been explored. The chapter relies on sustainable business models (SBMs) as a strategic requirement for businesses that want to positively impact society and the environment and be profitable. Then, Cosenz et al.'s Dynamic Business Modeling for Sustainability (DBMfS) approach has been presented to emphasize the creation of sustainable value through interconnected variables and feedback loops, and to provide a methodological framework to assist organizations in incorporating sustainability principles into their business models and so to shift from BM to SBM.

Lastly, we proposed a modified version of Cosenz et al. (DBMfS) that deepens the competitive dimension of SBM and sustainability-based adaptation, considering the literature reviewed in this chapter. In particular, the model allows us to understand the necessity of creating a systemic competitive advantage based on openness and dialogue with competitors that could be converted into partners (or "convertible competitors"). Then, this systemic competitive advantage should lead to environmental, economic, and social competitive advantages to obtain superior performance in these dimensions.

In conclusion, sustainability-driven adaptability through business model innovation becomes imperative in a world where societal expectations and environmental concerns pressure organizations. The framework described serves as a theoretical and practical guide for academics and professionals interested in deepening the links among sustainability, adaptability, and competitiveness in the contemporary business landscape. We discuss sustainability as a catalyst for innovation. In such a perspective, organizations can position themselves as contributors to a more sustainable and resilient global economy by staying profitable and thriving.

References

Abell, D. F. (1993). *Managing with Dual Strategies: Mastering the Present, Preempting the Future*, The Free Press, New York.

Bansal, P. (2005). Evolving sustainably: A longitudinal study of corporate sustainable development. *Strategic Management Journal*, 26, 197–218. http://dx.doi.org/10.1002/smj.441

Barney, J. (1991). Firm resources and sustained competitive advantage. *Journal of Management*, 17(1), 99–120.

Bocken, N. M. P., Rana, P., & Short, S. W. (2015). Value mapping for sustainable business thinking. *Journal of Industrial and Production Engineering*, 32(1), 67–81.

Bocken, N. M. P., Short, S. W., Rana, P., & Evans, S. (2014). A literature and practice review to develop sustainable business model archetypes. *Journal of Cleaner Production*, 65, 42–56.

Brandenburger, A. M., & Nalebuff, B. J. (1996). *Co-opetition*. Harper Collins Press, London.

Coffay, M., & Bocken, N. M. P. (2023). Sustainable by design: An organizational design tool for sustainable business model innovation. *Journal of Cleaner Production*, 427, 139294.

Cosenz, F. (2017). Supporting start-up business model design through system dynamics modelling. *Management Decision*, 55(1), 57–80.

Cosenz, F., & Noto, G. (2018). A dynamic business modelling approach to design and experiment new business venture strategies. *Long Range Planning*, 51(1), 127–140.

Cosenz, F., Rodrigues, V. P., & Rosati, F. (2020). Dynamic business modeling for sustainability: Exploring a system dynamics perspective to develop sustainable business models. *Business Strategy and the Environment*, 29(2), 651–664.

Cramer, J., & Krueger, A.B. (2016). Disruptive change in the taxi business: The case of Uber. *American Economic Review*, 106(5): 177–82.

Cusumano, M. A., & Gawer, A. (2002). The elements of platform leadership. *MIT Sloan Management Review*, 43(3), 58–66.

Dagnino G.B. (2009). Coopetition strategy: A new kind of interfirm dynamics for value creation. In: Dagnino G.B. & Rocco E. (Eds.). *Coopetition Strategy: Theory Experiments and Cases*. 25–43. Routledge, London, ISBN: 978-0-415-43898-8

Delmas, M. A., & Toffel, M. W. (2008). Organizational responses to environmental demands: Opening the black box. *Strategic Management Journal*, 29(10), 1027–1055.

Delmas, M. A., & Toffel, M. W. (2010). Institutional pressures and organizational characteristics: Implications for environmental strategy. *Business & Society*, 49(3), 431–455.

Di Vaio, A., Varriale, L., Di Gregorio, A., & Adomako, S. (2022). Corporate social performance and non-financial reporting in the cruise industry: Paving the way towards UN Agenda 2030. *Corporate Social Responsibility and Environmental Management*, 29(6), 1931–1953.

DiMaggio, P. J., & Powell, W. W. (1983). The iron cage revisited: Institutional isomorphism and collective rationality in organizational fields. *American Sociological Review*, 48, 147–160.

Dyer, J. H., & Singh, H. (1998). The relational view: Cooperative strategy and sources of interorganizational competitive advantage. *Academy of Management Review*, 23(4), 660–679.

Eisenhardt, K. M., & Martin, J. A. (2000). Dynamic capabilities: What are they? *Strategic Management Journal*, 21(10–11), 1105–1121.

Elkington, J. (1997). *Cannibals with forks: The triple bottom line of 21st century business*. Capstone, Oxford.

Engert, S., Rauter, R., & Baumgartner, R. J. (2016). Exploring the integration of corporate sustainability into strategic management: A literature review. *Journal of Cleaner Production*, 112, 2833–2850. http://dx.doi.org/10.1016/j.jclepro.2015.08.031

Foss, N. J., & Saebi, T. (2018). Business models and business model innovation: Between wicked and paradigmatic problems. *Long Range Planning*, 51(1), 9–21.

Freeman, R. E. (1984). *Strategic management: A stakeholder approach*. Pitman Publishing, Boston.

Geissdoerfer, M., Bocken, N. M. P., & Hultink, E. J. (2016). Design thinking to enhance the sustainable business modelling process: A workshop based on a value mapping process. *Journal of Cleaner Production*, 135, 1218–1232. http://dx.doi.org/10.1016/j.jclepro.2016.07.020

Girotra, K., & Netessine, S. (2013). Business model innovation for sustainability. *Manufacturing & Service Operations Management*, 15, 537–544.
Hart, S. L. (1995). A natural-resource-based view of the firm. *Academy of Management Review*, 20, 986–1014.
Hill, C. W. (2014). *International business: Competing in the global marketplace*. McGraw-Hill Education, New York.
Hinterhuber, A., & Liozu, S. M. (2016). Is innovation in pricing your next source of competitive advantage? *MIT Sloan Management Review*, 57(4), 69–76.
Hu, Y., Zhang, S., Li, J., & Sørensen, O. J. (2015). Gaining relational competitive advantages: A conceptual framework on rent generation and appropriation. *European Journal of International Management*, 9(5), 566–592.
Johnson, M. W., Christensen, C. M., & Kagermann, H. (2008). Reinventing your business model. *Harvard Business Review*, 86(12), 50–59.
Kim, W. C., & Mauborgne, R. (2014). *Blue ocean strategy, expanded edition: How to create uncontested market space and make the competition irrelevant*. Harvard Business Review Press, Boston, Massachusett.
Kirchherr, J., Reike, D., & Hekkert, M. (2017). Conceptualizing the circular economy: An analysis of 114 definitions. *Resources, Conservation and Recycling*, 127, 221–232.
Kramer, M. R., & Porter, M. E. (2006). Strategy and society: The link between competitive advantage and corporate social responsibility. *Harvard Business Review*, 84(12), 78–92.
Lozano, R. (2015). A holistic perspective on corporate sustainability drivers. *Corporate Social Responsibility and Environmental Management*, 22(1), 32–44.
Lüdeke-Freund, F. (2020). Sustainable entrepreneurship, innovation, and business models: Integrative framework and propositions for future research. *Business Strategy and the Environment*, 29(2), 665–681.
Markides, C. (2013). Business model innovation: What can the ambidexterity literature teach us? *Academy of Management Perspectives*, 27(4), 313–323.
Maurya, A. (2012). *Running Lean: Iterate from Plan A to A Plan that Works* (2nd Ed.). "O'Reilly Media, Inc.", Sebastopol, CA.
Maurya, A. (2022). *Running Lean: Iterate from Plan A to A Plan that Works* (3th Ed.)."O'Reilly Media, Inc." Beijing.
Mont, O., & Plepys, A. (2012). Sustainable consumption progress: Should we be proud or alarmed? *Journal of Cleaner Production*, 22(1), 1–4.
Morioka, S. N., Bolis, I., Evans, S., & Carvalho, M. M. (2017). Transforming sustainability challenges into competitive advantage: Multiple case studies kaleidoscope converging into sustainable business models. *Journal of Cleaner Production*, 167, 723–738. https://doi.org/10.1016/j.jclepro.2017.08.118
Osterwalder, A., & Pigneur, Y. (2010). *Business model generation: A handbook for visionaries, game changers, and challengers*. Wiley, Hoboken, NJ.
Osterwalder, A., Pigneur, Y., & Etiemble, F. (2020). *The Invincible Company: How to Constantly Reinvent Your Organization with Inspiration From the World's Best Business Models*. Wiley, Hoboken.
Porter, M. E. (1979). How competitive forces shape strategy. *Harvard Business Review*, 57(2), 137–145.
Porter, M. E. (1985). *Competitive advantage: Creating and sustaining superior performance*. Free Press, New York.
Porter, M. E., & Kramer, M. R. (2011). Creating shared value: How to reinvent capitalism and unleash a wave of innovation and growth. *Harvard Business Review*, 89, 62–77.

Ramfelt, L., Kjellberg, J., & Kosnik, T. (2014). *Gear up: Test your business model potential and plan your path to success*. John Wiley & Sons, Hoboken.

Roome, N., & Louche, C. (2016). Journeying toward business models for sustainability: A conceptual model found inside the black box of organisational transformation. *Organization & Environment*, 29, 11–35. http://dx.doi.org/10.1177/1086026615595084

Ruisi, M. (2022). Reconceptualizing business models in light of the COVID-19 experience: Insights from the world of start-ups for a renewed corporate finalism. In G. Campisi, A. Mocciaro Li Destri, C. Amenta (Eds.) *COVID-19 and communities: The University of Palermo's voices and analyses during the pandemic* (pp. 257–264). Springer International Publishing, Cham.

Schaltegger, S., Lüdeke-Freund, F., & Hansen, E. G. (2012). Business cases for sustainability: The role of business model innovation for corporate sustainability. *International Journal of Innovation and Sustainable Development*, 6(2), 95–119.

Schuler, D. A., & Jackson, S. E. (1987). Linking competitive strategies with human resource management practices. *Academy of Management Executive*, 1(3), 207–219.

Seuring, S., & Müller, M. (2008). From a literature review to a conceptual framework for sustainable supply chain management. *Journal of Cleaner Production*, 16(15), 1699–1710.

Sharma, S., & Henriques, I. (2005). Stakeholder influences on sustainability practices in the Canadian forest products industry. *Strategic Management Journal*, 26(2), 159–180.

Sterman, J. (2000). *Business dynamics: System thinking and modeling for a complex world*. McGraw-Hill, London.

Sullivan, R., & Gouldson, A. (2019). Exploring the social and organisational dynamics behind the adoption of sustainability-driven innovation. *Ecological Economics*, 165, 106418.

UN (2015). *Transforming our world: The 2030 agenda for sustainable development*. Resolution adopted by the United Nations General Assembly on 25 September 2015. https://www.un.org/en/development/desa/population/migration/generalassembly/docs/globalcompact/A_RES_70_1_E.pdf

Waddock, S. A., & Bodwell, C. (2004). Managing responsibility: What can be learned from the quality movement? *California Management Review*, 47(1), 25–37.

Wasserman, N. (2013). The Netflix effect: Teens, binge watching, and on-demand digital media trends. *Jeunesse: Young People, Texts, Cultures*, 5(1), 119–138.

Zervas, G., Proserpio, D., & Byers, J. W. (2017). The rise of the sharing economy: Estimating the impact of Airbnb on the hotel industry. *Journal of Marketing Research*, 54(5), 687–705.

9

INTERNATIONALIZATION AND DIGITALIZATION COMPETITIVE STRATEGIES IN HIGH-TECHNOLOGY COMPANIES

Multiple case studies

Marco Figueiredo and João J. Ferreira

9.1 Introduction

Markets today are not dense as they once were. In fact, markets have changed substantially, being a volatile and constantly evolving reality (Paul & Benito, 2018; Martins et al., 2021). These transformations require changes in companies, both at a strategic level and regarding growth and innovation. Technological progress, communications, and transport have a significant impact on companies and the way they operate in the market. Andersson et al. (2016) point out that since the mid-1950s, there have been significant changes and technological innovations that have boosted markets and business development at the international level.

The internationalization of companies has emerged as a decisive process for keeping up with changing markets. In this sense, Sapienza et al. (2006) state that internationalization is the most profound business phenomenon, and there is no consensus on the strategies needed for successful internationalization (Paul, 2020). Mintzberg and Westley (1992) and Porter (2001) emphasize that global transaction markets not only present companies with new challenges but also new opportunities.

Research into the internationalization of companies has sparked growing interest (Steinhäuser et al., 2021). As a result, research in this field is fragmented (Paul et al., 2017), given the existence of multiple fields of study, including international entrepreneurship, entry modes, strategies or resources used to internationalize, and internationalization models (Dabić et al., 2020).

Despite the diversity of topics found on the subject of internationalization, the current predominance related to the organization and the singularity of globalization is highlighted, as well as the innovation inherent in this process (Bahl et al., 2021), in the field of digitalization (Bergamaschi et al., 2020). For Piaskowska et al. (2021), digitalization allows companies to improve the efficiency of their processes or

DOI: 10.4324/9781032695969-10

replace manual and human capital-intensive tasks with digital alternatives, thereby also boosting their competitiveness.

Digitalization emphasizes a process of capturing, processing, and organizing knowledge, making it accessible and reliable. This includes customer perception, operational efficiency, customer analysis, and organizational learning (Tuomisalo & Leppäaho, 2019). As such, digitization enables digital approaches to accessing, organizing, storing, and using products and services (Singh et al., 2017).

This topic of internationalization through digital means is still under-researched (Castaldi et al., 2019; Chen et al., 2019; Hervé et al., 2020; Lee et al., 2021; Steinhäuser et al., 2021; Taylor et al., 2021; Teruel et al., 2021), considering the rapid development expected through digitalization. Digitalization will respond to companies' needs and behaviors, and will be a consequence of evolutionary lines, whether in terms of location and supply or even sustainable business models (Bergamaschi et al., 2020). According to Monaghan et al. (2020), the theme of internationalization through digital means is based on the growing need to identify the main challenges companies face when entering international markets. This can contribute to the survival of companies, particularly in periods of uncertainty, such as caused by the recent COVID-19 epidemiological crisis (Martins et al., 2021) and the current conflict in Eastern Europe.

In fact, the growing prevalence of digital technology is changing the way companies compete and create value (Bergamaschi et al., 2020) and is therefore considered a topic that needs further investigation, given the rapid and continuous technological changes, the variety of products and the continuous changes in customer expectations and preferences (Vrontis & Christofi, 2021). Future customers will probably be digital natives, leading to the need to produce more digital content on the one hand and increase interactions on the other (Castaldi et al., 2019; Hughes et al., 2021). Hence, companies that are early adopters of digital technologies will have the potential to lead the development of new competences, based on social media interactions and a deeper understanding of the customer (Syam & Sharma, 2018).

Consequently, this study proposes the analysis of the relationship between internationalization strategies and digital transformation in an attempt to ascertain whether companies were founded in the globalized market itself, the so-called Born Global companies (Taylor et al., 2021) or whether they were originally digital, known as Born Digital, companies that operate in the global digital space, and their connection to world markets can be almost instantaneous (Monaghan et al., 2020).

To this end, we will carry out a qualitative analysis of five high-tech companies through case studies using semi-structured interviews (Yin, 2017) with the company's directors/managers in an attempt to highlight the implications that internationalization and digitalization have on their companies' strategies.

Our research has revealed some evidence that contributes to the existing literature, providing a broad understanding of the internationalization behavior of high-tech companies, focusing on corporate internationalization through the global birth "Born Global" (Taylor et al., 2021) and, similarly, internationalization through the digital birth "Born Digital" (Monaghan et al., 2020).

First, our study shows that the strategies adopted for the internationalization of high-tech companies arise from the aggregation of different theoretical models, namely Born Global, Born Digital, network theory, Resource-Based View (RVB), and International New Ventures (INV). In this context, the internationalization of these companies does not exclusively reflect one theoretical model, as this is insufficient to explain the breadth of internationalization, and it is necessary to conglomerate different theories in order to improve the understanding of this phenomenon.

Second, we concluded that companies with digital technologies/digitization quickly achieve internationalization, avoiding the relocation processes typical of internationalization in stages, as referred to by the Uppsala model. We agree that digitalization boosts internationalization by opening up new markets and promoting entry in a simple, economical, and accessible way. Digitalization has become an essential condition for business competitiveness at a global level.

Third, the use of digital technologies/digitization promotes a wider involvement (customers, suppliers, partners), fostering greater interaction between customers and the company, suppliers and the company, and partners, which in turn increases organizational performance.

Fourth, it was also possible to see that entrepreneurs' motivation and determination to operate their company in a new international market are clearly drivers of internationalization. The entrepreneur's vision of the essential nature of internationalization is also a decisive factor in achieving it. Finally, we conclude that the digital strategy must be reconciled with the company's overall strategy, although it must be developed in a particular way as a special strategy. In this sense, the digital business strategy should be broader, more prominent, integrated, comprehensive, and sustained than other strategies. The companies need to understand these requirements of digital evolution and the necessities to adapt to new potential customers and also to global market trends. This innovative composition can be achieved through the development of organizational ambidexterity.

The research is organized into seven sections. The introduction is followed by a literature review that defines the main concepts and approaches under study. The third section outlines the methodology used and explains how the data was collected and analyzed. In the fourth section, we emphasize the main results obtained, discussing them in relation to existing literature and highlighting implications for theory and practice. The fifth section defines the limitations of the present study and suggests possible areas for future research. Finally, in the sixth section, we present our conclusions.

9.2 Conceptual background

9.2.1 Theories and strategies of internationalization

Global growth and commercial dynamics provide new opportunities for companies to act internationally (Martineau & Pastoriza, 2016; Witt, 2019). The momentum of the globalization process has brought new challenges and opportunities for companies, consequently leading to increased research (Paul & Mas, 2020). With this dynamic, international business transactions have increased exponentially, allowing companies to rethink their global strategies (Hänle et al. 2021).

The internationalization of companies arises from a growing shortage of companies, for reasons of competitiveness or limited demand in domestic markets (Paul & Sánchez-Morcilio, 2019). Internationalization provides opportunities for growth and the exploration of new markets (Moreira et al., 2019), offering a basis for international competitive advantage (Christofi et al., 2021), a strategic option for economic sustainability and competitiveness (Paul et al., 2017; Martins et al., 2021).

Although most of the studies on internationalization mainly focus on large companies (Steinhäuser et al., 2021), more recent literature has focused on the internationalization processes of small- and medium-sized companies (Dabić et al., 2020; Martins et al., 2021; Vrontis & Christofi, 2021), producing a new vision of internationalization, considering that these companies also have the capacity to compete internationally, sharing the same competitive space (Steinhäuser et al., 2021). For Dabić et al. (2020), competition in international markets was traditionally the realm of large companies and small companies remained local or regional. With recent market developments, this phenomenon has become unreal, as business world is more competitive and globalized.

Recent research therefore focuses on the analysis of how small- and medium-sized enterprises (SMEs) and family SMEs (Mondal et al., 2022) share the same opportunities embedded in the international markets (Moreira et al., 2019; Dabić et al., 2020; Lee et al., 2021), and it is true that most internationalization procedures are conducted by these companies (Zahoor et al., 2020). The internationalization of companies can be examined from different perspectives (Zahoor et al., 2020) through different theories and models that investigate the internationalization process, which is crucial for evaluating it. Table 9.1 encapsulates the main internationalization theories and models mentioned in the literature.

9.2.2 Digitalization and digital transformation strategies

The revised internationalization theories and models have not been properly adapted to the new challenges posed by digital environments, as emphasized by Johanson and Vahlne's (1977) model, which stresses progressive international involvement. Currently, the borders between countries are dematerializing, allowing new scientific debates around the potential impact of the digital context on the internationalization of companies (Hervé et al., 2020).

The introduction of new digital technologies leads to a shift from material goods or services transactions to the digital market. These markets generate innovations, new products, services, and processes, as well as new forms of interaction with suppliers and customers (Steinhäuser et al., 2021), which influence companies' ability to internationalize (Teruel et al., 2021).

According to Hervé et al. (2020), the integration of new digital technologies creates new opportunities for companies and it allows the emergence of different ways of reaching potential customers on a global scale. In a similar vein, Castaldi

TABLE 9.1 Summary of the main internationalization theories/models

Theories/models	*A few pieces of evidence*
Uppsala model	It emerges as one of the most developed and decisive models in business studies, explaining the most prominent characteristics of the internationalization processes (Johanson & Vahlne, 1977, 2009; Vahlne & Johanson, 2017). Business strategy should be processed gradually through incremental decisions, to the extent and in proportion to the learning and knowledge acquired through its experiences. In our opinion and following the line of research of Paul and Rosado-Serrano (2019), the Uppsala model has restrictions and ambiguities, as it does not explain the concept of accelerated internationalization.
Born globals	They rely on technology and innovation (Paul & Rosado-Serrano, 2019; Petricevic & Teece, 2019; Taylor et al., 2021), outlining technological strategies that consequently enable global communications and access to international markets, bypassing the traditional steps inherent in the internationalization processes. These companies depend on the development of knowledge to achieve competitive advantage (Taylor et al., 2021). Internationalization has been the ideal strategy for these companies because it enables them to access primary resources, go global, follow their customers, exploit the potential of markets and gain access to knowledge (Paul & Rosado-Serrano, 2019; Mondal et al., 2022) to improve their competitive advantage (Steinhäuser et al., 2021; Vrontis & Christofi, 2021).
Network theory	It assumes that companies achieve competitive advantages by developing mutually supportive interactions with other companies (Johanson & Mattsson, 1992; Moreira et al., 2019; Zahoor et al., 2020; Steinhäuser et al., 2021), offering a good understanding of internationalization phenomenon through the interpretation of business relationships (Dabić et al., 2020). Markets are portrayed as systems of social and professional relationships between customers, suppliers, and/or competitors (Martineau & Pastoriza, 2016), being a strategic resource and a competitive necessity in international markets (Moreira et al., 2019; Zahoor et al., 2020). The strategic approach to the network is very useful for understanding the initial capacity of entrepreneurs and companies (Mondal et al., 2022), in terms of strategic alliances and joint ventures (Dabić et al., 2020; Zahoor et al., 2020; Pereira et al., 2022).

(*Continued*)

TABLE 9.1 (Continued)

Theories/models	*A few pieces of evidence*
International entrepreneurship theory	According to Zahoor et al. (2020), this theory emerges as the third most prominent theory, inspiring a combination of innovation, proactivity, and risk-seeking that leads companies to start their international operations. These authors suggest that managers' entrepreneurial characteristics (Niittymies & Pajunen, 2020) and business behavior simplify internationalization and the achievement of growth in international markets. This theoretical field emphasizes the internationalization of small businesses, addressing companies that internationalize from birth, international new ventures (Tuomisalo & Leppäaho, 2019), or so-called Born Globals (Zahoor et al., 2020; Taylor et al., 2021), differing from gradual internationalization (Johanson & Vahlne, 2009), due to the speed with which the company internationalizes (Paul & Rosado-Serrano, 2019).
Resource-based view (RBV)	This theory, fundamentally investigated by Barney (1991), is the second most well-founded theory of the internationalization process (Zahoor et al., 2020). In the internationalization context, companies' internal resources and capabilities, such as entrepreneurs, technological, and financial resources, simplify international collaboration, increasing business performance (Catanzaro et al., 2018). According to Hamdoun (2020), the RBV is based on an internal analysis of the companies and complements Porter's (1980) valuable strategic approach, aiming to understand their growth and diversification. Singh et al. (2020) point out that when the resources are critical, rare, inimitable, and irreplaceable by alternative resources, the organization achieves superior and longer-lasting performance (Umrani et al., 2022) and a continuous competitive advantage gain from these resources. Likewise, Umrani et al. (2022) state that the evolution of business performance is only possible when managers improve organizations internally.

Source: Authors.

et al. (2019) reflect on the adoption of digital technologies by companies, arguing that it has a profound impact on business activities, business models, borders, cultures, and value chains. For Berger (2015), digital transformation is proliferating at company and market level and at macroeconomic level in the business economic environment. For the same author, digital transformation can be defined by connectivity in all areas of the economy and the process by which the various players adapt to the new conditions emerging from the digital economy.

In fact, new digital technologies have the potential to reduce the distance and costs of entering new markets, overcome trade barriers, provide an additional channel for business relations, marketing, and sales, and increase knowledge about foreign markets and potential competitors (Teruel et al., 2021). Ross et al. (2017) identify two stages in the adoption of new digital technologies: digitalized companies and companies becoming digital. The former shows progress at an operational level, involving the standardization of business processes and optimization of operations through the implementation of technologies and software. The latter involves digital technologies to personalize alternative offerings, aiming for a new model of value creation.

The literature often recognizes that digital technology plays an important role in connecting geographically dispersed production networks, although it confines this to the perspective of the infrastructural component (Castaldi et al., 2019). The growing prevalence of digital technology is changing the way companies create value. Vendrell-Herrero et al. (2021) state that digital technologies are a fundamental and widespread aspect of the progress made in the business organization. Notwithstanding the above, technology must be allied to the business strategy, which leads to digital transformation and ultimately provides a competitive advantage (Kindermann et al., 2021).

In the view of Monaghan et al. (2020), companies that become digital can create and leverage their business, regardless of the degree of digitalization, as this can vary between the digital transition phase and the digitalization of some processes. These authors point out that digital infrastructure exposes an identifiable presence online (i.e. in "space"), while at the same time, parts of the organization can be physically based (i.e. in "place"), with offices, warehouses, or data centers. The "space-place" relationship is, therefore, the first differentiating indicator of Johanson and Vahlne's (2009) internationalization model and the internationalization processes in digital companies.

In this way, digital technologies based on the Internet represent one of the drivers of globalization, transforming work patterns and divisions of labor, and consequently emerging as an influence on value creation processes (Castaldi et al., 2019). Nevertheless, digitalization in itself is not replacing traditional sales methods, but is asserting itself with new potential to encompass new learning and opportunities. The challenge is not just to automate existing processes, but to reinvent the entire interactive process, processing and developing automation for decision-making (Singh et al., 2017). Furthermore, future customers will probably be digital natives, leading to the need to produce more digital content on the one hand and to increase interactions with salespeople on the other (Castaldi et al., 2019). Therefore, companies that are early adopters of sales technology and artificial intelligence will have the potential to lead the development of new sales competences based on social media interactions and a deeper understanding of the customer (Syam & Sharma, 2018).

In the study by Singh et al. (2017), it is emphasized that strategic orientation reflects the company's philosophy on the direction of business through a deeply rooted set of values and beliefs that guide it to achieve superior performance (Haug et al., 2020; Zahoor et al., 2020; Kahn & Candi, 2021). Strategic orientation has been conceptualized for several domains, including market orientation, learning orientation, entrepreneurial and technological orientation (Paul & Mas, 2020; Kindermann et al., 2021). In fact, strategic orientation represents valuable intangible capabilities that are difficult to imitate and therefore provide competitive advantage in the market (Schweiger et al., 2019).

The company's vision of strategic alignment will have to be directed and combined with technological strategy (Zahoor et al., 2020), as companies with a digital structure will benefit from increased interconnections between products, processes, and services (Ross et al., 2017; Hänle et al., 2021). In this dynamic, digital technologies are seen as combining information, technology, computing, communication, and connectivity (Taylor et al., 2021). At their core, these change business strategies, business processes, company capabilities, products and services, and inter-company relationships in business networks (Bharadwaj et al., 2013).

Thus, the effects of digitalization prove that it is a marked antecedent of internationalization, and internationalization also amplifies the benefits of digitalization (Monaghan et al., 2020). This phenomenon has a dynamic relationship. Specifically, considering this dynamic relationship (i.e. the impact of digitalization on internationalization and vice versa) offers a unique image, recognizing innovative avenues for further research.

In short, new digital technologies are a precondition for the internationalization of companies (Teruel et al., 2021), and there is widespread recognition that they bring changes and have positive effects on companies and markets, marked by a benign and dynamic relationship.

9.3 Method

This research follows a subjectivist approach, applying the inductive research method by conducting multiple case studies. The case study approach is one of the most appropriate research strategies when questions of "how" and "why" are proposed, as well as when the researcher has limited control over events and when the focus is on current phenomenon within a given real-life context (Yin, 2017).

We used qualitative methods, drawing on primary sources through interviews. Understanding how high-tech companies vary in their internationalization and digitalization processes and strategies, warrants in-depth exploratory research using qualitative methods and a case study approach (Welch et al., 2022). We therefore selected five high-tech companies based in Portugal. The semi-structured interviews focused on the directors/managers of the companies in an attempt to highlight the implications that internationalization and digitalization have on their daily lives.

9.3.1 Data collection

The companies were reached to take part in this study via electronic communications sent to the company's institutional address and via LinkedIn. These interviews were conducted with appointments on different platforms, such as Google calendar, Zoom, and Teams. The interviews lasted between 20 and 40 minutes and were recorded with explicit permission using the Voice Recorder application, transcribed, and subsequently subjected to rigorous analysis. The insights gathered

TABLE 9.2 Data collection summary of companies and interviewees

No	*Company (business sector)*	*A brief description*	*Typology*	*Location*	*Creation year*	*Position within the company*	*No. of employees*
1	Uniplaces – service industry	Uniplaces is a company that provides rental brokerage service (medium and long term). The services operate via a web platform, which allows for rapid internationalization and growth. The rental services, which connect tenant and landlord, are characterized by being simple and unbureaucratic, without guarantors and other hassles and red tape.	B2C	Portugal	2013	CMO	25
2	Outsystems – service industry	OutSystems is a software and IT consultancy company that provides IT services with different characteristics to other companies, enabling them to innovate and boost their commercial value. This company is a pioneer in low-code and is transforming the concept of business software. They are currently market leaders, with an application platform that operates in 87 countries.	B2B	Portugal	2001	CIO	>1,000
3	We Say Digital – service industry	We Say Digital is a company that provides digital services aimed at creating a digital strategy, supporting the digital transformation of companies and private clients. The company has specialized professionals to provide personalized support, in line with the business plan, to find the right marketing strategy. The company offers consultancy services, digital marketing, email marketing, PPC campaigns, social media management and web design.	B2B/B2C	Portugal	2021	CEO/ co-Founder	4

4	Incognit. Cloud – service industry	Incognit.Cloud is an IT consultancy services company. Its focus is to support companies in the world of work, maximizing the impact and return on their investments, based on digital transformation. The company operates through a ServiceNow workflow platform and in low-code, executing processes in real time in a management system and in a cloud environment. The company has a group of experienced programmers who focus on customers and understand their needs. The company offers solutions to help customers identify and prioritize processes, automate workflows based on digital operations and accelerate digital innovation.	B2B	Portugal	2021	CEO/Founder	10
5	Link & Grow – service industry	Link & Grow is a company that offers a range of digital services. This company seeks to leverage its clients' digital businesses, promoting success through digital strategies. This organization provides inbound marketing, e-commerce, web design, automation, leads, PPC campaigns, social media management, email marketing, content marketing, SEO, sales, and CRM services. They use marketing automation software and are partners with Google. They also offer consultancy and diagnostic services, strategic planning, and metrics evaluation using Google analytics.	B2B/B2C	Portugal	2017	CEO/Founder	18

Note: CEO (Chief Executive Officer); CIO (Chief Information Officer); CMO (Chief Marketing Officer).

from these interviews enabled a critical deepening of the themes of internationalization, digitalization/digital transformation, and strategic orientation in high-tech business practice (Table 9.2).

In the interviews, we asked all the participants to discuss the internationalization of their company, specifically the criteria for choosing markets and their perspective on the phenomenon of Born Global companies. In the second phase of these interviews, the questions focused on digitalization/digital transformation initiatives, referring to their success or failure and operations within the company, as well as interactions with external partners and customers, the development of capabilities and measuring the success of digital transformation/digitalization initiatives from a Born Digital perspective. The aim of these interviews was also to understand the influence of advanced technologies on digitalization/digital transformation, clarify the essential capabilities for digital transformation, and understand the benefits gained through internationalization. As these interviews progressed, we asked our participants to clarify their company's core capabilities and the factors that can influence these capabilities and innovation strategies.

9.3.2 *Data analysis*

This research followed the qualitative data analysis guidelines (Yin, 2017), which involved coding the interviews and classifying the codes into themes and patterns. We carried out a cross-case analysis to discover the similarities and differences between the cases as performed by Ghosh et al. (2021). With this in mind and starting from the conceptual framework and data structure (Figure 9.1), we graphically illustrate the development of our research from first-order codes to second-order theoretical categories, describing the interrelationships between them and aggregate dimensions of the model (Gioia et al., 2013).

9.4 Findings

9.4.1 *Internationalization*

The aggregate dimension, known as internationalization, provides an overview of the main results of each question (shown in the first-order codes) and their respective correspondence to their theoretical categories (second-order theoretical categories).

9.4.1.1 *Internationalization strategies*

This subsection aims to identify the different forms of business internationalization to understand the motivations and objectives for internationalization.

Our results show some particularities associated with each of the companies interviewed in terms of internationalization strategies, motivations, and objectives. At the same time, they share similarities that we will emphasize in presenting these results.

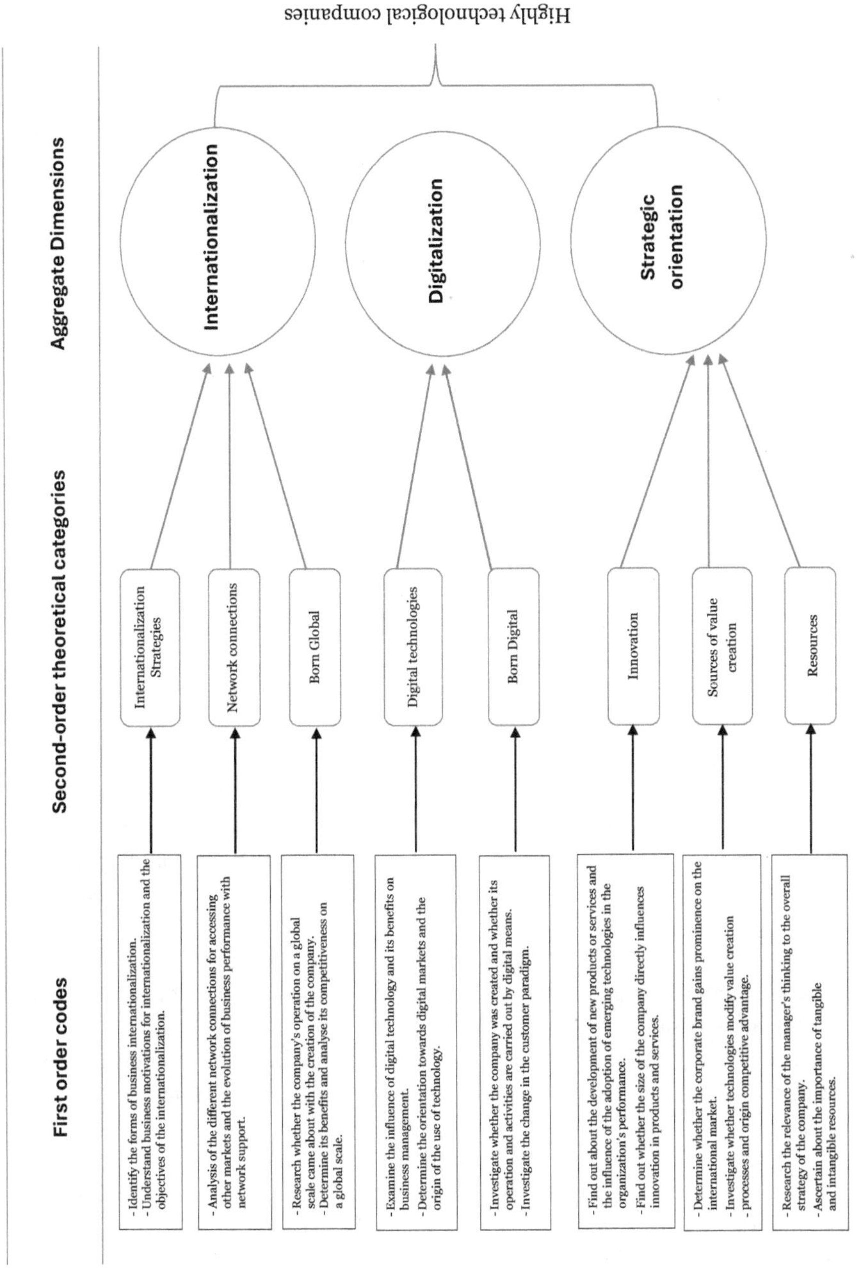

FIGURE 9.1 Data structure: general overview

First, we found that all the companies interviewed are internationalized, and three of them are internationalized in more than one foreign market. "Our company operates digitally in different international markets, it's not a physical presence. We operate in around 30 European countries, Australia, the USA and Brazil" (C1). "Yes, we have clients in more than 87 countries and in around 22 industries" (C2).

These results also show differences in the motivations for internationalization, the choice of markets and the strategies adopted. These strategies differ between companies, and they focus on using marketing to internationalize in a particular market "For internationalization, marketing is central to positioning the company, whether through indexing on Google, social networks, partnerships and then working offline" (C1), because "in the past, internationalization depended on relocating people who could speak the language and on the support of partners" (C1).

Our results show that more recent companies are present in fewer markets; their strategy is based on following up existing clients,

> until now… and as we're a small and recent company…. we've limited ourselves to create the website… then we set up the company and as we already had these clients, we just decided to bet on these clients' markets… that is, we segmented the adverts on our website to specific locations with the support of Google.
>
> *(C3)*

As for the motivations for internationalization, we found that companies internationalize with the aim of evolution, expansion, and growth

> primarily we think about evolving and growing, but we also have to have the means to evolve and grow… we don't have investors and our main objective is not to make money… our clients have led us to internationalize, we started with a few clients, we've done and continue to do our work and through them and the good work done, they've passed it on to others who are now our clients too.
>
> *(C4)*

These companies see internationalization as indispensable and beneficial to growth, helping them with brand recognition and development.

We also note that all of the interviewees consider the size of the domestic market to be insufficient, unable to satisfy the parameters of the companies' growth and survival, referring them to an international solution.

> The foreign market values the brand as an international reference. The national brand has little scale and ends up not being known. International recognition helps bring in new clients. A brand can only be built with effort, investment, partnerships and visibility.
>
> *(C1)*

Despite having clients in Portugal, these highly technological companies realize that the domestic market is very small. As they have clients in other countries, they are strengthening their support by internationalizing in those countries, to attract new clients and expand their brand.

In fact, the international scope and negotiation present these companies with greater challenges, since they are no longer restricted to a single geography, as (C2) says – "The company competes internationally, from the moment we rely on these technologies, we can compete in any region of the world" and (C4) – "There is more competition, but there are also more customers and bigger companies, which creates more opportunities".

Internationalization, in particular, emerges as an evolving need that struggles against the restrictions of development and performance at a national level. Internationalization requires adapting to markets and triggering structural changes in the company.

The selection of markets is centered on markets that foster greater business development, greater corporate visibility, and greater brand recognition.

9.4.1.2 Network connections

In this subsection, we analyze the importance of the different network connections for accessing other markets and their association with the evolution of business performance.

Networks and international market orientation explain some strategic options and are important for internationalization decisions.

Networks allow companies to acquire useful knowledge for internationalization, new market knowledge, information, opportunities, internationalization routes and technology, which can represent an important source of competitive advantage.

Based on our results, in four of these companies, the use of digital technology/digitization involves external actors (suppliers, customers, and partners),

> The business involves external partners. In terms of marketing, we use external platforms and request partnerships with universities. In terms of supply, we don't have ownership, we contact the owners who become partners. In terms of technology, we use our own technology, which serves as a database and supports the website, and in terms of operations, it's all internal technology, except for CRM, which is done via chat and is provided by an external supplier.
>
> *(C1)*

The majority of these highly technological companies do not have their own platforms, although the use of digital technologies/digitization involves a wide range of stakeholders (customers, suppliers, partners), promoting interaction between customers and the company, suppliers and the company, and partners and the company, which in turn increases organizational performance.

Our results corroborate that digitalization has boosted internationalization, with all five companies saying that digitalization/digital transformation has triggered the opening of new markets, making it easier for them to enter, as said:

> Digitalization completely opens the door to internationalization, all you need is a website in several languages, an address indexed by Google, an international Linkdin or a Facebook profile in the language appropriate to the country. Digitalization brings this flexibility and makes it possible to be present in countries where the company doesn't physically operate. Any company that wants to internationalize must use the digital sphere to make itself known. If the company wants to increase its size, it's almost unavoidable to turn to digital.
>
> *(C1)*

Digital transformation/digitization in these companies has broadened the parameters of negotiation. The company's horizons are no longer restricted to its country of origin, opening up the opportunity for international negotiation. We can, therefore, conclude that companies with digital technologies/digitization achieve faster internationalization, avoiding the relocation processes typical of internationalization by stages.

Regarding the effectiveness of internationalization and the international environment in which they operate, these companies were asked if they knew their competitors, how they assessed this competition, and whether it posed a threat to their development.

> We don't have a monopoly, we have competitors, but we are market leaders, we are aware of our competition. The market is dynamic, the target addressable market is huge and there are many potential customers, but we want to maintain our leadership position.
>
> *(C2)*

In this sense, we can confirm that when companies decide to enter a particular market, they strategically assess their competitors and their market methodologies, looking for differentiation to maximize their competitive advantage.

9.4.1.3 Born global

With this theoretical dimension, we ascertain whether the company's operation on a global scale came about concomitantly with the creation of the company, driving its growth, and competitiveness on a global scale.

Analyzing the results, most of the companies interviewed said that they immediately envisaged operating in other markets when the company was set up.

> Of course, in our field we can't just stop in Portugal, the outside world is more interesting... we have more clients in Germany and in the Netherlands than

> in Portugal. (…) our IT field horizon has to be infinite…. there can't be any restrictions, because the restrictions stagnate the company.
>
> *(C4)*

So, we analyzed the aggregate dimension of internationalization using the first-order concepts and the aforementioned theoretical categories. Based on these concepts, we were able to highlight that the main motivations for internationalization are boosting business capacity and growth, benefiting from new opportunities at international level (Martins et al., 2021).

In line with Paul and Mas (2020) and Hänle et al. (2021), we can see that globalization has provided new challenges and opportunities for companies wishing to internationalize, as it has enabled the creation of a dynamic environment with an increase in commercial transactions, driven by changes in business strategies.

With the results obtained and referencing the perspective of Taylor et al. (2021), we identified that the strategies adopted for internationalization by these high-tech companies arise from the aggregation of different theoretical models, such as Born Global, network theory, RVB, and "INV". These high-tech companies have a high capacity to adapt to markets and find growth restrictions with the small size of the domestic market, proactively focusing on the global market.

Through internationalization, these high-tech companies create new opportunities and access new customers (Castaldi et al., 2020; Hughes et al., 2021), thereby managing to grow, boost their performance, and create value.

In the same optics as Martineau and Pastoriza (2016), we see that some of these highly technological and global companies have recognized customer follow-up as the main impetus for internationalization and a key factor in the selection of markets.

As we have pointed out, customer follow-up drives internationalization, and the way to enter a given foreign market is digital. For these highly technological companies the use of digital technologies/digitization promotes rapid internationalization, overcoming barriers to entry in another market (Niittymies & Pajunen, 2020) and becoming the ideal mode of market entry, influencing business models, and supporting them digitally (Piaskowska et al., 2021).

In these highly technological companies, technology is an extremely important resource in developing labor skills, with a stimulating and differentiating effect. Digital technologies/digitization play a specific and substantial role in growth, providing the means to connect human resources, customers, suppliers, and partners worldwide.

In our results, entrepreneurs' motivation and determination to operate in new international markets are clearly drivers of internationalization. The entrepreneurial vision of ownership, with the perspective of the essentiality of internationalization, is also one of the main factors determining it.

Compared to Li et al. (2022), we can see that the resources that create value inhabit both inside and outside the company, corroborating corporate ambidexterity (Hughes et al., 2021; Bhandari et al., 2022; Li et al., 2022), which is central to increasing process efficiency, developing operations management and creating value, to achieve legitimacy, responsibility, reliability, and sustainability in the short term, while seeking new opportunities and viable products in the medium and long term (Hughes et al., 2021).

9.4.2 Digitization

The aggregate dimension defined as digitization, as specified in Figure 9.1, provides an overview of each question's main results, shown in the first-order codes, and their respective resemblance to their theoretical categories (second-order theoretical categories).

9.4.2.1 Digital technologies

In this second-order theoretical category, it was proposed the analysis of the influence of digital technology on business management and its benefits, determining market orientation and the use of digital technology.

The results show that all the companies interviewed use numerous digital technologies, both for internal support and for contact with the external environment.

"We programme in wordpress, make add-ons in Google and produce analyses in Google analytics, as well marketing in social networks, namely Facebook and Instagram, email marketing and everything within digital marketing" (C3).

In fact, these highly technological companies rely heavily on digital technologies and digitalization for internal and external management, leveraging their business.

Notwithstanding the highly technological capabilities of these companies, when we asked the interviewees about the impact of digital technologies on the company's performance, the response was peremptory in all the companies, all of them emphasized the importance of digital technologies in their business performance.

"The use of technology is inherent in what we do and in our work. It would be impossible to do what we do without technology, without the internet… Performance… there was no performance, there was no company…" (C3).

It should be noted that these highly technological companies are highly dependent on technology. Technology is central, both internally and externally. The companies that took part in this research mention that digital technologies and digitization generate new business strategies, creating value for the company and its customers.

"We put our innovation at the service of our customers and offer them this vision of achieving success, without commercial interest. We help clients innovate through technology, like Tesla, Google or Netflix" (C2).

We can see that digital technologies are closely associated with customer relationships. The speed of digital contact, through applications or digital platforms, allows customers to act together and solve problems, changing the paradigm in customer service.

> The customer is changing as they adapt to technology. Of course, the digitalization of companies and the use of other technologies promotes this change, because the customer goes and uses their mobile phone to buy anything that is actually online.
>
> *(C3)*

In this way, digital technologies help these companies innovate and create business value through constant interaction. In fact, digital technologies and digitalization are constantly evolving and represent a permanent challenge for business innovation.

9.4.2.2 Born digital

In this section we set out to investigate when the company was set up, if it was immediately envisaged to operate and carry out its activities using digital means, while also asking about the change in the customer paradigm.

In this sense, we found through the interviews made, that management in these highly technological companies is strongly influenced by the agglomeration of digital technologies, digitalization, and other technologies.

> There is a high influence on company management, because everything is digital.... and reciprocally influences the decision-making.
>
> *(C1)*

In this context, it is also important to note that most interviewees emphasize that the digital environment creates new business opportunities.

> In terms of opportunities, the digital environment creates new opportunities, given the ease of integrating another market and finding new clients.
>
> *(C1)*

We should point out that many interviewees don't have a physical space to interact with customers, suppliers, and partners. Their interaction and service are exclusively via technology, as opposed to the traditional business model.

> We don't have traditional support...only digital, as far as opportunities are concerned...these arise with the globalised market, when you have an online site... you can have clients from everywhere.... No, we don't have our own platform and in our field we have to work with others platforms like Google....
>
> *(C3)*

We can see that most of these companies don't have their own platforms but use platforms created by other companies, which allows them to create innovative services with greater organizational development and performance, boost the brand and ambidextrous value, and create internal and external value for the company, customers, and suppliers.

In this context, we end this subsection by observing that around 80% of these highly technological companies are Born Digital, i.e., they are designed from the outset as digital companies.

> The business is based on digital technology, it's a service company that intermediates rentals. Everything was digitally designed and everything is combined this way, both product communication and sales.
>
> *(C1)*

Considering the above, we assume the growing preponderance of digital technologies, in line with the theory presented by Kindermann et al. (2021), which indicates that digital technologies and digitization are transforming how companies create and deliver value.

Digital technologies and digitization have an evolutionary impact on these highly technological companies, promoting changes to business models.

As we have seen, the digital strategy must be positioned in line with the company's general strategy but developed as a special strategy.

We, therefore, corroborate the projection made by Bharadwaj et al. (2013), which is not far removed from today's reality. These authors confirmed that companies and sectors that go digital have more information, communication, connectivity, and functionality, and it was thought that the digital business strategy would be integrated into the company's general business strategy. In this way, it wouldn't have been expected that this digital strategy would become as important as it is today and has been proven in these highly technological companies. With the natural evolution and innovation of technologies, digital strategy will become increasingly important and the main business strategy underpinning this type of company, especially high-tech and Born Digital companies (Monaghan et al., 2020).

In this context, the digital business strategy should be broader, more prominent, integrated, comprehensive, and sustained than other strategies. Companies who recognize their digital evolution needs, adapt to new potential customers, and to global market trends. This innovative composition can be achieved by developing internal capabilities (Ghosh et al., 2021).

As mentioned above, the configuration of digital technologies and digitization requires capabilities for transforming business models and an antagonistic change to traditional models, centered on models focused on digital services (as stated by interviewees C1, C3, and C5).

In this regard, we can see that digital technologies and digitization originate new opportunities for development and value creation and expose companies to different transformations (Hervé et al., 2020).

In a similar vein to Bergamaschi et al. (2020), the current pandemic context has triggered new opportunities for innovations in business models, particularly in the field of digital technologies and digitalization, allowing for greater internal and external interactions through multi-technological innovation (Lee et al., 2021). Therefore, it is clear that digitalization is metamorphosing and dematerializing companies, consequently producing changes in the international markets.

Our results confirm that digital technologies and digitization are overcoming international barriers, enabling companies to engage in international markets (Hervé et al., 2020). Digitalization is an essential condition for business competitiveness at the international level (Bergamaschi et al., 2020).

In short, integrating new digital technologies drives internationalization (Teruel et al., 2021). Considering that any innovations in digital technologies allows business environment to reshape, providing new opportunities for companies (Ghosh et al., 2021; Kindermann et al., 2021), expanding connectivity within and outside business organization, between employees, suppliers, partners, and customers, as well as recognizing new business opportunities, reducing physical distance, and location dependencies (Kindermann et al., 2021; Vendrell-Herrero et al., 2021; Lee et al., 2022).

These new products and services, offered by these highly technological companies and especially implemented by digital technologies, do not require any adaptation to the stages of internationalization or their traditional models; they spread quickly, like a virus (Urbinati et al., 2020).

9.4.3 Strategic orientation

With this aggregate dimension called strategic orientation, we harmonize the general results, emphasizing the strategies adopted. In this way, we present an overview of the main results of each question (shown in the first-order codes) and their respective correspondence to their theoretical categories (second-order theoretical categories).

9.4.3.1 Innovation

With this theoretical category, we set out to find whether the adoption of emerging technologies, development, and innovation in new products or services directly influence the organization's performance.

The data gathered in our interviews shows that the five companies involved in this research show that digital strategy is effective in accelerating and launching new products and services.

> Of course it is. The speed and effectiveness of launching new products could not be achieved in any other way.
>
> *(C1)*

Based on the answers received, we can infer that digital strategy is faster and more effective in launching new products or services and promotes changes in innovation and operationalization. We can assume that this ability to create and launch new products or services quickly and efficiently is a crucial capability for a digital operating model. In this way, these high-tech companies show some restraints in making products or services available, since the launch of new products or services is carried out in phases, anticipating the testing and evaluation phases, after which the decision is made on making the product or service available.

Following on, our results show that the analysis of the main success factors in a digital business is essential. Through our interviewees' responses, we found numerous factors that influence business success, namely: C1 –

> The main success factors for a digital business, are having a good product that has added value and stands out from the rest. Since the start of the company, it is essential to meet users' expectations and what they really need. The way you communicate is very important. Google indexing is crucial, as is the dissemination of information on social networks and digital partnerships.

From the answers we received, we could ascertain that making products or services available requires them to add value to the company and the customer and distinguish themselves from other competitors' products or services.

These highly technological companies focus on these factors for their organizational development, focusing on customer relationships. It should be noted that this terminology is evolutionary; the company's analysis of the value attributed, through services and products, to the customer is a huge innovation operationalized in high-tech companies, which translates into competitive advantage.

9.4.3.2 Sources of value creation

In this theoretical dimension, we try to determine whether the corporate brand acquires prominence in the international market, examining whether technologies modify value creation processes and originate competitive advantage.

For this analysis, we found that digital technologies and digitalization lead to a strategic commitment to foreign markets, as mentioned in the five interviews with these five companies.

> As I said, the digital environment brings flexibility and makes it possible to internationalize quickly in other markets. If the company uses digital technologies to make itself known and this is its main mode of operation, it is clear that the company has a strategic commitment in any market in which it is present.
>
> *(C1)*

We conclude that these high-tech companies use advanced digital technologies and digitalization to join new markets and with this integration they make a strategic commitment. With this strategic commitment, the corporate brand acquires visibility, reference, and relevance.

We can also see from the results of all the companies interviewed (100% of the companies contributing to this study) that digital strategy is becoming increasingly important. When it is successfully established, it produces counterparts such as leveraging corporate value, differentiation from competitors, competitive advantage, and growth.

> What sets our company apart is our brand marketing methodology. It's a methodology that only four or five agencies are working on. We differentiate ourselves because of our working methods that brings value. We choose to define the strategy with the business manager that includes a set of actions for a final result. I see my clients' business as my own.
>
> *(C5)*

Based on these results, we can infer that these high-tech companies are governed by the strategic and differentiated proposals of their services, which is the main distinguishing factor. In this context, we also found that high-tech companies have different working methodologies and constantly look for innovative factors, anticipating technological changes. These constant changes also reveal some difficulties, particularly in the dependence on specialized human resources.

9.4.3.3 Resources

In this theme, we asked about the relevance of the manager's thinking to the company's overall strategy, emphasizing the importance of tangible and intangible resources.

Our results show that these highly technological companies have various technological and organizational factors that enable them to compete globally. It should be noted that these unique and valuable resources differentiate them in a globalized and international market.

> It's very difficult to find good IT development companies on this service now platform. It's much easier to get clients than specialised human resources.
>
> *(C4)*

We found that these companies with innovative technologies have some shortcomings, such as those consistently mentioned by the CEO of Company 4. These shortcomings stem from the difficulty in obtaining and maintaining specialized human resources, even though they provide technological training, high salaries, and a good business environment.

Based on our results, we asked the five interviewees about the impact of specialized human resources on their relationships with partners, customers, and suppliers.

> Human resources are essential.
>
> *(C2)*

As mentioned, human resources are essential and establish the connection between the company's digital technology, partners, suppliers, and customers.

On the other hand, based on all these results, we examined the CEO's importance in defining the company's overall and digital strategies.

We found that in 100% of these highly technological companies, the CEO defines the company's global strategies, with a hierarchical, top-down centrality.

> It is the CEO who defines the strategy. That's his responsibility. Our company operates vertically, there is a management board where expansion and internationalization are decided and discussed.
>
> *(C1)*

We therefore conclude that the CEO's role remains vital. He is responsible for making decisions and managing all the organization's initiatives and strategies.

Similarly to Jinzhi and Carrick (2019), we emphasize the relevance of the CEO with innovative development and management skills in high-growth and highly technological companies, alluding to the relevance of human capital for business growth.

In fact, it is evident the positive impact that strategic orientations have on business performance. Referencing the research of Singh et al. (2017), we found that strategic orientation directs the company through a set of values and beliefs to trigger superior performance (Haug et al., 2020; Zahoor et al., 2020; Kahn & Candi, 2021). As a rule, values and beliefs are provided by the vision of the CEO, who molds them and adapts them to the reality of his company to achieve constant and innovative superior performance.

Therefore, and in line with the study by Umrani et al. (2022), the evolution of business performance is only possible when managers improve their organizations internally. As evidenced by Kindermann et al. (2021) and Paul and Mas (2020), strategic orientation is conceptualized in market orientation, learning orientation, entrepreneurial orientation, and technological orientation. Based on these highly technological companies, we were able to underline that it is through a strategic orientation that intangible, valuable, unique, and hard-to-imitate capabilities are enhanced and that competitive advantage (Schweiger et al., 2019), superior performance, and corporate brand recognition are achieved.

The company's overall strategic alignment is directed toward a combined technological strategy (Zahoor et al., 2020) with the digital strategy, considering that these highly technological companies have an optimal digital structure and benefit from increases in the interconnections between products, processes, and services (Ross et al., 2017; Hänle et al., 2021). Ultimately, we can say that digital technologies modify corporate strategies, business processes, company capabilities, products, and services (Bharadwaj et al., 2013) and relationships, both internally (between employees) and externally with (customers, partners, suppliers, and competitors).

The results also make it possible to do an association with the analysis by Giones and Miralles (2020), given that CEOs uses networks to reduce the scarcity of resources, in particular the strong dependence on specialized human capital (Rydehell, 2020). These unique characteristics of the human capital typology are evident as a determining factor, a source of competitive advantage, being a pillar of these highly technological companies (Jinzhi & Carrick, 2019; Piaskowska et al., 2021), based on knowledge (knowledge-based view – KBV) (Nonaka & Takeuchi, 1995; Grant, 1996; Grant & Phene, 2021), as the company's most significant strategic resource (Camisón-Haba et al., 2019).

In these highly technological companies, internal resources, and capabilities, namely CEO/entrepreneurs, human resources, technological resources, digital resources, and financial resources, simplify intra- and inter-institutional collaboration and increase business performance (Catanzaro et al., 2018).

Notwithstanding the above and as is evident from our results, these highly technological companies get new ideas from customers, identifying new needs, understanding, and motivating future needs, and acquiring opinions on future developments of new products or services.

In this way, the development of new capabilities or the reconfiguration of existing ones is intrinsically correlated with the organizational structure, processes, and resources that the organization creates, allowing it to develop new products and competences and strengthen its competitiveness.

In short, the high-tech companies featured in this research are based on successful innovation (technological level and complexity) (Aydin, 2020), differentiated products and services, developing economic positioning, and customer orientation (Urbinati et al., 2019; Morgan & Anokhin, 2020).

9.4.4 Implications

Our research has significant implications for internationalization theory. To better understand the extent of internationalization in these highly technological companies, we require the association of different theoretical models.

This research presents opportunities for investigating different international competitive strategies through digital transformation and digitalization, as in the research made by Monaghan et al. (2020).

As our results show, digital transformation and digitization have broadened the parameters of negotiation, opening new horizons for companies, and dematerializing borders between countries (Hervé et al., 2020). This has created new opportunities for international negotiation and allowed new scientific debates to be fostered on the impact of the digital context in the internationalization of high-tech companies.

We have also contributed to the entrepreneurial vision, establishing that the motivation and determination shown by entrepreneurs for their company to operate in new international markets is the main and the most determining factor in internationalization.

In terms of business strategy theory, we can corroborate the findings that these highly technological, global, and digital companies recognize the importance of customer support as a stimulus for internationalization (Martineau & Pastoriza, 2016; Paul & Rosado-Serrano 2019) and a crucial factor for choosing markets, achieving faster internationalization and avoiding relocation processes, typical of internationalization by stages (i.e. Uppsala model).

We agree that digitalization boosts business internationalization by opening new markets and promoting this entry in a simple, affordable, and accessible way. In this sense, our results add understanding to the growing literature on digital internationalization, providing new evidence and knowledge of the distinct conditions and simultaneously capturing its dynamics in these highly technological companies.

Complementing the theoretical contribution of our research, our results also suggest multiple practical implications.

Firstly, we affirm that digitalization is an essential condition for rapid and effective internationalization, contributing to business competitiveness at a global level. In this context, we motivate managers to adopt and use digital technologies and digitalization, given that it is a vital condition for internationalization and can promote a broad involvement of (customers, suppliers, partners), fostering greater interaction between customers and the company, suppliers and the company and partners and the company, which in turn promotes an increase in organizational performance.

On the other hand, we contribute to business practice with our findings on digital strategy, changing its perspective, and demonstrating that it should be reconciled with the company's overall strategy, although developed in a particular way as a special strategy.

In this sense, we encourage managers to outline a broad, prominent, integrated, comprehensive, and sustained digital business strategy plan compared to other strategies. Companies must understand the necessity of digital evolution and adapt to new potential customers and global market trends. This innovative composition can be achieved through the development of organizational ambidexterity.

In short, our research provides a rationale for managers to support innovation, differentiated products and services, developing digital economic positioning, and customer orientation.

9.5 Limitations and future research

Considering the preliminary nature of our study, we believe that any limitations have a minimal effect on the results presented. In this sense, our research is within the parameters of the qualitative tradition, promoting new perspectives for other studies of this emerging phenomenon.

Our limitations stem from the structure of this research, which was based on interviews with five high-tech companies; if more interviews had been carried out, the results would have benefited. The Portuguese context may limit the generalizability of our results, although these digital companies operate in the global market.

On the other hand, the companies included in this research are primarily focused on providing services, which limits the extrapolation of the results and conclusions obtained to other potential business areas, namely the sale of products.

Another limitation is that this study is based on qualitative data (mainly semi-structured interviews) and does not use quantitative methods or methodological triangulation. The qualitative study allows us to investigate in detail but makes it impossible to generalize conclusions.

Nevertheless, these results will be useful for developing new methods and structures for future research focusing on internationalization and the use of digital technologies. In turn, this research is essential for companies and managers who wish to expand into international markets or globalize their business by setting up a company or adopting digital technologies.

We therefore encourage future researchers to take advantage of our proposals. Our aim is to analyze the new challenges that companies face with internationalization, understand these motivations, probable consequences, and expected results through internationalization, and provide practical solutions and fruitful strategic visions that support decision-makers in their decisions.

The potential for future studies in this area could be boosted by addressing the following research questions:

- What drives and what are the motivations for companies to internationalize in different contexts and to different markets?
- Are digital technologies and digitization the necessary means for companies to survive internally and externally? Do they inspire superior performance and value creation?
- What's the customer's perspective on interaction, relationships, and purchases of certain products or services provided by high-tech companies?

It is important to emphasize the need for in-depth research into corporate ambidexterity, associating it with the company's various strategies and business models.

9.6 Conclusion

This research focused on analyzing the connection between internationalization strategies and digital transformation, investigating whether companies were founded on the globalized market. To carry out this research, we based ourselves on the research objectives of understanding the organizational competitive advantages intrinsic to digital internationalization, the reasons for digital internationalization, relating internationalization strategies to digital transformation and understanding how companies have internationalized and leveraged their possible competitive advantages in the context of digitalization.

The research revealed some evidence that contributes to the existing literature on the subject, providing a broad understanding of the internationalization behavior of high-tech companies. The motivations for internationalization, the choice of markets, and the strategies adopted are not uniform among high-tech companies. Companies that have been set up more recently are present in fewer markets. Their strategy is based on customer follow-up, i.e., they reinforce customer follow-up in different markets, internationalizing in those countries to succeed in that market by attracting new customers and promoting their brand.

In turn, we conclude that high-tech companies resort to internationalization with the aim of evolutionary and expansionary growth, seeing internationalization as indispensable and essential. Since the size of the domestic market is insufficient to satisfy these types of company's growth and expansion parameters, internationalization helps with international recognition and brand development in new markets. We hope that this study on digital internationalization and its strategy will be beneficial and allow this phenomenon to evolve and grow, contributing to the theory of internationalization and the business practice field.

Acknowledgments

This work is financed by national funds through FCT – Fundação para a Ciência e a Tecnologia, I. P., under the project "UIDB/04630/2020".

References

Andersson, U., Dasí, À., Mudambi, R., & Pedersen, T. (2016). Technology, innovation and knowledge: The importance of ideas and international connectivity. *Journal of World Business*, 51(1), 153–162. https://doi.org/10.1016/j.jwb.2015.08.017

Aydin, H. (2020). Market orientation and product innovation: The mediating role of technological capability. *European Journal of Innovation Management*, 24(4), 1233–1267. https://doi.org/10.1108/EJIM-10-2019-0274

Bahl, M., Lahiri, S., & Mukherjee, D. (2021). Managing internationalization and innovation tradeoffs in entrepreneurial firms: Evidence from transition economies. *Journal of World Business*, 56(1), 101150. https://doi.org/10.1016/j.jwb.2020.101150

Barney, J. (1991) Firm resources and sustained competitive advantage. *Journal of Management*, 17, 99–120. http://dx.doi.org/10.1177/014920639101700108

Bergamaschi, M., Bettinelli, C., Lissana, E., & Picone, P. M. (2020). Past, ongoing, and future debate on the interplay between internationalization and digitalization. *Journal of Management and Governance*, 0123456789. Springer US. https://doi.org/10.1007/s10997-020-09544-8

Berger, R. (2015). The digital transformation of industry. The study commissioned by the Federation of German Industries (BDI), Munich. www.rolandberger.com/publications/publication_pdf/roland_berger_digital_transformation_of_industry_20150315.pdf

Bhandari, K. R., Ranta, M., & Salo, J. (2022). The resource-based view, stakeholder capitalism, ESG, and sustainable competitive advantage: The firm's embeddedness into ecology, society, and governance. *Business Strategy and the Environment*, November 2021, 1–13. https://doi.org/10.1002/bse.2967

Bharadwaj, A., El Sawy, O. A., Pavlou, P. A., & Venkatraman, N. (2013). Digital business strategy: Toward a next generation of insights. *MIS Quarterly*, 37, 471–482. https://doi.org/10.25300/MISQ/2013/37:2.3

Camisón-Haba, S., Clemente-Almendros, J. A., & Gonzalez-Cruz, T. (2019). How technology-based firms become also highly innovative firms? The role of knowledge, technological and managerial capabilities, and entrepreneurs' background. *Journal of Innovation and Knowledge*, 4(3), 162–170. https://doi.org/10.1016/j.jik.2018.12.001

Castaldi, L., Iscaro, V., Maresca, P. & Mazzoni, C. (2020). Digital Transformation and Internationalization: a Complexity Approach / Iscaro, Valentina; Castaldi, Laura; Maresca, Paolo; Mazzoni, Clelia. - Proceedings of 15th International Forum of Knowledge Asset Dynamic (IFKAD:Knowledge in Digital Age, pp. 1166–1180.

Catanzaro, A., Messeghem, K., & Sammut, S. (2018). Effectiveness of export support programs: Impact on the relational capital and international performance of early internationalizing small businesses. *Journal of Small Business Management*, 57. https://doi.org/10.1111/jsbm.12489

Chen, L., Shaheer, N., Yi, J., & Li, S. (2019). The international penetration of ibusiness firms: Network effects, liabilities of outsidership and country clout. *Journal of International Business Studies*, 50(2), 172–192. https://ideas.repec.org/a/pal/jintbs/v50y2019i2d10.1057_s41267-018-0176-2.html

Christofi, M., Iaia, L., Marchesani, F., & Masciarelli, F. (2021). Marketing innovation and internationalization in smart city development: A systematic review, framework and research agenda. *International Marketing Review*, 38(5), 948–984. https://doi.org/10.1108/IMR-01-2021-0027

Dabić, M., Maley, J., Dana, L. P., Novak, I., Pellegrini, M. M., & Caputo, A. (2020). Pathways of SME internationalization: A bibliometric and systematic review. *Small Business Economics*, 55(3), 705–725. https://doi.org/10.1007/s11187-019-00181-6

Ghosh, S., Hughes, M., Hodgkinson, I., & Hughes, P. (2021). Digital transformation of industrial businesses: A dynamic capability approach. *Technovation*, November, 102414. https://doi.org/10.1016/j.technovation.2021.102414

Gioia, D. A., Corley, K. G., & Hamilton, A. L. (2013). Seeking qualitative rigor in inductive research: Notes on the Gioia methodology. *Organizational Research Methods*, 16(1), 15–31.

Giones, F., & Miralles, F. (2020). Bound for glory or cursed for life? Exploring the impact of initial resources on the venture emergence of new technology-based firms. *International Journal of Entrepreneurial Venturing*, 12(2), 143–160. https://doi.org/10.1504/IJEV.2020.105532

Grant, R., & Phene, A. (2021). The knowledge based view and global strategy: Past impact and future potential. *Global Strategy Journal*, March, 1–28. https://doi.org/10.1002/gsj.1399

Grant, R. M. (1996). Toward a knowledge-based theory of the firm. *Strategic Management Journal*, 17, 109–122. https://doi.org/10.1002/smj.4250171110

Hamdoun, M. (2020). The antecedents and outcomes of environmental management based on the resource-based view: A systematic literature review. *Management of Environmental Quality: An International Journal*, 31(2), 451–469. https://doi.org/10.1108/MEQ-12-2019-0280

Hänle, F., Cambré, B., & Weil, S. (2021). A systematic review on the internationalization of Chinese SMEs: Thematic expansion, new impulses and potential avenues for future research. *Journal of Entrepreneurship in Emerging Economies*. https://doi.org/10.1108/JEEE-05-2021-0197

Haug, A., Adsbøll Wickstrøm, K., Stentoft, J., & Philipsen, K. (2020). The impact of information technology on product innovation in SMEs: The role of technological orientation. *Journal of Small Business Management*, 00(00), 1–27. https://doi.org/10.1080/00472778.2020.1793550

Hervé, A., Schmitt, C., Baldegger, R., & Preston, S. (2020). Internationalization and digitalization: Applying digital technologies to the internationalization process of small and medium-sized enterprises. *Technology Innovation Management Review*, 10(7), 29–41. http://doi.org/10.22215/timreview/1373

Hughes, M., Hughes, P., Morgan, R. E., Hodgkinson, I. R., & Lee, Y. (2021). Strategic entrepreneurship behaviour and the innovation ambidexterity of young technology-based firms in incubators. *International Small Business Journal: Researching Entrepreneurship*, 39(3), 202–227. https://doi.org/10.1177/0266242620943776. ISSN: 2547-8516 (n.d.).

Jinzhi, Z., & Carrick, J. (2019). The rise of the Chinese Unicorn: An exploratory study of Unicorn Companies in China. *Emerging Markets Finance and Trade*, 55(15), 3371–3385. https://doi.org/10.1080/1540496X.2019.1610877

Johanson, J., & Mattsson, L. (1992). Network positions and strategic actions—An analytical framework. In: Axelsson, B. and Easton, G., Eds., *Industrial Networks: A New View of Reality*. Routledge, London, 205–217.

Johanson, J., & Vahlne, J. E. (1977). The internationalization process of the firm—A model of knowledge development and increasing foreign market commitments. *Journal of International Business Studies*, 8, 23–32. https://doi.org/10.1057/palgrave.jibs.8490676

Johanson, J., & Vahlne, J. E. (2009). The Uppsala internationalization process model revisited: From liability of foreignness to liability of outsidership. *Journal of International Business Studies*, 40, 1411–1431. https://doi.org/10.1057/jibs.2009.24

Kahn, K. B., & Candi, M. (2021). Investigating the relationship between innovation strategy and performance. *Journal of Business Research*, 132(March), 56–66. https://doi.org/10.1016/j.jbusres.2021.04.009

Kindermann, B., Beutel, S., Garcia de Lomana, G., Strese, S., Bendig, D., & Brettel, M. (2021). Digital orientation: Conceptualization and operationalization of a new strategic orientation. *European Management Journal*, 39(5), 645–657. https://doi.org/10.1016/j.emj.2020.10.009

Lee, J., Hwang, J., & Kim, H. (2022). Different government support effects on emerging and mature ICT sectors. *Technological Forecasting and Social Change*, 174(August 2021), 121253. https://doi.org/10.1016/j.techfore.2021.121253

Lee, J. Y., Colpan, A. M., Ryu, Y. S., & Sekiguchi, T. (2021). What do we know about the internationalization of Asian business groups? A systematic review and future research agenda. *Asian Business and Management*, 0123456789. https://doi.org/10.1057/s41291-021-00164-0

Lee, J. Y., Irisboev, I. O., & Ryu, Y. (2021). Literature review on digitalization in facilities management and facilities management performance measurement: Contribution of Industry 4. 0 in the global era. *Sustainability*, 13(23), 13432. https://doi.org/10.3390/su132313432

Li, L., Shan, S., Shou, Y., Kang, M., & Park, Y. W. (2022). Sustainable sourcing and agility performance: The moderating effects of organizational ambidexterity and supply chain disruption. *Australian Journal of Management*, December 2021. https://doi.org/10.1177/03128962211071128

Martineau, C., & Pastoriza, D. (2016). International involvement of established SMEs: A systematic review of antecedents, outcomes and moderators. *International Business Review*, 25(2), 458–470. https://doi.org/10.1016/j.ibusrev.2015.07.005

Martins, R., Farinha, L., & Ferreira, J. J. (2021). Analysing stimuli and barriers, failure and resilience in companies' internationalization: A systematic and bibliometric review. *Review of International Business and Strategy*. https://doi.org/10.1108/RIBS-07-2021-0103

Mintzberg, H., & Westley, F. (1992). Cycles of organizational change. *Strategic Management Journal*, 13(2 S), 39–59. https://doi.org/10.1002/smj.4250130905

Monaghan, S., Tippmann, E., & Coviello, N. (2020). Born digitals: Thoughts on their internationalization and a research agenda. *Journal of International Business Studies*, 51(1), 11–22. https://doi.org/10.1057/s41267-019-00290-0

Mondal, A., Ray, S., & Lahiri, S. (2022). Family ownership, family management, and multinationality: Evidence from India. *Journal of Business Research*, 138(December 2020), 347–359. https://doi.org/10.1016/j.jbusres.2021.09.017

Moreira, J., Marques, C. S., Braga, A., & Ratten, V. (2019). A systematic review of women's entrepreneurship and internationalization literature. *Thunderbird International Business Review*, 61(4), 635–648. https://doi.org/10.1002/tie.22045

Morgan, T., & Anokhin, S. A. (2020). The joint impact of entrepreneurial orientation and market orientation in new product development: Studying firm and environmental contingencies. *Journal of Business Research*, 113(November 2017), 129–138. https://doi.org/10.1016/j.jbusres.2019.06.019

Niittymies, A., & Pajunen, K. (2020). Cognitive foundations of firm internationalization: A systematic review and agenda for future research. *International Business Review*, 29(4), 101654. https://doi.org/10.1016/j.ibusrev.2019.101654

Nonaka, I., & Takeuchi, H. (1995). *The Knowledge-Creating Company: How Japanese Companies Create the Dynamics of Innovation*. Oxford University Press, New York.

Paul, J. (2020). SCOPE framework for SMEs: A new theoretical lens for success and internationalization. *European Management Journal*, 38(2), 219–230. https://doi.org/10.1016/j.emj.2020.02.001

Paul, J., & Benito, G. R. G. (2018). A review of research on outward foreign direct investment from emerging countries, including China: What do we know, how do we know and where should we be heading? *Asia Pacific Business Review*, 24(1), 90–115. https://doi.org/10.1080/13602381.2017.1357316

Paul, J., & Mas, E. (2020). Toward a 7-P framework for international marketing. *Journal of Strategic Marketing*, 28(8), 681–701. https://doi.org/10.1080/0965254X.2019.1569111

Paul, J., Parthasarathy, S., & Gupta, P. (2017). Exporting challenges of SMEs: A review and future research agenda. *Journal of World Business*, 52(3), 327–342. https://doi.org/10.1016/j.jwb.2017.01.003

Paul, J., & Rosado-Serrano, A. (2019). Gradual internationalization vs born-global/international new venture models: A review and research agenda. *International Marketing Review*, 36(6), 830–858. https://doi.org/10.1108/IMR-10-2018-0280

Paul, J., & Sánchez-Morcilio, R. (2019). Toward a new model for firm internationalization: Conservative, predictable, and pacemaker companies and markets. *Canadian Journal of Administrative Sciences/Revue Canadienne des Sciences de l'Administration*, 36(3), 336–349

Pereira, V., Temouri, Y., Shen, K. N., Xie, X., & Tarba, S. (2022). Exploring multilevel innovative ecosystems and the strategies of EMNEs through disruptive global expansions – The case of a Chinese MNE. *Journal of Business Research*, 138(September 2020), 92–107. https://doi.org/10.1016/j.jbusres.2021.08.070

Petricevic, O., & Teece, D. J. (2019). The structural reshaping of globalization: Implications for strategic sectors, profiting from innovation, and the multinational enterprise.

Journal of International Business Studies, 50(9), 1487–1512. https://doi.org/10.1057/s41267-019-00269-x

Piaskowska, D., Tippmann, E., & Monaghan, S. (2021). Scale-up modes: Profiling activity configurations in scaling strategies. *Long Range Planning*, 54(6). https://doi.org/10.1016/j.lrp.2021.102101

Porter, M. E. (1980). *Competitive Strategy: Techniques for Analyzing Industries and Competitors*. Free Press, New York.

Porter, M. E. (2001). Strategy and the Internet. *Harvard Business Review*, 79(3). https://doi.org/10.2469/dig.v31.n4.960

Ross, B., Pechenkina, E., Aeschliman, C., & Chase, A. M. (2017). Print versus digital texts: Understanding the experimental research and challenging the dichotomies. *Research in Learning Technology*, 25, 1–12.

Rydehell, H. (2020). Stakeholders roles in business model development in new technology-based firms. *International Journal of Innovation Management*, 24(4). https://doi.org/10.1142/S1363919620500310

Sapienza, H. J., Autio, E., George, G., & Zahra, S. A. (2006). A capabilities perspective on the effects of early internationalization on firm survival and growth. *Academy of Management Review*, 31(4), 914–933. https://doi.org/10.5465/AMR.2006.22527465

Schweiger, S. A., Stettler, T. R., Baldauf, A., & Zamudio, C. (2019). The complementarity of strategic orientations: A meta-analytic synthesis and theory extension. *Strategic Management Journal*, 40, 1822–1851. https://doi.org/10.1002/smj.3042

Singh, J., Flaherty, K., Sohi, R. S., Deeter-Schmelz, D., Habel, J., Meunier-FitzHugh, K.L., Malshe, A., Mullins, R., & Onyemah, V. (2017). Sales profession and professionals in the age of digitization and artificial technologies: Concepts, priorities, and questions. Oklahoma State University. https://ueaeprints.uea.ac.uk/id/eprint/71361/1/Sales_Profession_and_Professionals_2019.pdf

Singh, S. K., Giudice, M. D., Chierici, R., & Graziano, D. (2020). Green innovation and environmental performance: The role of green transformational leadership and green human resource management. *Technological Forecasting and Social Change*, 150(September 2019), 119762. https://doi.org/10.1016/j.techfore.2019.119762

Steinhäuser, V. P. S., Paula, F. de O., & de Macedo-Soares, T. D. L. v. A. (2021). Internationalization of SMEs: A systematic review of 20 years of research. *Journal of International Entrepreneurship*, 19(2). https://doi.org/10.1007/s10843-020-00271-7

Syam, N., & Sharma, A. (2018). Waiting for a sales renaissance in the fourth industrial revolution: Machine learning and artificial intelligence in sales research and practice. *Industrial Marketing Management*, 69, 135–146. https://doi.org/10.1016/j.indmarman.2017.12.019

Taylor, M., Jack, R., Madsen, T., & Alam, M. A. (2021). The nature of service characteristics and their impact on internationalization: A multiple case study of born global firms. *Journal of Business Research*, 132(May), 517–529. https://doi.org/10.1016/j.jbusres.2021.04.050

Teruel, M., Coad, A., Domnick, C., Flachenecker, F., Harasztosi, P., Janiri, M. L., & Pal, R. (2021). The birth of new HGEs: Internationalization through new digital technologies. *Journal of Technology Transfer* (Issue 0123456789). Springer US. https://doi.org/10.1007/s10961-021-09861-6

Tuomisalo, T., & Leppäaho, T. (2019). Learning in international new ventures: A systematic review. *International Business Review*, 28(3), 463–481. https://doi.org/10.1016/j.ibusrev.2018.11.005

Umrani, W. A., Ahmad, I., Rasheed, M. I., Ahmed, U., Pahi, M. H., Jhatial, A., & Abbsai, G. A. (2022). Managing intellectual capital: Role of corporate entrepreneurship and absorptive capacity on firm performance. *Knowledge Management Research and Practice*, 00(00), 1–13. https://doi.org/10.1080/14778238.2022.2041374

Urbinati, A., Chiaroni, D., Chiesa, V., & Frattini, F. (2019). The role of business model design in the diffusion of innovations: An analysis of a sample of unicorn-tech companies. *International Journal of Innovation and Technology Management*, 16(1). https://doi.org/10.1142/S0219877019500111

Urbinati, A., Chiaroni, D., Chiesa, V., & Frattini, F. (2020). The role of digital technologies in open innovation processes: An exploratory multiple case study analysis. *R and D Management*, 50(1), 136–160. https://doi.org/10.1111/radm.12313

Vahlne, J. E., & Johanson, J. (2017). From internationalization to evolution: The Uppsala model at 40 years. *Journal of International Business Studies*, 48, 1087–1102. https://doi.org/10.1057/s41267-017-0107-7

Vendrell-Herrero, F., Bustinza, O. F., & Vaillant, Y. (2021). Adoption and optimal configuration of smart products: The role of firm internationalization and offer hybridization. *Industrial Marketing Management*, 95(February), 41–53. https://doi.org/10.1016/j.indmarman.2021.04.001

Vrontis, D., & Christofi, M. (2021). R&D internationalization and innovation: A systematic review, integrative framework and future research directions. *Journal of Business Research*, 128(March), 812–823. https://doi.org/10.1016/j.jbusres.2019.03.031

Welch, C., Paavilainen-Mäntymäki, E., & Piekkari, R. (2022). Reconciling theory and context: How the case study can set a new agenda for international business research. *Journal of International Business Studies*, 53, 4–26. https://doi.org/10.1057/s41267-021-00484-5

Witt, M. A. (2019). De-globalization: Theories, predictions, and opportunities for international business research. *Journal of International Business Studies*, 50(7), 1053–1077. https://doi.org/10.1057/s41267-019-00219-7

Yin, R. K. (2017). *Case Study Research and Applications: Design and Methods*. Sage Publications.

Zahoor, N., Al-Tabbaa, O., Khan, Z., & Wood, G. (2020). Collaboration and internationalization of SMEs: Insights and recommendations from a systematic review. *International Journal of Management Reviews*, 22(4), 427–456. https://doi.org/10.1111/ijmr.12238

10

FIRM COMPETITIVENESS FIT STRESS-TEST

Marco Arraya and João J. Ferreira

10.1 Introduction

Business prosperity may sometimes conceal a firm's shortcomings in competitiveness, which can be exposed during an economic downturn. Nonetheless, it is crucial to identify weaknesses that truly matter and initiate necessary changes as soon as possible, as these weaknesses may not persist indefinitely.

Managing change can be challenging due to resistance from people, uncertainty surrounding new measures, and the impact on markets. However, the most significant obstacle to successfully implementing transformation initiatives is the need for more consensus among business owners, C-suites, directors, and managers regarding the dimensions and factors that have the greatest influence on the competitiveness of a business model. If multiple individuals with decision-making and execution responsibilities within the same organization are asked to identify critical dimensions and factors, the business model needs to be modified or transformed to remain competitive and keep pace with the market. In this case, each person is likely to provide a different answer. This is because each individual has its own unique perspective and experience, and prefers to focus on approaches that align with their comfort zone. To address this challenge effectively, a tool that presents the core dimensions of competitiveness and incorporates questions that all firm collaborators must be able to answer.

When a firm is operational, it typically seeks to compete, achieve its objectives, and surpass rival firms that share the same goals (Porter, 1990). Competitive firms are more likely to succeed, flourish, and generate economic profit (Drucker, 1999; Srivastava et al., 2006). From a strategic standpoint, focusing on core activities and efficiency can lead to growth and enhanced competitiveness, which

DOI: 10.4324/9781032695969-11

often necessitates a shift in continuity. Therefore, the quality of market-oriented decisions, work, resources, skills, competencies, effort, and adaptability in which a firm invests in outperforming competitors is typically referred to as a competitive factor (Walzel, 2021). In essence, competitiveness is the state of being competitive, and in organizational management, it is the ability to compete successfully in an overcrowded field of competitors.

Competitiveness encompasses more than the various dimensions and factors necessary to achieve a significant market position and generate value (Porter, 2008). Nevertheless, maximizing the exploitation of these competitive dimensions and factors depends on a firm's capacity to orchestrate them (Lafuente et al., 2016). Ultimately, competitiveness is a systemic construct that interconnects dimensions with strong interdependencies and coherence, and must be understood from a holistic perspective to better understand how the firm competes and operates in the marketplace (Edwards, 2001; Lafuente et al., 2016).

In this study, the concept of firm competitiveness fit is understood as a firm's capacity and skill to thrive in highly competitive and demanding markets. This encompasses the proficiency and efficiency of each component while also emphasizing that the coherence and functionality of the entire system cannot be determined by evaluating a single dimension alone.

The primary objective of our study is to examine the fundamental aspects that significantly impact competitiveness in the context of firms' competitive adjustments. These dimensions enable organizations to identify and capitalize on opportunities or defend themselves against potential threats, ultimately fostering growth, efficiency, and long-term sustainability (Teece, 2018).

The assessment of the system's functioning, referred to as the stress test, enables firms to concentrate on key issues that need to be addressed, specifically firm competitiveness fit, regardless of prevailing economic conditions. By posing decisive and precise questions about the business and focusing on critical dimensions, a firm can pinpoint errors, inefficiencies, and weaknesses in its competitiveness. Therefore, we introduce the firm competitiveness fit stress-test, which has three distinct characteristics. First, firms can measure their competitiveness directly. Second, a firm can convey the outcomes of a stress test and its significance to stakeholders. Finally, and most importantly, the firm obtains information to analyze, adjust, or transform the business model.

10.2 The firm competitiveness fit seven key dimensions

Our investigation of the crucial aspects of firm competitiveness revealed that most financial and non-financial measures did not indicate organizational performance. Following an extensive search of management and strategic management literature, we identify the competitive dimensions that contribute to a firm's performance. Subsequently, we developed a firm competitiveness fit stress-test (FCFST) to measure organizational competitiveness. The FCFST instrument we created collectively aids in assessing the overall competitiveness of firms and in determining which dimensions are most strongly associated with organizational performance.

Empirical research has identified a set of competitiveness dimensions—purpose, leadership, passion for work, people-centered, customer-centric, infrastructure, and viability—that predict performance. By utilizing a tool designed to assess these seven dimensions, it is possible to evaluate a firm's level of competitiveness, identify areas of strength and weakness, and link improvements or declines in specific dimensions over time to overall competitiveness and organizational performance.

10.2.1 Purpose

This study defines purpose as the principles that provide direction and meaning to an organization. The purpose is the path the firm wishes to pursue, while values are moral and ethical guidelines that reflect appropriate conduct (Coleman, 2022; Slåtten et al., 2021). The values act as a roadmap for behavior. The combination of purpose, values, and inherent behaviors contributes to organizational culture (Ghavifekr et al., 2013). A clear vision offers focus, coherence, and guidance (Kraaijenbrink, 2021).

No evidence suggests that a formal firm outperforms its peers (Kraaijenbrink 2021). However, it is crucial that the organizational purpose is deeply ingrained in employees' mentality and serves as an inner voice that directs and influences their behavior (Kohles et al., 2012).

When employees share a purpose, they connect with a common goal that generates energy and focuses on their efforts (Avery, 2005). Aligning personal values with those of the firm results in a unified direction that transforms the workplace into a unique environment that addresses the needs of employees and stakeholders (Avery, 2005; Kraaijenbrink, 2021). As Coleman (2022) points out, vision, values, behavior, adaptation, and alignment are all essential elements of a successful organizational purpose.

10.2.2 Leadership

As Peter Drucker (1999) posits, a leader's guiding light should concentrate on doing the right things. According to Drucker (1999), this mindset is rooted in four key aspects: a people-centric approach, customer-centric approach, sound business strategy, and leadership style grounded in character and values.

When a leader prioritizes a people-centric culture, they feel valued. By involving people directly in strategic and operational decisions and providing support to help them reach their full potential, a leader fosters an environment in which people's voices are heard, and their needs are considered and addressed (Ettlin, 2019).

A leader who prioritizes a customer-centric approach aligns customer needs with the value that arises from the business model, strategies, and tactics (Senn et al., 2013). This requires all individuals to be aligned when developing a customer-centric environment.

The literature on strategy emphasizes the well-established impact of leadership on firm performance (Herrmann & Nadkarni, 2014) and the influence of individual soft and hard skills on performance (Hendarman & Cantner, 2018).

10.2.3 Passion

Work passion is a strong and positive emotion that drives individuals to pursue their goals with perseverance, enabling them to overcome the challenges encountered during their daily work. This involves devoting time, energy, and mental effort (Cardon et al., 2017; Forest et al., 2011).

Individuals who possess work passion are deeply invested in their jobs and can easily dedicate time, energy, and effort (Vallerand et al., 2008). This attitude has a significant impact on individuals' self-esteem (Baumeister et al., 2003), which motivates them to improve their performance. Consequently, work passion increases productivity, efficiency, and strength, making the individual a valuable and rare resource (Srivastava, 2012).

Work passion is contagious and positively affects all stakeholders when genuine and sincere (Cardon & Mueller, 2016). Research indicates that work passion is a significant predictor of commitment and directly affects creativity, perseverance, and performance (Astakhova & Porter, 2015; Cardon et al., 2017; Mol et al., 2020).

10.2.4 People-centric

Skilled, committed, and dedicated individuals comprise a select group with unique, non-transferable knowledge, skills, and competencies that enable them to generate value for the organization and competitive advantages (Becker & Gerhart, 1996; Colbert, 2004). This is consistent with Barney's (1991) definition of valuable, rare, and difficult-to-imitate resources. Therefore, people are the most important assets for any firm, but many leaders often overlook this resource (Lepeley, 2017).

A people-centric firm that prioritizes employees alongside customers fosters a culture of care, inclusiveness, and a learning-oriented mindset (Ettlin, 2019; Lepeley, 2017; Nold, 2019), which has a direct impact on a firm's performance (Ettlin, 2019; Nold, 2019). Creating a nurturing and compassionate work environment involves ensuring that everyone feels respected, acknowledged, supported, and valued (Romansky et al., 2021).

Inclusiveness allows all individuals to participate in decisions made across an organization and to access development opportunities within a firm (Romansky et al., 2021). It fosters diversity, improves decision-making, increases work engagement and satisfaction, and consequently enhances work passion, dedication, innovation, and performance in a holistic manner. Absence of inclusiveness hampers the energy of diversity, leaving the potential energy of untapped diversity (Geldenhuys et al., 2014; Romansky et al., 2021).

Learning orientation describes a firm's ability to utilize knowledge to create value for stakeholders (Arraya, 2022). The existing literature considers learning orientation a strategic guiding factor and a valuable internal organizational resource for value creation and success (Melton & Hartline, 2013; Tajeddini, 2011). For example, it enables a firm to understand customer needs more effectively and mitigate threats, leading to new product success, customer retention, and improved profitability (Farrell et al., 2008). Learning orientation also fosters inclusiveness by encouraging individuals to question work processes and propose and test new procedures and routines (Franco & Almeida, 2011).

Effective learning orientation and participative decision-making promote people's sense of empowerment and proactivity, enabling them to promptly satisfy expressed and latent customer needs (Zacharatos et al., 2005).

10.2.5 Customer-centric

Customer-centric culture refers to a firm's ability to identify and meet customers' specific needs and behaviors, retain them, and enhance sales by providing appropriate services and products. This involves creating satisfied customers, which implies a firm in which strategic and operational boundaries are integrated into customer-centric processes and routines. The key components of a customer-centric culture include understanding the customer's explicit and hidden needs to build up a database of interactions that support customized activities, strong involvement with customers in innovation, marketing, and product or service decision-making processes, and a vision that focuses on implementing customer-centric processes and aligning cross-functional activities to deliver value to the customer.

To foster a customer-centric culture, executives must possess a mindset that is adaptable to the external environment and can execute internal modifications in the short term to fulfill market requirements. They must also empower people to make decisions and take action to solve customer needs or problems.

10.2.6 Infrastructure

A firm's formal organizational structure comprises systems, work processes, routines, workflows, and practices that support its customer-centric vision and objectives (Carew et al., 2009; Grant, 2010). Effective infrastructure enables an organization to swiftly adapt and innovate in response to external circumstances, enhance the quality and customer experience of its products and services, streamline internal processes, and promote seamless coordination among various departments (Carew et al., 2009; Lamberti, 2013).

10.2.7 Viability

A business entity is deemed viable when all its stakeholders derive value, such as shareholders through dividends, suppliers through new orders, partnerships

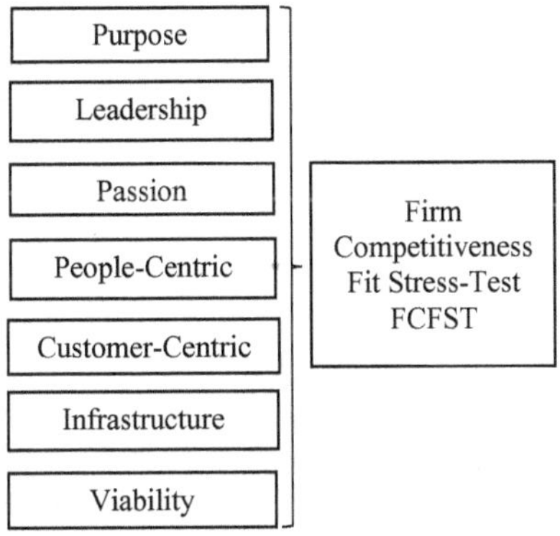

FIGURE 10.1 Tool's dimensions.

through joint ventures, and employees through benefits (Chesbrough et al., 2006). In practical terms, business viability implies that a product or service is either successful or has the potential to survive (Magretta, 2002).

The measurement of viability plays a critical role in ongoing learning that supports a firm's strategic and business model (Sainaghi et al., 2017) and is an essential factor to consider when planning, strategizing, and reorganizing (Bourne et al., 2013). Therefore, it is valuable for managers' decision-making regarding what is essential for the survival and growth of any business, such as vision, leadership, employee passion, customer focus, and infrastructure (Feng et al., 2019; Sainaghi et al., 2017). The ultimate goal is to assess the extent to which outcomes are sustainable and enhance a firm's overall capabilities, competencies, and effectiveness, leading to improved performance (Evans, 2017).

Figure 10.1 shows the firm competitiveness fit stress-test (FCFST) tool.

10.3 Creating the tool

Research on these seven dimensions has created a tool that enables firms to evaluate their competitiveness. This tool employs a scoring system based on the variables that impact each dimension. Employees from various positions and roles within a firm, regardless of their standing (Kianto, 2009), can contribute to the assessment of a firm's competitiveness by assigning scores to seven dimensions.

Evaluations are inherently subjective; however, this tool provides businesses with an unbiased framework for informed strategic decisions. The scoring mechanism also ensures that executives compare different periods to determine whether a firm's competitiveness has improved, remained stagnant, or declined. Utilizing these seven dimensions, executives can comprehensively assess a firm's progress and identify its strengths and weaknesses. This exercise applies to an entire organization or individual business unit.

The FCFST items were inspired by several studies, including Alqahtani et al. (2022), Avci et al. (2011), Bassi and McMurrer (2007), Carew et al. (2009), Leinwand and Mainardi (2011), and Sigmundsson et al. (2020).

The FCFST is a method that is applied iteratively, with each assessment indicating the firm's current state of competitiveness and its impact on organizational performance. Depending on the results, the firm may choose to implement changes such as reconfiguration or transformational measures. It is recommended that the FCFST be conducted periodically to ensure that a firm remains competitive. However, as a firm evolves in response to changes in its internal environment, stakeholders, and market, the dimensions that have the greatest influence on competitiveness may also change. Therefore, it is crucial to measure competitiveness and align it with the firm's strategic goals, processes, and routines. Table 10.1 presents the FCFST tool and its interpretation.

10.4 Recognize the interdependence of dimensions

Experience has demonstrated, and the literature has affirmed (Arraya, 2024; Leinwand & Mainardi, 2011), that it is not feasible for a firm to concentrate its change efforts, focus, and resources on all its capabilities and competencies simultaneously. Similarly, it is not advisable to intervene simultaneously in these seven dimensions.

A firm should prioritize addressing emergencies as these can compromise its competitiveness, long-term growth, and sustainability. Rather than dispersing energy without purpose, executives should concentrate their efforts on two or three dimensions. This involves identifying the dimensions with the most significant impact on a firm's strategy, competitiveness, and sustainability.

Although the focus is crucial, it is necessary to recognize that the dimensions are interconnected and mutually dependent. Therefore, although rationality may suggest that only two or three dimensions should be addressed simultaneously, it is important to acknowledge that all dimensions are correlated and do not exist in isolation. This implies that minimal intervention may be required to prevent jeopardization of the overall system. For instance, more than customer-centric behavior is required; the firm needs to possess a leadership mindset that prioritizes employees and their learning, innovation, and infrastructure, consisting of organizational resources and capabilities, processes, and routines that allow it to deliver value to customers. Hence, improvements in any one dimension can positively impact others.

10.5 Conclusion

Have you attempted to assess the competitiveness of your firm? Yes! Therefore, what is the firm's competitive level? Scores in the range of 148–210? Did you score minus 5% on items like "I'm not sure/don't know"?

TABLE 10.1 Firm competitive fit stress-test (FCFST)

		1 = strongly disagree to 10 = strongly agree	*Not Sure / Don't Know*
Purpose	Leadership in our firm aligns with a shared purpose and value.		
	The people in our firm have a passion for shared purposes and values.		
	In our firm, the values and purpose are properly defined and understood by people.		
	Add items in above section | Add items Not Sure / Don't Know | **Subtotal**		
Leadership	Our firm is effective in taking action based on the feedback that people provide.		
	In our firm, leaders believe that leading is about serving and not being served.		
	In our firm, leaders remove barriers to helping people focus on their work and customers.		
	Our managers are effective in keeping the firm track and executing the business model strategy.		
	Add items in above section, then multiply by 0.75 | Add items Not Sure / Don't Know | **Subtotal**		
Work Passion	I work hard enough to fulfil my goals.		
	I have enough passion to become very good in my area/skills.		
	I am motivated to build a career in our firm or this industry.		
	I have invested in my personal development.		
	I really like what I do.		
	Add items in above section, then multiply by 0.6 | Add items Not Sure / Don't Know | **Subtotal**		
People-centric	People in our firm are actively supported in the development of new skills and competencies.		
	Our firm continually incorporates new learning into standard ways of conducting business.		
	In our firm, people are willing to exchange and combine ideas with co-workers.		
	In our firm, people have easy access to the information they need to perform their jobs effectively.		
	Our firm communicates plans and decisions so that people can be clearly understood.		
	Our firm provides people with appropriate information about important changes.		
	In our firm, everyone has the opportunity to influence decisions that affect them.		
	In our firm, work teams can influence decision-making.		
	Add items in above section, then multiply by 0.375 | Add items Not Sure / Don't Know | **Subtotal**		

(Continued)

TABLE 10.1 (Continued)

		1 = strongly disagree to 10 = strongly agree	*Not Sure / Don't Know*
Customer-centric	In our firm, everyone maintains the highest quality and service standards.		
	In our firm, all work processes are designed to make it easier for customers to do business with us.		
	Our firm has a clear way to create value in the market.		
	Our firm has a clearly stated set of capabilities–that is, things you do better than anyone else–that customers' value and competitors cannot beat.		
	Our firm anticipates market changes and responds proactively.		
	Our firm is systematically looking for new ways to sell more.		
	Our firm can easily adapt to the challenges imposed by the market.		
	Add items in above section, then multiply by 0.42857 | Add items Not Sure / Don't Know | **Subtotal**		
Infrastructure	In our firm, the systems, structures, and formal and informal practices are integrated and aligned.		
	In our firm systems, structures and formal and informal practices make it easy for people to get their jobs done.		
	In our firm, people, processes, and work routines allow us to do things better than competitors, which rivals cannot imitate, and customer value.		
	Add items in above section | Add items Not Sure / Don't Know | **Subtotal**		
Viability	Our firm's overall performance has improved over the last two to three years.		
	Our firm's overall sales revenue improved in the last two to three years.		
	Customer satisfaction in our firm has increased over the last two to three years.		
	Customer perception of our brand has increased over the last two to three years.		
	Employee satisfaction in our firm has increased over the last two to three years.		
	The introduction of innovations or new products/services to the market has increased in the last two to three years.		
	Add items in above section, then multiply by 0.5 | Add items Not Sure / Don't Know | **Subtotal**		
	TOTAL (Sum of seven section subtotals above | The sum "Not Sure / Don't Know" must be divided by 36)		

Scoring Taking the sum of the seven subtotals from the dimensions above (note that all dimensions have the same weighting), refer to the chart below for the interpretation. This interpretation is accurate only if people's answers are honest. The total score of FCFST is (01–63) — We have a low level of competitiveness. (64–147) — We are almost there, but we still have a way to go. (148–210) — We are where we want to be, but we cannot fall asleep.	The tally of times the "**Not Sure/Don't Know**" box was checked on the FCFST measurement system, as follows: ≤5% — Excellent. This indicates the tool can be employed to enhance competitiveness. >5% to ≤10% — Acceptable. It is likely that there were significant gaps in the tool. ≥10% — Poor. This suggests that there is inadequate fundamental data to improve the competitiveness of firms.

Evaluate a firm's performance on a scale of 1 to 10 (1 = strongly disagree to 10 = strongly agree) for each listed dimension. If someone is unsure about any item, please provide the best guess and select the "Not Sure/Don't Know' option. After all participants completed the survey, they followed the instructions provided to calculate the estimated effectiveness of the firm competitive fit stress-test (FCFST).

If the responses to any or all of these three inquiries are negative, this could indicate that the enterprise lacks the necessary competitive edge for current market conditions, compromising its long-term viability and, ultimately, its survival.

The increased competitiveness in global markets resulting from the aggressive nature of competitors necessitates that firms reach a performance level above the industry average to achieve sustainability and growth. Unfortunately, there is only one solution for this challenge. To determine the most and least important dimensions contributing to performance, executives must thoroughly assess their competitiveness. This analysis allows them to make informed decisions about where to invest resources to achieve the maximum impact. Over time, this process leads to a baseline useful for benchmarking, continuity, or disruption in the firm's evolution.

We believe that a firm's competitive fit stress-test plays a crucial role in promoting the sustainability and growth of its organizational performance. This, in turn, enhances the firm's purpose, employee satisfaction, and customer focus; fosters innovation in the market; and ultimately contributes to organizational sustainability, serving as an accelerator for the growth of the firm's profitability.

We also hold the view, consistent with the insights shared by other authors throughout the various chapters of this book, that a people-centric mindset is crucial to a firm's competitive edge. When individuals embody a firm's purpose, possess the appropriate passion, and are guided by inclusive leadership that fosters growth, they are more inclined to engage in efforts to enhance competitiveness, sustainability, and growth. However, it is essential to couple a customer-centric approach rooted in the relationship and understanding of customers for the firm to allocate its organizational capabilities, resources, people, and processes to identify and capitalize on opportunities for disruption and innovation in the business model.

Ultimately, displaying bravery is crucial in endeavoring to gain insight and to examine and implement strategies that elevate one's competitive standing. Consequently, we extend the challenge to you by undertaking a firm competitiveness fit stress-test. As Drucker (1999) articulated, change cannot be managed; it can only be anticipated, and only those who lead the change process can survive.

References

Alqahtani, N., Uslay, C. and Yeniyurt, S. (2022). Entrepreneurial marketing and firm performance: Scale development, validation, and empirical test. *Journal of Strategic Marketing*, 2–22. https://doi.org/10.1080/0965254X.2022.2059773

Arraya, M. (2022). The relationship between distinctive capabilities system, learning orientation, leadership and performance. *European Journal of Management Studies*, *27*(2), 205–227.

Arraya, M. (2024). Capabilities configurational method for organizations' sustainability: Antecedents and consequences. *International Journal of Management Concepts and Philosophy*, *17*(2), 215–233.

Astakhova, M. N. and Porter, G. (2015). Understanding the work passion–performance relationship: The mediating role of organizational identification and moderating role of fit at work. *Human Relations*, *68*(8), 1315–1346

Avci, U., Madanoglu, M., and Okumus, F. (2011). Strategic orientation and performance of tourism firms: Evidence from a developing country. *Tourism Management*, *32*, 147–157.

Avery, G. C. (2005). *Leadership for sustainable futures*. Edward Elgar.

Barney, J. (1991). Firm resources and sustained competitive advantage. *Journal of Management*, *17*(1), 99–120.

Bassi, L. and McMurrer, D. (2007) Maximizing your return on people. *Harvard Business Review*, March, 1–9.

Baumeister, R. F., Campbell, J. D., Krueger, J. I., and Vohs, K. D. (2003). Does high self-esteem cause better performance, interpersonal success, happiness, or healthier lifestyles? *Psychological Science in the Public Interest*, *4*(1), 1–44.

Becker, B. and Gerhart, B. (1996). The impact of human resource management on organizational performance: Progress and prospects. *Academy of Management Journal*, *39*(4), 779–801.

Bourne, M., Pavlov, A., Franco-Santos, M., Lucianetti, L., and Mura, M. (2013). Generating organizational performance: The contributing effects of performance measurement and human resource management practices. *International Journal of Operations & Production Management*, *33*(11/12), 1599–1622.

Cardon, M. and Mueller, S. (2016). Passion is contagious, to customers, partners, employees, and investors. *Entreprendre & Innover*, *29*, 60–63.

Cardon, M. S., Post, C., and Forster, W. R. (2017). Team entrepreneurial passion: Its emergence and influence in new venture teams. *Academy of Management Review*, *42*(2), 283–305.

Carew, D., Kandarian, F., Parisi-Carew, E., and Stoner, J. (2009). Is your organization high performing? In Ken Blanchard (Ed.). *Leading at a Higher Level, Revised and Expanded Edition: Blanchard on Leadership and Creating High Performing Organizations*, 2nd Edition (pp. 3–16). Pearson.

Chesbrough, H., Vanhaverbeke, W., and West, J. (2006). *Open innovation: Researching a new paradigm*. Oxford University Press.

Colbert, B. A. (2004). The complex resource-based view: Implications for theory and practice in strategic human resource management. *The Academy of Management Review*, *29*(3), 341–358.

Coleman, J. (2022). It's time to take a fresh look at your company's values. *Harvard Business Review*, March 28, 1–10.

Drucker, P. F. (1999). *Management challenges for the 21st century*. HarperCollins.

Edwards, J. R. (2001). Multidimensional constructs in organizational behavior research: An integrative analytical framework. *Organizational Research Methods*, *4*, 144–192.

Ettlin, M. (2019). *What does it really mean to be people-centric?* Forbes, Dec 11. https://www.forbes.com/sites/forbestechcouncil/2019/12/11/what-does-it-really-mean-to-be-people-centric/?sh=7d648e824789. Accessed: 30 March 2024.

Evans, J. R. (2017). *Quality & performance excellence: Management, organization, and strategy*, 8th edition. Cengage Learning.

Farrell, M. A., Oczkowski, E., and Kharabsheh, R. (2008). Market orientation, learning orientation and organizational performance in international joint ventures. *Asia Pacific Journal of Marketing and Logistics*, *20*(3), 289–308.

Feng, T., Wang, D., Lawton, A., and Luo, B. (2019). Customer orientation and firm performance: The joint moderating effects of ethical leadership and competitive intensity. *Journal of Business Research*, *100*, 11–121.

Forest, J., Mageau, G. A., Sarrazin, C., and Morin, E. M. (2011). Work is my passion: The different affective, behavioural, and cognitive consequences of harmonious and obsessive passion toward work. *Canadian Journal of Administrative Sciences (CJAS)*, *28*, 27–40.

Franco, M. and Almeida, J. (2011). Organizational learning and leadership styles in healthcare organizations: An exploratory case study. *Leadership & Organization Development Journal*, *32*(8), 782–806.

Geldenhuys, M., Laba, K., and Venter, C. M. (2014). Meaningful work, work engagement, and organizational commitment. *SA Journal of Industrial Psychology, 40*(1), 1–10.

Ghavifekr, S., Afshari, M., Zabidi, A. H., and Razak, B. A. (2013). Vision-driven strategies and policies for managing educational systemic change: A qualitative analysis. *Australian Journal of Basic and Applied Sciences*, *7*(4), 333–341.

Grant, R. M. (2010). *Contemporary strategy analysis,* 7th edition. Wiley.

Hendarman, A. F. and Cantner, U. (2018). Soft skills, hard skills, and individual innovativeness. *Eurasian Business Review*, *8*, 139–169.

Herrmann, P. and Nadkarni, S. (2014). Managing strategic change: The duality of CEO personality. *Strategic Management Journal*, *35*(9), 1318–1342.

Kianto, A. (2009). Development and validation of a survey instrument for measuring organisational renewal capability. *International Journal of Technology Management*, *42*(1/2), 69–88.

Kohles, J. C., Bligh, M. C., and Carsten, M. K. (2012). A follower-centric approach to the vision integration process. *The Leadership Quarterly*, *23*(3), 476–487.

Kraaijenbrink, J. (2021). Why your mission and vision statements don't work (and what to do about it). *Forbes*, April. https://www.forbes.com/sites/jeroenkraaijenbrink/2021/04/13/why-your-mission-and-vision-statements-dont-work-and-what-to-do-about-it/?sh=24997d1234e2. Accessed: 30 March 2022.

Lafuente, E., Szerb, L., and Rideg, A. (2016). A system dynamics approach for assessing business competitiveness. *Organizations & Markets: Policies & Processes eJournal*. Available at SSRN 2892221.

Lamberti, L. (2013). Customer centricity: The construct and the operational antecedents. *Journal of Strategic Marketing*, *21*, 588–612.

Leinwand, P. and Mainardi, C. (2011). *The essential advantage: How to win with capabilities-driven strategy*. Harvard Business Review Press.

Lepeley, M. T. (2017). *Human centered management: The five global pillars of organization quality and sustainability*. Routledge.

Magretta, J. (2002). Why business models matter. *Harvard Business Review*, *80*(5), 86–92.

Melton, H. L. and Hartline, M. D. (2013). Employee collaboration, learning orientation, and new service development performance. *Journal of Service Research*, *16*(1), 67–81.

Mol, E. de, Cardon, M., and Khapova, S. N. (2020). When entrepreneurial passion backfires. *Harvard Business Review*, February 20, 1–12.

Nold, H. (2019). Dynamic capabilities for people-centric management in turbulent times. In: M. F. Brandebo and A. Alvinius (eds). *Dark sides of organizational behavior and leadership*. Intechopen, pp. 110–124.

Porter, M. E. (1990). *The competitive advantage of nations*. Free Press.

Porter, M. E. (2008). The five competitive forces that shape strategy. *Harvard Business Review*, *86*, 79–93.

Romansky, L., Garrod, M., Brown, K., and Deo, K. (2021). How to measure inclusion in the workplace. *Harvard Business Review*, May 27, 1–10.

Sainaghi, R., Phillips, P., and Zavarrone, E. (2017). Performance measurement in tourism firms: A content analytical meta-approach. *Tourism Management*, *59*, 36–56.

Senn, C., Thoma, A. M., and Yip, G. S. (2013). Customer-centric leadership: How to manage strategic customers as assets in B2B markets. *California Management Review*, *55*, 27–59.

Sigmundsson, H., Haga, M., and Hermundur F. (2020). The passion scale: Aspects of reliability and validity of a new 8-item scale assessing passion. *New Ideas in Psychology*, *56*, 100745.

Slåtten, T., Mutonyi, B. R., and Lien, G. (2021). Does organizational vision really matter? An empirical examination of factors related to organizational vision integration among hospital employees. *BMC Health Services Research*, *21* (483), 2–17.

Srivastava, D., Shah, H., & Talha, M. (2006). Determinants of competitiveness in Indian public sector companies: An empirical study. *Competitiveness Review*, *16*(3), 212–222.

Srivastava, M. (*2012*) *Stress, Workahol-ism and Job Demands: A Study of Executives in Mumbai*. NMIMS Management Review, XXII, pp. 94–116.

Tajeddini, K. (2011). Customer orientation, learning orientation, and new service development: An empirical investigation of the Swiss hotel industry. *Journal of Hospitality & Tourism Research*, *35*, 437–468.

Teece, D. J. (2018). Dynamic capabilities as (workable) management systems theory. *Journal of Management and Organisation*, *24*(3), 359–368.

Vallerand, R. J., Pelletier, L. G., and Koestner, R. (2008). Reflections on self-determination theory. *Canadian Psychology/Psychologie Canadienne*, *49*(3), 257–262.

Walzel, S. (2021). Fundamentals of sports economics and sports management. In: S. Walzel and V. Römisch (eds). *Managing sports teams, management for professionals*, pp. 1–22. Springer.

Zacharatos, A., Barling, J., and Iverson, R. D. (2005). High-performance work systems and occupational safety. *Journal of Applied Psychology*, *90*, 77–93.

11

CURRENT AND FUTURE CHALLENGES FOR ORGANIZATIONS

Forewarned is forearmed!

André de Waal and Julie Linthorst

11.1 Introduction

The current decade has so far turned out to be extremely challenging for organizations and all the signs are there that the coming decade will be the same. Organizations have to deal with an increasing number of challenges, many of which are already having an impact. Thus, for organizations to deal adequately with these challenges, they need to be innovative enough to prepare themselves for these. Unfortunately, the current academic literature does not give much guidance in this matter, as preciously little has been published on this matter yet (Linthorst and de Waal, 2020). The literature is mainly backward-looking, i.e., it looks at what organizations have done (past tense) to deal with current changing circumstances to survive but does not discuss how they can deal with future challenges (Cozzolino et al., 2017). To address this gap in the literature, we started a study with the goal of identifying how organizations should adapt to challenges in such a way that they not only will survive these challenges but even thrive during trying periods. Our research question, therefore, was: What are the challenges that can be found in the literature for which organizations have to prepare themselves?

Our research consisted of a descriptive literature review with the goal to identify which challenges will impact or are already influencing organizations (de Waal and Linthorst, 2022; Linthorst and de Waal, 2022). From each of the identified challenges, their postulated impact and consequences for organizations are described.[1] In practice, we notice that many of these challenges cannot be seen separately because they influence each other. This is the case for three of the most threatening challenges for organizations: speed of technological advancement, the changing labor market and the misalignment between the skills that people have and the skills organization need, now and in the (near) future (the so-called skills

DOI: 10.4324/9781032695969-12

mismatch). The downward spiral of these three mutually influencing challenges is discussed in more detail as these challenges are the ones organizations have to worry most about in the short and midterm.

The remainder of this chapter is structured as follows. In the next section the research approach for the identification of the challenges is describe. Subsequently, the challenges are described in more detail, including their impact on organizations. Then, the three most threatening challenges are discussed and their mutual impact on the future of organizations reviewed. The chapter ends with a discussion of several strategies that can help organizations prepare and deal with the challenges.

11.2 Research approach

Our research is based on a descriptive review as it focuses on trying to discern an interpretable pattern from the extant literature (Guzzo *et al.*, 1987). This type of review covers many studies which are directly or indirectly related to our topic and summarizes information about the results obtained by the researchers (Bhamu and Singh Sangwan, 2014; Costa and Godinho Filho, 2016; Rowley and Slack, 2004). The descriptive method uses a systematic procedure including searching, filtering and classifying processes so trends and patterns among the papers surveyed can be detected (King and He, 2005). We used the content analysis technique, in the form of the SLIP technique (Sort, Label, Integrate, Prioritize) to process the collected articles (Maeda, 2006).

The descriptive literature review started with a search of the various academic databases (EBSCO, Emerald, Google Scholar), using the keywords 'Megatrends', 'Disruptors', 'Future of Work' and '4th Industrial Revolution'. To focus on the latest insights, making sure that the findings in these studies are relevant, we narrowed the scope of our search to the previous decade (2010–2019). We did not only look at the academic literature as it was rather scarce on the topic of challenges (Malik and Janowska, 2018), but also the professional literature was examined, using the same keywords, as the future of work and organizational challenges are prominent topics in descriptive studies conducted by consultants and professional associations (Mahlendorf, 2014). The chosen keywords delivered many results from which we took a sample of 250 articles, books and papers which seemed most promising judging by their synopsis. Duplications were eliminated and our final sample contained 162 relevant articles. We grouped the challenges for organizations in categories of similarity (for example, 'millennials/generation Z', 'crowded planet' and 'demographic/aging' formed category 'changing workforce composition') to initially arrive at 14 challenges. Since the literature review took place in 2021, for this chapter we made an update of the review and identified an additional challenge which we have included here. In Appendix 1, the results of the literature review are given. In Appendix 2, we have listed the interdependencies between the challenges and their (combined) effect on organizations.

11.3 The identified challenges

In this section, the 15 identified challenges are described (based on de Waal and Linthorst, 2022; Linthorst and de Waal, 2022).

11.3.1 Challenge 1: Speed of technological advancement

Technological advancement is the collective term for the progress of technological and digital tools such as automation, Big Data and advanced analytics that increase productivity and provide better access to information and ideas (de Waal *et al.*, 2022). Organizations have been automating work for decades, but it is specifically the increasing speed of change that makes technological advancement such a force of change. Technological advancement is the main theme in 'Industry 4.0', also called the 'Fourth Industrial Revolution'. Industry 4.0 is originally a German project that discusses the strategic approach to digitalization and automation and consist of nine pillars (Erboz, 2017): Big Data and analytics that affect decision-making in organizations, autonomous robots having the ability to learn and perform certain tasks, simulations based on mathematical modeling to optimize processes, horizontal and vertical system integration leading to smart factories, the industrial internet of things connecting physical objects and systems, the cloud-enabling work through shared platforms, additive manufacturing such as 3D printing-enabling customization, augmented reality making human-machine interaction possible and cyber-security awareness leading to implementation of defense mechanisms against cyber-attacks.

In regard to the last, a challenge within this challenge is the increasing risks of cyber-attacks as these are becoming larger, more intricate and more relentless (Gilad and Tishler, 2023; Green, 2023). They are a significant threat to individual organizations and national security. Organizations are facing a widespread ransomware issue, sometimes paralyzing essential services, including power grids, water supply networks and transportation systems, thus having severe consequences including loss of life and economic damage.

The impact of speed of technological advancement on organizations can be summarized as follows. There are fewer employees needed for lower-level tasks because of increasingly automated tasks, resulting in fear among employees for job losses. Many tasks disappear and are replaced by new tasks, resulting in an increasing mismatch between the skills needed in the workplace and those offered by employees. A continuing increase in remote working requires different leadership styles. Changes in the organization of work, processes and the way employees collaborate, require the learning of new skills and changes in how organizations organize themselves and their networks with suppliers and customers. Technological considerations play an ever-increasing role during the decision-making process, requiring more technological awareness from management and employees. Training is needed to not only increase the knowledge level of technology but also to take away fear of technology and what it can and will do to their organization and the industry it operates in. Changes in external communications are needed as organizations have to show their customers and other stakeholders that they are on top of technological developments and are capable of dealing with these adequately.

11.3.2 Challenge 2: Flexible employment

Flexible employment refers to the increasing variety in working arrangements and work practices, variation in working time/hours, working locations, amount and type of work contracts and employment contract forms. Traditional nine-to-five jobs decrease in favor of mobile and on-demand employment, and because of mobile technology and the internet, employees no longer work in the same location. There is a rise in 'fluid' positions and jobs where people have multiple roles within one organization or sign on as independent contractors (Anani, 2018). The economy now is a 'gig-economy' or 'network-economy': a labor market in which temporary positions are common and organizations have contracts with independent workers for short-term engagements rather than long-term employment contracts (Anani, 2018; Batt, 2018). Digital labor platforms outsource work through an open call to a geographically dispersed crowd (such as Upwork and Clickworker), and location-based applications allocate work to workers in a specific geographical area (such as Uber and Airbnb). Consequently, a growing number of workers are no longer employed but hired for a specific task.

The impact of flexible employment on organizations can be summarized as follows. There is a decrease in employment contracts for indefinite periods as well as for fixed terms, in favor of an increase in self-employed contract workers. This results in more insecurity for (certain categories of) people and less loyalty to organizations. It is more common that workers have multiple contracts with multiple organizations at the same time, potentially resulting in more burn-out and more difficultly scheduling work in organizations. There is an increase in remote working, as well as working at different times and with varying working hours, which requires different leadership styles of managers and more complex scheduling of work and meetings. Fewer employees are physically present in the office, requiring changes in the organization of work and the way employees collaborate.

Society increasingly looks at the business sector to focus on and foster sustainability by creating social value, as organizations in general possess the financial, technological and managerial resources that can be used to deal with social issues. Social value creation is in this respect the process that results in the creation of something of value for society by providing solutions to social issues (de Waal *et al.*, 2023b). It consists of ESG (environment, social and governance), CSR (corporate social responsibility) and EDI (equality, diversity and inclusivity), and thereby is a 'super challenge' encompassing challenges 2, 4, 7 and 8.

11.3.3 Challenge 3: Changing workforce composition

The changing workforce composition addresses both the aging of the worldwide population and generation shifts. By 2050, one in six people in the world is over age 65, up from one in 11 in 2019 (United Nations, 2019). Older employees are not only a growing proportion of the workplace, they also work longer. Older adults remain in the workforce longer for a variety of reasons, including concerns about maintaining healthcare benefits and income, and the desire to remain active and engaged as they will live longer than earlier generations (Rudolph *et al.*, 2018). The generation shifts from baby boomers (generation X, 1960s–1970s) to millennials (generation Y, 1980s–1990s), followed by generation Z (2000s–2010s) and generation A (2010s and onward) cause major changes to the composition of the workforce as by 2025; millennials are then making up the majority of the workforce (Appel-Meulenbroek *et al.*, 2019). All these different generations have different interests and needs and thus different demands from the organizations they work in.

The impact of changes in workforce composition on organizations can be summarized as follows. The workforce has aged, and organizations need to make sure aging at work can take place successfully, through vitality and well-being programs for older employees. Younger people who are entering the workforce are more sensitive to sustainability and climate change, they want purposeful and varied work. Thus, to attract and retain these younger generations, organizations create (more) meaningful and sustainable work with enough learning opportunities, sufficient variety in work tasks and personalized working conditions. Thus, to meet the diverse needs and wishes of the different generations, organizations offer for more flexible employment conditions.

11.3.4 Challenge 4: Sustainable employment

Sustainable employment (or similar concepts such as sustainable work and decent work) refers to the extent to which workers are willing and able to remain working now and, in the future (United Nations, 2019, World Economic Forum, 2018). It is about offering work and working conditions that keep workers happy, healthy and motivated. There is rising interest and concern around sustainable employment amongst management as there is in many (Western) countries an imminent worker shortage arising from the aging of the population, coupled with a growing awareness of the need for sustainability in general among the population (and thus the clients of the organization) (Annunziata and Bourgeois, 2018).

The impact of increasing attention toward sustainable employment on organizations can be summarized as follows. There is increased awareness of successful aging and staying healthy at work, and increased inclusion of worker groups with special needs, such as disabled people. Organizations offer a safe working environment, safe working conditions and challenging and meaningful jobs that lead to self-development, and promote vitality and well-being. There is increased attention to workforce self-development, and gender equality and equal pay. Organizations offer more flexibility in the type of work, what they demand of their employees and the make-up of their workforce. They eliminate the factors that discourage or hinder employees from staying in or entering their workforce and match the needs and abilities of the individual with the quality of job on offer.

11.3.5 Challenge 5: Environmental issues

Climate change refers to changes in the world's climate, caused by human activity and its consequences. Flooding, the rise in sea level, extreme weather conditions and natural disasters caused by climate change result in major impacts on daily life. Climate change has a huge negative impact on economic growth because much investment has been made available for reducing the ecological footprint of people and businesses, fostering sustainability and protecting the environment and dealing with the expected migration of people from countries that are at risk of sea level rising and flooding (Kiel *et al.*, 2017; Peetz, 2019).

The impact of climate change on organizations can be summarized as follows. Because of the consequences of climate change, there is great awareness of the ecological footprint of organizations and increased pressure on governments to enforce clean and sustainable value creation. This requires increased and continuous innovation in production methods and use of resources by organizations, and for the population, customers and stakeholders visible measures dealing with the negative consequences of processes on the environment.

11.3.6 Challenge 6: Continued globalization

Globalization is the process by which businesses or other organizations develop international influence or start operating on an international scale, or alternatively, the growing interaction and integration among people, companies and governments worldwide (Guttal, 2010). Globalization of course is not new, and we noticed that this challenge had a 100% overlap in the literature with the challenges 'speed of technical advancement' and 'flexible employment', which suggests that there is a connection between the three. We, therefore, assumed for this analysis that the consequences of globalization are the same as those mentioned for technical advancement and flexible employment.

11.3.7 Challenge 7: Skills mismatch

Skills mismatch refers to the gap between the skills of the existing/current workforce and the skills that are needed for jobs in the future workplace. Learning new skills to adapt to the changing work environment is not a new phenomenon but with the increasing speed of change it has become a serious challenge to prepare organizations, employees and educational systems in time for these changes. The

World Economic Forum (2018) states that in many industries and countries, the currently most in-demand occupations or specialties did not exist ten or even five years ago, and the pace of change in occupations is accelerating. Most of the literature highlights the imperative of ensuring that organizations and workers focus on lifelong learning to maintain a smooth transition to new ways of working, new jobs or to other forms of employment contract (Cassells *et al.*, 2018; Lent, 2018).

The impact of an increased skills mismatch on organizations can be summarized as follows. There is a shortage of workers with the right skills and a surplus of workers with skills that do not match the jobs of the future. As a consequence, organizations are unable to deliver the performance needed which threatens their continuity. Organizations invest more and more often in educating their workforce in the new skills required, requiring more investment in both these educational programs as well in the people that organize and run them.

11.3.8 Challenge 8: Increasing inequality

There is a growing concern about increasing wage and income inequality. Although employment rates have gone up, there are groups of workers that are not benefiting, and their situation seems to be deteriorating (Annunziata and Bourgeois, 2018). Particularly low-skilled employees, employees with jobs that are likely to disappear due to automation, self-employed employees (gig-workers) and employees with a migrant background are at risk; in addition, the gender gap (which also creates differences in pay between workers) is not disappearing (enough) in the near future (Peetz, 2019). Thus, there is an increasing need for social protection of vulnerable employees, with measures ranging from legal protection for flexible working arrangements to the introduction of a universal income.

The impact of increasing inequality on organizations can be summarized as follows. There is an increase in governmental policies eliminating inequalities and protecting vulnerable employees. Organizations offer training programs for lower-skilled employees, which leads to sustainable employment for this type of employee, and they offer equal and sustainable pay and working conditions. The legislation results in an increasing administrative burden for organizations as they need to be able to 'prove' that they are compliant with the new legislation.

11.3.9 Challenge 9: Individualism

Individualism is the trend to distinguish oneself from others as a result of a shift from a more collectivist society to a focus on the individual and the increasing expectations from society of instant the availability of goods and services. According to Boumphrey and Brehmer (2018), the consumers of today focus on obtaining the most out of life, reassessing values and priorities. People and organizations expect tailored or personalized products, services and solutions. Furthermore, the pace of societies, round-the-clock use of services in combination with ICT pervasiveness drive e-commerce, e-shopping and mobile service expansion (von der Gracht and Darkow, 2010). Client experience and employee experience are key performance indicators that need close monitoring. In response to individualization, much more specialized goods, services and even education are offered.

11.3.10 Challenge 10: Urbanization

Urbanization is the worldwide population shift from rural to urban areas, as a consequence of which an increasing number of people are permanently concentrated in relatively small areas (cities or metropolitan areas). This has an impact on organizations in rural as well as urban areas (Diong, 2017; Retief *et al.*, 2016).

The impact of urbanization on organizations can be summarized as follows. In rural areas there is a drain of qualified workers leading to organizational issues while urban areas are becoming too crowded leading to higher cost of living, competition for jobs and a more hectic/less balanced life and, as a consequence of that, health issues. On the other hand, urbanization comes with opportunities for skilled (e.g. professional services), as well as non-skilled workers (e.g. construction, housing services).

11.3.11 Challenge 11: Cross-border migration

Cross-border migration refers to the migration of employees to another country with the aim of finding (better) work. Cross-border migration has been a natural consequence of a world in which people do not find attractive work opportunities in their country of origin, at a time when other economies are not adequately filling their skills gaps (Woetzel *et al.*, 2016). It changes the workforce composition and creates social issues. In addition, cross-border migrants are more vulnerable than native employees and have a higher unemployment rate – especially when they have a non-Western background.

The impact of cross-border migration on organizations is as follows. There is an increase in migration which changes the workforce composition in 'receiving countries' while at the same time causing a knowledge and skills drain in the home countries of the migrants (countries with low wages, subject to climate change, politically instable). Organizations are prepared for a more diverse workforce (in culture, religion and language) to accommodate immigrant workers, and at the same time are more aware of sustainable value creation.

11.3.12 Challenge 12: Economic powershifts

By economic powershifts it is meant the shift in economic power from the traditional West to the upcoming East. Countries in Asia such as China and to a lesser extent in South America and Africa are becoming bigger and more important globally, due to an increase in their middle class (Hajkowicz, 2015; Hoppe *et al.*, 2014). The impact of economic powershifts can be summarized as follows. Emerging markets are rewriting the rules of work and work culture because, as a result of economic growth in these areas, their political power is increasing. This has an impact on the competitive position of organizations in the developed countries, making these more vulnerable and at the same time creating opportunities for growth.

11.3.13 Challenge 13: Resource scarcity

Resource scarcity refers to the problem of an increasing demand for resources such as water, food, energy, land and minerals which is causing scarcity and inherent cost increases. Global consumption has increased dramatically over the past century, which has caused resources to be scarcer and falling in quality (Diong, 2017; Retief *et al.*, 2016). Organizations increasingly address and reconsider their dependence on raw materials and resources. Finding new ways of working, innovation and the use of alternative resources is key for organizations to survive. And when leaders are not responding to this, society forces them to minimize the negative impacts on society and the environment through regulation.

11.3.14 Challenge 14: Pandemics

Pandemics, such as the recent Corona pandemic, place extraordinary and sustained demands on the public health and medical care systems and strain the operations, and even survival, of all organizations. Thus, major outbreaks leave severe, often long-lasting, effects on the economy and society as a whole, with economic and fiscal impacts outlasting the epidemiological impact due to severe shocks to investment, production and consumption (Calero and Soledad, 2020). Often response systems and capabilities for disease outbreaks are not sufficient to deal with the enormous impact, rapid spread and shock to health, social and economic systems. Thus, the consequences of a pandemic are severe for individual organizations, the business world and society at large. These crises impact the free movement of people and goods across borders and across the world negatively, thus revitalizing local industries. The use of digital communication tools and advanced technologies such as 3D printing, digital solutions, digital currencies and AI are increasing. Organizations expand the use of home office practices and digital activities, eliminating face-to-face meetings and introducing online meetings.

11.3.15 Challenge 15: Geopolitical unrest and instability

Unrest and instability are expressed in regional conflicts with worldwide consequences. The geopolitical pressures and tensions created by the Ukraine war and Russia's expansionist drive, and the conflict in Israel and Palestine have affected organizations, amongst other with the economic blockades they had to adhere to, and abnormal returns on their investment. Many more economic and political repercussions will follow and in general trade is severely affected in a negative way with additional much destruction of human capital, institutions and infrastructures (Aliu *et al.*, 2023; Bhattacharjee *et al.,* 2023; Magidu, 2010; Sedrakyan, 2022). Conflicts thus have significant adverse economic consequences, both for organizations and the regions, which contribute to less investment or even disinvestment, in turn leading to lower economic growth and more poverty and inequality (Chisadza and Clance, 2021).

11.4 The 'unhappy triad'

The future of work, defined as a projection of how, by whom, when and where work will get done in the years ahead (Gartner, 2022; SHRM, 2021), is now one of the most pressing issues for organizations (Gratton, 2020). This is because currently organizations are experiencing an almost perfect storm caused by the unhappy triad of three simultaneously occurring challenges that reinforce each other: the changing workforce composition, the speed of technological advancement and the skills mismatch.

The changing workforce composition coincides with a collapse of career assumptions, i.e. previously atypical career paths are becoming mainstream with rising retirement ages, midcareer breaks, shifts of employment across industries and the embracement of contingent work and other nontraditional employment models. This is already creating havoc in many organizations as they experience an acute shortage of labor power, which translates into increasing difficulty in retaining good people from the current employee base and attracting good new employees. This actually is a downward spiral: there are less people to do the work so they experience more pressure, which causes them to either physically quit their job or practice 'quiet quitting'. In a recent survey, 9% of respondents said they planned to leave their job in the next three to six months (Simon *et al.,* 2023). People are revising their attitudes toward work and at work. Professionals who leave say it is not just money, work-life balance, their professional development or an inspiring organizational vision that will get them back to work: it is a combination of all of these things. Quiet quitting occurs when employees are mentally less involved with their work. They do not actually quit or leave the labor force but do their work, putting in the bare minimum amount of time and effort, due to a lack of commitment and putting excessive value on better work-life balance (Lee *et al.*, 2024). Examples of quiet quitting can be arriving and leaving just on time, not speaking up when necessary, refusing to work at the office, taking long breaks, not going the extra mile for a client (Serenko, 2024).

One of the ways forward which is increasingly taken by organizations is increased automation (OECD, 2023). In fact, many organizations are experiencing a digital revolution, which is a change in how an organization employs digital technologies to modify existing or create new business processes, new business models, culture and customer experiences, with the purpose to meet changing internal business and external market and client requirements (de Waal *et al.*, 2023a). In general, the transformation is made possible by the availability of new hardware and especially software which is generated increasingly rapidly by continuous technological developments (Morgan, 2020; Trianz, 2020; Verhoef *et al.*, 2021). No modern-day organization can function without an effective IT architecture; thus, there is a great need for successful digital transformations. Automation/technological advancement can provide a solution to staff shortage and make work more sustainable, for example, when robots take over boring or heavy tasks.

Unfortunately, many digital transformations are difficult and turn out to be not successful. In fact, the literature reports that only one-third of organizations had their expectations regarding the results of the digital transformation met, while two-thirds state that their expectations were only partly or not at all satisfied (Morgan, 2020; Trianz, 2020). The literature indicates the main reason for this is employees are insufficiently prepared for the digital transformation (Gartner, 2021; Lawson *et al.*, 2019; Pratt and Sparapani, 2021; Verbeeten and Heinen, 2019). It turns out that employees do not have enough knowledge about IT and/or there is too little internal training to make them more knowledgeable. The result is that digitalization and automation only lead to frustration because employees are struggling to get to grips with the new tools and applications.

The logical solution for organizations is to hire qualified personnel that can handle the new (digital) tools. Unfortunately, the third leg of the unhappy triad now comes into play: the skills mismatch between what organizations need in their (new) employees and what employees can actually offer in skills, a situation which is expected to be around for quite some time (Kwok, 2022). Technological progress causes an increasing skills gap as it is undoable for many people to keep up with the current pace of automation and the skills required for that. This mismatch in skills has direct consequences for organizations because employees with missing skills cannot deliver the required performance. This situation may also create reputational, regulatory and legal issues around the use of artificial intelligence (AI), if companies do not provide employees with adequate training on how to do their work using AI and on how to develop judgment around how to use information in a valid and permissible manner.

Add to this the personnel shortage and the problems increase. The work gets assigned to the available staff even if they are not yet qualified. It is already noticeable that less experienced workers are placed in jobs for which they are actually not yet ready. Although clients are already getting used to longer waiting times to get work and goods delivered, they may not accept lower quality standards. This situation causes tension in the workplace, leading to stress, burnout, sick leave, complaints, labor disputes and legal proceedings. As a consequence, there is a need for more skilled managers who can manage, rather than silence, interpersonal conflict among employees. To resolve these tensions, organizations, therefore, need to hire specialists such as confidential advisors, coaches or lawyers, which is also quite costly. In combination with the decrease in tenures (or higher turnover rates) this is a toxic formula, because it leads to short-term thinking, volatile approaches, an emphasis on quick wins and stop-gap solutions, creating lacking efficiency and lower long-term effectiveness.

11.5 The way forward

So, is the situation hopeless, will we experience a prolonged period of economic difficulties because of this 'unhappy triad'? Not necessarily. A possible way forward is to prioritize and focus on dimensions and characteristics that, according to the literature, lead to long-term success – even in a fast-changing environment. A suggested approach, for example, is to transform the organization into a high-performance organization (HPO). An HPO is defined as an organization that achieves results that are better than those of its peer group over a longer period of time (de Waal, 2021). The literature shows that such an organization experiences many advantages over lesser performing ones (de Waal, 2020): more innovative, a greater ability to improve, more openness, better cooperation internally in the organization and externally with third parties, a better reputation, easier to gain new clients and – most importantly in the context of this chapter – its people are happier with more focus and discipline and it is more attractive to current and potential employees.

In fact, there is research that shows that employees in an HPO experience more happiness at work (HAW), where HAW consists of the three factors work engagement, job satisfaction and affective organizational commitment (de Waal, 2018; Mroueh and de Waal, 2020). The latter is a measure for how committed people are to the organization where they work and whether they feel an emotional connection with their workplace. Thus, becoming an HPO increases the happiness of work of employee and this in turn raises the feeling of how attractive the organization is to the employees themselves and to the external world. An HPO is seen as 'a winning team' for which people like to work. This is also reflected in the time it takes HPOs to fulfill bottleneck vacancies (de Waal, 2022). The bottleneck vacancies fulfillment time measures the time between posting a vacancy on the job market and fulfilling that vacancy with a new employee. The measurement is not used for all vacancies but only for those historically hard to fill positions in organizations, such as technical occupations. The research shows that the shorter the average fulfillment time for bottleneck vacancies in the organization, the more attractive this organization is, as it does not take the organization much time to attract new employees to these vacancies.

One of the main reasons that people in an HPO are so happy is that their organization keeps investing in them, even in difficult economic times (see, for examples, of this, de Waal, 2020). Recent research shows that many activities of HPOs are directly focused on increasing the happiness and the feelings of worth among employees (de Waal et al., 2023c):

- they involve employees as much as possible in organizational activities (such as decision-making);
- they improve communication, dialogue and feedback processes;
- they invest in the training and development of their employees;
- they give their employees the time to learn to work as an HPO and to incorporate HPO in their daily activities;

- they use the organization's core values (which include HPO) as guideline for all their operations (thus providing employees clear guidelines for their work processes);
- they have and keep an HPO support structure in place to support employees;
- they have an excellent onboarding process for new employees.

In summary, organizations have a need for more responsible and future-oriented managers who continuously monitor and weigh upcoming trends and challenges, and translate these into actions for a positive future of work for everyone; prioritize social and psychological safety; work together with employees, and break silos between functional areas, creating collective intelligence and incorporate the UN SDG's and social value targets in their strategies and act upon these. The world needs leaders who not only manage this for their own organization but set the right example and expect the same from other organizations in their ecosystem.

11.6 Conclusion

These are trying times for organizations as they need to deal with an increasing number of challenges that are becoming ever more threatening for their welfare and continuation. As the saying goes, forewarned is forearmed, so in this chapter the most impactful challenges are identified and discussed. In addition, the three challenges that currently and in the near future will have the most prolonged impact – speed of technological advancement, the changing labor market and skills mismatch – and which form a 'unhappy triad' as they are mutually reinforcing, are discussed. Fortunately, there is a way forward to deal with this unhappy triad, which is transforming the organization into a high performing one, the so-called HPO. Research shows that HPOs are able to increase the happiness at work of their employees, thus becoming and staying an attractive employer for current and future employees. This also shows in the reduced time they need to fulfill their bottleneck vacancies. Thus, despite the challenges organizations nowadays have to deal with, there is hope at the end of the tunnel for them!

Note

1 The postulated impact of the challenges and their consequences for organizations as discussed in this chapter are necessarily generic in nature, the reader will have to adapt them to the specific context of their own organization.

References

Aliu, F., Mulaj, I. and Hašková, S. (2023), "Consequences of the Russia-Ukraine war: evidence from DAX, ATX, and FTSEMIB", *Studies in Economics & Finance*, Vol. 40, Issue 3, pp. 549–568.

Anani, N. (2018), "Paving the way for the future of work", *Canadian Public Policy*, Vol. 44, Issue S1, pp. S167–S176.

Annunziata, M. and Bourgeois, H. (2018), "The future of work: how G20 countries can leverage digital-industrial innovations into stronger high-quality jobs growth", *Economics: The Open-Access, Open-Assessment E-Journal*, Vol. 12, Issue 42, pp. 1–23.

Appel-Meulenbroek, H. A. J. A., Vosters, S. M. C., Kemperman, A. D. A. M. and Arentze, T. A. (2019), *Workplace Needs and Their Support; Are Millennials Different from Other Generations?* Paper presented at the twenty fifth annual Pacific Rim Real Estate Society conference (PRRES 2019), Melbourne, Australia.

Batt, R. (2018), "The financial model of the firm, the 'future of work', and employment relations", in Wilkinson, A., Dundon, T., Donaghey, J. and Colvin, A. (eds), *The Routledge Companion to Employment Relations*, Routledge: London, pp. 465–479.

Bhamu, J. and Singh Sangwan, K. (2014), "Lean manufacturing: literature review and research issues", *International Journal of Operations & Production Management*, Vol. 34, Issue 7, pp. 876–940.

Bhattacharjee, A., Gaur, D. and Gupta, K. (2023), "Russia–Ukraine war and the impact on Indian economy", *Journal of Economic Studies*, Vol. 51, Issue 4, pp. 841–858.

Boumphrey, S. and Brehmer, Z. (2018), "Megatrend Analysis: Putting the Consumer at the Heart of Business", *Euromonitor International*, available at: http://go.euromonitor.com/rs/805-KOK719/images/wpMegatrendAnalysis.pdf

Calero, D. and Soledad, M. (2020), "An X-ray of pandeconomics: a look at pandemics past puts coronacrisis into perspective", *Caribbean Business*, Vol. 6, Issue 10, pp. 8–11.

Cassells, R., Duncan, A., Mavisakalyan, A., Phillimore, J., Seymour, R. and Tarverdi, Y. (2018), *Future of Work in Australia: Preparing for Tomorrow's World*, BCEC Report, Bankwest Curtin Economics Centre.

Chisadza, C. and Clance, M. (2021), "Conflict heterogeneity in Africa", *South African Journal of Economics*, Vol. 89, Issue 4, pp. 459–479.

Costa, L. B. M. and Godinho Filho, M. (2016), "Lean healthcare: review, classification and analysis of literature", *Production Planning & Control*, Vol. 27, Issue 10, pp. 823–836.

Cozzolino, A., Rothaermel, F. T. and Verona, G. (2017), "Business model innovation after disruptions: a process study of an incumbent media organization", *Academy of Management Proceeding*, Vol. 1, pp. 1–6.

de Waal, A. (2018), "Increasing organisational attractiveness: the role of the HPO and happiness at work frameworks", *Journal of Organizational Effectiveness: People and Performance*, Vol. 5, No. 2, pp. 124–141.

de Waal, A. A. (2020), *High Performance Managerial Leadership*, Praeger: New York.

de Waal, A. (2021), "The high performance organisation: proposed definition and measurement of its performance", *Measuring Business Excellence*, Vol. 25, Issue 3, pp. 300–314

de Waal, A. (2022), "Measuring organizational attractiveness", *International Journal of Management and Applied Research*, Vol. 9, Issue 1, pp. 1–20.

de Waal, A. and Linthorst, J. (2022), *Futurize! Dealing with Megatrends and Disruptors*, Routledge: New York.

de Waal, A., Bilstra, E. and Bootsman, J. (2022), "Digital transformation of finance functions: status, obstacles and courses of action", *EURAM Conference 2022*, June, Winterthur.

de Waal, A., Bilstra, E. and Bootsman, J. (2023a), *De hoogpresterende financiële functie, handboek voor de toekomstgericht professional* [The high-performance financial function, handbook for the future-oriented professional], Vakmedianet: Zeist.

de Waal, A., Patel, S., de Jong, A., den Uil, K., Eegdeman, N. and van der Gaast, R. (2023b), *Capabilities Needed for Social Value Creation: A Multinational Enterprise Perspective*, Paper presented during the 1st Interdisciplinary Workshop on Sustainability and ESG Dynamics 2023, Castellanza, Italy, October 26–27.

de Waal, A., Burrell, J., Drake, S., Sampa, C. and Mulimbika, T. (2023c), "How to stay high-performing: developing organizational grit", *Measuring Business Excellence*, Vol. 27, Issue 1, pp. 25–39.
Diong, T. (2017), "The future of management systems", *Quality*, September, Vol. 56, pp. 52–54.
Erboz, G. (2017), *How to Define Industry 4.0: Main Pillars Of Industry 4.0*, Paper presented on the 7th International Conference on Management (ICoM 2017), Nitra, Slovakia, 1–2 June.
Gartner (2021), *The Digital Future of Finance, 10 CFO Opportunities to Accelerate Digital Transformation*, Gartner Inc., London.
Gartner (2022), *Definition of Future of Work*, Gartner Human Resources Glossary, www.gartner.com/en/human-resources/glossary/future-of-work
Gilad, A. and Tishler, A. (2023), "Mitigating the risk of advanced cyber attacks: the role of quality, covertness and intensity of use of cyber weapons", *Defence & Peace Economics*, Vol. 34, Issue 6, pp. 726–746.
Gratton, L. (2020), "Five Insights From Davos on the Future of Work", *MIT Sloan Management Review*, https://sloanreview.mit.edu/article/five-insights-from-davos-on-the-future-of-work/
Green, C. (2023), "Best practices in supplier relationship management and response when supply is disrupted by cyber attack: an incident response framework", *Journal of Business Continuity & Emergency Planning*, Vol. 17, Issue 1, pp. 6–15,
Guttal, S. (2010), "Globalisation", *Development in Practice*, Vol. 17, Issue 4/5, pp. 523–531.
Guzzo, R. A., Jackson, S. E. and Katzell, R. A. (1987), "Meta-analysis analysis", *Research in Organizational Behavior*, Vol. 9, pp. 407–442.
Hajkowicz, S. (2015), *Global Megatrends Seven Patterns of Change Shaping our Future*, CSIRO Publishing: Melbourne.
Hoppe, M., Christ, A., Castro, A., Winter, M. and Seppanen, T.M. (2014), "Transformation in transportation?", *European Journal of Futures Research*, Vol. 2 No. 1, pp. 1–14.
Kiel, D., Müller, J. M., Arnold, C. and Voigt, K. I. (2017), "Sustainable industrial value creation: benefits and challenges of industry 4.0", *International Journal of Innovation Management*, Vol. 21, Issue 8, pp. 1740015.
King, W. R. and He, J. (2005), "Understanding the role and methods of meta-analysis in IS research", *Communications of the Association for Information Systems*, Vol. 16, article 32.
Kwok, L. (2022), "Labor shortage: a critical reflection and a call for industry-academia collaboration", *International Journal of Contemporary Hospitality Management*, Vol. 34, Issue 11, pp. 3929–3943.
Lawson, R., Hatch, T. and Desroches, D. (2019), *Achieving a Competitive Advantage in the Digital Age—The Value of Training and Certification*, IMA® Institute of Management Accountants, New Jersey.
Lee, D., Park, J. and Shin, Y. (2024), "Where are the workers? From great resignation to quiet quitting", *Review* (00149187), 1st Quarter, Vol. 106, Issue 1, pp. 59–71.
Lent, R. W. (2018), "Future of work in the digital world: preparing for instability and opportunity", *The Career Development Quarterly*, Vol. 66, Issue 3, pp. 205–219.
Linthorst, J. and de Waal, A. (2020), "Disruptive forces and their postulated impact on organizations", *Proceedings of the EURAM 2020 Conference*, Dublin, Ireland, 4–6 December 2020.
Linthorst, J. and de Waal, A. (2022), "Megatrends and disruptors and their postulated impact on organizations", *Sustainability*, Vol. 12, Issue 20, paper 8740.
Maeda, J. (2006), *The Laws of Simplicity: Design, Technology, Business, Life*, MIT Press Ltd: Cambridge.
Magidu, N. (2010), "Causes and consequences of fragility in Africa: the experience of the greater lakes region", *Economic Papers*, Vol. 29, Issue 4, pp. 490–496.

Mahlendorf, M. D. (2014), "Discussion of: the multiple roles of the finance organization: determinants, effectiveness, and the moderating influence of information system integration", *Journal of Management Accounting Research*, Vol. 26, Issue 2, pp. 33–42.

Malik, R. and Janowska, A. A. (2018), *Megatrends and Their Use in Economic Analyses of Contemporary Challenges in the World Economy*, Research Papers of the Wroclaw University of Economics, No. 523, pp. 209–220.

Morgan. B. (2020), "Is COVID-19 forcing your digital transformation? 12 Steps to move faster", *Forbes*, https://www.forbes.com/sites/blakemorgan/2020/04/05/is-covid-19-forcing-your-digital-transformation-12-steps-to-move-faster/

Mroueh, M. and de Waal, A. (2020), "Measuring happiness at work in a Takaful organization", *Journal of Organizational Effectiveness: People and Performance*, Vol. 7, Issue 2, pp. 139–154.

OECD (2023), *Under Pressure: Labour Market and Wage Developments in OECD Countries*, OECD Employment Outlook, Paris.

Peetz, D. (2019), *The Realities and Futures of Work*, Australian National University Press: Acton.

Pratt, M. K. and Sparapani, J. (2021), *What Is Digital Transformation?* TechTarget, https://searchcio.techtarget.com/definition/digital-transformation

Retief, F., Bond, A. J., Pope, H., Morrison-Saunders, A. and King, N. (2016), "Global megatrends and their implications for environmental assessment practice", *Environmental Impact Assessment Review*, Vol. 61, pp. 52–60.

Rowley, J. and Slack, F. (2004), "Conducting a literature review", *Management Research News*, Vol. 27, Issue 6, pp. 31–39.

Rudolph, C. W., Marcus, J., Mah, R. and Zacher, H. (2018), "Global issues in work, aging, and retirement", in Shultz, K. S. and Adams, G. A. (eds.), *Aging and Work in the 21st Century*, Routledge: New York, pp. 292–324.

Sedrakyan, G. S. (2022), "Ukraine war-induced sanctions against Russia: consequences on transition economies", *Journal of Policy Modeling*, Vol. 44, Issue 5, pp. 863–885.

Serenko, A. (2024), "The human capital management perspective on quiet quitting: recommendations for employees, managers, and national policymakers", *Journal of Knowledge Management*, Vol. 28, Issue 1, pp. 27–43.

SHRM (2021), *Future of Work*, www.shrm.org/resourcesandtools/pages/future-of-work.aspx

Simon, P., Maor, D., Guggenberger, P., Park, M., Luo, M., Klinger, D., D'Auria, G, Weddle, B., De Smet, A., Fletcher, B., Thaker, S. and Di Lodovico, A. (2023), *The State of Organizations 2023*, McKinsey & Company: New York.

Trianz (2020), *State of Digital Transformation Worldwide: 2020*, Trianz, New York City.

United Nations (2019), *World Population Prospects 2019*, United Nations: New York.

Verbeeten, F. and Heinen, J. (2019), *Finance Transformation in the Digital Era, Acquiring New Skills to Drive the Digital Transformation*, Finance on a Mission (University of Amsterdam/Workday/PLUC!/Finance Transformation Forum), Amsterdam.

Verhoef, P. C., Broekhuizen, T., Yakov, B., Bhattacharya, A., Qi Dong, J., Fabian, N. and Haenlein, M. (2021), "Digital transformation: a multidisciplinary reflection and research agenda", *Journal of Business Research*, Vol. 122, pp. 889–901.

von der Gracht, H. A. and Darkow, I. L. (2010), "Scenarios for the logistics services industry: a delphi-based analysis for 2025", *International Journal of Production Economics*, Vol. 127, Issue 1, pp. 46–59.

Woetzel, J., Madgavkar, A., Khaled, R., Mattern, F., Bughin, J., Manyika, J. and Hasyagar, A. (2016), *People on the Move: Global Migration's Impact and Opportunity*, McKinsey Global Institute: New York.

World Economic Forum (2018), *The Future of Jobs Report 2018*, World Economic Forum: Geneva.

APPENDIX 1 – OVERVIEW LITERATURE REVIEW RESULTS

This appendix provides an overview of the results of the literature review. For each relevant literature source it is indicated (with an X) which challenges are discussed in that source.

Literature source	*C1 Technology*	*C2 Flexibility*	*C3 Workforce*	*C4 Sustainability*	*C5 Environment*	*C6 Globalization*
Allen, R. C. (20X7), "Lessons from history for the future of work", Nature News, Vol. 550, Issue 7676, p. 32X.	X			X		
Anani, N. (20X8), "Paving the way for the future of work", *Canadian Public Policy*, Vol. 44, Issue SX, pp. SX67–SX76.	X	X	X	X		X
Annunziata, M., and Bourgeois, H. (20X8), "The future of work: how G20 countries can leverage digital-industrial innovations into stronger high-quality jobs growth", *Economics: The Open-Access, Open-Assessment E-Journal*, Vol. X2, Issue 20X8–42, pp. X–23.	X	X		X		X
Anthes, E. (20X7), "The shape of work to come", *Nature News*, Vol. 550, Issue 7676, p. 3X6.	X	X		X		
Anxo, D. (20X8), "Shaping the future of work in Sweden: the crucial role of social partnership", in *Reducing Inequalities in Europe*, Edward Elgar Publishing.						
Appel-Meulenbroek, H. A. J. A., Vosters, S. M. C., Kemperman, A. D. A. M., and Arentze, T. A. (20X9), Workplace needs and their support; are millennials different from other generations?. X-X4. *Paper presented atTwenty fifth annual Pacific Rim Real Estate Society Conference* (PRRES 20X9), Melbourne, Australia.			X			
Bakhshi, H., Downing, J. M., Osborne, M. A., and Schneider, P. (20X7), *The Future of Skills: Employment in 2030*, Pearson.	X	X	X		X	X

C7 Skills	*C8 Inequality*	*C9 Individualization*	*C10 Urbanization*	*C11 Migration*	*C12 Powershifts*	*C13 Resources*	*C14 Pandemics*	*C15 Geopolitical*
X								
X	X							
	X							
X	X							

(*Continued*)

Literature source	*C1 Technology*	*C2 Flexibility*	*C3 Workforce*	*C4 Sustainability*	*C5 Environment*	*C6 Globalization*
Baldassari, P., and Roux, J. D. (20X7), "Industry 4.0: preparing for the future of work", *People & Strategy*, Vol. 40, Issue 3, pp. 20–23.	X					
Baldwin, R. (20X9), *The Globotics Upheaval: Globalization, Robotics, and the Future of Work*, Oxford University Press.	X	X		X		X
Batt, R. (20X8), "The financial model of the firm, the 'future of work', and employment relations", in *The Routledge Companion to Employment Relations* (pp. 465–479), Routledge.	X	X		X		X
Behrendt, C., and Nguyen, Q. A. (20X8), "Innovative approaches for ensuring universal social protection for the future of work", *Future of Work Research Paper Series* (X).	X	X		X		
Behrendt, C., and Nguyen, Q. A. (20X9), "Ensuring universal social protection for the future of work", *Transfer: European Review of Labour and Research*, Vol. 25, Issue 2, pp. 205–2X9.		X	X			
Beier, G., Niehoff, S., Ziems, T., and Xue, B. (20X7), "Sustainability aspects of a digitalized industry–a comparative study from China and Germany", *International Journal of Precision Engineering and Manufacturing-Green Technology*, Vol. 4, Issue 2, pp. 227–234.	X				X	
Belet, H., Glorieux, I., and Laurijssen, I. (20X7), "The transition from school to work in Flanders: gender inequality and the role of household formation", in *The Future of Work in Europe* (pp. X57–X77), Routledge.			X			
Bell, M., Bristow, D., and Martin, S. (20X7), "The future of work in wales", Retrieved from January, X4, 20X9.	X		X	X	X	

C7 Skills	*C8 Inequality*	*C9 Individualization*	*C10 Urbanization*	*C11 Migration*	*C12 Powershifts*	*C13 Resources*	*C14 Pandemics*	*C15 Geopolitical*
	X							
X								
X	X							

(*Continued*)

Literature source	*C1 Technology*	*C2 Flexibility*	*C3 Workforce*	*C4 Sustainability*	*C5 Environment*	*C6 Globalization*
Berg, J., Furrer, M., Harmon, E., Rani, U., and Silberman, M. S. (20X8), *Digital Labour Platforms and the Future of Work: Towards Decent Work in the Online World*, International Labour Organization: Geneva.		X				
Berik, G. (20X8), "Toward more inclusive measures of economic well-being: debates and practices", *Future of Work Research Paper* (2).				X		
Bhalla, V., Dyrchs, S., and Strack, R. (20X7), "Twelve forces that will radically change how organizations work", *BCG Perspectives*.	X	X	X	X	X	X
Bhamu, J., and Singh Sangwan, K. (20X4), "Lean manufacturing: literature review and research issues", *International Journal of Operations & Production Management*, Vol. 34, Issue 7, pp. 876–940.						
Bhattacharyya, S. S., and Nair, S. (20X9), "Explicating the future of work: perspectives from India", *Journal of Management Development*, Vol. 38, Issue 3, pp. X75–X94.	X	X		X		X
Biggs, S., McGann, M., Bowman, D., and Kimberley, H. (20X7), "Work, health and the commodification of life's time: reframing work–life balance and the promise of a long life", *Ageing & Society*, Vol. 37, Issue 7, pp. X458–X483.			X			
Bissell, D., and Del Casino, V. J. (20X7), "Whither labor geography and the rise of the robots?", *Social & Cultural Geography*, Vol. X8, Issue 3, pp. 435–442.	X					
Biswas, A. K., and Tortajada, C. (20X8), "Assessing global water megatrends", in Biswas, A. K., Tortajada, C. and Rohner, P. (eds), *Assessing Global Water Megatrends*, Springer: Singapore. Chapter X, pp. X–26.	X			X	X	
Blit, J., Amand, S. S., and Wajda, J. (20X8), "Automation and the future of work: scenarios and policy options".	X					

C7 Skills	*C8 Inequality*	*C9 Individualization*	*C10 Urbanization*	*C11 Migration*	*C12 Powershifts*	*C13 Resources*	*C14 Pandemics*	*C15 Geopolitical*
X	X			X				
X								
			X					
	X							

(*Continued*)

Literature source	*C1 Technology*	*C2 Flexibility*	*C3 Workforce*	*C4 Sustainability*	*C5 Environment*	*C6 Globalization*
Boobier, T. (20X8), *Advanced Analytics and AI: Impact, Implementation, and the Future of Work*, John Wiley & Sons.	X					
Borker, D. R. (20X7), "Russia and Ukraine: a comparison of cultural accounting orientation", *The Business & Management Review*, Vol. 8, Issue 4, p. 269.						
Boudreau, J. (2016), "Work in the future will fall into these 4 categories", *Harvard Business Review Digital Articles*, 3/17/2016, pp. 2–6.	X			X		X
Boumphrey, S., and Brehmer, Z. (20X7), *Megatrend Analysis, Putting the Consumer at the Heart of Business*, Euromonitor International: United Kingdom.	X		X		X	
Boyd, J. A., and Huettinger, M. (20X9), "Smithian insights on automation and the future of work", *Futures*, Vol. XXX, pp. X04–XX5.	X					
Breheny, M. J., and McQuaid, R. (20X8), *The Development of High Technology Industries: An International Survey*, Routledge.	X					
Brotchie, J., Hall, P., Newton, P., and Nijkamp, P. (20X7), *The Future of Urban Form: The Impact of New Technology*, Routledge.	X					
Brougham, D., and Haar, J. (20X8), "Smart technology, artificial intelligence, robotics, and algorithms (STARA): employees' perceptions of our future workplace", *Journal of Management & Organization*, Vol. 24, Issue 2, pp. 239–257.	X					
Brown, J., Gosling, T., Sethi, B., Sheppard, B., Stubbings, C., Sviokla, J., and Zarubina, D. (20X7), "Workforce of the future: the competing forces shaping 2030", *PWC*. Retrieved on-line at: https://www.pwc.com/gx/en/services/workforce/publications/workforce-of-the-future.html			X			

C7 Skills	*C8 Inequality*	*C9 Individualization*	*C10 Urbanization*	*C11 Migration*	*C12 Powershifts*	*C13 Resources*	*C14 Pandemics*	*C15 Geopolitical*
								X
					X			
			X					

(*Continued*)

Literature source	*C1 Technology*	*C2 Flexibility*	*C3 Workforce*	*C4 Sustainability*	*C5 Environment*	*C6 Globalization*
Buckingham, M., and Goodall, A. (20X9), *Nine Lies about Work*, Boston, MA, 20X9, X42.				X		
Bukowski, A., and Rudnicki, S. (20X9), "Not only individualism: the effects of long-term orientation and other cultural variables on national innovation success", *Cross-Cultural Research*, Vol. 53, Issue 2, pp. XX9–X62.						
Burgess, A. (20X7), *The Executive Guide to Artificial Intelligence: How to Identify and Implement Applications for AI in Your Organization*, Springer.	X					
Campbell, Stacy M., Twenge, Jean M., and Keith Campbell, W., "Fuzzy but useful constructs: making sense of the differences between generations, work", *Aging and Retirement*, Vol. 3, Issue 2, pp. 130–139.			X			
Carney, M. (20X8), *The Future of Work*, Whitaker Lecture at the Central Bank of Ireland, Dublin, September, X4.	X			X		
Cassells, R., Duncan, A., Mavisakalyan, A., Phillimore, J., Seymour, R., and Tarverdi, Y. (20X8), "Future of work in Australia: preparing for tomorrow's world".	X	X				
Chapman, T. B., and Sonne, L. (20X8), "Conceptualising an inclusive future of work in India", *ORF Occasional Paper*, (X66).	X					
Cheung-Judge, M. (20X7), "Future of organizations and implications for OD practitioners", *Summary. Od Practitioner*, Vol. 49, Issue 3, pp. 7–X3.	X	X	X	X		X
Choi, J., Dutz, M., and Usman, Z. (20X9), *The Future of Work in Africa*.	X	X			X	
Colombino, U. (20X9), *Is Unconditional Basic Income a Viable Alternative to Other Social Welfare Measures?* IZA World of Labor.						
Cook, J. W. (Ed.) (20X9), *Sustainability, Human Well-Being, and the Future of Education*, Palgrave Macmillan.					X	

C7 Skills	*C8 Inequality*	*C9 Individualization*	*C10 Urbanization*	*C11 Migration*	*C12 Powershifts*	*C13 Resources*	*C14 Pandemics*	*C15 Geopolitical*
		X						
X	X							
X								
X								
X	X			X				
	X							

(*Continued*)

Literature source	*C1 Technology*	*C2 Flexibility*	*C3 Workforce*	*C4 Sustainability*	*C5 Environment*	*C6 Globalization*
Cook, N. (20X7), *Enterprise 2.0: How Social Software Will Change the Future of Work*, Routledge.	X					
Cottey, A. (20X9), "The future of work: disciplined useful activity", *Journal of Global Responsibility*, Vol. X0, Issue 3, pp. 27X–286.				X	X	
de Lima, Y. O., and de Souza, J. M. (20X7, April), "The future of work: insights for CSCW", in *20X7 IEEE 2Xst International Conference on Computer Supported Cooperative Work in Design* (CSCWD) (pp. 42–47), IEEE.	X	X	X			X
De Stefano, V., and Aloisi, A. (20X9), "Fundamental labour rights, platform work and human rights protection of non-standard workers", in *Research Handbook on Labour, Business and Human Rights Law*, Edward Elgar Publishing.		X		X		
Degryse, C. (20X7), "Shaping the world of work in the digital economy", *ETUI Research Paper-Foresight Brief.*	X	X				
Di Fabio, A. (20X7), "The psychology of sustainability and sustainable development for well-being in organizations", *Frontiers in Psychology*, Vol. 8, p. X534.					X	
Dignan, A. (20X9), *Brave New Work: Are You Ready to Reinvent Your Organization?*, Penguin UK.				X		
Diño, M. J. S., and Ong, I. L. (20X9), "Research, technology, education & scholarship in the fourth industrial revolution [4IR]: influences in nursing and the health sciences", *The Journal of Medical Investigation*, Vol. 66, Issue X.2, pp. 3–7.						
Diong, T. (20X7), "The Future of management systems", *Quality*, September, pp. 52–54	X	X	X	X	X	X
Dølvik, J. E., and Steen, J. R. (20X8), *The Nordic Future of Work: Drivers, Institutions, and Politics*, Nordic Council of Ministers.	X	X	X		X	X

C7 Skills	*C8 Inequality*	*C9 Individualization*	*C10 Urbanization*	*C11 Migration*	*C12 Powershifts*	*C13 Resources*	*C14 Pandemics*	*C15 Geopolitical*
	X							
X				X				
X								
		X	X		X	X		X

(*Continued*)

Literature source	*C1 Technology*	*C2 Flexibility*	*C3 Workforce*	*C4 Sustainability*	*C5 Environment*	*C6 Globalization*
Drahokoupil, J., and Piasna, A. (20X7), "Work in the platform economy: beyond lower transaction costs", *Intereconomics*, Vol. 52, Issue 6, pp. 335–340.		X				X
Dregger, J., Niehaus, J., Ittermann, P., Hirsch-Kreinsen, H., and ten Hompel, M. (20X8), "Challenges for the future of industrial labor in manufacturing and logistics using the example of order picking systems", *Procedia CIRP*, Vol. 67, pp. X40–X43.	X					
Edgell, S., and Granter, E. (20X9), *The Sociology of Work: Continuity and Change in Paid and Unpaid Work*, SAGE Publications Limited.	X	X				X
Eichhorst, W. (20X7), "Labor market institutions and the future of work: good jobs for all?", (No. X22). *IZA Policy Paper*.	X	X		X		X
Erboz, G. (20X7, November), "How to define industry 4.0: main pillars of industry 4.0", in *7th International Conference on Management* (ICoM 20X7).	X					
Ernst, E., Merola, R., and Samaan, D. (20X8), "The economics of artificial intelligence: implications for the future of work", *ILO Future of Work Research Paper Series*, Vol. 5, p. 4X.	X					
Esposito, M., and Tse, T. (20X8), "DRIVE: the five megatrends that underpin the future business, social, and economic landscapes", *Thunderbird International Business Review*, Vol. 60, Issue X, pp. X2X–X29.			X			
European Environment Agency (20X5), *The European Environment – State and Outlook 20X5: Assessment of Global Megatrends*, European Environment Agency: Copenhagen.	X			X	X	
Faith, B. (20X7), "Automation, women, and the future of work".	X					

C7 Skills	*C8 Inequality*	*C9 Individualization*	*C10 Urbanization*	*C11 Migration*	*C12 Powershifts*	*C13 Resources*	*C14 Pandemics*	*C15 Geopolitical*
				X				
X								
	X		X			X		
			X				X	X

(*Continued*)

Literature source	*C1 Technology*	*C2 Flexibility*	*C3 Workforce*	*C4 Sustainability*	*C5 Environment*	*C6 Globalization*
Fernández-Macías, E., Gómez, E., Hernández-Orallo, J., Loe, B. S., Martens, B., Martínez-Plumed, F., and Tolan, S. (20X8), "A multidisciplinary task-based perspective for evaluating the impact of AI autonomy and generality on the future of work", *arXiv preprint* arXiv:X807.024X6.	X					
Fitch Solutions (2020), *Towards 2050: Megatrends in Industry, Politics and the Global Economy*, fitchsolutions.com	X		X		X	X
Florito, J., Aneja, U., and de Sanfeliu, M. B. (20X8), *A Future of Work that Works for Women*, G20 Insights.	X	X		X	X	X
Forrester (2024), "Tech trends to watch for", accessed at https://www.forrester.com/what-it-means/ep352-tech-trends-2024/	X					
Fuller, J. B., Raman, M., Walllenstein, J. K., and de Chalendar, A. (20X9), "Your workforce is more adaptable than you think", *Harvard Business Review*, Vol. 97, Issue 3, pp. XX8–X26.	X	X	X			
Galinska, B. (20X8), "Logistics megatrends and their influence on supply chains", *Proceedings of theX8th International Scientific Conference Business Logistics in Modern Management.* October XX–X2, 20X8 - Osijek, Croatia, pp. 583–602.	X		X	X	X	
Gelderblom, A., de Hek, P., Gravesteijn, J., van der Toorn, A. J., and Prince, Y. (20X9), *Toekomst Van Werk.*	X	X	X			X
Gernandt, K. (20X2), *Megatrends and Their Impact on Logistics, Think Logistics 20X2: The Impact of Severe Disruptions on Global Supply Chains*, Singapore, 6 November 20X2.	X		X	X	X	X
Graham, M., Lehdonvirta, V., Wood, A., Barnard, H., Hjorth, I., and D Simon, P. (20X7), "The risks and rewards of online gig work at the global margins".		X		X		X

C7 Skills	*C8 Inequality*	*C9 Individualization*	*C10 Urbanization*	*C11 Migration*	*C12 Powershifts*	*C13 Resources*	*C14 Pandemics*	*C15 Geopolitical*
							X	X
X	X							
X								
X	X							
			X					

(*Continued*)

Literature source	*C1 Technology*	*C2 Flexibility*	*C3 Workforce*	*C4 Sustainability*	*C5 Environment*	*C6 Globalization*
Gratton, L. (20XX), "Lynda Gratton investigates: the future of work", *Development and Learning in Organizations*, Vol. 25, Issue 3, pp. X6–22.		X		X	X	
Gregg, M., and Lodato, T. (20X8), "Managing community: coworking, hospitality and the future of work", in *Affect in Relation* (pp. X75–X96). Routledge.		X				
Gregosz, D. (20X2), "Economic megatrends up to 2020", in *What Can We Expect in the Forthcoming Years?* Konrad-Adenauer-Stiftung Facts & Findings: Berlin.	X		X		X	
Greve, B. (Ed.) (20X7), *Technology and the Future of Work: The Impact on Labour Markets and Welfare States*, Edward Elgar Publishing.	X	X		X		X
Gruen, D. (20X7), "The future of work", *Policy: A Journal of Public Policy and Ideas*, Vol. 33, Issue 3, p. 3.	X					
Hagel, J., Schwartz, J., and Bersin, J. (20X7), "Navigating the future of work", *Deloitte Reviews*, Vol. 2X, pp. 27–45.	X	X	X	X		X
Hajkowicz, S.A., Cook, H., and Littleboy, A. (20X2), *Our Future World: Global Megatrends That Will Change the Way We Live, The 20X2 Revision*, Commonwealth Scientific and Industrial Research Organization (CSIRO): Australia.	X				X	
Haldane, A. (20X7), *Work, Wages and Monetary Policy*, Speech at the National Science and Media Museum, Bradford, 20.		X		X		
Hancock, P. A. (20X7, June), "Whither workload? Mapping a path for its future development", in *International Symposium on Human Mental Workload: Models and Applications* (pp. 3–X7), Springer: Cham.	X				X	

C7 Skills	*C8 Inequality*	*C9 Individualization*	*C10 Urbanization*	*C11 Migration*	*C12 Powershifts*	*C13 Resources*	*C14 Pandemics*	*C15 Geopolitical*
						X		
					X			X
X	X							
X				X				
			X			X		X
	X							

(*Continued*)

Literature source	*C1 Technology*	*C2 Flexibility*	*C3 Workforce*	*C4 Sustainability*	*C5 Environment*	*C6 Globalization*
Harteis, C. (20X8), "Machines, change and work: an educational view on the digitalization of work", in *The Impact of Digitalization in the Workplace* (pp. X–X0), Springer: Cham.	X					
Harvey, G., Rhodes, C., Vachhani, S. J., and Williams, K. (20X7), "Neo-villeiny and the service sector: the case of hyper flexible and precarious work in fitness centres", *Work, Employment and Society*, Vol. 3X, Issue X, pp. X9–35.		X				
Healy, J., Nicholson, D., and Gahan, P. (20X7), "The Future of Work in Australia: anticipating how new technologies will reshape labour markets, occupations and skill requirements", Department of Education.	X			X		
Healy, J., Nicholson, D., and Parker, J. (20X7), "Guest editors' introduction: technological disruption and the future of employment relations".	X					
Hegewisch, A., and Heidi, H. (20X9), "Women, automation, and the future of work", Institute for Women's Policy Research.	X					
Hertel, G., Stone, D. L., Johnson, R. D., and Passmore, J. (Eds.) (20X7), *The Wiley Blackwell Handbook of the Psychology of the Internet at Work* (Vol. 7696), John Wiley & Sons.	X	X		X		
Héry, M., and Levert, C. (20X7), "The future of work", *Futuribles*, Issue 5, pp. 5–X8.	X					
Hessel, V. (20X4), "Megatrends – megascience?", *Green Processing and Synthesis*, Vol. 3, Issue 2, pp. 99–X00.	X	X	X		X	X
Hickman, C. R., and Silva, M. A. (20X8), *The Future 500: Creating Tomorrow's Organisations Today*, Routledge.	X	X		X	X	

C7 Skills	*C8 Inequality*	*C9 Individualization*	*C10 Urbanization*	*C11 Migration*	*C12 Powershifts*	*C13 Resources*	*C14 Pandemics*	*C15 Geopolitical*
X								
X	X							
X								
		X				X		

(*Continued*)

Literature source	*C1 Technology*	*C2 Flexibility*	*C3 Workforce*	*C4 Sustainability*	*C5 Environment*	*C6 Globalization*
Higgins, V. (20X7), "Augmented and virtual reality: the future of work, not just play", *Professional Safety*, Vol. 62, Issue 6, p. 86.	X					
Hines, A. (20XX), " A dozen surprises about the future of work", *Employment Relations Today*, Vol. 38, Issue X, pp. X–X5.	X	X				
Hoppe, M., Christ, A., Castro, A., Winter, M., and Seppanen, T. M. (20X4), "Transformation in transportation?", *European Journal of Futures Research*, Vol. 2, Issue X, pp. X–X4.			X		X	X
Howard, J. (20X9), "Artificial intelligence: implications for the future of work", *American Journal of Industrial Medicine*, Vol. 62, Issue XX, pp. 9X7–926.	X					
Huws, U. (20X7), "Where did online platforms come from? The virtualization of work organization and the new policy challenges it raises", in *Policy Implications of Virtual Work* (pp. 29–48). Palgrave Macmillan: Cham.		X		X		X
Hyder, S. (20X4), *7 Things You Can do to Build an Awesome Personal Brand*, Retrieved January 9, 2020.						
Ibrahim, M., El-Zaart, A., and Adams, C. (20X8), "Smart sustainable cities roadmap: readiness for transformation towards urban sustainability", *Sustainable Cities and Society*, Vol. 37, pp. 530–540.						
Illanes, P., Lund, S., Mourshed, M., Rutherford, S., and Tyreman, M. (20X8), "Retraining and reskilling workers in the age of automation", *McKinsey Global Institute*. Available at https://www.mckinsey.com/featured-insights/future-of-work/retraining-and-reskilling-workers-in-the-age-of-automation	X					

C7 Skills	*C8 Inequality*	*C9 Individualization*	*C10 Urbanization*	*C11 Migration*	*C12 Powershifts*	*C13 Resources*	*C14 Pandemics*	*C15 Geopolitical*
X								X
	X	X	X					
		X						
			X					
X								

(*Continued*)

Literature source	*C1 Technology*	*C2 Flexibility*	*C3 Workforce*	*C4 Sustainability*	*C5 Environment*	*C6 Globalization*
ILO (20X7), *A Study on the Future of Work in the Pacific*, ILO Office for Pacific Island Countries, International Labour Organization.	X	X		X	X	X
Islam, I. (20X8), "Automation and the future of employment: implications for India", *South Asian Journal of Human Resources Management*, Vol. 5, Issue 2, pp. 234–243.	X					
Istrate, E., and Harris, J. (20X7), *The Future of Work: The Rise of the Gig Economy*, National Association of Counties, November.		X				
Jarosławska-Sobór, S. (20X9), "Megatrends – challenges and threats for the contemporary labour market", *Scientific Papers of Silesian University of Technology, Organization & Management Series*, Issue X40, pp. X33–X45.	X		X		X	X
Jarrahi, M. H. (20X8), "Artificial intelligence and the future of work: human-AI symbiosis in organizational decision making", *Business Horizons*, Vol. 6X, Issue 4, pp. 577–586.	X					
Jayakumar, S., and Goh, E. (20X7), *The Future of Work: New Underclass*, Dystopian Reality?	X					
Jayne, T. S., Yeboah, K., and Henry, C. (20X7), "The future of work in African agriculture trends and drivers of change (No. 994987492X02676)", *International Labour Organization*.	X	X	X	X	X	X
Jesuthasan, R., and Boudreau, J. W. (20X8), Reinventing jobs: a 4-step approach for applying automation to work.	X	X		X		
Jesuthasan, R., and Boudreau, J. W. (20X8), "The future of work: can you answer these strategic questions?", www.ihrim.org, Workforce Solutions Review, October–December 20X8.	X	X				
Jones, C. (20X7), "The value of work and the future of the Left", *Counter Futures*, Vol. 4, pp. X3–X66.					X	

C7 Skills	*C8 Inequality*	*C9 Individualization*	*C10 Urbanization*	*C11 Migration*	*C12 Powershifts*	*C13 Resources*	*C14 Pandemics*	*C15 Geopolitical*
				X				
X								
X								

(*Continued*)

Literature source	*C1 Technology*	*C2 Flexibility*	*C3 Workforce*	*C4 Sustainability*	*C5 Environment*	*C6 Globalization*
Kaivo-Oja, J., Roth, S., and Westerlund, L. (20X7), "Futures of robotics. Human work in digital transformation", *International Journal of Technology Management*, Vol. 73, Issue 4, pp. X76–205.	X	X	X			X
Kara, D., Kim, H. L., Lee, G., and Uysal, M. (20X8), "The moderating effects of gender and income between leadership and quality of work life (QWL)", *International Journal of Contemporary Hospitality Management*.						
Karabag, S. F. (2020), "An unprecedented global crisis! The global, regional, national, political, economic and commercial impact of the coronavirus pandemic", *Journal of Applied Economics and Business Research*, Vol. X0, Issue X, pp. X–6.	X			X		
Kasriel, S., and Upwork, C. E. O. (20X8), "The future of work won't be about college degrees, it will be about job skills", *CNBC*. Retrieved, 8.	X	X				X
Kavanagh, M. M., Thirumurthy, H., Katz, R., Ebi, K. L., Beyrer, C., Headley, J., Holmes, C. B., Collins, C., and Gostin, L. O. (20X9/2020), "Ending pandemics: U.S. foreign policy to mitigate today's major killers, tomorrow's outbreaks, and the health impacts of climate change", *Journal of International Affairs*, Vol. 73, Issue X, pp. 49–68.					X	
Kessler, S. (20X8), *Gigged: The Gig Economy, the End of the Job and the Future of Work*, Random House.	X	X				
Kiel, D., Müller, J. M., Arnold, C., and Voigt, K. I. (20X7), "Sustainable industrial value creation: benefits and challenges of industry 4.0", *International Journal of Innovation Management*, Vol. 2X, Issue 08, pp. X7400X5.	X			X	X	

C7 Skills	*C8 Inequality*	*C9 Individualization*	*C10 Urbanization*	*C11 Migration*	*C12 Powershifts*	*C13 Resources*	*C14 Pandemics*	*C15 Geopolitical*
X				X				
	X							
							X	
X								
				X				
X								

(*Continued*)

Literature source	*C1 Technology*	*C2 Flexibility*	*C3 Workforce*	*C4 Sustainability*	*C5 Environment*	*C6 Globalization*
Kim, K. H., and Bok Ree, S. (20X7), "A study on the development of the key promoting talent in the 4th industrial revolution-utilizing six sigma MBB competency", *Journal of the Korean Society for Quality Management*, Vol. 45, Issue 4, pp. 677–695.						
Kiss, M. (20X7), "The future of work in the EU. Inventory of what various committees are planning to work on", *Interesting Read.*	X	X				
Kochan, T. A. (20X9), "Shaping the future of work: challenges and opportunities for U.S. labor management relations and workplace dispute resolution", *Dispute Resolution Jounal*, Vol. 74, Issue X, pp. XX–3X.	X	X		X		
Kohlbacher, F. (20X7), "Skills 4.0: how CEOs shape the future of work in Asia".	X		X		X	X
Kotler Ph., and Kotler M. (20X3), *Market Your Way to Growth: Eight Ways to Win*, John Wiley and Sons: Hoboken, NJ.	X			X		X
Kotynkova, M. (20X7), "Re-industrialization of europe: industry 4. 0 and the future of work", *European Scientific Journal*, Vol. 788X, pp. 249–256.	X			X		
Kubicek, B., and Korunka, C. (20X7), "The present and future of work: some concluding remarks and reflections on upcoming trends", in *Job Demands in a Changing World of Work* (pp. X53–X62). Springer: Cham.	X		X	X		
Lamb, C., and Doyle, S. (20X7) "Future-proof: preparing young Canadians for the future of work", *Brookfield Institute for Innovation Entrepreneurship.*	X	X			X	
Lanier, K. (20X7), "5 Things HR professionals need to know about generation Z: thought leaders share their views on the HR profession and its direction for the future", *Strategic HR Review*, Vol. X6, Issue 6, pp. 288–290.		X				

C7 Skills	*C8 Inequality*	*C9 Individualization*	*C10 Urbanization*	*C11 Migration*	*C12 Powershifts*	*C13 Resources*	*C14 Pandemics*	*C15 Geopolitical*
X	X							
X	X							
				X				
			X		X			
X								

(*Continued*)

Literature source	*C1 Technology*	*C2 Flexibility*	*C3 Workforce*	*C4 Sustainability*	*C5 Environment*	*C6 Globalization*
Lent, R. W. (20X8), "Future of work in the digital world: preparing for instability and opportunity", *The Career Development Quarterly*, Vol. 66, Issue 3, pp. 205–2X9.	X			X		
Liao, Y., Loures, E. R., Deschamps, F., Brezinski, G., and Venâncio, A. (20X8), "The impact of the fourth industrial revolution: a cross-country/region comparison", *Production*, 28.						
Liu, C. (20X7), International competitiveness and the fourth industrial revolution. *Entrepreneurial Business and Economics Review*, Vol. 5, Issue 4, pp. XXX–X33.						
Loprest, P., and Nightingale, D. (20X8), *The Nature of Work and the Social Safety Net*, Urban Institute, Washington, DC.		X		X		
Lund, S., Manyika, J., and Segel, L. H. (20X9), "The future of work in America: people and places, today and tomorrow".	X					
Lusmagi, Sandra (n.d.)	X	X	X			
MacEachen, E. (Ed.) (20X8), *The Science and Politics of Work Disability Prevention*, Routledge.			X	X		
Malik, R., and Janowska, A. A. (20X8), "Megatrends and their use in economic analyses of contemporary challenges in the world economy", *Research Papers of the Wroclaw University of Economics*, Issue 523, pp. 209–220.	X		X		X	
Malone, T. W. (20X8), "How human-computer 'Superminds' are redefining the future of work", *MIT Sloan Management Review*, Vol. 59, Issue 4, pp. 34–4X.	X					
Manyika, J., Chui, M., Madgavkar, A., and Lund, S. (20X7), *Technology, Jobs, and the Future of Work*, McKinsey Global Institute.	X	X		X		X

C7 Skills	*C8 Inequality*	*C9 Individualization*	*C10 Urbanization*	*C11 Migration*	*C12 Powershifts*	*C13 Resources*	*C14 Pandemics*	*C15 Geopolitical*
X								
					X			
					X			
	X							
X								
	X							
			X					X
X	X			X				

(*Continued*)

Literature source	*C1 Technology*	*C2 Flexibility*	*C3 Workforce*	*C4 Sustainability*	*C5 Environment*	*C6 Globalization*
Manyika, J., Lund, S., Chui, M., Bughin, J., Woetzel, J., Batra, P.,… and Sanghvi, S. (20X7), *Jobs Lost, Jobs Gained: Workforce Transitions in a Time of Automation*, McKinsey Global Institute.	X			X		
Marshall, J., Coleman, G., and Reason, P. (20X7), *Leadership for Sustainability: An Action Research Approach*, Routledge.					X	
McEncroe, R. (20X8), "How the GIG economy exploits workers", *Green Left Weekly*, Issue X205, p. 24.		X				
McKay, C., Pollack, E., Fitzpayne, A., and Aspen Institute/Future of Work Initiative (20X8), *Modernizing Unemployment Insurance for the Changing Nature of Work*, https://assets.aspeninstitute.org/content/uploads/20X8/0X/Modernizing-Unemployment-Insurance_Report_Aspen-Future-of-Work.pdf.						
Mcquay, L. (20X8), "Will robots duplicate or surpass us? The impact of job automation on tasks, productivity, and work", *Psychosociological Issues in Human Resource Management*, Vol. 6, Issue 2, pp. 86–9X.	X					
Means, A. J. (20X8), "Platform learning and on-demand labor: sociotechnical projections on the future of education and work", *Learning, Media and Technology*, Vol. 43, Issue 3, pp. 326–338.		X				
Méda, D. (20X7), "The future of work: the meaning and value of work in Europe".	X	X		X	X	X
Meged, J. W., and Christensen, M. D. (20X7), "Working within the collaborative tourist economy: the complex crafting of work and meaning", in *Collaborative Economy and Tourism* (pp. 203–220), Springer: Cham.		X				

C7 Skills	*C8 Inequality*	*C9 Individualization*	*C10 Urbanization*	*C11 Migration*	*C12 Powershifts*	*C13 Resources*	*C14 Pandemics*	*C15 Geopolitical*
	X							
X								
X	X			X				

(*Continued*)

Literature source	*C1 Technology*	*C2 Flexibility*	*C3 Workforce*	*C4 Sustainability*	*C5 Environment*	*C6 Globalization*
Mittelstaedt, J. D., Shultz II, C. J., Kilbourne, W. E., and Peterson, M. (20X4), "Sustainability as megatrend: two schools of macromarketing thought", *Journal of Macromarketing*, Vol. 34, Issue 3, pp. 253–264.				X		
National Intelligence Council (20X2), *Global Trends 2030: Alternative Worlds,* National Intelligence Council, www.dni.gov/nic/globaltrends	X		X		X	
Ng'weno, A., and Porteous, D. (20X8), *Let's Be Real: The Informal Sector and the Gig Economy are the Future, and the Present, of Work in Africa*, Center for Global Development, October, X5.		X				
Nica, E., Manole, C., and Stan, C. I. (20X8), "A laborless society? How highly automated environments and breakthroughs in artificial intelligence bring about innovative kinds of skills and employment disruptions, altering the nature of business process and affecting the path of economic growth", *Journal of Self-Governance & Management Economics*, Vol. 6, Issue 4.	X					
Ovaskainen, M., and Tinnilä, M. (20XX), "Megatrends in electronic business – an analysis of the impacts on SME's", *International Journal of E-Entrepreneurship and Innovation*, Vol. 2, Issue X, pp. X–X5.	X	X				
Peetz, D. (20X9), *The Realities and Futures of Work*, Australian National University Press, Acton.	X		X		X	X
Peters, M. A., Jandrić, P., and Hayes, S. (20X9), "The curious promise of educationalising technological unemployment: what can places of learning really do about the future of work?", *Educational Philosophy and Theory*, Vol. 5X, Issue 3, pp. 242–254.	X					

C7 Skills	*C8 Inequality*	*C9 Individualization*	*C10 Urbanization*	*C11 Migration*	*C12 Powershifts*	*C13 Resources*	*C14 Pandemics*	*C15 Geopolitical*
		X	X			X		X
					X			
X								

(*Continued*)

Literature source	*C1 Technology*	*C2 Flexibility*	*C3 Workforce*	*C4 Sustainability*	*C5 Environment*	*C6 Globalization*
Pieriegud, J. (20X5), "Wykorzystanie megatrendów do analizy przyszłościowego rozwoju sektorów gospodarki", in Gajewski, J., Paprocki, W. and Pieriegud, J. (eds), *Megatrendy i ich wpływ na rozwój sektorów infrastrukturalnych*, Instytut Badań nad Gospodarką Rynkową, Gdańsk.	X		X	X	X	X
Pulkka, V. V. (20X9), ""This time may be a little different" – exploring the Finnish view on the future of work", *International Journal of Sociology and Social Policy*, Vol. 39, Issue X/2, pp. 22–37.	X					
Puri, R. (20X7), "Gig economy: the road ahead", *IMI Konnect*, Vol. 6, Issue 5.		X				
PWC (20X9), "Talent trends 20X9, upskilling for a digital world, Part of PwC's 22nd Annual Global CEO Survey trends series", *PWC*, ceosurvey. pwc						
Qian, J., Yang, F., Wang, B., Huang, C., and Song, B. (20X9), "When workplace ostracism leads to burnout: the roles of job self-determination and future time orientation", *The International Journal of Human Resource Management*, Vol. 30, Issue X7, pp. 2465–248X.				X		
Quiggin, J. (20X9), "Labour market policy and the future of work", *Revisiting Henderson: Poverty*, social security and basic income.						
Ransome, P. (20X9), *Sociology and the Future of Work: Contemporary Discourses and Debates*, Routledge.	X	X				
Retief, F., Bond, A., Pope, J., Morrison-Saunders, A., and King, N. (20X6), "Global megatrends and their implications for environmental assessment practice", *Environmental Impact Assessment Review*, Vol. 6X, pp. 52–60.	X		X	X	X	X

C7 Skills	*C8 Inequality*	*C9 Individualization*	*C10 Urbanization*	*C11 Migration*	*C12 Powershifts*	*C13 Resources*	*C14 Pandemics*	*C15 Geopolitical*
			X			X		
X								
	X							
			X			X		X

(*Continued*)

Literature source	*C1 Technology*	*C2 Flexibility*	*C3 Workforce*	*C4 Sustainability*	*C5 Environment*	*C6 Globalization*
Rubery, J. (20X9), "A gender lens on the future of work", *Journal of International Affairs*, January 22.			X			
Rubery, J., Grimshaw, D., Keizer, A., and Johnson, M. (20X8), "Challenges and contradictions in the 'normalising' of precarious work", *Work, Employment and Society*, Vol. 32, Issue 3, pp. 509–527.		X				
Sargeant, M. (20X7), "The gig economy and the future of work", *Ejournal of International and Comparative Labour Studies*, Vol. 6, Issue 2, pp. X–X2.		X				
Schwarzmüller, T., Brosi, P., Duman, D., and Welpe, I. M. (20X8) "How does the digital transformation affect organizations? Key themes of change in work design and leadership", mrev *Management Revue*, Vol. 29, Issue 2, pp. XX4–X38.	X					
Scotch, R. K., and McConnel, C. E. (20X7), "Disability and the future of work: a speculative essay", in *Factors in Studying Employment for Persons with Disability: How the Picture Can Change* (pp. 249–266). Emerald Publishing Limited.				X		
Sinar, E. (20X8), *6 Leadership Megatrends from the Global Leadership Forecast, Global Leadership Forecast 20X8 report*, Development Dimensions International Inc.,	X		X			
Smidt, M., Becker, K., and Bradley, L. (20X5), "Forces shaping the future of work in a changing regional economy", *Australasian Journal of Regional Studies*, Vol. 2X, Issue 3, pp. 349–372.	X		X			X
Smith, P. A., and Sharicz, C. (20XX), "The shift needed for sustainability", *The learning Organization*, Vol. X8, Issue X, pp. 73–86.				X	X	

C7 Skills	*C8 Inequality*	*C9 Individualization*	*C10 Urbanization*	*C11 Migration*	*C12 Powershifts*	*C13 Resources*	*C14 Pandemics*	*C15 Geopolitical*
	X							
	X							
X								

(*Continued*)

Literature source	*C1 Technology*	*C2 Flexibility*	*C3 Workforce*	*C4 Sustainability*	*C5 Environment*	*C6 Globalization*
Sousa, M. J., and Wilks, D. (20X8), "Sustainable skills for the world of work in the digital age", *Systems Research and Behavioral Science*, Vol. 35, Issue 4, pp. 399–405.						
Spencer, D. A. (20X8), "Fear and hope in an age of mass automation: debating the future of work", *New Technology, Work and Employment*, Vol. 33, Issue X, pp. X–X2.	X					
Stanford, J. (20X8), "The future of work, and the future of skills", *Australian TAFE Teacher*, Vol. 52, Issue X, p. 20.						
Tinnilä, M. (20X2), "Impact of future trends on banking services", *Journal of Internet Banking and Commerce*, Vol. X7, Issue 2, pp. X–X5.	X		X			X
Toops, L. M. (20X4), "5 megatrends that will revolutionize insurance: will you be prepared?", *National Underwriter*, July, pp. 20–2X.	X		X		X	
Torii, K., and O'Connell, M. (20X7), "Preparing young people for the future of work: policy roundtable report".	X	X		X		X
Utikal, H., and Wothe, J. (20X5), "From megatrends to business excellence: managing change in the German chemical and pharmaceutical industry", *Journal of Business Chemistry*, Vol. X2, Issue 2, pp. 4X–47.	X		X			X
Van Doorn, N. (20X7), "Platform labor: on the gendered and racialized exploitation of low-income service work in the 'on-demand'economy", *Information, Communication and Society*, Vol. 20, Issue 6, pp. 898–9X4.		X		X		
Vielmetter, G., and Sell, Y. (20X4), *Leadership 2030: The Six Megatrends You Need to Understand to Lead Your Company into the Future*, AMACOM: New York.	X	X	X		X	X

C7 Skills	*C8 Inequality*	*C9 Individualization*	*C10 Urbanization*	*C11 Migration*	*C12 Powershifts*	*C13 Resources*	*C14 Pandemics*	*C15 Geopolitical*
X								
	X							
X								
		X						
			X			X		X
X				X				
		X				X		

(*Continued*)

Literature source	*C1 Technology*	*C2 Flexibility*	*C3 Workforce*	*C4 Sustainability*	*C5 Environment*	*C6 Globalization*
Vielmetter, G., and Sell, Y. (20X4), *Leadership 2030: The Six Megatrends You Need to Understand to Lead Your Company into the Future*, AMACOM: New York.	X		X		X	X
Volberda, H., Heij, K., and Bosma, M. (n.d.), *Innovatie Jij.nu. Niet de robots*, maar wij zijn aan zet.	X			X		
Von der Gracht, H., and Darkow, I. L. (20X0), "Scenarios for the logistics services industry: a Delphi-based analysis for 2025", *International Journal of Production Economics*, Vol. X27, Issue X, pp. 46–59.	X	X	X	X	X	X
West, D. M. (20X8), "Chapter thirteen the future of work", *Government for the Future: Reflection and Vision for Tomorrow's Leaders*, 2X3.	X	X		X		
West, D. M. (20X8), *The future of Work: Robots, AI, and Automation*, Brookings Institution Press.	X			X		
Woetzel, J., Madgavkar, A., Khaled, R., Mattern, F., Bughin, J., Manyika, J.,…, and Hasyagar, A. (20X6), *People on the Move: Global Migration's Impact and Opportunity*, McKinsey Global Institute: New York.	X					
World Bank (20X9), *World Development Report 20X9: The Changing Nature of Work*, World Bank: Washington, DC.	X	X	X	X	X	X
World Economic Forum (20X8a), *The Future of Jobs Report 20X8*, World Economic Forum: Geneva.	X			X		
World Economic Forum (20X8b), *Eight Futures of Work Scenarios and Their Implications*, Whitepaper (Jan, 20X8) in preparation of The Future of Work Project. World Economic Forum: Geneva.	X	X	X	X	X	X

C7 Skills	*C8 Inequality*	*C9 Individualization*	*C10 Urbanization*	*C11 Migration*	*C12 Powershifts*	*C13 Resources*	*C14 Pandemics*	*C15 Geopolitical*
X		X						
	X			X				
X	X			X				
X	X							
X	X			X				

APPENDIX 2 – OVERVIEW OF THE INTERDEPENDENCIES AND IMPACT OF THE CHALLENGES

This appendix provides an overview of the interdependencies between the challenges and the (combined) impact they (will) have, according to the literature, have on organizations.

Challenge	*Inter-dependencies between challenges*	*Impact of (combined) challenges on organizations*
[C1] Technological advancement	[C2], [C7], [C4], [C6], [C3], [C8]	Potential drop in organization performance and results if organization cannot keep up with pace, threatening continuity of organization Increase in automation of work, depletion of, changes in and creation of new jobs Feeling of insecurity, fear of job loss for workers Feeling of insecurity, fear of not being to cope with technological advancements as managers Skills mismatch, reskilling programs Remote working, less office space, need for social networks/hangouts for workers Changes in organization design, organization of work and work environment (such as suppliers, customers) Need for other leadership styles and reskilling of management More data and advanced analytics tools, changes in decision-making processes Technological awareness of leadership Prepare for internal and external communications being able to prove that organization is on top of technological developments Being able to handle security issues

[C2] Flexible employment	[C1], [C4], [C3], [C8], [C11]	Decrease in employment contracts (indefinite and definite period), increase in self-employed workers and multiple contracts for workers (working for more organizations at the same time) Greater variety in contracts in terms of working hours and working location Shorter tenures for workers as well as managers Decrease in workforce stability, potentially leading to miscommunications, not fully counting the opinions of flex workers, decrease in worker engagement Remote working, less office space, need for social networks/hangouts for workers Changes in organization design, organization of work and work environment (such as suppliers, customers) Need for other leadership styles and reskilling of management Better or worse work-life balance for workers, depending on whether workers have work, the amount of work and the working conditions Deteriorating economic situation for flex workers (lack of social protection) Challenges in planning and oversight of work and workers Comply with changing employment legislation (being able to prove compliance) Potential drop in organization performance and results if organization lacks skills in oversight, management and decrease in engagement of workers
[C3] Changing workforce composure	[C1], [C2], [C7], [C4], [C11]	Aging workforce, investments in programs for successful aging at work including continuous development Increasing variety in needs of workers because of generation shifts, investments in flexible working conditions (flexible benefits, customization of work environment), adjustment to cultures and backgrounds of foreign workers Potential loss of productivity and engagement workers, a potential drop performance and results, threatening the continuity of the organization

(Continued)

Challenge	*Inter-dependencies between challenges*	*Impact of (combined) challenges on organizations*
[C4] Sustainable employment	[C2], [C7], [C3], [C8], [C5]	Increased awareness for the needs of employees, work culture, inclusion, working conditions and safety at work Investments in programs such as vitality, well-being, adjusting the workplace, remote working, self-development, gender equality including implementation of tools to measure and improve employee experience Leadership development to reduce unsustainable working environments such as fear culture, or expectations on availability for work Communicate/advertise to stakeholders (workers, customers, shareholders) that sustainable work is important for the organization Not adapting to sustainability expectations from society may lead to burn-out, workers leaving or reduced engagement, a potential drop in performance of the organization and results, threatening the continuity of the organization
[C5] Environmental issues	[C4], [C11]	Increasing awareness in ecological footprint of organization, investments in clean and sustainable value creation (including the value chain of the organization) Investments in innovation Increased customers and stakeholder awareness leading to visible measures and refusing to work with organizations who are not working in a sustainable way, potentially leading to loss of results threatening the continuity of the organization
[C6] Continued globalization	[C1], [C2]	See impact mentioned at [C1] and [C2]
[C7] Skills mismatch	[C1], [C4], [C3], [C8]	Focus on skills and capabilities here and now, for a specific work task, instead of relying on former achievements such as college degrees – lifelong learning – skills passport Need for workers with skills such as agility, adaptability, critical thinking, entrepreneurship and interpersonal skills – currently underrepresented in school curriculums Shortage of workers with the right skills, surplus of workers with a skill mismatch Higher investments in education programs and those who run them Increasing inequality specific worker groups Potential drop in organization performance and results, threatening the continuity of the organization

[C8] Increasing inequality	[C1], [C2], [C7], [C4], [C11]	Increase in government policies, investments in the development of workers and compliance with legislation treating workers equally Increasing administrative burden
[C9] Individualization		24/7 – round the clock 'readiness' Increased specialization of goods and services Increasing attention for customer experience and employee experience Personalization of goods and services for clients as well as employees Increasing demand will lead to shortages and scarcity of energy
[C10] Urbanization		Increase in difficulty to attract enough employees in urban areas Exodus and shortage of employees in rural areas
[C11] Cross-border migration	[C2], [C3], [C8]	Increase in workers with different cultural background, tensions in workforce, increase in languages, investments in culture programs Possibility to fill skills and workforce gaps with migrant workers Knowledge and skills drain in home country organizations
[C12] Economic powershifts		Shift from West to East (emerging countries) making Western companies more vulnerable Powerhouses India and China are unleashing endless opportunities for growth International logistics sector may increase Organizations who want to compete should adopt ways of working, and business culture of Eastern countries Business environment will become less stable as they are impacted by political power
[C13] Resources scarcity		Rates of raw materials and consumer goods will rise and/or quality will drop New production methods must be found, especially for water intensive production processes Renewed focus on risks of overconsumption and waste for generations to come Legislation on/regulated use of resources i Tax rates may rise in specific countries for specific resources

(Continued)

Challenge	*Inter-dependencies between challenges*	*Impact of (combined) challenges on organizations*
[C14] Pandemic		Increase in illness and absence rates Investments in safe work environment Increase in digitization and working from home Pressure on health sector Worldwide negative impact on various sectors and economy Focus on local products, avoiding dependency on global suppliers Increase in online learning platforms
[C15] Geopolitical unrest and instability	[C8]	Destruction of human capital, institutions and infrastructures. Adverse economic consequence Less investment, more disinvestment Lower economic growth, more poverty and inequality

INDEX

Note: **Bold** page numbers refer to tables; *italic* page numbers refer to figures and page numbers followed by "n" denote endnotes.

Kolibri 360 GmbH
Ferdinand-Jühlke-Straße 7
99095 Erfurt, Deutschland
produktsicherheit@kolibri360.de